TORONTO, THE BELFAST OF CANADA

The Orange Order and the Shaping of Municipal Culture

In late nineteenth-century Toronto, municipal politics were so dominated by the Irish Protestants of the Orange Order that the city was known as the "Belfast of Canada." For almost a century, virtually every mayor of Toronto was an Orangeman and the anniversary of the Battle of the Boyne was a civic holiday. *Toronto, the Belfast of Canada* explores the intolerant origins of today's cosmopolitan city.

Using lodge membership lists, census data, and municipal records, William J. Smyth details the Orange Order's role in creating Toronto's municipal culture of militant Protestantism, loyalism, and monarchism. One of Canada's foremost experts on the Orange Order, Smyth analyses the Orange Order's influence between 1850 and 1950, the city's frequent public displays of sectarian tensions, and its occasional bouts of rioting and mayhem.

WILLIAM J. SMYTH is the president emeritus of the National University of Ireland, Maynooth, and a past president of the Geographical Society of Ireland and the Association of Canadian Studies in Ireland.

D1596246

WILLIAM J. SMYTH

Toronto, the Belfast of Canada

The Orange Order and the Shaping of Municipal Culture

UNIVERSITY OF TORONTO PRESS
Toronto Buffalo London

© University of Toronto Press 2015
Toronto Buffalo London
www.utppublishing.com
Printed in the U.S.A.

ISBN 978-1-4426-4687-2 (cloth)
ISBN 978-1-4426-1468-0 (paper)

Printed on acid-free, 100% post-consumer recycled paper with vegetable-based inks

---

Library and Archives Canada Cataloguing in Publication

Smyth, William J., 1949–, author
Toronto, the Belfast of Canada : the Orange Order and the shaping of municipal culture / William J. Smyth.

Includes bibliographical references and index.
ISBN 978-1-4426-4687-2 (bound)   ISBN 978-1-4426-1468-0 (pbk.)

1. Orangemen – Ontario – Toronto – History.   2. Orange Order – History.
3. Toronto (Ont.) – Politics and government.   I. Title.

HS1550.C32T67 2015   369'.2713541   C2015-900127-7

University of Toronto Press gratefully acknowledges the financial assistance of the Jackman Foundation in the publication of this book.

University of Toronto Press acknowledges the financial assistance to its publishing program of the Canada Council for the Arts and the Ontario Arts Council, an agency of the Government of Ontario.

 Canada Council   Conseil des Arts
for the Arts   du Canada

 ONTARIO ARTS COUNCIL
CONSEIL DES ARTS DE L'ONTARIO
an Ontario government agency
un organisme du gouvernement de l'Ontario

University of Toronto Press acknowledges the financial support of the Government of Canada through the Canada Book Fund for its publishing activities.

In memoriam
Professor Tom Jones Hughes, 1922–2011
Professor Don Kerr, 1920–2008

Contents

Figures and Tables

Figures

Tables

Acknowledgments

The present study represents a continuation of a research journey that commenced more than thirty years ago in the company of Cecil Houston. That fruitful partnership generated two books and several dozen articles, but it was interrupted by each of us turning increasingly towards a career in academic administration and management. Archives, libraries, and fieldwork were necessarily forfeited in the face of demands from the boardrooms and council chambers of academia. For my own part, eight years as a university vice-president were followed by ten years as a university president and eventual release to an extended period of sabbatical leave. Cecil, meanwhile, continues to toil as an academic Dean. The Centre for Celtic Studies, St Michael's College, University of Toronto hosted my sabbatical leave, 2004–6, and I remain indebted to it for provision of an office, solace, and intellectual stimulation as I negotiated my return to active research. Mark McGowan, Principal of the College, generously facilitated this sabbatical transition, and David Wilson, Ann Dooley, Mairin Nic Diarmada, and Jean Talman provided a camaraderie that will be forever appreciated. The sabbatical research was supported by The Atlantic Philanthropies.

David Wilson, under the auspices of a 2005 conference on the Orange Order in Canada, reawakened my interest in the field, and in subsequent years he has been a tremendous source of advice, intellectual challenge, and generous support. Navigating his way through his award-winning publications on Thomas D'Arcy Magee, David still found time to engage with Magee's nemesis, the Orange Order, in the guise of frequent discussions with me in the convivial surrounds of Mullins of Bay Street. Gunter Gad and the late Don Kerr provided a sounding board and advice on source material over the gestation of the present book and with consummate skill and wisdom they eased my return to the world of archives and libraries. Gunter also provided me with the photograph of the banner of the Giuseppe Garibaldi Lodge. John Talman provided me with a copy of the 1930 postcard of a Toronto Orange parade. Peter Toner, Tom Mclwraith, Cecil Houston, Deryck Holdsworth, and Cole Harris provided help, encouragement, and enduring friendship at different stages in the research odyssey. Fred McEvoy assisted with provision of source material in Ottawa. Rev. Edward Jackman introduced me to the archives of the Roman Catholic Archdiocese of Toronto many years ago and he has continued to offer support and encouragement. Officers of the Loyal Orange Association of Canada, especially David Griffin and John Chalmers, were courteous and helpful in providing access to source material, as were the staff in the Baldwin Room of the Toronto Reference Library, the Provincial Archives of Ontario, the Toronto City Archives, the Archives of the Roman Catholic Archdiocese of Toronto, and Library and Archives Canada. Robarts Library in the University of Toronto provided a rich haven of secondary reading material.

I first encountered Toronto in the early 1970s as a young professor in the Geography Department of the University of Toronto, and, ever since, the city has held an especial fascination for me. In particular, I have continued to be intrigued by its cultural transformation as it reached out from narrow beginnings to become a centre of global significance. Until the mid-twentieth century, Toronto projected an identity that was an unambiguous derivative of immigrant source regions in the British Isles, and especially Ulster. Civic culture and alignments in municipal politics in Toronto reflected the social fissures and political ideologies of that tension-ridden part of Ireland, and comparisons with contemporary Belfast were apt. The extremism of the Irish city was undoubtedly moderated in the Canadian setting but the badges of identity politics were transferred intact. In the present study, the descriptor "The Belfast of Canada" is employed not as a pejorative term but rather as an explanatory tool in historical analysis. Contemporaries in the period 1850–1950 were not *ad idem* in their use of the term. Catholics hurled it as a label of ghetto bigotry: Protestants took pride in the inferred origins. Only the integrity of the transplanted quarrel was common to all.

Ultimately, the present study is an exploration of how power, both formal and informal, operated within a specific context, creating a distinctive culture in the process. Anyone familiar with academic politics would be well aware of the operation of formal and informal power bases and in many ways nineteenth-century Toronto exhibited a comparable weilding of power, not only by responsible office holders but also by a self-appointed power broker, the Orange Order. Elected officials in City Hall and the informal network of Orange lodges that sustained them constructed a system of municipal governance that privileged sections of the population and made little space for others. The model was not unique to Toronto or even Belfast. Other variants of ethno-religious identities were apparent in the formal and informal power networks of contemporary American cities. Nuances in early migration streams had determined that Orange rather than green would be the badge of distinction in Toronto. Equally, altered nuances in post-war migration streams rendered the previous power alignments of Toronto redundant – creating a multicultural city in the process. It is a moot point whether present-day Toronto is an outgrowth of its past or a "born again" creation: a triumph of change over continuity.

This book has been written at a time of significant changes in the personal world of my family. Weddings and the arrival of two grandsons, Thomas and Culann, have enriched and extended the family experience. Fiona provided the skill set for the construction of the diagrams, Sinead and Cathal provided technical advice. In the midst of an environment of transformation, Rosemary has remained firm, wise, and supportive and has provided much-needed editorial assistance. To all, a debt is owed.

The book is dedicated to two men, now deceased, who were significant influences on my professional career. Professor Tom Jones Hughes was my mentor during my undergraduate and postgraduate years in Geography and he provided unflinching support at critical points in my early career. Professor Don Kerr guided my development in the University of Toronto and was a friend and constructive critic thereafter. Both men were quiet determined scholars, possessed of the highest standing and integrity. I am indebted also to Rev. Edward Jackman for generously supporting the publication of the book. At all stages in the production process I have been privileged by the editorial assistance and support of Len Husband of University of Toronto Press.

TORONTO, THE BELFAST OF CANADA

The Orange Order and the Shaping
of Municipal Culture

Introduction

Toronto in the twenty-first century has little memory of an earlier and formative era in its history when an assemblage of transplanted Irish cultures created in the Canadian city a social and political environment that bore close resemblance to that of Belfast. Toronto may have forgotten, but many in Belfast still remember, some with pride and others with misgivings, the depth and significances of the Ulster contribution to the shaping of Canadian history and the bonds that formerly united two cities within a British imperial outreach. Transference from Belfast was embedded in Toronto's history, culture, image, and personality. The specifics of geography and the accidents of history helped create a distinctive civic culture in the Canadian city and, although it was never a replica of Belfast, it did sustain over many generations a resemblance that was always more complex than simply being a site for the re-enactment of immigrant Irish quarrels. Sectarian violence was part of Toronto's past, but its identity as the "Belfast of Canada" extended well beyond that to include a distinctive manifestation of municipal governance – one wherein the political machinery of Orangeism was able to develop a remarkable grip on power and patronage within the city. To some extent there were similarities with the system operated by ward bosses and their political machines in contemporary American cities, but in Toronto it was religion, not ethnicity, that provided the unifying bonds for the dominant group. The descriptor "Toronto the Belfast of Canada" was in common usage for the better part of one hundred years, losing its relevance and application only in the 1950s and being largely forgotten by most Torontonians thereafter. It was a name that signified much more than the record of demographic links that had routinely directed tens of thousands of Ulster migrants to the Ontarian city: the appellation was also a metaphor for a reconstructed cultural geography in which a Protestant and British set of values, bearing the distinctive and often divisive inflections of Belfast society, found a fertile new environment. Loyalty to Empire and the Protestant monarch was a cherished belief of the majority of citizens in both cities, but their urban cultures were infused also with a latent suspicion of Catholics and a general unwillingness to make space for them in public life and employment. Indeed, in both Belfast and Toronto there were occasions when the inter-group suspicions escalated into religious animosities that spilled over into street riots and neighbourhood violence, but the incidence of such extremism was most pronounced in the Ulster city. Ulster Protestant settlers in Toronto celebrated with enthusiasm their construction of a replica of their homeland and over time they came to set the standard for loyalty and British Protestantism in the new setting. To them the epithet "Belfast of Canada" was a badge of pride; conversely, the epithet represented for Catholics a stark reminder of sectional triumphalism and of a social experience that was less than inclusive and inherently prone to discriminatory practice. "Belfast of Canada" was a term of abuse hurled by Catholics at opponents in municipal life, an accusation of political corruption and self-serving elitism. The stark difference in meaning attributed to the single descriptor reflected clearly the lack of a shared vision for the shaping of Toronto prior to the mid-twentieth century.

Toronto had originated as a conservative British and Protestant town, but early in its history it became apparent that the dominant influence shaping the nuances of its political and social life was the transplanted culture of Irish Protestantism with all of its fractious history and defensive mentality. Canadian historian Maurice Careless has suggested that by the 1820s it was evident that "the long Orange Walk through Toronto history was already underway."[1] The Orange Order had originated in Ulster in 1795, only two years after Lieutenant-Governor Simcoe had founded the Canadian town, and many of Toronto's earliest Irish settlers were men who had personal experiences of the battles, group massacres, and sectarian attacks of the 1798 Rebellion. They had grown up in an Ireland where the Orange Order was undergoing rapid geographical expansion throughout the island: a self-appointed counter-revolutionary force of loyalists that, at certain times, enjoyed the pragmatic favour of government, but which was generally distrusted by officialdom. In many respects the extension of the Order to the Canadian colonies was merely a transatlantic manifestation of a process of spatial diffusion that had emanated from Co Armagh, spreading with some rapidity throughout Ireland and into Scotland and England.[2] Prior to 1850 in Canada, successive waves of immigrants from Ulster and other Protestant enclaves in Leinster and Munster constituted upwards of 60 per cent of all immigrants from the British Isles, and at least two-thirds of them were Protestant. Throughout Ontario, its rural settlements, towns, and cities, they proved to be particularly adept at manipulating the levers of political power. Nowhere was this more apparent than in Toronto, where they secured control of municipal politics as early as the 1840s, retaining it almost continuously for the next one hundred years. Second- and third-generation Irish Canadians shared lodge membership and political ambitions with newer waves of immigrants from Ireland, England, and Scotland, and the Orange Order moved resolutely to the centre of Toronto's civic culture. Orangeism established itself as the arbitrator of loyalty and Protestantism in the city, setting the standards to which others might aspire and endowing the city with a personality for which it became internationally renowned. No understanding of the evolution of Toronto history is attainable without an identification of the central role played by the transplanted organization.

At the macro level, the Orange Order helped formulate, support, and lead political sentiment centred upon maintenance of the connection with the British motherland, and, although it was not the only support for such sentiment, it was certainly one of the most vociferous. Throughout more than a century, Orange leaders managed to link the ambitions of their organization with a projected Canadian national identity. Active in defeating Mackenzie's 1837 Rebellion, Orangemen claimed prominence in resisting the Fenian invasions of Canada in the decade of Confederation, and took especial pride in thwarting the Riel Rebellions in the Canadian West, avenging in the process the death of Thomas Scott, himself a lifelong Orangeman. Such national political crises, in combination with a long-standing suspicion of French and Catholic populations in Quebec, helped sustain an Orange garrison mentality. Simultaneously, defence of the imperial connection, a central concern of many Canadians especially in the nation-building period 1870–1920, was adapted to Orange thinking by reference to the Empire as a bulwark of Protestantism and portrayal of the Irish Home Rule movement as a threat to not only imperial unity but, by implication, Canada's own political identity.[3] At a more local level the Order, through its control of municipal power in Toronto, supported a version of machine politics that ensured that Catholic representation in political life and public employment was kept to a minimum and oversaw the creation of a set of municipal by-laws that helped support a strong sabbatarian flavour in city life. Sunday prohibition of public transport and organized games in the city parks were symptomatic of a generally conservative Protestant influence, but their advocates were most likely to be found especially in the city's annual Twelfth of July parade, which involved thousands of Orangemen, many of them city officials and public employees whose attendance was facilitated by time off with pay. The centrality of the Order in Toronto politics was remarkably long-lived and, although not identical to its counterpart in Belfast, its influence was sufficiently similar to warrant the cultivation of the nickname "The Belfast of Canada" for the Queen City of Ontario.

The social and political dynamics that characterized both Belfast and Toronto in the period 1850–1950 not only depended upon the operation of the Orange Order as a successful political machine but also implied a functional relationship with a Catholic population that was never more than one-third, or fewer than one-eighth, of the population of either city. By the way it dealt with a Catholic minority that was always too large to ignore, the Orange Order in both Belfast and Toronto constructed a civic culture in which identity politics were to the fore. Catholics, because of their religion, were viewed as different, and their "otherness" generated suspicion and sometimes hostility. In both places an identification of Catholicism and Irishness added a further ingredient of complexity and grounds for animosity.

At frequent intervals throughout the nineteenth century, the two cities experienced street rioting and sectarian murders, but there was a vast difference between the intensity of violence in Toronto and that in Belfast, where sectarian mayhem has persisted until recently. Violence, however episodic, was an extreme manifestation of deep-set community divisions; similarities in the civic culture of the two cities were also recognizable in other behaviour of lower intensity but longer duration. Discriminatory practices in the manner in which patronage, especially in respect of employment and procurement of services, was distributed were uncannily similar in both places. The New World setting did make a difference, but not enough to disguise a common reluctance to make space for Catholics when largesse from the public purse was being distributed. Municipal officialdom presented a cold environment for the Catholic minority over many decades.[4] So too did the employment patterns in Toronto-based federal and provincial government offices. Recent analyses of the identity of the Catholic Irish community in Toronto have emphasized, especially for the post-1880 period, their significant upward social mobility, their unequivocal loyalty to their new home, and their integration into mainstream Canadian society.[5] The present study suggests that, notwithstanding their credentials as good citizens, unqualified integration was still some way off by the end of the century, and that it was not until the 1950s that the environment of official Toronto became less cold for Catholics. The transformation of civic culture that became most apparent in mid-twentieth-century Toronto was founded not so much upon a defined uplift of Catholic fortunes as upon a demographic transition that completely diluted the principles that had sustained city politics for so long, destroying in the process the preserved parochialism of the old regime. Henceforth, Little Italy, Chinatown, and Greek Town became the community names for immigrant districts within the city. A celebration of ethnic heterogeneity and an implicit cosmopolitanism were proposed as the new civic culture. The "Belfast of Canada" disappeared not because either of the traditional adversaries won but because both were subsumed within a new environment wherein the religious wars of seventeenth-century Europe and the fortunes of imperial Britain had become irrelevant within the wider schema of Toronto life. Civic culture and its attendant social and political conditions altered much more slowly in contemporary Belfast.

The present study focuses upon the period 1850–1950, during which Toronto grew from a small provincial city to a metropolitan centre of continental significance. In the process it developed its economic base, adding a significant industrial component to its original commercial and administrative functions. Its population expanded from 30,000 to 675,000 over the course of that century, and, by the time of the First World War, it had attained parity in size with Belfast. Thereafter it grew much more rapidly than the Ulster city, drawing upon a diverse migration stream that introduced a much greater plurality of ethnic groups, particularly eastern and southern Europeans, to the city in the early twentieth century. The impact of the new migration stream was initially slow and, as late as 1950, almost 70 per cent of Torontonians still claimed British origins. Two decades later that charter group contained less than half the citizenry and a fundamental transformation of the civic culture was evident to all. Initially, demographic growth and increasing cultural diversity had been accommodated within a comparatively narrow framework of social and cultural change, but from the mid-twentieth century onwards national and global transformations diluted the restraining influences of Toronto's conservative past.

Arguably, the culture of City Hall altered at a pace slower than that of the citizenry in general, but ultimately change became an inescapable condition for the mayor's office, the Council Chamber, and the administrative mandarins alike.

Genesis, Consolidation, and Demise of Orange Power

In the 1840s and 1850s the Orange Order emerged as a distinctive power bloc within municipal politics, contributing to the demise of the established Tory Family Compact group and forging a new power base for immigrant Irish Protestants. But electoral strength did not immediately deliver social or political respectability. From the outset the Order and its electoral machinery were viewed with suspicion not only by Catholics but also by the older social elite who still retained personal power, wealth, and influence. Orange performance justified those suspicions. The organization and its hangers-on were frequently associated with personal intimidation and group violence, and its public parades were at times subject to official censure and legislative prohibition. Respectability and power did ultimately coalesce, and by the 1890s the Orange Order was the largest voluntary organization in the city, claiming a membership that was composed predominantly of skilled and unskilled labourers but also included many representatives of the professional and commercial elites. Throughout the first half of the twentieth century, Orange parades in Toronto usually included the premier of Ontario, the mayor of the city, several judges, senior administrators, managers, and civil servants, including the chairmen of Ontario Hydro and the Toronto Transit Commission, respectively. Businessmen, lawyers in frock coats, teachers, doctors, and journalists paraded from the Legislature in Queen's Park to Exhibition Park in the company of firemen, policemen, and streetcar drivers – all of them formally arrayed behind banners depicting scenes of seventeenth-century Irish battles. The silk banners had probably been hand-painted in Belfast, the sashes were of Canadian manufacture, and the prevailing ideology was transnational but scarcely progressive. As an organization the Order embodied decades of continuous power and influence, and nowhere was that more apparent than in City Hall. In Toronto virtually all mayors in the period 1850–1950 were Orangemen – and while most of them were Irish in origin, the two most outspoken anti-Catholic mayors in the twentieth century, Horatio Hocken and Leslie Saunders, were born in England. Elsewhere, the Ontario government and the federal Parliament in Ottawa also contained many Orangemen, several of them in positions of power, and

Englishmen, Scots, and Canadians were prominent among the membership at large. Among the first twelve prime ministers of Canada there were four Orangemen – John A. Macdonald, John Abbott, Mackenzie Bowell, and John Diefenbaker – and it is indicative of the breadth of appeal of the fraternity that none of them were of Irish ethnic origin.

Despite the apparent simplicity of its beliefs and prejudices, the Orange Order in Toronto was a complex political and social machine. It was also an organization that was well able to adjust to changing economic and social environments, but there were limits to its chameleon-like qualities. It could, for example, cope with changing demographic conditions, but only as long as the majority of the population were of British background. It was at an impasse when Toronto's population changed to include migrations that were dominated by European Catholics and diverse groups from Asia, the Caribbean, and the Middle East. Its demise, however, must be seen also in a wider context of political and social change. The collapse of the British Empire, the waning of an imperial spirit, and the growth of a self-confident Canada all challenged the macro-scale relevance of the tenets of Orangeism in the decades after the First World War. By the time Orange servicemen returned to Canada after the Second World War, their fraternal organization appeared old-fashioned and ill equipped to operate in a country then undergoing fundamental social and economic change. The intimacy of old workplace loyalties was diminished, suburbanization had fractured community networks, and a new multinational society was increasingly to the fore in political, social, and religious life. Apart from such fundamental alterations to the national political environment, other threats of a more social nature operated to its detriment. The Orange Order was not the only voluntary organization to face collapse in the second half of the twentieth century. In America and in Canada alike, ongoing migration to the suburbs, the emergence of new forms of recreational activity, and an overall diminution of a sense of community have combined to challenge the older form of social and recreational activity represented by voluntary societies. Late twentieth-century society emerged as more individualistic and more atomized than that of preceding generations; secular as well as religious organizations suffered accordingly.[6] Patterns of engagement with civic society and the nature of civic society itself have been transformed, and in combination they have sounded the death knell of very many organizations, none more obviously than the Orange Order in Toronto. Even in contemporary Belfast the impact of modernity on social organizations has resulted in a decline in Orange membership and a narrowing of the class profile of members.[7] A process of generational change and a transformation of the demographic components of Toronto have completely altered the ecological niche wherein the Order had flourished for so long, and in so far as its shrunken number of lodges retain a sense of vibrancy they are most likely to express it in certain suburbs where recent immigrants from Ulster and Scotland have congregated.

When a new Canadian national anthem, "O Canada," was selected to replace "God Save the Queen" in the 1960s, the much-weakened Orange Order expressed outrage on two counts. The new anthem was condemned as a composition of a Catholic priest in Quebec, and the Orange ode, "The Maple Leaf Forever," had been ignored. The protests had little impact. Contemporaneous adoption of a new national flag served only to confirm that a new reality had emerged and much of it had little recall of Orange heritage or history.

The present study is therefore about Toronto at a particular period in its history and it examines the nature and processes of socio-political engagement that were then characteristic of the city. The Orange Order is employed as a means to unravelling and understanding the city, but this is ultimately a study that transcends the boundaries of institutional history. It explores core elements in the formation and sustenance of civic culture and municipal politics, evaluating ethnic transplants that adjusted to become central components in the adopted new environment. By way of comparison with Belfast, the common and distinctive elements of Canadian and Irish Orangeism are explored, and the mediating influences of the new environment are assessed. In so doing the present study builds upon the seminal work published thirty years ago by Houston and Smyth,[8] but it goes beyond their findings by reference to nominal census data and municipal records, many of which were not available to the earlier authors. Patterns of municipal, provincial, and federal employment in Toronto are identified and assessed in the context of the civic culture. Contemporary Orange, church, city, and newspaper archives have been drawn upon in a reconstruction of core aspects of that civic culture. The study terminates at a juncture that is commonly recognized as pivotal in the evolution of Toronto and presents an interpretation of the timing and causality of cultural change. The Orange Order did not die in Toronto in 1950; it still persists, albeit in much-reduced circumstances, but its trajectory had altered fundamentally and irreparably by the mid-twentieth century.

1 Canada and Ireland: The Imperial Context

Greater than life size, the ornate granite and metal monument in the grounds of Belfast City Hall depicts a son of the locality, Frederick Temple Blackwood, First Marquis of Dufferin and Ava. The perimeter of the plinth is adorned with two additional carved figures – a fur-capped Canadian voyageur sitting on a moose, and a turbaned Indian complete with sabre sitting on a cannon. The sculpture memorializes an Ulster landlord who was appointed as Canada's third governor-general in 1872 and eighth viceroy of India more than a decade later. The far-flung and diverse geography of the British Empire epitomized by Dufferin's appointments as Queen Victoria's representative reflects well the importance and complexity of Ireland, Belfast, and its Ulster hinterland in the imperial outreach of contemporary Britain. Ireland's contribution to empire building may be measured by its contribution of soldiers, settlers, administrators, and ecclesiastical figures who helped structure, defend, and populate colonies across the globe. But the nature of that contribution was complex and sometimes contradictory. Internal differences fractured the Irish population, and the relationship that bound Ireland and Britain was often volatile. Ireland was undoubtedly part of the heartland of imperial power, represented in Westminster by more than a hundred elected parliamentarians and dozens of aristocratic denizens in the Upper House. But yet it was, in many respects, peripheral to the core and retained many of the characteristics of a long-established colony. The administration in Dublin Castle bore many similarities to colonial administrations around the world, and the presence of an armed police force and military garrison bases throughout the island reflected an environment wherein local resentments could, and sometimes did, spill over into revolutionary insurrection.

Prior to the Irish Church Act of 1869, the Church of Ireland, which catered to the minority Anglican population, was supported financially by taxes levied on all citizens – the overwhelming majority of whom were Catholic. Civil power rested in the hands of administrators appointed from London, not Dublin, and they ruled an Ireland that was incredibly complex in its political, religious, and social composition. Ireland was not a homogeneous entity, and while elites within it supported the imperial agenda fully and creatively, the majority of the population were more marginal to the imperial project. As soldiers, administrators, and settlers, they participated, however willingly, in the expansion and retention of Empire, but an ambiguity persisted as to whether Ireland was really part of the core or merely part of the colonized periphery, and whether Irish settlers were really colonial adventurers or merely hapless exiles.[1] Certainly, Ireland was less apparently British than was Scotland, England, or Wales, and, recognizing this reality, Linda Colley, in her seminal analysis of British culture, excluded Ireland from her exploration of Britishness, declaring that "Ireland was cut off from Great Britain by the sea; but it was cut off still more effectively by the prejudice of the English, Welsh and Scots, and by the self-image of the bulk of the Irish themselves, both Protestants and Catholics."[2]

Yet the impact of Ireland on diverse parts of the Empire has been both considerable and enduring. Across the Atlantic, over a period spanning four centuries and at geographical scales ranging from continent to region to city, the presence and contributions of the Irish were easily discernible. Group identities, transferred by the accident of early population movements and fostered by vibrant and prolonged chain migrations, created ties that bound places on both sides of the ocean. The Scotch Irish of eighteenth-century Pennsylvania, the Catholic Irish ghettoes of early nineteenth-century eastern seaboard cities, and the Orangemen of Toronto all exemplified geographical relocations but not necessarily authentic reconstructions of regional Irish identities in New World settings. Those relocations, however modified, were constructed within the context of a dynamic and expansive British imperial outreach.

The first British Empire, commencing circa 1500, lasted until the loss of the American colonies in 1783, and it formed part of a wider pattern of European expansion that was driven especially by the Iberian powers, France, Holland, and England. Irish migrants were strongly represented in the British outreach to both the Caribbean and American settlements of the seventeenth century, and in the century before 1775 more than a quarter of a million Irish may have crossed the Atlantic. The scale of the migration, emanating from such a small source area, was unprecedented. To put it in perspective, it may be noted that the number of French who settled permanently in Canada before the Conquest was approximately ten thousand. Both were part of an emigration flow of an estimated aggregate total of 1.4 million European migrants who, during the period 1500–1783, made the transoceanic voyage to French, Portuguese, Spanish, Dutch, and British colonies in the Americas. Ireland supplied between one-sixth and one-quarter of this cohort, although at the time it was home to less than 2 per cent of the population of Europe. Throughout this period, Ireland had the highest proportion of emigrants per one thousand population of any European country or region. Within the British Isles, the degree of over-representation of Ireland's emigration was stark. In the 1770s, for example, Ireland had a total population of about 3.5 million, England had 6.5 million, and Scotland had about 1.5 million, but the Irish emigrants outnumbered the English and Scots combined.[3] The vast majority of these Irish settled within the North American territories of the First British Empire, and by the time of the American Revolution they were the largest ethnic group in the nine American colonies south of New England. More than any other group, the Irish moved early in conjunction with the logistics of imperial trade, availing themselves of the settlement opportunities that emerged with the overseas outreach of an expanding "Greater Britain." For the most part, they worked as indentured servants or settled independently on the agricultural frontier, although their role in commerce and administration may have been greater than has been traditionally acknowledged. The majority of them were Protestant, mostly Presbyterian, but upwards of a quarter may have been Catholic.[4]

The Irish, therefore, constituted a primary ingredient in the rise of early emigration from Europe, and this demographic dynamic was replicated in the nineteenth century, a period when world demography entered its modern phase of mass migration. A revolution in transportation, world trade, and political circumstances created conditions in which the remaining temperate grasslands and forested areas of the mid-latitudes and, later, the rising industrial cities would be targeted in a migration frenzy of Europeans seeking opportunities abroad. In the century 1815–1914, emigrants from the British Isles contributed 22.6 million to that migration flow, and within it the Irish amounted to at least 7 million. Throughout this period Ireland contributed 15 per cent of all European migrants, and for eight of the ten decades that preceded

the First World War, Ireland was ranked first among European countries in terms of the annual average rate of emigration per one thousand
population.[5]

The Irish migrant stream initially followed the established pattern of
the eighteenth century, moving northward along the eastern seaboard
of North America, seizing opportunities as they arose within the tim-
bered resources of the Miramichi and Saint John valleys in New Brunswick, the Ottawa Valley, and the rich agricultural land of the Lake Erie
and Lake Ontario shores. In tens of thousands they moved upstream
along the St Lawrence River. Some settled in Montreal and Quebec City,
a few found agricultural possibilities in the Eastern Townships, but the
vast majority continued westward to the settlement frontier of Ontario.
It was the Ulster counties of Ireland that contributed the majority of
the emigrants, probably two-thirds of whom were Protestant. But as
economic conditions worsened, and the relative cost of ocean passages
fell, the lure of emigration cascaded through Irish society. By the 1840s
all parts of Ireland and all religious groups were contributing to the
emigration mania. In the thirty years prior to the mid-century famine
that drove more than one million people out of Ireland in the years
1845–50 and caused the death of a comparable number, the Canadian
colonies were the preferred destinations for slightly more than half of
the Irish emigrants who crossed the Atlantic, although very many of
them proceeded south of the border either immediately or quite soon
after disembarking. The numbers of Irish famine migrants peaked in
1847. Thereafter, an alteration in the statutory regulation of Canadian
immigration had the effect of directing the overwhelming bulk of the
Irish emigrants to the United States. Canada attracted but a trickle. With
the exception of the 1880s and the first two decades of the twentieth
century, migration to Canada from Ireland remained at a low level, surpassed by both the English and the Scots. The nature of the Canadian
Irish population, therefore, was shaped primarily by its pre-famine
origins and by its concomitant religious complexion, two-thirds Protestant and one-third Catholic – an inverse ratio to that of the nineteenth-
century Irish community in the United States, and indeed the inverse
of the religious demography of Ireland itself.[6] This distinctive manifestation of Irish emigration was not a simple repetition of the eighteenth-century Scotch-Irish emigration to colonial America. The Irish
Protestant immigrants to Canada were more likely to be Anglican than
Presbyterian, and they had left an Ireland that was increasingly polarized by events such as the 1795 formation of the partisan Orange Order,

the bloodshed of the 1798 United Irishmen's rebellion, and the abolition of the Irish Parliament in 1800. Nineteenth-century Ireland moved
increasingly in a direction wherein Irishness was equated with Catholicism and, conversely, Protestantism was identified with loyalty to the
newly constituted United Kingdom of Great Britain and Ireland. In the
process, innate sectarian and political tensions became much more visible, and those tensions were an intrinsic part of the cultural baggage
transferred to Canada.

The Irish in Canada

It has been estimated that in the period 1815–50, at least 960,000 people left the British Isles for Canada. The ethnic composition of that
outflow was approximately 60 per cent Irish, 20 per cent English, and
20 per cent Scots.[7] The pattern of emigration emphasized a geography
of the United Kingdom's periphery. Both Scotland and Ireland were
over-represented in the exodus, but it was the latter country that was
most aberrant. Ontario attracted the greatest share of the migrants,
and within that destination the Irish outnumbered the combined
numbers of English and Scots. Their relative strength was even more
apparent in urban centres, especially Toronto. In 1851 Toronto was
very much an immigrant city – almost two-thirds of its population
had been born in the British Isles and, of those, 61 per cent had been
born in Ireland, 27 per cent in England, and 12 per cent in Scotland.
Seventy-five per cent of its citizens were Protestant. The Irish presence
inserted a particularly distinctive personality into the city, and that
personality developed and flourished over several decades within a
congruent Canadian political environment.

The political realities of early nineteenth-century Canadian society
were embedded in a geographical reality that contained within it the
twin strands of French and British imperial ambitions and juxtaposed
contrasting social, linguistic, and religious cultures. Confessional states
had been the norm in early modern Europe, and sets of symbiotic relationships between Church and State were transferred, in much of their
detail, to the New World, where they informed the development of
colonial societies – lending emphasis to the development of popular as well as "official" culture. Canada embraced the legacy of both
the earlier Catholic French heritage and a more recent Protestant British heritage. The British conquest of French Canada, 1759–60, "reposi-
tioned the French-speaking people along the lower St. Lawrence in a

British empire that had warred with France, would do so again, and was deeply suspicious of Roman Catholicism."[8] Throughout the next two centuries, Canada's emerging identity was constructed within the context of a rapidly expanding British Empire, and the country became a favoured and indispensable component of imperial greatness. Cartographic distortions inherent in Mercator map projections may have created a visual exaggeration of the scale of the broad swathe of British red on contemporary maps of the world, but the strategic location, settlement geography, and resource base of British North America made that region a vital component in an Empire that covered, at its peak, one-quarter of the land surface of the earth. Britain and its Empire were part of what might be described as "an imagined political community,"[9] and a fundamental trait of that community was an identity that had been forged and developed from the early eighteenth century onwards. Linda Colley has argued that a sense of Britishness emerged only after the Union of Scotland and England 1707, and only then in reaction to a sense of "the other beyond their shores." Central to this emerging identity was an affirmed dependence upon Protestant culture – "Protestantism was the foundation that made the invention of Great Britain possible," she argues, emphasizing that, by way of contrast, Britons viewed Catholic nations and Catholic communities as subservient to the Pope, poverty-ridden, and misguided, and within this infrastructure of prejudice there was little room for inclusive tolerance.[10] The Empire was Protestant; loyalty and Protestantism were synonymous, and Catholics were perceived as being inherently disloyal. Within this general imperial context, the specifics of Canada's developing social and political identity were guided by the dynamic juxtaposition of an inherited Catholic French population, a predominantly Protestant British immigration, and a significant population of Irish Catholics, all united under a single imperial authority.

The geography of settlement was to eventually create two distinct cultural regions within Canada. Language and religion were the badges of distinctiveness that separated the "two solitudes" of French and English Canada. Within the British-settled areas, and none more so than in what was to become the province of Ontario, religion created its own divisions and tensions, the precise nature of which owed much to the early numerical dominance of immigrants from Ireland who transferred deep-seated antagonisms to the New World setting. Writing at the end of the nineteenth century, George Grant, Canadian philospher and president of Queen's University in Kingston, commented:

Even in cities where there is the closest association of Protestants and Romanists in commercial, industrial and political life, the two currents of religious life flow side by side as distinct from each other as the St. Lawrence and the Ottawa after their junction. But the rivers do eventually blend into one. The two currents of religious life do not.[11]

From such an imperial perspective we can look afresh at the Irish in Canada. It was in Canada, and especially in Ontario, that the Irish immigrants constructed a unique colonial society, one that was very different from the Irish communities of either the United States or Australia. Ability to provide for early emigrant passage, a predisposition towards greater mobility emanating from their tradition of migration in the previous century, and perhaps also a perception of the role and nature of the British colony were combined in a filtration process that affected the timing and composition of the migration stream leaving Ireland, influencing also their regional distribution subsequent to arrival in Canada. The St Lawrence shipping artery delivered Catholic and Protestant Irish simultaneously to the Canadian gateway, Quebec City, but of those who settled in French Canada, a majority were Catholic. Conversely, Protestants were in the majority among those settling in Ontario. Behavioural differences manifested themselves upon arrival, and a feedback mechanism of emigrant letters and kin-based patterns of migration created a potent chain migration that reinforced the initial settlement geography.[12]

Irrespective of their religion, all immigrants arriving from Ireland in the period 1815–45 brought to Canada a sense of leaving a country in which a spiralling population had created the most densely settled rural landscape of western Europe. Tensions, ambition, and the frustrations of thwarted opportunity fractured long-standing generational ties with regional and local niches and prompted a search for a new beginning. Not all could realize their dreams by migrating; those with access to a small amount of capital were best positioned to make the break with the homeland. By virtue of their social position, Protestants were advantaged to move early. Consequently, the growing mania for emigration was initially most apparent in Ulster and regional enclaves in Leinster and Munster where Protestants formed localized majorities. Anglicans, socially and politically akin to the landed ascendancy of contemporary Ireland, were the largest component of the migration and, importantly, it was they who had been to the fore in defending power, position, and privilege in the bitter sectarian environment of a generation earlier. In the 1790s, it was Anglicans of all social strata who had been instrumental in organizing the Orange Order to combat the rising social and political claims of Catholics, and Anglicans too were very much central in the bitter sectarian and political events that had led to the death of thirty thousand people in the summer months of the 1798 United Irishmen's rebellion. In a short-lived accommodation of views, liberal Presbyterians, inspired by political events in contemporary France, had sided with Catholics during that Rebellion, but in the aftermath of the Act of Union they too had progressively identified with the Establishment's anti-Catholic stance. Few of the early pioneers in Ontario would have been participants in the 1798 Rebellion, but almost all would have been the children or grandchildren of those who had lived through, or perhaps died, in that turbulent event.

By the 1830s, however, it was apparent that no region of Ireland was immune to the lure of emigration, and only the poorest, and predominantly Catholic, landless classes remained immobilized by their poverty. Ultimately these were most affected by the famine, 1845–50, and hundreds of thousands of this vulnerable agricultural underclass died of disease and starvation. Canadian geographer Cole Harris has described the migrations of this period as constituting a conservative defence of a pre-existing value system – the migrants were not social revolutionaries, and through relocation they hoped to improve, or at least maintain, the social standing into which they had been born.[13] This innate conservative trait was, of course, further intensified by the possibility that dissatisfied immigrants could, and many did, continue their journey on to the United States, thereby insulating and preserving among those remaining in Canada an ethos that was fundamentally conservative in values and attitudes.

It was that conservative mindset which helped define the Protestant Irish in Canada, presenting a clear continuity with the cultural environment of their unique homeland region on the Atlantic fringe of Europe. The Canadian context was that of a colonial outreach in which British law, the English language, and Protestant religion provided at the macro level a supportive and familiar environment for the settlers. Canada was not an isolated outpost, far removed from the value system and social realities of the British homeland.[14] The scale of the Irish influx ensured that there was sufficient mass to support cherished aspects of their transplanted culture, and the infusion of continuous migration ensured that organic relationships were maintained with the homeland. The 1871 Canadian census, the first enumeration since

Confederation, recorded 850,000 persons of Irish descent, one-quarter of the national population. They were second only to the French, and significantly more than those of English and Scottish origin. More than half of the Irish had been drawn from Ulster, a relatively small region of little more than 150 kilometres in either an east-west or north-south extent, and even that small geographic region was further characterized by certain sub-districts that were especially associated with the Canadian migrations. Given that prepaid fares and emigrant remittances helped fund the passage of many, it was hardly surprising that an

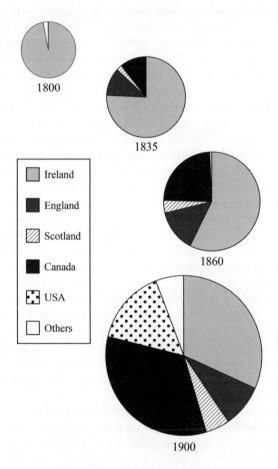

1.1 Global distribution of Orange lodges, 1800–1900

intrinsic networking dynamic operated within the chain migration process, facilitating the successful transfer of many aspects of the regional culture of their homeland. By means of such transfers, the immigrants reconstructed their community identity, supported by a networks of church memberships and voluntary associations, and, undisputedly, the Orange Order was the most important of their transplanted secular organizations.

The male fraternal organization of the Orange Order operated as an integral part of community life on the frontier, providing a range of social facilities for the immigrant Protestant population and acting as a focal point for community development. Protestants of other ethnic origins were welcome to join the quintessential Irish cultural transplant, and they did so in considerable numbers. Early lodge buildings, usually log structures capable of accommodating meetings of forty or fifty members, were located in the corner lots of farms and in village settlements, and were rarely more than a few miles apart. At the conclusion of monthly meetings, at which Scripture was read and politics discussed, brown sugar and hot whiskeys helped while away the long winter evenings, and in summer the annual Twelfth of July parade offered the opportunity for public spectacle and family picnics. Orange funerals, assistance to members whose barns or houses had burnt down, and privileged access to off-farm employment all signified the supportive role of the Order in forging community consciousness. With very little alteration, the details of initiation ceremonies, the symbols, sashes and officers' regalia, drums and banners, were directly transferred from the 1795 Irish prototype. Orangemen from different parts of Ireland, and representing different denominations of Protestantism, found common cause under the familiar auspices of an organization that saw nothing strange about celebrating the victory of King William over the Catholic King James at the battle of the Boyne in July 1690 amid the tree stumps of a partially cleared landscape on the margin of the Canadian wilderness. There was even a Boyne River in Ontario, and plenty of other evocative place names such as Orange Corners, Enniskillen, Derry, and Belfast. Orangemen, processing from the partially cleared farms in annual celebration of a defining moment in British and European history, articulated clearly the wider dynamic of imperial relationships that imparted local meaning to life on the frontier.

Irish Protestants, at home and abroad, did not lack certitude about the significance of being part of the British colonial outreach and they were unambiguous advocates of the innate superiority of British

Protestant and monarchical culture. They did, however, retain in their layered identity a sense of Irishness and an enduring affinity with their homeland. Many Catholic Irish settlers, on the other hand, were more ambiguous in their attitude towards the experiment of Empire building, and by virtue of their religion they were always conscious of their difference within the wider schema of the geopolitical realities that characterized the English-speaking world in which they found themselves. Within Canada, they were part of a double minority – an ethnic minority within a Catholic Church populated largely by French Canadians and a religious minority within English-speaking regions outside of Quebec. The transferred sectarian fissures of Ireland meant that the Catholic Irish in Canada were viewed with some suspicion by their Protestant countrymen, and they themselves, conscious of their minority status, sought to construct religious, community, and political structures that would protect their distinctive identity while facilitating their engagement in the emergent civic society. In time they would win the right to operate their own separate confessional schools – a provision that facilitated greatly the retention of their distinctive ethno-religious value system.

Among Protestant communities, the Orange Order with its belief system and geographical network of local, district, and county lodges proved well able to adapt to the new environment. Ultimately, Orangeism was but an Irish manifestation of an ideology that differed only in degree of emphasis and public presentation, but not in kind, from the more general Protestant ethos of British colonial society. In their rhetoric of "No Surrender," Orangemen articulated, with fervour, an attitude in which the colonists saw themselves as an ideological garrison on the Canadian frontier. At one stage Canada could claim more Orange lodges than Ulster, and at the time of Canadian Confederation one-third of all adult male Canadian Protestants were, or had been, members of the organization. A century after its introduction to Canada, the Order still proclaimed its slogan "Keep Canada British and Protestant" and proudly asserted that the organization "has been developing Empire sentiment since its inception."[15] Central to its success was its ability to transcend its original ethnic basis, projecting itself as an important barometer of loyalty and authenticity in Canadian politics. Nowhere was this more obvious than in Toronto, where, at the peak of its organizational strength, the Order contained more men who had been born in Canada, England, and Scotland than in Ireland, and where its influence in municipal governance and civic power was apparent to all. An Irish eighteenth-century creation had proven remarkably adaptable to the colonial context of Canada's foundation and its subsequent national maturation.

In the drumlin country of south Ulster and in the gridiron streets of Toronto alike, the watch cry of "No Surrender" was not merely a historical evocation; it was an integral part of a colonial mindset that unambiguously proclaimed its belief in an imperial civilization that had constructed an Empire on which the sun never set. As colonists, and as the previously colonized, the Irish (Protestant and Catholic) negotiated and constructed their own distinctive identities within the Canadian component of that Empire. Significantly, because of their numerical preponderance, their widespread geographical distribution, and their ease of access to the centrality of power, the Protestant Irish shaped in a very real sense the overall mentality. Toronto emerged, therefore, as a place where continuity and change within the community cultures of the Irish were indicative of much wider imperial and colonial contexts. In very many ways, Toronto was a metaphor for the understanding of Ontario in the century prior to 1950 and its culture that may have been simplified, but which was never simple.

In both Ireland and Canada, the social, cultural, and political divisions that distinguished Catholics from Protestants were not static. The identities of both groups continued to evolve along ever-diverging paths as the nineteenth century progressed. In Ireland, this led, eventually, to territorial partition and the creation of two separate political jurisdictions. In Canada, Irish communities and the pan-British Orange Order were not immune to the fundamental political debates and developments underway in the original homeland, and their reactions had significant implications not only for inter-group relations in Canada but also for Canadian society in general. In the 1860s and 1870s, national unrest in Ireland spilled over into Canadian affairs in the form of the Fenian invasions, and, although it was condemned by Church leaders such as Archbishop Lynch of Toronto and lay leaders such as Thomas D'Arcy McGee, many Catholics did retain a sneaking regard for the invaders. An alleged Fenian assassinated McGee, a Canadian government minister, in Ottawa, and to many the extremities of the Irish political spectrum appeared to have crossed the Atlantic with a vengeance. However, more moderate voices prevailed, and the Irish impact on Canadian political development was largely contained within the framework of constitutional behaviour. Passions, nonetheless, could run high, and developments in Ireland were closely monitored by regular newspaper copy and visits of leading political figures. By way of reaction to macro-scale political developments in their respective homelands, the actions and attitudes of Orangemen, in Canada and in Ireland, evolved in directions that sometimes placed them at the centre of political activity, and at other times consigned them to the margins of acceptability.

Traditionally, the Orange Order has been regarded as an emblem of Protestant Irish culture, both at home and abroad, and in no other country outside of the British Isles did the Order achieve the strength, power, and notoriety that characterized the Canadian organization. Nonetheless, it would be simplistic to view the Order as an unchanging entity, either at home or abroad. Its power waxed and waned over the years, and so also did the esteem in which it was held. The volatility of its actions, especially during its first half-century of existence, resulted in the Order being proscribed (1825–8) in the United Kingdom; subsequently its parades were banned, 1850–70. In Canada, the Order was never proscribed, but its parades were banned, 1843–51.[16] Civil disturbance, associated with its public parades and electoral forays, was the primary reason for the legal censure. Although the Order attained a majority on the municipal council of Toronto by the late 1840s, in the eyes of many citizens it still lacked respectability, and for many years thereafter it continued to be castigated for its fractious contributions to civic life. Nowhere was this more apparent than when the city's Orangemen declared their intent of parading to greet the Prince of Wales on the occasion of the Royal visit in 1860. Ironically, a fear of extreme manifestations of loyalty on the part of Orangemen deterred the Prince from landing in Kingston and was the cause of much negotiation on the part of his officials when he did eventually land in Toronto. The Prince refused to participate in meetings with the Order on the basis that Orange parades were banned in Britain at the time and he did not wish to condone their public activities in the colony. Tensions in Toronto climaxed with a riotous attempt to forcibly drag the Prince's carriage under an Orange arch as he made his way to Sunday service in St James' Cathedral. As the historian Ian Radforth has observed, "Public ceremonies intended to enhance imperial relations ended up exposing long-standing social tensions."[17] The Orange reception accorded to the Prince of Wales demonstrated a latent instability within the organization. But that image was to be transformed in the final third of the nineteenth century when the Order's grip on power strengthened, and political responsibility and social respectability coalesced to bring the organization to a more central position in Canadian life.

The Growth of Orange Respectability in the Belfast of Canada

In the final third of the nineteenth century, the Orange Order experienced a significant improvement in its public image. The forces of change had many origins, and factors local to Canada, as well as international developments, were involved. Within Canada, a cohort of second-generation recruits helped broaden the demographic base of the organization, minimizing its purely immigrant identity. A professed commitment to harmony, stability, and progress in the city and a broadening of the social standing of membership also helped. The Order, although still numerically dominated by labouring and semi-skilled workers, now included many skilled artisans and clerical and professional classes in its ranks, and a maturing generation of immigrants who had arrived in the 1830s and 1840s now included many who had prospered in their new home. Irish-born Francis Medcalf, for example, had settled in Toronto as a blacksmith in 1839, but within a few years he had become a wealthy industrialist and owner of the very successful Don Foundry, specializing in the manufacture of agricultural machinery and heavy castings for water-powered mills. He became the founding grand master of the newly created Toronto County Orange Lodge in 1859 and served as provincial grand master of Canada West, 1862–4. In 1864 he was elected mayor of Toronto on an explicit Orange ticket, serving in that capacity for five years. His abrasive style and unconcealed antipathy towards progress for the Catholic community were redolent of an early style of Orange politics, but as Toronto and its civic culture matured and became more complex, a more socially aware leadership replaced Medcalf's style. The growing political complexity and sophistication of post-Confederation Canada also added a new dynamic that impacted directly on the Order, offering additional foci for its activities. An Ontario legislature based in Toronto and a federal Parliament in Ottawa provided new avenues to power for those who could harness the support of political machines, and henceforth Orangemen aspired to elected positions, spanning a range of offices from City Hall and the provincial legislature in Queen's Park in Toronto, to the federal government, headed initially by Sir John A. Macdonald, himself a member of an Orange lodge in Kingston.

Contemporaneous developments in Britain also lent momentum to the organization's trajectory of social ascent. The ban on Party Processions was rescinded in 1870, and, in both Ulster and Westminster, the cause of Orangeism now evolved in tandem with developments in the arena of mainstream politics. The British Conservative party, who had endorsed the Orange position that Home rule would equate with Rome rule, attacked Gladstone's espousal of Home Rule for Ireland and his introduction in 1886 of a bill to that effect. At a monster meeting in the Ulster Hall in Belfast, the leading Conservative, Lord Randolph Churchill, coined the memorable slogan "Ulster will fight, and Ulster will be right," thereby initiating a political flirtation with Orangeism, anti-Catholic bigotry, and thinly veiled treasonable disloyalty that was to shape British and Irish politics for the next three and a half decades.[18] The debate over Irish Home Rule was not confined to the British Isles. It soon spilled over to Canada, where trenchant opposition to it was espoused by Orangemen and employed as a strategy for harnessing a wide array of support. Home Rule for Ireland was portrayed as a threat to the future integrity of the Empire. Fragmentation of the motherland would, it was argued, have immediate and disastrous implications for the imperial project in which Canada was a central component. Little heed was paid to the obvious fact that Canada itself, recently confederated and endowed with a national parliament, was very similar to the model proposed for Ireland by Gladstone and the British Liberal party.

Orange concerns about the future of the Empire resonated with the leaders of the Canada First movement then seeking to impart an energetic concept of nationalism to post-Confederation Canada. Central to their philosophy was an overriding belief in the fundamental importance of British racial stock, institutions, and culture for the development of a new northern civilization. Far from projecting a Canadian rivalry to the greatness of Britain, the Canada First proponents presented the Empire as an insulating and supportive framework within which Canada could prosper.[19] Underlining its philosophy was a clear sense that the best of the Canadian character was derived from Protestant and English-speaking citizens. As a political movement, Canada First survived for only a few years, but its philosophy found a much broader and lasting base among intellectuals and political leaders at large. This sense of a national destiny, made manifest within a flourishing British imperial system, fitted comfortably with views expressed by the contemporary Orange Order, and a communion of interests was signalled clearly when Goldwin Smith, Canada's leading public intellectual of the day, accepted an invitation to address thousands of Orangemen and their sympathizers at the July Twelfth celebrations in Toronto in 1888 – two years after Gladstone had introduced his first Home Rule bill. With vigour, Smith articulated a vision of a seamless historical link between

William of Orange's contribution to the principles of constitutional freedom, the historical and current roles of the Orange Order, and the future direction of Canada. For its part, the Order continued to promulgate a set of political stances inspired by Irish developments, but tailored to the nuances of Canadian conditions. Issues such as compensation of the Jesuits for property seized in the eighteenth century, the festering issue of separate schools and bilingualism in Manitoba, ongoing concerns about demographic growth, and the geographical expansion of French Canada preoccupied Orangemen. These issues were also the foci of national politics. The confluence of interests allowed the Order to occupy a political space near to that of mainstream society, generating a dynamic relationship that helped enlarge membership and attract many men of high social standing to an organization now deemed to be respectable.

In so doing, the Order, particularly in Toronto, proved itself to be an effective political machine. As a mass organization of several thousand men, it established a strong grip on municipal power and engaged with some success in Canadian provincial and national politics, while at the same time projecting an attractive and continuing appeal to immigrants from the British Isles. As befitted a body then operating in the city for more than eighty years, the Orange Order, in the 1890s, was an effective local construct – about half of its members were Canadian-born, but, strikingly, the other half of its membership was derived from recent immigrants. It spanned two universes. On the one hand, the persistence of an Irish-born cadre of officers in the County Lodge and a stream of enthusiastic recruits from the British Isles helped maintain a vigorous interest in political developments in Ireland. On the other hand, the presence of a large cohort of Canadian-born members, the sense of mission in shaping the Canadian nation along British and Protestant lines, and the realizable worth of local political power combined to give the Order a strong interest in Canadian affairs. The union of Orange concerns about developments in Ireland and about the future prospects of Canada were well illustrated in 1893 when the Toronto County Orange Lodge, spurred on by the publication of the second Irish Home Rule Bill, issued a public statement of support for their Orange brethren in Ireland.

Resolved: That the *Orangemen of Toronto* in County Lodge assembled avail themselves of the earliest opportunity of expressing the warmest sympathy with the Loyalists of Ireland in their present great struggle to preserve the union and the integrity of the British Empire. We fully believe that the adoption of the mischievous and dangerous legislation now proposed by the Government of Great Britain is fraught with the greatest danger to the Empire at large and as loyal subjects of the Empire living in Canada, we enter our most emphatic protest against the passage of the present or any legislation of a similar character which will of necessity tend to the ultimate dismemberment of the Empire. *We* look with confidence to the Imperial Grand Master, the Earl of Erne and the loyalists, noble men associated with him in the House of Lords, to stand nobly in the breach and by voice and vote defeat the impious designs of the enemies of Our Faith and Fatherland and that a Copy of this Resolution be forwarded to the Earl of Erne, Imperial Grand Master and Grand Master of Ireland, Colonel Thomas Waring M.P., Grand Master of England; Colonel Edward G. Saunderson M.P., Grand Master of Scotland: William Johnston M.P., Deputy Grand master of Ireland. *And* we would respectfully intimate to the honourable gentlemen named that when they consider it necessary they may call upon this Loyal City for material aid, which we can assure them will be cheerfully given.[20]

Two years previously, the Imperial World Council of Orangeism had been held in Toronto and, undoubtedly, it had been an occasion for briefing the Canadian Orange leadership on the details of contemporary Irish politics. Reporting back on that meeting to Orangemen gathered in Clifton Street Orange Hall in Belfast, the legendary Irish Orange leader William Johnston MP paid tribute to

The intelligence and energy of the Protestant Canadian emigrants from the North of Ireland. Everywhere Ulstermen were pushing ahead in that great country – men who had gone away from Down and Antrim, and Tyrone and other parts of the province, who had carried with them their Orange certificates, who were standing true to the Protestant cause and who were sober, honest and faithful citizens of the land in which they lived. He was sure that if any Orangemen went out to Canada they would have the warm hand of friendship and fellowship extended to them by their brethren and more than that, they would be told what was best for them to do, and they would find that the Institution was as active, flourishing and thriving as in Ireland and that the brethren were standing by the good old Orange cause as steadfastly as they in Belfast.[21]

Johnston's comments conveyed a sense of a continuing strong Protestant Irish influence in Toronto, and it was that group which provided immediacy and transferred relevance to the Canadian debates about

Irish Home Rule. Through the medium of the Order, Canadians and immigrants from Scotland and England also acquired a passionate interest in the Home Rule debate, and, as the relevant legislation made its way torturously through Westminster, it became increasingly clear that participation in public meetings organized in Toronto by the Order reflected a high level of respectability and social inclusion.

In 1912 a third Home Rule Bill was introduced into the British Parliament, finally passing all stages in 1914, although its scheduled implementation was postponed until after the war. These two years, 1912–14, witnessed vociferous demands from the Toronto Orangemen that the bill be abandoned, and large-scale political rallies were organized with increasing frequency for the city. John Ross Robertson, prominent Torontonian and owner of the *Telegram*, addressed Cameron Orange Lodge, of which he was a member, and asserted in stirring language, "We are all Ulstermen, Ulstermen after the flesh or Ulstermen after the spirit."[22] The sentiment articulated by Robertson was one in which Home Rule for Ireland and imperial disintegration were linked disasters, capable of being averted only through the resistance of Ulster Protestants, aided by their Canadian counterparts. The Westminster debates were not merely of Irish interest, they were projected as being central to the very future of Canada itself, and through public meetings, reams of newspaper coverage, and personal appeals of leading citizens, a successful union of Irish and Canadian political interests was constructed. The strategy was driven by the Orange Order, but was not confined to it, and every effort was made to project a national mood of concern rather than a partisan preoccupation of the few. Within their lodges Orange leaders were more expressive, linking the proposed political developments with a potential rise in Catholic influence, thereby creating a situation where Protestants would be "ruled from the Tiber instead of the Thames."[23] Orchestrated by the Order, a massive rally was organized for Toronto in October 1912, and so great was the attendance that it exceeded the 3,500 seating capacity of Massey Hall and additional accommodation had to be sought in the nearby County Orange Hall on Queen Street. The mayor and aldermen of the city, several prominent non-Orange citizens, and members of the Canadian Parliament and the Ontario legislature took their places on the platform alongside visiting parliamentarians from Britain. Outside, Orange bands played their sectional music on the streets.[24] It was one of many such public protest meetings held in Toronto. In May 1914, for example, a reported 6,000 Ulster sympathizers attended yet another rally in Queen's Park, and to emphasize the general appeal of the cause, Orangemen in attendance were specifically requested by their leaders not to appear in Orange regalia. Instead, every man wore a badge commemorating the Ulster Unionist leader, Sir Edward Carson, and there was widespread support from the crowd for Carson's telegraphed request, "Will Canada help us?"

The *Sentinel* reported:

> The demonstration was more of a religious than of an Orange nature, and hymns such as "Onward Christian Soldiers" and the "Recessional" were the favourites. Citizens of all walks of life, including prominent professionals and businessmen, and men who are leaders in public life, gave the lie to the report that Canada is "heart and soul on the side of the nationalists." A resolution was passed proclaiming Canada's willingness to assist Ulster loyalists with both moral and financial assistance in their "struggle to maintain their rights of full citizenship under the flag of the great and glorious British Empire, of which we, as Canadians, are justly proud to form a part.[25]

It is impossible to ascertain, at this remove, just how many non-Orangemen participated in that rally. At the time there were about 10,000 Orangemen in the city. At least twice as many more had once been members. The 6,000-strong crowd in Queen's Park included several prominent citizens who had never sworn the Orange oath, but the vast majority of those in attendance would have been members of the Order. The tone of religious revivalism which coloured proceedings was very much in keeping with Toronto's civic culture of the day and, in depicting its opposition to a piece of legislation enacted by the Parliament of the United Kingdom as a moral crusade, it was virtually identical in tone and content to the politics of contemporary Belfast.

Orange public rallies fell into abeyance during the wartime years; a quarter of the members were on military service in Europe, and the suspension of the implementation of the Irish Home Rule Act for the duration of the war had removed a stimulus for action. The 1916 Easter Rising in Dublin provoked outrage in Toronto Orange circles, as did the subsequent War of Independence, but mass Orange rallies did not appear in Toronto until 1920, when the partition of Ireland emerged as the likely political settlement to the Irish crisis. Toronto Orangemen rallied in political support for the Protestant and Orange character of the projected state of Northern Ireland and, once more, the strength of the Belfast connection was displayed. A group of Irish Protestant church leaders, touring North America in early 1920 as part of a propaganda exercise mounted by Ulster Unionists, were invited to Toronto, where the leader of the delegation, Rev. William Coote, MP, proclaimed on arrival, "Toronto is the Belfast of Canada. Being so it ought to be the most loyal city in the British Empire ... Toronto could never look with pleasure on a class of men who refused to fight for the Empire and now wish to tear it in two."[26] This was a clear reference to Irish opposition to conscription, but it contained also an implicit allusion to the recent French Canadian conscription crisis. The argument was designed to strategically link the causes of Ulster and English-speaking Canada. The Rev. Coote spoke as guest of honour at a public meeting in Massey Hall, the proceedings of which had been formally opened by prayers led by the Anglican Archbishop of Toronto. Howard Ferguson, future premier of Ontario, shared the platform, and the meeting was chaired by Mayor Church, who deemed "it a great pleasure to welcome to the Belfast of Canada, the brilliant and eloquent representatives of Ulster, the province that has done so much for the building up of this city and the Empire." Both Church and Ferguson were prominent figures in Toronto Orangeism, and their attendance, together with that of several thousand fellow Orangemen, prompted Coote to remark:

> We are delighted with the city [Toronto], with its memory-haunting associations of the Old Land, and with its kindly people. We have been delighted with our welcome from the industrial capital. It reminds us of Belfast, and I cannot say anything more than that, for in that city, friendship means more than mere acquaintainship [sic]. From the first moment we entered the city, until our departure we felt at home in the fullest sense of the word. We have felt that we were in the atmosphere of Ulster. I cannot say more.[27]

The cultural familiarity and social intimacy of Toronto that was recognized by the visiting delegation was an embodiment of the particular nuances of civic culture honed over several generations. The public profile of engagement with the politics of Irish Home Rule was but one, albeit then noteworthy, expression of Toronto's cultural inheritance. For years, commentary on the Irish political crisis had appeared regularly in the mainstream Toronto papers, and was an unsurprising preoccupation of the editor of the Orange organ, the *Sentinel*. That latter publication interspersed its coverage of the Home Rule crisis with reports of the progress of the Empire and the growth of the Orange

Order, and frequent condemnation of the Catholic Church, its *Ne Temere* decree that restricted interfaith marriages, and the anti-British conduct of Daniel Mannix, Archbishop of Melbourne and former president of Maynooth. The Toronto public was kept abreast of Irish developments by telegraphed news reports, reprinted articles from the Ulster and Scottish editions of the *Weekly News,* and the circulation of recent copies of the *Belfast Newsletter* and the *Belfast Telegraph.* There was an intensity to the communications that transcended mere emigrant nostalgia. Its vitality was derived from a constructed interrelated relevance of Canadian, imperial, and Irish politics, orchestrated in large measure under the aegis of the Orange Order and its sympathizers among the wider Canadian political establishment.

From the beginning of the Irish crisis, Toronto's Orangemen had expressed a readiness to provide moral, financial, and even military assistance to the Protestants of Ulster. A few Canadian volunteers did go to Belfast to lend armed support to Protestant paramilitaries, and, more generally, financial aid was provided. However, no systematic records were created for the monetary transfers, and it is impossible to construct an accurate assessment of the scale of the support. American historian Robert McLaughlin has argued that "Orange-Canadian unionists contributed hundreds of thousands of dollars to the arming of the Ulster Volunteer Force."[28] The scale of his suggested flow is surprising. In total, the UVF spent £70,000 on illegal arms, the bulk of it subscribed in Ulster. Recent research suggests that the organization would have had access to little more than £100,000 at the peak of its development. The Canadian contribution, important though it was, could not have been as large as that proposed by McLaughlin. Certainly, the Grand Orange Lodge of British America did send $1,000 in 1914, the Grand Black Chapter sent $2,500, several lodges sent sums of about $50, and individual Orangemen sent modest contributions. But the amount subscribed was a long way from totalling hundreds of thousands of dollars. The records of the County Orange Lodge of Toronto contain only passing references to lodge donations, and the available records for local lodges in the city are equally scarce on the details of expenditure on the Ulster cause – where mentioned, it was generally in amounts of a few dollars.

Moral support was not lacking, however, and the resolutions passed at public meetings in Toronto and expressed in the columns of its newspapers lent credence to the belief that the city was indeed the Belfast of Canada. Some Canadians did avail themselves of the opportunity

to sign the Ulster Covenant – a pledge to resist Home Rule signed in
Ulster in 1912 by a quarter of a million Ulster Protestant men, with a
similar number of Ulster women signing an ancillary pledge. A total of
fifty-six Canadians signed that covenant, but their addresses were all
in Edmonton and Winnipeg.[29] Toronto did not feature, though it is possible that this represented an organizational glitch rather than a lack of
local ardour. Whether that moral support would ever have been translated into the provision of large numbers of fighting volunteers is a
matter for speculation. On commencement of the First World War, the
Ulster Volunteer Force was inserted as a distinctive unit into the British
army; its Canadian supporters merged into the ranks of the Canadian
army. There was, however, no doubting the strength of imperial sentiment in Toronto, and the Orange Order proved itself to be very adroit
in both supporting that sentiment and deriving institutional sustenance
from it.

In the inter-war period, that imperial sentiment waned in the face
of an evident decline in British power and the gradual collapse of the
Empire. Within this altered geopolitical scenario, and suffering also
from a context of fundamental economic, demographic, and cultural
changes, the Orange Order began its inexorable drift to the margins of
municipal significance. But even as late as 1950, when Sir Basil Brooke,
prime minister of Northern Ireland, visited the city, he was able to meet
with thousands of Orangemen at a public rally and could identify readily with them.[30] Significantly, however, an official Canadian government communiqué on this visit noted, "There was too much insistence
upon 'British' and 'Empire' to make his speeches completely compat-
ible to Canadian audiences."[31] That official record of the 1950 visit captured well the transformation of the Toronto and Canadian mindsets,
although Brooke himself was oblivious to the subtleties of the altered
circumstances. The transformation of the city's culture was even more
obvious eight years later during an official visit by the lord mayor of
Belfast. The lord mayor spent four days in Toronto, more than in all
other Canadian cities combined, and his schedule included at least two
lengthy meetings with the local Orange Order. However, cognizant that
the Order no longer retained the power or prestige of earlier decades,
the trip organizers arranged that "Orange events have been left to the
last minute to avoid any possible publicity repercussions, no matter
how remote."[32] By the mid-twentieth century, Toronto had ceased to be
the "Belfast of Canada," and in the altered circumstances the Orange
Order appeared increasingly redundant.

2 A Tale of Two Cities: Belfast and Toronto

Few residents or visitors familiar with Toronto today are aware of the earlier close identification of the Canadian city with its counterpart, Belfast, capital of Northern Ireland. The cosmopolitanism of Toronto stands as the antithesis of the perceived insularity of the Irish city, and the commonality of former political linkages, social patterns, and cultural attitudes is largely forgotten – now irrelevant in a new era of global connectedness and post-modern thinking. Those historians and writers who do have an awareness of the interwoven history of the two cities are largely uncomfortable with the descriptor of Toronto as "the Belfast of Canada" and often suggest in their analyses that the term was, at most, merely partially accurate and relevant only to the third quarter of the nineteenth century. Canadian historian Mark McGowan has argued recently that use of the term produces a history that "is skewed, romanticized, distorted and mythologized."[1] His apparent unease with employment of the metaphor of a Canadian Belfast arises from its implicit connotations of religious bigotry, riotous behaviour, ritualized violence, and naked sectarianism. To McGowan, and many others, it is inconceivable that Toronto should be classified, however fleetingly, in the same genre. Such reservations are understandable. Toronto has never approximated Belfast in the scale of its sectarian murders or street violence, yet the metaphor is capable of being applied and interpreted in ways appropriate to an urban culture that was always more complex than that conveyed merely by the record of sectarian violence. Unquestionably, Toronto has never experienced levels of such violence common in Belfast, where the number of deaths resulting from a single evening of rioting often exceeded the total number of such fatalities accrued over a century in the Canadian city. But, nonetheless, suspicion, tension, and animosity were characteristic features of Protestant-Catholic relations in both Toronto and Belfast, and, most significantly, over several generations the two cities have exhibited many common elements in their municipal power structures and civic cultures. A comparative analysis of the two places has much to offer. Orange celebrations on the Twelfth of July, for example, have been hosted annually in Toronto since 1820, a record of continuity that is almost as long as that of Belfast.[2] However, Orange parades that once brought tens of thousands onto Toronto's main thoroughfares are now almost forgotten, although in Belfast they remain significant, and divisive, public spectacles.

The appellation "Belfast of Canada" would appear to have come into popular use only in the second half of the nineteenth century. McGowan has traced its usage back to the 1860s – a period described by Gregory S. Kealey as one of increasing sectarianism in Toronto politics.[3] Initially, the descriptor was used as a term of abuse hurled by the Catholic Irish community at the Protestant Irish who dominated city politics and fashioned municipal affairs along what were perceived as sectarian lines. Street riots and public affrays, not unknown in earlier decades, had become increasingly common in the city during the 1850s, especially on festive occasions such as St Patrick's Day and the anniversary of the battle of the Boyne on the Twelfth of July. Orangemen had been to the fore in municipal politics since the 1840s, and, for ninety years after the election of F.H. Medcalf as Toronto's first avowedly Orange mayor in 1864, that administrative office rested almost exclusively in the hands of the Orange brethren. The introduction of the term "Belfast of Canada" was also a sign of the rising confidence and frustrations of Toronto Catholics, who, through their own religious and social organizations, were gradually becoming better organized and more self-conscious.[4] To them, progress and societal standing could be achieved only if they could identify and eradicate the political and economic discrimination that had impeded them in Ireland, and which now appeared in resurrected form in their new homeland. To their minds, Belfast was certainly not a desirable role model for Canada. The Canadian journalist Hector Charlesworth, writing in 1925, recalled the bitterness of the Toronto of the 1880s: "In those days the city perhaps really deserved the epithet, 'the Belfast of Canada,' which I have always thought a disgusting and insulting accusation."[5]

Indicative of the unsavoury community relations of that time was the stoning of the newly appointed Catholic archbishop in 1888. However, the incidence of sectarian street riots diminished considerably from the late 1880s onwards, a development attributed by some historians to the two Irish communities becoming less self-conscious of their ethnic background and more focused upon their assimilation into mainstream Canadian life.[6] It is reasonable to infer that as the immigrant generations declined in relative importance, the realities of the New World would have taken precedence over the memories of the Old. McGowan has specifically identified the period 1887–1922 as the era wherein the relevance of the older attitudes waned in the context of greater social and cultural assimilation of Catholics, and has protested that the "Belfast of Canada label has been particularly obstructive to those scholars wanting to probe beyond the myth and fantasy enveloping the English-speaking Catholics of Toronto after the 1890s."[7] Unquestionably, Catholics in Toronto did regard themselves as loyal and committed citizens, and they may well have been increasingly so regarded, but McGowan's argument underestimates the lingering potency of old suspicions and animosities prevalent among those who continued to control municipal affairs. Analysis of the machinations of City Hall, the skewed employment profile of those paid from the public purse, and the obvious political power of the Orange Order all demonstrate that the "Belfast of Canada" label was to remain an appropriate epithet well into the twentieth century. The Catholic community may well have become more embedded in "the social, occupational, economic, and political structure of Toronto ... developing and adapting its sense of Catholicity to local circumstances,"[8] but those local circumstances still imposed limits on acceptance – life in the city remained characterized by fissures that reflected politico-religious divisions. Certainly, the fluidity of New World society did preclude a rigid imposition of sectarianism as practised in Belfast, but until 1954 the influential position of Toronto mayor was under the virtually continuous control of Orangemen, most senior positions in municipal government remained in the hands of Protestants, and city employees continued to be given a day's holiday with pay in July to enable them to participate in the city's Orange parade. Up until the 1950s, City Hall recorded the religion of employees along with details of membership in the Masons and Orange Order for all aldermen and the mayor – according an unambiguous official recognition to the specifics of power-based politics in the city. It is a matter of perspective as to whether a preference for Protestants in municipal employment, the police force, or the fire brigade represented legitimate patronage or anti-Catholic discrimination, but, in either case, the effect was the same. Catholics were no longer downtrodden immigrants and they occupied private positions of prestige and wealth in a rapidly growing commercial and manufacturing city, but, until the mid-twentieth century, they remained somewhat marginal to "official" Toronto. Parallel universes of separate schools and confessional university colleges, counterpoised religion-based fraternal societies such as the Knights of Columbus and the Orange Order, the prevalence of Orange commemorative processions on public streets, and the deliberate absence of St Patrick's Day parades all served to demonstrate that religion extended well beyond matters of private beliefs and Sunday worship. Greater numbers of interfaith marriages, mixed residential street patterns, and the growing opportunities of diverse private-sector employment injected greater fluidity into Toronto life than was ever the case in the much more rigid society of Belfast, but, nonetheless, up until the 1950s a continuing stream of immigrants and visitors from the Ulster metropolis continued to find much that was familiar when they arrived in Toronto. Those arriving would have been aware of a common social conservatism in both Toronto and Belfast, and although other citizens, not just those of Irish Protestant or Orange background, had played a part in creating the atmosphere of "Toronto the Good," there is no denying the potency of the Irish contribution to the stifling moral atmosphere of the city. An abiding sense of dullness characterized both places.

Urban Genesis and Comparable Developments

Despite its Old World setting and notwithstanding a nomenclature that is suggestive of a much earlier Irish settlement, Belfast is a relatively recent urban creation. Owing much to its strategic significance as an early seventeenth-century plantation town, the settlement at the head of Belfast Lough remained small and compact throughout the first two centuries of its existence – suffering many vagaries in its economic fortunes in the process. In 1657 the town had only 589 inhabitants, but a century later this had grown to 8,549, and by 1791 the population had risen to 18,320.[9] It is quintessentially a modern city – predominantly a creation of the nineteenth century, and an offshoot of the Industrial Revolution *par excellence*. In the dominant phases of their growth, Belfast and Toronto bear many similarities, and the latter half of the nineteenth century, in particular, witnessed the emergence of distinctive Victorian architectural expressions in both places. Their evolving social geographies likewise displayed visible commonalities that persisted well into the twentieth century, when much more vibrant demographic and economic dynamics projected Toronto onto a growth trajectory that was recognizably North American and much less imitative of contemporary Britain.

As garrison and administrative centres, Belfast and Toronto originated in the strategic requirements of British-directed land colonization processes. They were, however, sufficiently distinct in the timing of their respective foundations that they shared no immediately identifiable morphological traits such as had emerged in the plantation towns of early seventeenth-century Ireland and the contemporaneous colonization ventures in colonial America. Belfast was one of a number of Ulster towns established by Royal charter as part of the scheme known as the Ulster Plantation. Acquisition of native Irish land and in-migration of Scottish and English settlers were twin components of the British planter-colonization of the northern part of Ireland, following on from a period of prolonged warfare. The town charter granted by King James in 1613 gave legal existence to a defensive urban centre that possessed the strategic advantages of easy maritime communication to Britain via Belfast Lough and interior access to a fertile hinterland in the Lagan Valley. The initial population was predominantly English in origin and Anglican in religion, but as trade and commerce slowly developed, an increasing number of Scottish settlers moved into the area. By the eighteenth century, Belfast had acquired a strong Presbyterian character – establishing a distinctive cultural emphasis that it retains to the present day.[10] The growth of the town was slow – half a century after establishment its population still did not exceed six hundred.[11] However, by the early eighteenth century the focus of economic activity in Ulster had shifted emphatically eastwards from the Foyle Valley and the city of Derry to the Lagan Valley and Belfast, engendering a rise in the status of the town as a commercial and trading port. Belfast developed strong shipping connections with colonial America, to which goods and people were transported in ever-increasing numbers. The historian J.C. Beckett has noted that throughout this period Belfast's Presbyterian community retained close links with Scotland and the sons of the mercantile families were educated in the universities of Glasgow and Edinburgh, bringing back to their home town a set of philosophical and political ideas that were to make Belfast renowned for its liberalism, educational institutions, and literary culture.[12] It was a reputation that was not to last; in the aftermath of the United Irishmen's rebellion of 1798, during which local Presbyterians had assumed a leadership role in opposing the British and largely Anglican establishment, the political culture of Ireland assumed a more binary aspect. Protestants and Catholics occupied increasingly rigid positions at either end of a political spectrum with monarchical and British loyalty at one end and Catholic-infused nationalism at the other. Out of this alignment there emerged the sectarian tensions and hatreds with which Belfast has remained identified for the past two hundred years. Coincidentally, this new period in Belfast's development coincided with the rapid transformation of the town from a commercial to an industrial metropolis, and the rows of hastily built working-class houses soon provided the most inflexible politico-religious segregated social areas of any city in the British Isles.

In common with Belfast, the urban genesis of Toronto owed much to its suitability as a strategic site for the unfolding administrative and settlement needs of a region undergoing British colonization. It replaced the original regional capital, Niagara-on-the-Lake, which was deemed to be too vulnerable to American attack, and under the direction of John Graves Simcoe, the first lieutenant governor of the territory, the new town of York was developed strategically on the Lake Ontario shore at the mouth of the Don River. York, later renamed Toronto, had the added advantage of being located at the intersection of traditional fur-trading routes. The low-lying muddy lakeshore site, like the mudflats at the mouth of the Lagan in Belfast, was not a place of much natural attraction. It did, however, have considerable potential as an access point to a resource-rich hinterland, and in that respect the colonization access provided by Yonge and Dundas streets for early nineteenth-century Ontario was similar in function to that provided by the Lagan Valley for seventeenth-century Ulster. From its beginning, the town of York was controlled by a tightly knit group of key figures who were decisively Tory in their political leanings, predominantly Anglican in religion, and "conspicuous in Government, on the Bench and on the Bar."[13] Known as the Family Compact, this group, which was often interrelated by marriage, was to control virtually all aspects of life in the town throughout the earliest decades of its history, and their legacy was to remain discernible long after they ceded municipal political power whenYork was incorporated as the city of Toronto in 1834. England, Scotland, and Ireland were all represented within this early elite, and in combination they set a distinctive British tone for the place, building upon its nomenclature honouring the Duke of York to replicate in the emerging geography of street and ward names an unambiguous assertion of the origins and desired future direction of the settlement. In the core of the town, Simcoe and John streets acknowledged the influence of the founding lieutenant governor, Jarvis Street celebrated a leading Family Compact family, Queen, King, Princess, Duke, and Duchess streets commemorated the British Royal family, and after 1834, four electoral wards – St George, St Andrew, St David, and St Patrick – recognized the patron saints of the homelands of existing and anticipated future settlers. The Irish were an influential ingredient within that early elite, and names such as Hincks, Russell, Baldwin, and Willcocks were synonymous with the early history of the town. Their ethnic commonality was reinforced by the specificity of their geographical origins; Cork and its merchant families, rather than Dublin, was the origin of many of these leading Irish immigrants. But while they were unquestionably Protestant in composition, they were socially and culturally very different from the waves of Orangemen who were soon to flock to the new settlement.

The urban dynamic of emergent York owed much to its administrative and commercial roles, for, although craft industry was undoubtedly present, the development of a significant industrial base awaited the second half of the nineteenth century. In that respect, early Toronto had more in common with eighteenth-century Belfast than it did with the vibrant factory economy of the Ulster town in the early nineteenth century. The rate of population growth was similarly discordant. In 1801 the population of York was little more than 600, and when it was elevated to city status as Toronto in 1834 its inhabitants numbered only slightly more than 4,000. The urban fabric was likewise slow to develop. A Scottish visitor in 1818 commented, "this town consists of one street lying parallel to the lake, and the beginnings of two or three more at right angles to it."[14] Four years later an Irish gentleman, Francis Stewart, witheringly described it as "not a pleasant place, as it is sunk down in a little amphitheatre cut out of the great bleak forest."[15] Toronto's harbour was shallow, subject to silting, and the local economy of its hinterland was very much subsistence-oriented. It was only with the development of the regional economy, in the second quarter of the nineteenth century, and the rapid and effective expansion of transportation arteries in the form of road, canal, and rail that the city revealed its potential significance in regional, national, and continental terms.

Demographic Change

Two distinct periods are discernible in the comparative urban demographics – Belfast was by far the larger of the two throughout the nineteenth century, but in the twentieth century Toronto far outgrew its Irish counterpart.

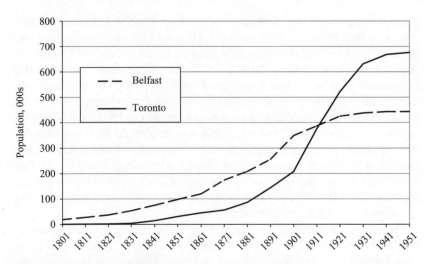

2.1 Belfast and Toronto, 1801–1951

Census returns for 1911 indicated that, for the first and last time, Belfast and Toronto were of comparable size. Belfast was then home to 386,947 citizens; Toronto had 376,538 (figure 2.1). The two cities had experienced phenomenal growth in the previous century and both had shared in a Victorian vision of unfettered progress, which, despite cyclical economic depressions, appeared to point towards linear improvement not only in industrial output, house construction, and street lighting but also in the social mores and spiritual well-being of the inhabitants

Superlatives reigned supreme in descriptions published in city directories and newspapers and in commissioned local histories. Sometimes described as "linenopolis," Belfast was recognized as the leading manufacturer of linen in the world. By 1901 some 164,000 people were employed in the textile, shipbuilding, and engineering industries in the city, and through its port activities it was closely linked with all the major importing centres of the world, including Toronto, where Irish linen was a prominent commodity in Eaton's retailing empire. On the eve of the First World War, it boasted of the largest rope works and the largest dry dock in Europe and was one of the premier shipbuilding yards in the world. It was by any standards an important hub in the industrial might of contemporary Britain. Toronto, likewise, laid claim to global pre-eminence. The Gooderham and Worts distillery claimed to be the largest of its kind in the world; meat packers, hide manufacturers, and the Massey farm machinery plant testified to the role of the city in the capitalization of Canadian agriculture; and the retail giant, Eaton's, was renowned across the country and beyond. The Royal York Hotel, commenced in 1926, claimed to be the largest free-standing structure in the British Empire, and the grandiose Romanesque architecture of the new City Hall opened in 1899 was as much a symbol of civic pride and wealth as the Italianate Belfast City Hall opened in 1906. Of the two places, Belfast was clearly the more industrial, and nowhere in Toronto was there an enterprise as large as Harland and Wolff's shipyard, which employed at its peak more than 20,000 men, or the linen industry that employed tens of thousands of men and women. With its heterogeneous mixture of administrative, commercial, and industrial functions, Toronto, however, was able to create and maintain a greater dynamic in employment patterns and social mobility.

Belfast was one of the fastest-growing cities in the British Isles in the nineteenth century, and at times its rate of growth outstripped that of quintessential industrial centres such as Manchester, Birmingham, and Glasgow. It was a city of teeming migrants, hastily developed row housing, factory chimneys, and imposing commercial edifices constructed in eclectic Victorian architectural styles. Unsurprisingly, it was a city marked by serious social problems ranging from attenuated life expectancy caused by adverse working and living conditions, through to dysfunctional families striving to establish some element of stability amid the turmoil of migration and resettlement in what was rapidly becoming one of the world's great industrial centres. All of this was inserted into, and filtered through, a context of omnipresent sectarian tensions, violence, and street riots. Those moving into Belfast were rural and small-town migrants, pushed out by the twin forces of declining agricultural labouring employment and the collapse of handloom weaving and domestic spinning. They sought new opportunities among the burgeoning linen factories of Belfast and its engineering and shipbuilding industries – part of a massed population in a large-scale urban economy where new technologies and transferred community tensions coexisted. Born in rural eighteenth-century Ulster amid intense competition for land and economic and political rivalry, the Orange Order and the rural migrants simultaneously adjusted to the circumstances of life in the urban centre, giving its emergent culture an indelible inflection.

Belfast became a clear locus for internal migration from within its rural Ulster hinterland – tens of thousands moved the comparatively short distances into the working-class terraced homes emerging from the shadows of the linen mills and the foundries and the gantries at the head of Belfast Lough. Increasing at an annual rate of 3 per cent throughout the nineteenth century, the population growth of Belfast was especially strong in the 1860s when an international shortage of raw cotton, occasioned by the American Civil War, facilitated a boom in linen production. It was an urban environment of relentless change, development, and growth: above all it was a city of migrants, and as late as 1901 only 20 per cent of Belfast's citizens were native to the city. Most Belfast residents at the beginning of the twentieth century had been born in Ireland, especially the east Ulster counties of Antrim and Down, but upwards of 10 per cent had come from England and Scotland, attracted by niche management and skilled engineering opportunities in the city. Coincidentally, Antrim and Down were the same counties that fed much of the flow of Irish migrants to Canada and Toronto. In both Ulster and Canada the process of urban adjustment would have been eased by the presence of kin and neighbours who had made the journey earlier,[16] but fundamental differences also shaped the local demographic and economic conditions. Belfast, one of a number of distinctive economic regions produced by the contemporary British industrial revolution, embodied all the tensions, problems, and challenges of economic liberalism and the civic culture of successful Victorian cities, but it also managed to inject its own distinctive personality into the mix.[17]

Given the religious composition of Antrim and Down, it was scarcely surprising that the migrants were predominantly Protestant, and, from its beginnings, the religious geography of Belfast was one in which Catholics were a minority (table 2.1). The years 1820–60 were the main period of Catholic in-migration, their numbers probably increasing threefold at that time to give them a one-third share of the urban population. However, all censuses, 1861–1901, recorded a proportionate drop in the Catholic population of the city, and although their absolute numbers did double in these years it was evident that Protestants were moving into the city in ever-greater numbers. There is also reason to believe that Catholics from the regional hinterland increasingly preferred emigration as a means to new beginnings.[18] It was a trend that was to continue well into the twentieth century.

The specifics of the migration stream likewise created in Toronto a city that was predominantly Protestant (table 2.1). In the case of Toronto, the growth of the Catholic population was in keeping with more general trends in the composition of transatlantic migration.[19] By 1841, Catholics

Table 2.1 Catholic population: Belfast and Toronto

	1808	1834	1841	1851	1861	1871	1881	1891	1901
Belfast	4,000	19,712	nd	nd	41,406	55,575	59,975	67,378	84,992
%	16.0	32.3	nd	nd	34.1	31.9	28.8	26.3	24.3
Toronto	nd	nd	2,401	7,940	12,135	11,881	15,716	21,830	23,699
%	nd	nd	16.8	25.8	27.1	21.2	18.2	15.1	15.2

Note: The data for Belfast prior to 1861 are to be found in Hepburn, *A Past Apart*, 4. Subsequent data are derived from the relevant national census reports. The data for Toronto are to be found in J.M.S. Careless, *Toronto to 1918: An Illustrated History* (Toronto: Lorimer, 1984), 201.

already constituted almost 17 per cent of the city's inhabitants, rising to a quarter by 1851 and peaking at 27 per cent in 1861– the same year that the proportion of Catholics of Belfast also peaked. Even more than its Irish counterpart, Toronto was predominantly a Protestant city, and this aspect of its identity became increasingly pronounced as the nineteenth century progressed. Toronto's annual rate of growth was greater than that of Belfast, but it had started from a much smaller base and, ultimately, it was to become the much larger place. Migration drove much of the demographic growth in each city, and it is striking that, despite the potentially disruptive impact of a continuous streams of new arrivals, each place retained a pronounced conservatism in its civic culture and practice of municipal governance. To a considerable extent this was due to the relatively narrow range of source regions from which the migrants were drawn. Belfast's migrants came mainly from within a radius of fifty miles; more than 90 per cent of Toronto's immigrants were sourced within the British Isles, a majority of them from Ireland. By 1851, a quarter of a century of sustained heavy immigration from Ireland had made Toronto the most Irish of all cities in North America. Thirty-seven per cent of Torontonians were Irish-born, and probably half as many again had been born in the city of Irish parents; the English-born constituted only 16 per cent. Contemporary Boston, widely regarded as the most Irish centre in the United States, had an Irish-born component that amounted to just over a quarter of its total population.[20] The 1871 Canadian census was the first to include a question on ethnic background, and in that year 40 per cent of Torontonians still claimed to be Irish, notwithstanding the fact that for the previous decade and a half, immigration from England had swamped the numbers arriving from Ireland.[21] It is impossible to distinguish accurately the proportion of Catholics among the Irish in Toronto at mid-century. However, it has been estimated that among the overall Irish settlers in Ontario in 1871 about 30 per cent would have been Catholic,[22] and the proportion in Toronto would certainly have been higher. In a geographical analysis of the settlement patterns of the Irish in Ontario, Houston and Smyth estimated that Catholics were almost twice as likely as their Protestant counterparts to settle in an urban environment,[23] and the same methodology applied specifically to Toronto suggests that in 1851 about 43 per cent of the Irish in the city may have been Catholic.[24] In summary, Catholics may have been a much greater proportion of the Toronto Irish in mid-century than they were in contemporary Belfast, but among the city's population in general they measured only about a quarter. The reality of life in nineteenth-century Toronto was that Catholicism was identified almost exclusively with the Irish, and they took their place within a city that was overwhelmingly Protestant and where Orangeism came increasingly to be the defining characteristic of British and loyal citizenship.

Religion and Social Tensions

The British identity of Toronto was from the beginning shaped by a Tory elite within which Irish Protestants were prominent. This older elite retained their prominence in society and business long after they had ceased to control local politics, and their lasting influence in imparting a certain civility and grandeur to Toronto life should not be underestimated. However, within City Hall the presence of the more recent Irish arrivals was increasingly apparent. In 1847, when 38,000 Irish famine refugees arrived in the city, they encountered a resident population of little more than 20,000, half of whom were Irish. Fifteen of the eighteen aldermen were also Irish. In addition, probably eight of the aldermen were members of the Orange Order and no Catholic held municipal office.[25] This early Orange emphasis within municipal governance endured with slight modifications for almost a century, proving to be remarkably resilient to forces of changes that were to transform the hitherto small city into a major metropolitan centre of commerce and industry. Described by some as a "British Town on American Soil,"[26] Toronto was compared favourably in 1842 to an English country town by the visiting Charles Dickens, but he did lament, "It is a matter of deep regret that the political differences should have run high in this place, and led to the most discreditable and disgraceful results."[27] The incident to which

Dickens referred was the murder of a man during a recent Orange riot. The Orange tradition in Toronto had emerged early; there is evidence of a Twelfth of July parade in 1818 and by 1820 the parade had become a regular occurrence, attracting some recognition from the elite. In 1822 Rev. John Strachan, a future Anglican archbishop in the city, preached a sermon to about one hundred Orangemen at the conclusion of their festive celebrations. The following year he again attended the Orange celebrations, although he never became a member of the organization.[28]

Notwithstanding this early flirtation between Strachan and the Orangemen, it was clear that a sense of social difference propelled the Tory elite and the more recent Irish arrivals along diverging paths. The history of the Orange Order in Ireland was well known to the administrators and government officials in Canada and not all were convinced that it was a force for stability. In 1823 a bill outlawing Orange parades was introduced into the Upper Canadian Assembly by the Cork-born Dr William Baldwin, who argued that "no party ever cultivated greater animosity, or exhibited a higher degree of hostile distinction from the rest of their fellow subjects, than the Orange societies."[29] The bill failed to pass, but it was a clear signal of the mind of the Establishment, who feared the emergence of an unruly immigrant power bloc. There are no records of street disturbances in Toronto at this early period, but elsewhere in Upper Canada sectarian riots had occurred in the Perth district in 1824,[30] and a replication of Irish troubles seemed probable. With the creation of a Grand Lodge of British North America in 1830, Canadian Orangeism assumed a more coordinated approach to organizational development, and for a time, under the leadership of its grand master, Wexford-born Ogle R. Gowan, it flirted openly with the possibility of creating an immigrant political power bloc that would challenge the Family Compact.[31] The Order failed to gain political traction in the heady mixture of Upper Canadian politics of the 1830s, a decade of considerable turmoil, localized rebellion, and ambiguity in protestations of reform and loyalty. But the Order did find relevance as a mechanism for bringing like-minded immigrants together in fraternal gatherings wherein information on settling in and opportunities for personal advancement could be exchanged amid an atmosphere of conviviality and nostalgic reminiscences of life in the Old Country. Diversity of experience in the settlement regions of Upper Canada, and difficulties in communication between them, may have precluded the emergence of an Orange political party, but the contemporary experience of the Order in Ireland also revealed a similar lack of political evolution. It was not until 1886 that the Irish Order formally translated itself into a party political movement under the guise of the Ulster Unionist party in affiliation with the British Conservative party. Prior to that time, Orange interests had been expressed and advanced at the national level through the support of mainstream political parties, a practice which emerged early in Canada and persisted unchanged throughout the decades when the Order might be deemed to have wielded greatest political influence.

The real strength of the Order in Toronto rested in its ability to attract into its ranks large numbers of Protestants who were willing to affiliate within a fraternal body organized around a set of explicit core values. Central to those values was an attitude shaped and adapted to counter any, and all, advances of Catholicism – whether expressed internationally by growing ultramontanism, the revival of Catholic bishoprics in Britain, and the endowment of a national seminary at Maynooth, or, more locally, by the perceived threat of differentiated migration flows on neighbourhood communities and employment competition. It was an attitude that was remarkably enduring and resilient to changing circumstances, and it was easily transferred to Toronto and Belfast as well as many other places where it found much sustenance and many different expressions over succeeding generations.

In both Belfast and Toronto, community tensions escalated during the marching season of July when the main thoroughfares were filled by lines of men bedecked in Orange sashes, ceremonial swords, and (occasionally) guns – all accompanied by martial music, drums and fifes, and waving banners depicting heroes of past religious conflicts. In both cities there was a common reaction from Catholics – fear, resentment, and a sense of imposed social inferiority pervaded their local communities, especially if they resided along or adjacent to the routes taken by the parades. Catholic children were customarily taken inside, forbidden to watch the spectacles; youths and young men jeered and hurled abuse and sometimes missiles at those deemed to be challenging their sense of territoriality, civic status, and political loyalty.

To disinterested observers the annual pageantry was an outmoded and illogical throwback to the European religious wars of previous centuries, but protagonists saw it as a seamless and vital transference of hard-fought-for principles to a new environment where fresh battles might need to be fought under new guises. The manifestations of Orangeism, and the predictable Catholic reaction, represented transfers of tradition by migrant communities whose drums, sashes, and attitudes alike had been deliberately transported to the factory environs of

Belfast, the emerging colonial capital of Upper Canada, and many other places besides. Anticipated social improvement did not necessitate the discarding of cultural baggage. On the contrary it was used as a comforting mechanism that would facilitate the construction of familiar community relations amid unfamiliar physical environments. Catholics, a distinctive minority in both Toronto and Belfast, also found a resounding familiarity in the transferred culture. To them it was frightening and unwanted. Given the binary nature of Irish society, the cement of community cohesion among Protestant migrants was conversely perceived as hostile to the safety of fledgling Catholic communities. It was the interface of two passionately held, but diametrically opposed, belief systems that generated endemic tensions, sometimes spilling over into public violence on a large scale. Toronto and Belfast share such a history of episodic violence, as well as a common causative environment, but the Irish venue far exceeded its Canadian counterpart in terms of the scale, duration, intensity, and sheer viciousness of the engagements. In both places the prompts and circumstances that occasioned particular outbreaks of public violence were remarkably similar – election counts, offensive slogans and inflammatory public meetings, parades, and perceived infringements of assumed territorial boundaries all appear in the police reports on either side of the Atlantic.

Sectarian rioting in Toronto and Belfast has been frequently attributed to the destabilization of local demographic balances by the arrival of large numbers of impoverished Catholic famine migrants. However, such analysis tends to underestimate the presence of migrant streams of Catholics in the decades before the famine, and is unable to account for the intensification of violence after 1860, by which time the relative strength of Catholics in both Toronto and Belfast was on the wane. Toronto's population doubled in the 1840s, but only a fraction of this expansion was due to the Irish famine. The tragic events of the worst year of the famine, 1847, contributed fewer than two thousand Irish to the city's permanent population,[32] the remainder of the growth being attributable to natural increase and the continuation of a more regular stream of migrants. Furthermore, not all of the famine's destitute were Catholic. McGowan has demonstrated that in 1847 more than half of the Irish admitted to the House of Industry in Toronto were Anglicans; Catholics did not have a monopoly of suffering.[33] Belfast would likewise have included both Catholics and Protestants among its famine victims. Sectarian violence may have been temporarily intensified by the famine migrations, but it did not originate with them and it persisted long after the memory of the tragic event had faded.

Table 2.2 Incidence of major Orange riots in nineteenth-century Belfast and Toronto

	Belfast	Toronto
1813	Parade	
1825	Parade	
1832	Election	
1835	Election	
1839		Political meeting
1841		Election
1843	Parade	Party Processions Act
1844		Twelfth parade
1849		Rebellion losses debate
1852	Election	
1855		Municipal election
1857	Inflammatory sermon	Attack on Catholic cathedral
1858		St Patrick's Day parade
		Twelfth processions
1860		Visit of Prince of Wales
1863		Separate schools
1864	Parade	Corpus Christi parade
		Guy Fawkes Day
1872	Parade	
1875		Papal Jubilee parade
1878		O'Donovan Rossa visit
1886	Parade	
1887		O'Brien visit
1899	Parade	

Note: The information for Toronto is drawn from Gregory S. Kealey, "Orangemen and the Corporation: The Politics of Class during the Union of the Canadas," in Victor L. Russell, ed., *Forging a Consensus: Historical Essays on Toronto* (Toronto: University of Toronto Press 1984), 44. The information for Belfast is derived largely from Bardon, *A History of Ulster*.

Tensions that spilled over into riots or street violence were not merely short-term responses to long-term demographic shifts. They were violent episodic expressions of ingrained attitudes and endemic mutual distrust. The major incidents of street violence in Toronto and Belfast are indicated in table 2.2, but many smaller incidents occurred regularly in both places – eliciting, because of their apparent routine commonality, only passing comment in police and newspaper reports.

Kealey, in his study of Toronto's nineteenth-century working class, has demonstrated that in the period 1867–92 there were twenty-two clashes between Orangemen and Catholics in the city, but he dismisses most of them as being insignificant and mostly ritualistic affairs.[34] Brian Clarke has recently pointed out that sixteen of these incidents of public disorder occurred in the 1870s.[35] In agreement with Kealey, he argues that most of the affrays were of low intensity and short duration, predictable occurrences in the Toronto calendar of public events. The regularity, and indeed predictability, of street affrays created an image that not only was resented by the established Tory elite within the city but was also a cause of concern to Orange leaders seeking to bring their organization into the mainstream of municipal politics. Their aim was to attain the respectability to match the power they had already wrung from a compliant electorate, but their goal was not attained until the final quarter of the nineteenth century.

Early Orange riots in Toronto displayed a remarkable ability to find cause in political crises pertinent to Canada rather than Ireland. Government attempts to assuage feelings and provide compensation for losses in the aftermath of the 1837 Reformers' rebellion, which had been led by Toronto's first mayor, William Lyon Mackenzie, provoked outrage among Orangemen. Likewise, elections, at municipal and regional levels, were often translated into sectarian arguments about loyalty and reform as the partisan Order sought to establish a power base. Still other incidents stemmed from drunken responses to traditional parades on the Twelfth of July and St Patrick's Day – the latter celebration increasingly associated with the Catholic community, notwithstanding the strong Protestant involvement that was apparent in its early commemoration. In terms of severity, the most serious of these disturbances was undoubtedly the St Patrick's Day riot of 1858. A public demonstration against Thomas D'Arcy McGee, the leading Irish Catholic politician in Canada, who was attending a banquet in Toronto, escalated into a full-blown riot, and a Catholic stableman, Matthew Sheedy, was killed. Two further incidents of disturbance were directly related to political events in Ireland – the visits of O'Donovan Rossa in 1878 and of William O'Brien in 1887. O'Donovan Rossa, a Fenian leader living in exile in the United States, arrived in Toronto to deliver a lecture in March 1878 in St Patrick's Hall in the Toronto markets area. Two days of rioting by Orange opponents resulted in all the windows in the building being smashed, Cosgrove's tavern, a reputed Fenian meeting place, wrecked, and many stores along Queen Street damaged. It was, however, the last of such major confrontations in the city, and when William O'Brien brought the cause of Irish agricultural tenants to the city in 1887, in a calculated campaign to embarrass the Irish landlord and erstwhile governor-general of Canada, Lord Lansdowne, the resultant disturbances were little more than nocturnal scuffles on the downtown streets. The era of such public physical confrontation was drawing to a close in a city that was learning to live more peacefully with itself.

Two occasions of riots, 1864 and 1875 respectively, were, however, nakedly sectarian and aimed specifically at Catholic liturgical practices which had temporarily extended beyond church precincts to include public streets. The 1864 riot was occasioned by a Corpus Christi procession that was held customarily on the first Thursday after Trinity Sunday. The roots of this liturgical ceremony extended back to peasant springtime festivals in Europe, but the ultramontane Church of the nineteenth century had brought doctrinal orthodoxy to bear on the celebration and regulated it as a formal Eucharistic devotion. In Catholic countries, the feast of Corpus Christi was marked by a procession of clergy and their congregation through public thoroughfares. Under an ornate canopy held aloft by four laymen, the Eucharist, displayed in a gold monstrance, would be carried by the priest or bishop dressed in formal canonical robes. At intervals along the route, the procession would halt at temporary altars where participants would kneel and prayers would be recited. The ceremony extended the geographical remit of the Church to the residential neighbourhoods of its congregation. It was especially venerated by Catholics because it represented "a prolongation of the celebration of the Eucharist: Immediately after Mass, the Sacred Host, consecrated during the Mass, [was] borne out of the Church for the Christian faithful."[36] In Belfast, such processions usually passed off peacefully, since they were contained within the Catholic ghettoes, but the dispersed residential patterns of Toronto did not offer such exclusive neighbourhoods. Toronto may have been located on the same line of latitude as Rome but it was certainly not a Mediterranean town, and public displays of Catholic practice on its streets were not welcome. In May 1864, Archbishop Lynch had agreed to the organization of a Corpus Christi procession but wisely required that it be confined to the Cathedral grounds. But on the day, the large congregation not only filled the church grounds but spilled over into the street, thereby attracting the ire of some armed Protestant youths who tried to attack the monstrance and St Michael's Cathedral. The attack was perceived by Catholics not only as a personal assault but also as a sacrilegious attack on the Real Presence of Christ in the consecrated host in the monstrance. Civil commotion ensued.[37] Similar circumstances prevailed in 1875 when the Catholic archdiocese celebrated a Papal Jubilee by encouraging parishioners, in prayer, to process along a defined route between the Catholic churches in the city on a specific Sunday. Plenary indulgences were promised to participants. The liturgical event provoked one of the largest riots ever witnessed in Toronto with as many as eight thousand people being involved. Ten policemen were injured and considerable damage was caused to property. It has been claimed that over one-third of those arrested were members of the Orange Order.[38]

The Toronto experience of riot was very different from that of contemporary Belfast, where high fatality numbers were recorded throughout not only the nineteenth century but the twentieth century as well. The Belfast riots of 1886, for example, caused the deaths of more than thirty people, most of them Catholic. The sheer viciousness of Belfast sectarian passion was minimized considerably in Canada, and although group animosities were well established, the intensity of expression was much more modest.

In Belfast the first serious religious riot had occurred in 1813 on the occasion of a Twelfth of July parade, and at the end of that day's conflict two men had been shot dead and a further four had been seriously wounded.[39] Throughout the rest of the century, and at frequent intervals centred round elections and parades, Belfast would erupt into orgies of violence in which houses would be burnt, occupants forcibly evicted, and hundreds injured. Extending over several days, and simmering throughout the summer months with periodic conflagrations, the Catholic and Protestant mutual distrust metamorphosed into downright hatred. Deaths and serious injuries were common. The most prolonged of the early riots occurred in 1857 when the annual Twelfth Orange parade was prefaced by a particularly vitriolic anti-Catholic sermon by an evangelical clergyman. The rioting that commenced that evening lasted for six days and at least five people were killed. Community tensions remained high throughout the summer, fanned by more anti-Catholic sermons delivered not only in churches but also on the steps of the Customs House by clerical extremists such as the Rev. Hanna and the Rev. Drew who had no compunction about mingling evangelical theology with partisan politics. In September riots erupted once more, extending over a period of eleven days, during which police and military were stretched to their limits.[40] Seven years later another summer of rioting resulted in at least twelve deaths and required the intervention of "almost 1,000 constables, 150 Town Police, 600 special constables, 6 troops of the 4th Hussars, infantry of the 84th Regiment and half a battery of artillery."[41]

Residential Geography

There was no comparison between the scale of violence in Belfast and that in contemporary Toronto, where the smashing of windows in Cosgrove's tavern and rampages along Queen Street were confined in space and intensity, requiring the intervention of only a few dozen policemen. A further fundamental difference was that the Belfast riots emanated from clashes between large rival communities ensconced in adjoining but segregated residential districts, and an obvious and deliberate outcome of virtually every riotous incident was the burning of homes and the eviction of residents from streets of mixed religion on the boundaries of emerging ghettoes. Frequently also the evictions included forcible removal of Catholics from employment niches in some linen factories and in the shipyards. The 1860s, 1870s, and 1880s saw an increase in residential segregation in the city, a process that continued into the twentieth century and which was particularly dramatic in the 1920s and 1930s and more recently in the 1970s and 1980s. In an evocative description of Belfast, as revealed by the 1901 census, historian A.C. Hepburn has written:

> Balkan Street, Belgrade Street, Bosnia Street and Servia Street are adjacent terraces in the Lower Falls area of West Belfast. In 1901 they were home to a total of 1,237 Catholics and 2 Protestants. Genoa Street, Pisa Street and Venice Street housed 239 Protestants and 9 Catholics. Disappointingly, perhaps, there was no Adriatic Avenue flowing between these two clusters; they were divided by no greater barrier than a minute's walk across the Grosvenor Road.[42]

The micro-geography of this district was replicated in many other communities within the city, where Catholics, although less than one-third of the population, nonetheless amounted to more than 50,000 persons from the 1870s onwards. Comparable figures for Toronto in the 1870s suggest a community of about 12,000 Catholics. Scale did matter, for it not only dictated the geographical spread of street violence but also helped account for its prolongation over months in Belfast as

Table 2.3 Patterns of residential segregation in Belfast, 1901

Streets	< 10% RC	10–90% RC	> 90% RC	N =
RC households	7%	49%	44%	1,349
Protestant households	62%	38%	0%	4,098
All households	48%	40%	11%	5,461

Note: This table is derived from data presented in Hepburn and Collins, "Industrial Society."

compared with hours or days in Toronto. While some degree of seg-regation between neighbourhoods may have been manifested in early nineteenth-century Belfast, most analysts agree that there was more flu-idity in residential patterns than was the case in the second half of the century. Riots in the 1830s, but particularly during the 1850s, led to a progressive encirclement of districts that were predominantly Catholic. Eventually these districts became almost exclusively Catholic. Hepburn and Collins, using an aggregation of city wards, have determined that the index of social dissimilarity in some parts of west Belfast in 1901 was at a level comparable to those of ghettoes in American cities, and that the five most segregated areas in the city were all Catholic.[43] Their further analysis, based on sample households at the level of the street rather than the ward, reveals at a finer geographical scale the extremity of the pattern of segregation (table 2.3).

The reality of the urban geography was stark. Only 7 per cent of Cath-olic households were to be found in predominantly Protestant streets, and there were no Protestant households in predominantly Catholic streets. Almost two-thirds of Protestants lived in streets predominated by their co-religionists, and while Catholics had a wider distribution in mixed neighbourhoods, that percentage continued to shrink during the "Troubles" of the twentieth century. As recently as 1972, 70 per cent of Catholics lived in streets that were exclusive to their co-religionists and only 22 per cent of Catholics lived in mixed streets.[44] As a result of this segregated residential geography, half of all Catholics and 62 per cent of all Protestants had little community knowledge of citizens of the opposite religion, and places where they did interact – the margins of the ghettoes, the workplace, and the city centre – tended to be the points of conflagration. Streets that had a minority population of either Catho-lics or Protestants were especially targeted during riots, and in these it was common for whole terraces of houses to be set on fire with the evicted families fleeing to relatives, friends, or church groupings within the cores of segregated districts. It was a particular and effective form of urban violence and it drew on the experience of eighteenth-century rural Ulster when skirmishes that preceded the formation of the Orange Order in 1795 had been characterized by the wrecking of linen looms and houses belonging to Catholics. In Belfast, each such attack further intensified both the process and the sense of segregation and established for whole districts an identity that was self-perpetuating in that, once a neighbourhood was labelled as occupied by a particular group, future allocation of houses, either by municipal or private landlords, tended to confirm the recognized local majority population.

It has been observed that "Religion in Belfast was, indeed, a considerably more potent force for residential segregation than social class,"[45] a fact that is apparent in the analysis that indicated 74 per cent of Catholic manual workers in 1901 lived in predominantly Catholic districts, as did 60 per cent of the Catholic business and commercial class and 49 per cent of their professional co-religionists. Furthermore, it was obvious that the segregated districts were not simply home to recent migrants to the city – 76 per cent of Belfast-born Catholic householders as opposed to 66 per cent of those born elsewhere in Ulster were to be found within the seven most Catholic areas of the city.[46] These communities were well established, inclusive of the overall social mix of Belfast Catholics and representative of a defensive population that was conscious of its own distinctive culture and strongly aware of the inferior position to which it was consigned by the majority population. Within the apparent safety of their own neighbourhoods, Catholics had their own foci for everyday living. Churches, denominational schools, pubs, shops, recreational outlets, and patterns of socializing all confirmed the quasi-autonomous nature of the communities, and, for some, local employment cemented the pattern.

The residential geography of Toronto stood in sharp contrast to that of Belfast. It was never a city of recognizable ghettoes, and although it contained distinctive neighbourhoods they never exhibited the rigidity of those in the Ulster city. Scale was a factor. Toronto in 1871 was of approximately the same size (circa 56,000) as Belfast had been in the 1830s – the period when ghetto formation first became a pronounced trend. But by then Toronto Catholics were only about one-fifth of the population and declining. Furthermore, some of the second and third generations of Catholics in Toronto at that time had registered significant social mobility and were distributed across a variety of neighbourhoods in the city. In general, Toronto exhibited one of the most flexible residential patterns in North America in the last quarter of the nineteenth century, and Irish Catholics benefited accordingly. There were marked differences between the Toronto experience and that of contemporary American cities.

In places as diverse as Boston and New York, the early nineteenth-century Irish Catholics migrated into established urban environments whose charter population was predominantly Protestant and where upward mobility was limited even into the second generation.[47] Residential segregation, reflecting their low socio-economic status, contributed to a pattern of dockside and inner-city working-class neighbourhoods in these American cities, and initially a similar pattern was discernible in early nineteenth-century Toronto, where Irish slums were to be found along the mud flats of the Don River. But there were fundamental differences in the scale and duration of Irish Catholic migration to Boston and Toronto. The Catholic migrations to the Canadian city were associated primarily with a thirty-year period (1820–50), and by 1851 there were still fewer than eight thousand Catholic Irish in the city. Boston, with a total population of 137,000 in 1850, was almost five times larger, and its Irish-born population stood at 35,287 – almost all of them Catholic.[48] Strikingly, the Irish Catholic population of Boston continued to grow at a sustained heavy rate throughout the rest of the century and effected a renewal of group culture as well as replenishment of numbers – inner-city and dockside ghettoes always had a new generation of immigrant Irish willing to take up rooms in the boarding houses and seek opportunities in casual labouring jobs, many of them controlled by Irish ward bosses. Toronto was, by contrast, a maturing community in which the majority of those of Irish Catholic background were Canadian-born by the latter years of the century. The community, with an aging and declining percentage of immigrants among its cohort, displayed increasing evidence of social and geographical integration.

The geographer Peter G. Goheen's pioneering analysis of the factorial ecology of post-1850 Toronto identifies and maps the principal elements of the social geography of the city and charts its changing character as it evolved from a small-scale administrative and commercial centre into a large-scale industrial and commercial metropolis. Noting that residential segregation within the city in 1861 could be most accurately predicted at the extremes of the social scale, with the professional and commercial elite concentrated in the city centre and the unskilled located on the margins in the more remote and often less healthy environs of the Don River plain, he nonetheless identified a city wherein geographical scale did not encourage or facilitate pronounced segregation.[49] His analysis for that year did not include religion as a variable, and when it was entered into his data analysis of 1870 he found that "there may have been some systematic residential segregation within the city according to classes of occupation and religion."[50] In particular, he identified the sharpest segregation as being between Anglicans and Catholics, highlighting a very strong correlation between Catholics, low socio-economic status, and poorest housing conditions. He argued, "The Roman Catholic group alone was territorially identified."[51] One of the two largest concentrations of Catholics was in the northwest of the city in the emerging industrial area around King and Bathurst; the other was a relict community in the southeast of the city around St Paul's Church and adjacent to the original settlements along the Don River. Religion was obviously a potent force in social behaviour in the city at the time. By way of contrast, Goheen's analysis of 1890 and 1899 demonstrated the much greater significance of occupations as predictors of segregation within the rapidly growing and increasingly more complex city, although Catholics, significantly less clustered than in previous years, still provided some signs of concentration, notably at the mouth of the Don, around King and Bathurst streets, in the Junction district west of Dufferin Street, and in the extreme eastern part of the city.[52] His analysis does not extend to explaining the reasons underlying these trace elements of clustering – some new, others obviously relicts of a much earlier time. Neither does he detail the scale of the populations therein. At no time, however, were the Catholic concentrations as extensive or as exclusive as their Belfast counterpart; at all times Catholics were to found scattered across all residential areas.

Goheen does point to a Catholic community that was becoming increasingly diversified in socio-economic terms during the course of the second half of the nineteenth century, and identification of this process is supported by more recent studies by Clarke and McGowan. Clarke concedes that small-scale clustering of Irish Catholics remained in Toronto well into the late nineteenth century but argues that it was identifiable at the scale of the street and the block rather than large districts.[53] McGowan's study of Irish Catholics in Toronto is less accepting of the notion that Catholics tended to cluster in defined areas of the city. He has argued forcefully, "Unlike their co-religionists in major American and British cities, Toronto's English-speaking Catholics had no North End, South Side or Falls Road to call their own."[54] His difference with Goheen rests on a question of scale – neither author quantifies the size of what constituted a cluster, nor does he calibrate the data in a manner likely to assist in the identification of more precise boundaries for the recognized clusters. These clusters may well have emerged in streets around Catholic churches, or they may have preceded the establishment of the churches and the attendant parochial structure, but in either case their existence reflects a lingering geographical expression of difference and "otherness." Yet one must acknowledge the fundamental fact that the scale of such clusters was undeniably small and the vast majority of Catholics did not live in them. Social mobility and geographical mobility in the Canadian city were much more fluid than in the ghettoized Catholic communities of Belfast. Moreover, the smallness of the Toronto clusters meant that they did not provide fully self-contained commercial and social environments. Separated to only a limited extent, the Catholic districts of Toronto were functionally interdependent on the rest of the city to a much greater extent than was the case in Belfast.

Social Integration and Occupational Mobility

In terms of everyday service provisions, the segregated neighbourhoods of Belfast could claim a certain level of self-sufficiency, but although many factories were located within the segregated neighbourhoods of west Belfast, the majority of industrial and commercial employment was located in common areas or in specialized industrial quarters such as the docklands. In these central employment districts, allocation of jobs carried with it an unambiguous connotation of religion. Generally, rougher jobs in the mills and the less skilled jobs on the docks were the lot of Catholics, and, as the apprenticeship system for skilled jobs in engineering and shipbuilding matured, the patterns of difference became not only more established but also self-regulating. Cross-tabulation of male occupations and religion derived from the Irish 1871 census illustrates clearly the relative inequalities that existed within certain industries. With a value of 100 representing equality, the divergences are striking (table 2.4).

In general, Presbyterians were to the fore in the more highly skilled trades, followed closely by Anglicans, with Catholics a long way behind. There were notable exceptions, however. In the drinks trade and in butchering, Catholics predominated, and their outlets were to be found throughout the city, including in characteristically Protestant

Table 2.4 Weighted male participation in selected occupations by religion, Belfast, 1871

Occupation	(100 = equality)		
	Catholic	Anglican	Presbyterian
Shipbuilding	30	101	163
Engine/boiler makers	60	122	109
Printing	78	107	110
Linen workers	112	93	95
Joiners	66	86	144
Bricklayers	89	92	125
Carters	114	86	108
Dockers	136	103	79
Factory labourers	35	103	77
Tailors	122	74	104
Shoemakers	112	116	80
Hairdressers	188	69	66
Butchers	211	65	44
Publicans	163	68	79
Dealers	208	59	49

After Hepburn, *A Past Apart*, 75

districts. Among the unskilled tasks in which Catholics predominated, the most common were those of carter, docker, and general factory labourer. In the semi-skilled trades, shoemaking and hairdressing exhibited a similar over-representation of Catholics. The most extreme over-representation of Catholics was in the generalized occupation of dealer – an activity that could include anything from trading in rags and second-hand clothes and furniture to the collection of old fowl and sale of vegetables. Trades such as bricklaying and carpentry tended to be more associated with Protestants – confirmation of the restrictive mechanism of apprenticeships and the patterns of ownership in the major construction firms. Overall, the data confirm Belfast as a city in which Presbyterians and, to a lesser extent, Anglicans enjoyed a marked social advantage over Catholics.

Throughout the last third of the nineteenth century, and well into the twentieth century, the correlation of Catholics with insecure and low-paid employment remained a constant in Belfast – despite considerable technological change and alteration in employment patterns within the rapidly industrializing city.[55] An aristocracy of labour existed in so far as the preferred and skilled occupations were dominated by Protestants, but given the fact that they represented more than two-thirds of the total population there were many Protestants even in the lower employment niches in which Catholics were proportionately over-represented. Competition for these menial jobs, exclusion from more desirable occupations, and an overall restricted social mobility sustained a raw edge in community life and politics over the decades. The pattern of religious bias in public employment at the municipal level conformed to that exhibited in the private sector. Belfast operated as a Protestant city, and preference was given to that group not only in professional, administrative, and technical areas but also in semi-skilled and unskilled fields. When Northern Ireland was granted regional autonomy in 1920, the newly created local parliament and regional civil service continued with the discriminatory practices. Prime Minister Sir James Craig's famous assertion that the Belfast Parliament was "a Protestant Parliament for a Protestant people" had a long-established precedent as a recruitment philosophy in Belfast City Hall, where membership of the Orange Order was an irreducible qualification. In 1886, for example, fewer than 5 per cent of white-collar employees of Belfast Council were Catholic, despite the fact that as a group they constituted 28 per cent of the city's population. The position had altered little by 1911. Moreover, remuneration for those Catholics fortunate enough to be employed by the city was generally only 60 per cent of that received by their Protestant colleagues and they were usually assigned the least attractive tasks.[56]

Statistical analysis of the comparative occupational structure of different ethnic and religious groups in Toronto is not as complete as that for Belfast, but the corpus of research is sufficiently large to support some general inferences. The socio-economic status of Catholics is quite well documented, but comparisons with other ethnic and religious groups are weak. A census of Catholics was taken in the early 1860s by their Church in preparation for assembling a list of ratepayers who would be liable for support of the proposed Separate School Board, and, given the composition of the city's population at the time, it may be assumed that virtually all the Catholics were of Irish origin.[57] This data has been analysed by Clarke, who has demonstrated that the occupational distribution among heads of household was heavily skewed in

Table 2.5 Occupational characteristics of the Irish (Toronto and St David's Ward), c. 1860

| | Toronto* | St David's Ward** | |
	Catholics %	Catholics %	Protestant %
Unskilled	45.0	67.7	36.5
Semi-skilled	13.5	14.3	25.0
Skilled	12.1	15.7	11.5
Clerical	2.8	0	7.7
Business	16.7	2.9	11.5
Professional	3.3	0	0
Private means	6.6	1.5	7.7

* After Clarke, *Piety and Nationalism*, 19.
** After Houston and Smyth, "The Irish Abroad," 10.

favour of manual work with 70 per cent classified as unskilled, semi-skilled, or skilled. Labourers, carters, and teamsters were the most common occupations.[58]

The seemingly high proportion classified as business refers primarily to shopkeepers, tavern owners, and service providers that had a base not only in the Catholic neighbourhoods but also in the city in general. Analogous information of a comparative nature for 1860 is contained in Houston and Smyth's analysis of ethnic groups in St David's Ward (table 2.5).[59] There are obvious dangers in comparing the two studies, but the comparative perspective contained within the Houston and Smyth study does resonate to some extent with Clarke's analysis of the position of Catholics.

The preponderance of manual occupations is common to both studies, with the unskilled being clearly the largest category. The greatest variance is to be found in the professional and business categories, but this may be explained, in part, by the predominantly working-class character of St David's Ward. A primary outcome of the Houston and Smyth study is their demonstration of differences that may have separated the two Irish groups. Protestants and Catholics were both overwhelmingly associated with manual occupations, with Catholics being most likely to be unskilled. Interestingly, Toronto Catholics were the stronger of the two groups in the skilled occupations – a reference to

Table 2.6 Occupational characteristics of Catholic and Protestant Irish in urban Canada, 1871

	Catholic %	Protestant %
Unskilled	32.2	12.0
Semi-skilled	10.7	7.2
Skilled	33.8	39.3
Clerical	6.0	11.6
Business	11.3	13.4
Professional	3.9	8.1
Farmer	2.3	7.4

After Darroch and Ornstein, "Ethnicity and Occupational Structure," 324.

large number of tradesmen working in the construction field. Protestants were the stronger group in business.

The socio-occupational profiles of the two religious groups are confirmed in general terms by Darroch and Ornstein's analysis of the 1871 census, and although their study refers to Canadian urban centres in general, not Toronto in particular, they do emphasize that their results have wide applicability (table 2.6).[60]

The data suggest a considerable divergence between the religious groups, although, as in the previous studies, manual work predominated among both. Seventy-six per cent of Catholics were in the three lower occupation categories as compared with 70 per cent in Clarke's study, but, given the divergence in the data sets, it would be unwise to infer a pattern of social mobility. Nonetheless, it may be argued that, since the 1871 census was held at a time when second-generation Catholics were coming to the fore, their status might have been expected to be better than that of the earlier immigrant generation. Comparative analysis of Protestant and Catholic Irish in 1871 is supportive of a pattern of Protestant aristocracy of employment. In general, Catholics were less well off than their Protestant counterparts, but no explanation of the underlying causative forces is discernible from these data. In a separate study, McGowan's construction of the occupation profile of four Catholic parishes in Toronto in 1890 depicts a population in the closing years of the century wherein almost two-thirds were still classified in the three lower occupation categories. Unfortunately no comparable data is available for Protestants at that time.[61]

Unlike Belfast, Toronto's employment structure was dominated by neither a single industry nor any group of industries, but the two cities did have a common structure of public employment. Municipal governance, provision of services from street sweeping to building regulation and medical inspection, were statutory responsibilities in both places, and hundreds were employed at levels ranging from labourer to chief accountant. It has already been noted that Catholics did not exceed 5 per cent of clerical employees in Belfast City Hall in 1886, although they constituted 28 per cent of the overall population at the time. However, there was an equally cold climate for Catholics in public employment in Toronto, where in 1894 only 5 per cent of City Hall employees were Catholic; most of them were in manual jobs, and there were no Catholics at the level of head of department. In the Post Office and Customs and Revenue sectors the proportion was marginally better – 8 per cent and 7 per cent, respectively, were Catholic. But at the time Catholics amounted to 15 per cent of the city's population. Three per cent of the fire service was Catholic; the equivalent figure for the police was 5 per cent. When consideration is given to the status of jobs filled by Catholics, their disadvantaged position becomes even more apparent. In the city's waterworks, for example, three Catholics were employed as street turnkey operators and none were represented among the engineers and clerks in the extensive staff complement of the operation. Matters did not improve much in the early twentieth century. Officer positions in the police remained almost entirely in Protestant hands and little improvement was registered among firemen either. In 1920 the City Clerk's Office, the bureaucratic nerve centre of municipal governance, had twenty-one employees of whom three were Catholics, and they were employed as telephone operators and at salaries lower than that of the Protestant messenger boy in the same office. By 1930 the staffing levels in the City Clerk's Office had expanded to thirty-five; four were Catholics employed at the lower end of the salary scale. It was well known in the city that Protestants were at a significant advantage when seeking public employment, but, despite generations of protest by Catholics, little change was registered before the 1950s. Until the mid-twentieth century, City Hall maintained a tradition of granting leave with pay to employees wishing to participate in the annual Twelfth of July parade, and municipal business was traditionally suspended for the day. Belfast was the only other city in the world where commemoration of the 1690 Battle of the Boyne received such official acclaim.

Private companies, such as the giant retailing enterprise of Eaton's, were recognized as offering preferential treatment to Protestant applicants, and although this practice was more mythical than real by the 1950s, there is strong evidence to validate the description for earlier decades. Older patterns of employment bias altered in the post–Second World War era when massive expansion of the scale of industrial and commercial outlets and competition for labour diluted the rigidities of earlier times. Some businesses, however, did initially resist the forces of change, as was evidenced by the Consumer's Gas Company. A prominent trade unionist has recalled in his memoirs that when natural gas reached Toronto in 1958 there was a huge demand for labour to dig trenches and for skilled fitters to connect the new service. It was a time when large numbers of Italian and Portuguese labourers were entering the city, but the company maintained its tradition of giving preference to immigrants from the British Isles, specifically Protestants from Scotland and Ulster. Applicants were asked, "Which team d'ye support?" and if the answer was Glasgow Rangers a job was proffered.[62] Such behaviour was a throwback to a mindset that had persisted for more than a century in the city.

The religious dimension of that civic culture was emphasized further by the electoral geography of both cities. Toronto and Belfast constituencies elected between three and five representatives to the respective national parliaments in Ottawa and Westminster in the period under study. There was a striking similarity in the electoral records of both places. Their members of Parliament were almost invariably Protestant, very many of them members of the Orange Order who owed their electoral success to the support of the local lodges. The exceptions proved the rule. Belfast did elect a Catholic businessman, Bernard Hughes, and Toronto elected a Catholic labour lawyer, John O'Donoghue, in the last quarter of the nineteenth century. Frank Smith, Toronto's equivalent of the entrepreneurial Bernard Hughes, was allocated a seat in the Ottawa Senate through the patronage of the prime minister. But these men were exceptional personalities whose personal attributes and wealth enabled them to transcend traditional fissure lines. Of the parliamentarians elected to the Ontario Provincial Legislature in the first half of the twentieth century, more than one-third were Orangemen, and between 1923 and 1961 three of the province's premiers, who between them held office for a total of twenty-four years, were Orangemen.[63] Correspondingly, all six prime ministers of Northern Ireland who held power, 1920–72, were Orangemen, and while representatives elected to the regional parliament in Belfast always included some Catholic representatives, the majority was invariably Orange and Protestant. A similar pattern prevailed at municipal level. In Toronto City Hall, the elected Council contained very few Catholics in the years before 1950. In some years no Catholics were returned. The most senior Catholic representative in City Hall, and sometime member of the Board of Control during the 1940s and early 1950s, was David Balfour, and of him the president of the city's Irish Protestant Benevolent Society noted, "Balfour is a Roman Catholic whose father, a Scottish Presbyterian, married an Irish Catholic. Dave is really not a bad fellow but at times a silly ass in his pursuit of votes from all and sundry. Naturally he gets the Catholic votes when aspiring to Civic Office and also a number of votes from Protestants like myself who try to be broadminded."[64]

The description captured well the nature of politics in the city and hinted at a process of change that would become much more apparent over the next several years. Historically, the absence of large neighbourhood concentrations in Toronto had made the creation of a coherent electoral force of Catholics a very difficult task, whereas in Belfast the structure of the wards, and the strength of Catholic communities in at least two of them, always ensured the return of some Catholic representatives, although they never amounted to more than a recognized minority of those elected. Prior to 1954, all mayors of both Toronto and Belfast were Protestant – most were also Orangemen. In the council chambers of the respective cities Orangemen were an overall majority, the Twelfth of July was officially recognized, and civic culture was shaped accordingly.

Evolution of the Orange Order in Belfast and Toronto

The Orange Order had first emerged as a structured organization in rural Co Armagh in the autumn of 1795 and over the next few months it had spread through adjoining communities, reaching Dublin by early 1797.[65] Belfast at the time had been associated with the reform politics advanced by liberal Presbyterians and during the 1798 Rebellion it was identified with the rebels' cause. Nonetheless, at least three Orange lodges, LOL 145, LOL 238, and LOL 243, had been formed in Belfast by June 1797, and numerous other lodges were founded in the nearby adjoining Co Antrim villages of Derriaghy and Lambeg,[66] creating a sufficiency of Orangemen to support a parade in the city on the Twelfth of July 1797.[67] In the immediate aftermath of the 1798 Rebellion,

Orangeism found greater traction among a citizenry shocked by the bloody excesses of the insurrection. In October 1798 a leading Belfast citizen wrote to Lord Charlemont in Dublin: "The Orange mania has broken loose amongst us, and spreads with a rapidity almost incredible ... all denominations of Protestants are taking it up ... within these forty eight hours, the number of Orangemen is trebled in this town."[68] A report in 1810 referred to "the rooted animosity at present subsisting between those yeomen denominated Orangemen and the Roman Catholics," indicating clearly that the animosities of the countryside had been transferred to the city.[69]

The Orange Order continued to grow in Belfast well in advance of the famine-induced inflow of migrants in the late 1840s, and, as has been noted earlier, the first serious riot resulting in deaths occurred as early as 1813. By 1833 there were at least 33 lodges in the city, a number that grew slowly to 37 by 1858, and in that year the number of Belfast lodges was only marginally greater than the 34 to be found in Dublin.[70] Dramatic growth in lodge numbers and lodge size occurred in the second half of the nineteenth century. By 1900 there were 165 lodges in Belfast. A total of 199 were recorded for 1909 and Belfast was recognized as the undisputed capital of Irish Orangeism.[71] Growth during these years reflected the ongoing polarization that was taking place in a city that was increasingly segregated and riot-torn, but it is difficult to ascribe cause or effect to the relationship between lodge numbers and intensity of community tensions. Undoubtedly, Orange parades were the occasion for rioting, but, in reality, they were symptoms of a pre-existing cultural chasm, and there is little evidence to suggest that the formation of lodges was stimulated by the predictable annual clashes. Political developments, especially the emergence of national debates and associated legislative attempts to introduce Home Rule for Ireland, were more important stimuli for the expansion of Orangeism in Belfast, and this dynamic became especially important after the formation of a Unionist party in 1886. Henceforth, lodges were the constituency loci for political alignments and electoral support. In such a role the local lodges transcended their community functions and identities to become cogs in a political machine that was determined to maintain intact the United Kingdom of Great Britain and Ireland, protect the integrity of the British Empire, and defend the cause of the Protestant monarchy. However, there existed also a broad correlation between the number of lodges and the overall Protestant population of the city, indicating that new neighbourhoods, expanding suburbs, and the geographical realities of the most rapidly growing industrial city in the British Isles brought their own dynamic to the fortunes of the Order.

In Toronto a similar combination of factors contributed to the growth in lodge numbers, but, as in Belfast, much of the growth was generated by the demographic and geographic expansion of the city. In contradistinction to Belfast, however, the Order in the Canadian city had to adjust to a reality wherein its natural supporters, the Protestant Irish, did not have a monopoly on Protestantism or anti-Catholicism. It met the challenge, thrived on it, and within a few years the Order was attracting Englishmen and Scots as well as smaller numbers of other Protestant groups to its ranks. The Orange Order in Toronto was, therefore, always more varied in its composition than its Ulster counterpart, but there was no lessening of its fervour for all of that. In time, the Irish would become a minority in the Toronto body; in aggregate, Canadians, Englishmen, and Scots would become a majority, but policy formation and direction remained heavily influenced by the Irish. The Canadian Order never meshed into a political party in the same way as the Ulster Unionists and Orangemen bonded, although for most of its history it was associated with the national Conservative party, and when that party was in power three seats in Cabinet were allegedly reserved for Orangemen. The provincial legislature, whose seat was Queen's Park in Toronto, was even more clearly Orange in the composition of its Conservative governments, and, on occasion, a majority of that party's MPPs were members of the Order. Queen's Park was a fertile source of patronage for Orangemen in the city.

However, the political significance of Toronto Orangeism was most effectively, and obviously, expressed at the level of municipal politics, where clientalism and patronage supported an exercise of power comparable to the Belfast model. The Orange network in Toronto was divided into organizational districts coterminous with federal electoral districts, but for municipal elections to City Hall or to the School Board the network of lodges operated on a ward basis. Candidates for election were introduced at formal lodge meetings; Orange halls were recognized venues for electioneering. Given the fact that municipal electoral campaigns were held over the brief period of one week, candidates had few opportunities to address public meetings and they gained an advantage from meetings in lodge halls and their ready-made partisan audiences. Electioneering in Belfast and Toronto adhered to similar structures; the Orange vote was critical in both places. Notwithstanding differences in their scale and history, there was an unmistakable

Table 2.7 Number of Orange lodges: Belfast and Toronto

Year	Belfast	Toronto
1797	3	na
1833	33	4
1858	37	22
1900	165	55
1909	199	59

similarity between the cities, and that similarity would persist until the mid-twentieth century.

The data in table 2.7 present the comparable position of Belfast and Toronto in terms of their total lodge numbers in the period 1797–1909. The apparent lag in the growth of lodges in Toronto in the late nineteenth century masks the fact that lodge size was, on average, greater in the Canadian city. Nonetheless by 1909, when both cities were of comparable size, there was no doubt that Belfast was the more Orange of the two places. In terms of local political effectiveness, however, the Order in Toronto would have been close to its Belfast prototype and the Canadian organization would have been considerably more powerful than its counterparts in either Liverpool or Glasgow, other recognized bastions of Orangeism.

Measured in terms of membership, the Order grew rapidly in both Toronto and Belfast during the opening decades of the twentieth century. Heightened political feelings arising from the ongoing Irish Home Rule crisis lent new energy to the Order, especially in Belfast, where it was closely involved with the organization of a Protestant paramilitary group, the Ulster Volunteer Force under the leadership of Edward Carson and Sir James Craig. The political crisis in Ireland evoked a similar response in lodge growth in Toronto, but social and economic factors of a more local nature also remained to the fore in Canada. The Home Rule crisis certainly generated considerable interest in Toronto, where major rallies chaired by civic leaders attracted thousands of supporters of the Ulster Protestant cause, and statuettes of Carson were sold in large numbers for display in family homes. Carson sent a public message to the Toronto rallies – "We fight against betrayal and for civil and religious liberty. Will Canada help us?"

Funds were raised in the Canadian city and forwarded to Belfast for the purchase of arms, and some men prepared for armed insurrection in the event of the Home Rule Act being implemented.[72] A Belfast man, Sam McIlroy, who had recently settled in Toronto, wrote to a friend in the United States in June of 1912 stating, "If there is any assistance wanted when Home Rule comes, I suppose we will all have to return."[73] In the same year, a Toronto lodge, Aughrim Rose of Derry LOL 2159, passed a resolution that was disseminated widely, both in Toronto and in Ireland:

> The Aughrim Rose of Derry LOL 2159 desires to formally place on record the approval of its members of the firm stand for Imperial unity by the Orangemen and Unionists of Ulster. In our opinion the adoption of Home Rule would ultimately lead to the separation of Ireland from the British Empire and it would set up a force beside the United Kingdom that would become a menace to the Empire. We believe that the civil and religious liberties of the loyal minority living in Ulster would be threatened by an Irish parliament as it would be dominated and controlled by the servants of a foreign power which has for ten centuries increasingly striven to rule all the kingdoms of the earth and impose its will as a temporal as well as a spiritual power. We further pledge ourselves to do all we can both by moral and material support, to assist our brethren in Ireland in this dark hour of their history.[74]

The potential support of Toronto Orangemen was well understood by brethren in Ireland. A letter sent by the master of a Co Donegal lodge to his opposite number in a Toronto lodge in 1913 informed the Toronto brethren, "We are resolved to die sooner than submit to be ruled by Rome. We are all ready for them at anytime. As Brother Deane can tell you, we are drilled. We are expecting hard times anyway. Trusting your lodge is in a flourishing condition and that you will be able to send us a good contingent of men to fight a second Boyne when the time comes which won't be long."[75]

The Toronto lodges did not send men to fight in Ireland – the onset of the First World War injected a new cause. But the empathy to be found in the "Belfast of Canada" was, and remained, strong. Indeed a sub-stratum of this sentiment extended into much more recent times, as was exemplified by the proven involvement of some Toronto citizens in the provision of automatic rifles, grenade launchers, and ammunition to Ulster Protestant paramilitaries in the 1980s.[76]

Inter-group Relations

The tensions that traditionally pervaded inter-group relations in Belfast and Toronto were rooted in common sets of mutual distrust, supported by strong senses of group identity. But different demographic scales and the particularities of local conditions mediated the effect of those tensions in the two places. Catholics in Belfast were part of a larger national community that amounted to three-quarters of the population of Ireland, and their sense of religious cohesion was augmented by a political identification with a wider nationalist movement. Protestants, although a majority in Belfast and its adjoining hinterland of east Ulster, were very conscious that they were a minority within the total Irish population, and their sense of colonial precariousness was invigorated by a folk memory that recalled dangers from previous insurrections, the most recent of which had occurred in 1798. In Canada a different set of conditions prevailed. Irish Catholics in Toronto saw themselves as part of a double minority. They were a minority within a province and a city that were 75 per cent Protestant, and they were an English-speaking minority within a Canadian Catholic Church that was over-whelmingly French.[77] Their Protestant countrymen, on the other hand, found themselves part of local, provincial, and national majorities in their new homeland. The demography wrought its own logic. Irish Protestant marriages in Canada were not restricted to their own communities; they married into English and Scottish as well as German and United Empire Loyalist families and helped construct a pan-Protestant community. To a considerable extent they, and their organizational and ideological structures, came to define the Britishness and loyalty of that wider community in terms of Orangeism. At its organizational peak, possibly one-third of Protestant males in Ontario were, or had been, Orangemen; they was not a marginal minority movement. Conversely, as the nineteenth century came to a close, Toronto's Catholics were conscious that they were a small population of little more than twenty thousand persons – probably no more than 3,500 families. They did not have the demographic resilience of their counterparts in Belfast, where there were some eighty thousand Catholics, supported by another three and a half million elsewhere on the island of Ireland. Attitudes to cross-community interaction and marriage were accordingly very different in the two countries.

In 1864, cognizant of the religious demography of his adopted city, Toronto's Archbishop Lynch had railed against attempts to encourage further Irish Catholic arrivals, bluntly telling his episcopal colleagues in Ireland that the Irish who had come to Toronto in previous years found "Before them the Protestant religion and infidelity in the ascendant. No wonder therefore that a vast number of the youth have been absorbed into the pores of this society, through the medium of mixed marriages, common schools, living with Protestant employers, the great scarcity of priests to attend to their spiritual wants and the innumerable associations with the Protestant and infidel elements of the country."[78]

Leakage from the Catholic community remained a major concern for Archbishop Lynch, and, although he tried to stem it by restricting dispensations for interfaith marriages,[79] he was clearly aware that many of his flock simply married with no official permission from the archdiocese. Many others may have either abandoned religion entirely or formally joined a Protestant denomination. Lynch's successor, Archbishop Walsh, operated a much more flexible system of dispensations, and under his episcopacy as many as 20 per cent of all marriages taking place in Catholic churches in the city included non-Catholic partners.[80] In turn, his successor, Archbishop O'Connor, who took up office in 1899, was appalled at the apparent laxity of his predecessor and immediately initiated a restrictive regime wherein few dispensations for mixed marriages were granted. It was a short-lived restriction that bowed to the inevitable after his episcopacy ended in 1908.[81] Data for York County, of which Toronto formed by far the largest component, indicate that by 1905 at least 60 per cent of all marriages involving Catholics included a partner from another religion. Ninety per cent of those interfaith marriages took place outside of the Catholic Church. The degree of interfaith marriage in Toronto was the highest in Canada at this time, and it reveals an intriguing time-shot of the largely Irish Catholic Church on the eve of the introduction of large numbers of southern European Catholics into the city. There was a high degree of membership instability within the Irish Catholic community, and the very high proportion of interfaith marriages and the publicly expressed concerns of the Catholic bishops would suggest that there was a pattern of ongoing dilution of their flock. It was probably in response to this evident pattern that, in 1900, Archbishop O'Connor expressed a wish that Catholics should segregate themselves residentially, creating enclaves in the vicinity of Catholic churches where they could better protect their faith.[82] It was a wish that could not be realized, given the established fluidity of residential and social mobility in contemporary Toronto, although at the micro-scale of street blocks clusters of parishioners were sometimes evident. Bishop

Lacey, in his homily in St Michael's Cathedral at mass on St Patrick's Day in 2005, recalled how, growing up in Toronto in the 1930s, he was part of a defined Catholic community on St Clarens Ave, and he recalled that his generation on the street produced eleven priests and nineteen nuns. He remembered a unique community in the shadow of St Claren's Church of Christ, but official records show that even in that "Catholic neighbourhood" there were also many Anglican and Presbyterian neighbours.[83]

It was a religious geography that stood in marked contrast to that of Belfast. Traditionally, and until very recent years, the incidence of interfaith marriage was exceptionally low within the Irish city. A sample of more than five thousand households in Belfast in 1901 revealed less than 0.2 per cent of mixed marriages,[84] and partners in such relationships generally lived in Catholic areas. Those who did insist on living in Protestant districts were often the subject of intimidation and were burnt out of their homes during periods of community conflict. Within the Catholic communities the limited tolerance extended to mixed marriages was framed by a set of social and religious instruments that sought to prevent relationships developing across the religious divide. Donald Akenson has perceptively noted, "The Irish phrase for religious intermarriage is 'mixed marriage' and it is not an innocent term ... the phrase is more than merely descriptive; it is one of implicit opprobrium."[85] Demographic scale, residential segregation, separate schooling, self-sufficiency in service provision within the neighbourhood, and strong church leadership provided a set of self-reinforcing conditions that established the normality of marriage within community boundaries. In Toronto a system of separate schooling, a strong church leadership, universal canon law, and a consciousness of difference were not sufficient to maintain effective barriers against interfaith marriages. The contrast between the Belfast and Toronto experiences was evident and massive, and the key to it lay within the reality of social and concomitant residential patterns of mobility. Aspirations for improvement and change could be expressed and realized in nineteenth-century Toronto; in contemporary Belfast there was limited possibility of self-improvement, and within their tightly bounded universes the Catholic and Protestant communities folded in upon themselves, literally for protection. In many ways, the difference between the two urban experiences was rooted also in the difference between New World and Old World societies. As Cole Harris has consistently argued, the physical resources and social conditions of Canada were much more permissive than those which existed in Europe, and there was a much greater dynamic for change, less of a hidebound fixation with the past.[86] The Orange Order was an obvious transfer from the Old World and it did survive and prosper to the extent that it was able to replicate some aspects of the civic culture of its Belfast counterpart. But the nature of Canadian society ameliorated the extremes of the Belfast experience and contained within it a dynamic that would eventually lead to the demise of the Order after the Second World War.

Urban Images: Belfast and Toronto

For two centuries Belfast has been known throughout the world for its sectarian tensions and street politics. In poetry and prose its reputation has been expounded, extending beyond Ireland to virtually every corner of the globe. Poet and historian Maurice Craig has captured well this urban identity in his poem "Ballad to a Traditional Refrain," in which he describes a city that seems forever locked in its past, oblivious to the modernity of its urban landscape.[87]

> It's to hell with the future and live on the past;
> May the Lord in His mercy be kind to Belfast.

Toronto has been less evidently the inspiration for literary reflection on its Orange culture, but a doggerel verse published in the *Evening Telegram* on the occasion of the Twelfth parade of 1893 did capture the sense of the synonymous relationship that existed between Orangemen and the staff of the City Hall.[88]

> Like the temple of old Egypt
> Empty as a noxious mine
> Stood the City Hall deserted
> For "the byes" were all in line.

The all-pervading sense of the continued relevance of the 1690 Battle of the Boyne to life in rapidly modernizing urban centres on either side of the Atlantic struck many contemporary commentators as odd, but for the tens of thousands who made up the membership of Orange lodges there was no anomaly. The tradition of civil and religious liberty as established by King William's victory was not merely a historical fact; it was regarded as the cornerstone for the preservation of future democracy. Many Catholics would have agreed with the political interpretation; they regretted that it was bounded within a world of exclusive Protestantism.

A civic culture interwoven with Protestantism and tempered by temperance and Sabbatarianism was common to both Belfast and Toronto and was enshrined in city by-laws in both places. Shocked by the high social cost of alcohol abuse, both Catholic and Protestant communities supported temperance movements and restrictions on the consumption of alcohol, notwithstanding the fact that a disproportionately large number of publicans in Belfast, and very many in Toronto, were Catholic. However, municipal attempts to outlaw Sunday sports and games, theatre performances, and dances were regarded as being representative of a particularly inflexible Protestantism. Until the final quarter of the twentieth century, Belfast required cinemas and theatres to remain closed on Sundays, bars were licensed for six days only, and dances held their last waltz as the clock moved towards midnight on Saturdays. Catholic parish halls, operating under a club licence, extended their dances into the early hours of Sunday morning, and some were even scheduled for Sunday evenings. But on city property there was an inflexible prohibition of group recreation on the Lord's Day. Public parks were available for family strolls, but the swings and roundabouts were chained into immobility lest children be tempted by frivolity. Golf, cricket, and soccer were relegated to the other six days of the week, although in Catholic communities Gaelic football and hurling were played in private sports fields. Sunday in Belfast was for church-going; the city centre was closed to recreational and social activities and only in train and bus stations could *bone fide* travellers obtain a cup of tea, but not a beer. Anyone emigrating from Belfast to Toronto would have found a resounding familiarity in the prohibitions that were required by law to operate on a Sunday.

Observance of the Sabbath in Toronto was in keeping with the strict requirements of evangelical Protestantism, filtered through the churches and supported by the officers and politicians of the Orange Order. A visiting British scientist commented in 1897, "Sunday in Toronto is as melancholy and suicidal sort of day as Puritan principles can make it."[89] Indeed for five years commencing in the mid-1880s, municipal politics in Toronto were convulsed over the issue of whether streetcars should be allowed to operate on a Sunday. Since 1861 a city ordinance had prohibited Sunday operation of public transport and attempts to overturn that prohibition resulted in large-scale public meetings, bitterly contested mayoralty elections, and threats of imminent fire and brimstone.

Reform, assisted by votes from the Catholic and Jewish communities in the city, eventually won the day, but in the debate citizens had been asked to choose between a New York or European style Sunday and the moral strictures of "Toronto the Good."[90] Henceforth streetcars would operate on a Sunday, but the Eaton retailing company would still draw the blinds on its windows on that day and during the week it would still prohibit the sale of alcohol or tobacco products. The appellation "Toronto the Good" had been coined in 1898 by local writer C.S. Clarke and it remained a popular descriptive term for the next half- century.[91] Central to that image was the reinforcing attribute of its being a "city of churches." In 1891, with a population of 144,023, Toronto could boast of 102 churches and by 1895 it supported 178 churches and 41 missions, including the Salvation Army. In addition, street preaching by evangelicals could be heard in the downtown area on both Saturday night and Sunday, although as city historian Jesse Middleton wryly commented, "Whether or not it is effective no one can tell."[92] Arriving in 1923 from Paris to take up a post as journalist with the *Toronto Star*, Ernest Hemingway commented, with some exasperation, "In Toronto, as you know, 85% of the inmates attend a Protestant church on a Sunday. Official figures. I don't know what the other 15% do. Probably attend a catholic church."[93] A few weeks later his friend Ezra Pound similarly criticized Toronto, bemoaning his difficulty in purchasing a box of chocolates to take to a sick friend: "I had to buy them from the bootleggers. The Drug Stores cannot sell candy on Sunday."[94]

Belfast likewise could boast of a large number of churches, mission halls, and street preachers, and like Toronto it was a city where the intermingling of personal identity and church affiliation was the norm. Religion was much more than the codification of theological doctrines and liturgical practices; it was a vital determinant of personal, civic, and political behaviour. In keeping with Toronto's image of a citadel of temperance, the Scottish entrepreneur John McLaughlin developed, in 1890, a new soft drink for the local market – modelling it on the ginger ales that had been first developed in Belfast in 1851. His Belfast Style Ginger Ale proved to be an immediate success and was appropriately marketed with a map of Canada and a beaver on the label complementing the Irish origins implied by its title. Some years later a new name was decided upon – Canada Dry Pale Ginger Ale. In more ways than one, Toronto really was the "Belfast of Canada," although product differentiation operated in both places.

3 Toronto Orangeism: The Nature and Structure of the Orange Order

The Orange Order in Canada was, and remains, a recognizable cultural import from Ireland, and, through its organizational structure, codified rules, regulations, and rituals, the fraternal body has maintained an identity that has been sustained by immigrants and Canadian-born alike for several generations. Its transplantation, survival, and organizational success constitute some of the most striking ingredients in Canadian social and political history, and, although it may well be currently enduring a prolonged period of decline and decay, there is no doubt that its impact on the land of its adoption has been of fundamental and often controversial significance. Its legacy is enshrined in national, provincial, and local histories. Today its contributions are muted and largely discarded by a national culture that has outgrown its originating British imperial past, yet for almost two centuries the history and geography of Canada have borne the imprint of the Orange Order, and nowhere has that been more striking than in the city of Toronto, the "Belfast of Canada."

The longevity of Canada's Orange experience and its early entrenched Irish Protestant identity does not obviate the fact that the Order itself was the subject of considerable change and adjustment as it was transplanted to, and matured in, its new environment. Internally, its rules and ritual were amended to take account of altered circumstances and the political demands of its early leaders while simultaneously the social, ethnic, and denominational composition of the membership adjusted in compliance with the nature of society in general. The external perception of the Order by Catholics has remained constant throughout its history; to them it has always been a bigoted sectarian and secretive political organization that actively sought to restrict their social standing and access to power. By way of contrast, the attitude to Orangemen displayed by the Canadian Protestant majority became more accommodating and accepting, especially in the post-Confederation era and well into the twentieth century. Perceived in its early years as an immigrant rabble associated with riot and community strife, the Order had advanced its image by the first quarter of the twentieth century to a point where it was the largest fraternal body in the country, enumerating among its membership an inclusive range of occupational and social classes together with a hierarchy of political leaders at local, provincial, and national levels. Possessed of a chameleon-like quality, the organization proved itself capable of adapting to the complex social, cultural, and political dynamics not only of Ireland but also of the many colonial niches within which it established itself. The Orange Order was, and still remains, identifiable as an outgrowth of the sectarian conditions of late eighteenth-century Ireland, but an inherent organizational flexibility facilitated its transfer from rural Ulster to industrial Belfast, from pre-famine Ireland to the agricultural frontier of Canada and onwards to metropolitan Toronto.

As a formal, structured organization with written rules, elected officers, and a hierarchy of local, district, provincial, and national lodges, the Orange Order may trace its origins to a sectarian fight that occurred in Ireland, specifically Co Armagh, in September 1795. The newly created Order quickly became embroiled as a counter-revolutionary force in helping government forces quash the United Irishmen's rebellion of 1798, and its defence of Protestantism, power, and property became one of its earliest defining characteristics. Riotous excesses, naked sectarian aggression, and an organizational structure based on secret signs and passwords engendered a reputation that was anathema to Catholics and, at times, provoked the government to seek to limit its public activities. A central tenet of the Order's ideology was an identification of Catholics with disloyalty, or at best with a conditional loyalty to the secular state arising from their perceived overall subservience to papal authority. In these beliefs Orangemen were not remarkably different from many in mainstream contemporary British society, where celebration of Protestantism frequently verged on anti-Catholicism, and legal impediments restricted the participation of Catholics in public life prior to the ceding of Catholic Emancipation in 1829. Despite the passage of that Act, Benjamin Disraeli could still argue in 1852 that "hatred of the Pope" remained a defining feature of English public opinion – an attitude that remained prevalent in Britain until at least the 1880s.[1] Where the Orange Order did differ from societal norms was in the physical violence and language of sectarian extremism to which it sometimes resorted. As an organization, the Orange Order presented structured and powerful means of managing sectarian enmity and was initially acclaimed by the Irish Protestant community as a union of like-minded persons linked by fear of previous Catholic rebellions and united in vigilance against any enhancement of the position, privilege, or power of the agreed enemy. In the eyes of many Protestants, the Order represented an effective and necessary community organization. In the eyes of Catholics, the Order represented a marshalling of sectarian bigots capable of resorting to injury and killings to maintain their social, economic, and political superiority. No reconciliation of such opposing stances was possible, either in the Irish homeland or in the overseas destinations in which Catholic and Orange immigrants settled.

The earliest Orange lodges to operate in Canada were those introduced by military regiments to Halifax and Montreal in 1799 and 1800 respectively. Settlers introduced additional lodges in the following decade to the Ottawa Valley. However, sustained and systematic growth of the organization required the mass Irish immigration of the years following the ending of the Napoleonic wars in 1815. The settlers brought with them the structures and traditions of a dynamic organization, and for the next one hundred years the geographical expansion of the Order in Canada marched in step with the expansion of the settlement frontier. Eventually a network of lodges that stretched from Newfoundland to Vancouver Island was created, although Ontario, and especially Toronto, quickly attained, and long retained, positions of national pre-eminence.

From its inception the Orange Order had borrowed much of its ritual, symbolism, and organizational structure from the Masonic Order. It acquired elements such as elaborate initiation ceremonies, sworn secrets, cellular lodge structures, and intricate symbolism. Some of these elements had originated beyond Masonry, in bodies as diverse as the craft guilds and revolutionary movements of medieval and early modern Europe.[2] In all cases, the trappings of secret fraternalism served to bond members closely together in the embrace of organizational solidarity and protect them from infiltration by non-members. Goals of a political, economic, or religious nature were identified as their *raison d'être*, but ultimately they prospered or failed in accordance with their success in attracting, retaining, and motivating a membership of like-minded individuals. The Orange Order was not unique in some of its attributes but it did prove to be more successful and more durable than most of its counterparts. With the possible exception of Freemasonry, no other fraternal organization has survived for so long in the modern period – expanding in the process to virtually every English-speaking country in the world and achieving mass membership and considerable political influence in environments far removed from its cradle of origin.

Structurally, the Order was well equipped for geographical expansion. Stimulated by the rise of mass emigration, the development of modern communications, and the imperial outreach of the second British Empire, it created a flexible organizational network that was capable of functioning within diverse local environments. Its distinctive social and political geographies were adjusted to fit within different environments, but, nonetheless, it retained more than a semblance of fidelity to the circumstances and organizational requirements of its original heartland. By a combination of robust but flexible structures it expanded, survived, and prospered, recruiting new members and accommodating émigré Orangemen, all of whom found in the lodges of their new locality reassuring camaraderie, ritual, and ceremony. The Order was organized in a hierarchical structure – local primary lodges were responsible to a network of district lodges that, in turn, reported to a system of county lodges. Provincial and national lodges formed the two highest organizational levels in each country. In 1866, and largely at the instigation of the Canadian body, the Imperial Grand Orange Council of the World was created, forming a consultative and ceremonial body that still continues to meet every three years. In all countries where it had established a presence, the strength and vitality of the Order were dependent fundamentally upon the robustness of the network of local primary lodges, authorization for the formation of which always required written sanction and a formal warrant granted by the relevant provincial or national body. Each warrant in a national jurisdiction was numbered sequentially by order of date of formation, and although this system was compromised over the years by the reissuing of dormant warrant numbers and erroneous duplication, the system still retains a functionality that is transparent and organizationally effective. Establishment of new lodges has generally required the written support of at least five known Orangemen. By such means authenticity was guaranteed, tradition was preserved, and control exercised over an organization that, for more than a century, grew rapidly in spatial and numerical terms. Registers of all warrants are preserved in official manuscript records in both Ireland and Canada, and although the Irish records have been amended to take account of the temporary banning of the organization in the 1820s and other institutional revisions, there does exist a coherent set of records that purport to cover the development of the Order from its foundation in 1795. The Canadian register dates from 1830, the year of the establishment of the Grand Lodge of British North America, and it too has been amended to take account of the subsequent addition of unique warrant numbering systems operated initially by New Brunswick and Newfoundland.[3]

Territorial Organization

A sound geographical logic is discernible in the organizational structure of the Orange Order in Canada. At the time of its inception in 1830, the Grand Orange Lodge of British America claimed jurisdiction over the organization in Upper and Lower Canada; extent lodges in the Maritime provinces were added later. Newfoundland lodges were inserted into the national register more than half a century before the island colony became a province of Canada. The jurisdiction of the Grand Lodge expanded westward in harmony with the expansion of the settlement frontier, and eventually the Order could validly claim a hegemony stretching from the Atlantic to the Pacific.[4] In 1860 the Upper Canadian territory was divided into the two Orange provinces of Ontario East and Ontario West, with the division line being drawn a few miles to the east of Toronto. The Toronto lodges were originally administered as part of York County, but in 1859 the growth in numbers justified the subdivision of that area into four separate Orange counties, York East, York West, York North, and Toronto. At the time, there were nineteen lodges, with an average membership of sixty, in the city. The first county master was F.H. Medcalf, an immigrant blacksmith who had become a self-made industrialist and owner of the Don Foundry. He resigned his position one year later to assume the role of grand master of the newly formed Grand Orange Lodge of Ontario West,[5] and in 1864 he was elected mayor of Toronto on a specifically Orange platform. The first secretary of the Toronto county lodge was Harcourt P. Gowan, master of LOL 4 and son of Ogle R. Gowan, who had organized the first Grand Lodge of British America in 1830. The division of York County into four distinct Orange counties was part of a wider organizational strategy and was not prompted solely by the administrative requirements of an expanding cohort of lodges. The 4 February 1859 meeting of the York County Lodge, at which the decision to subdivide the area was taken, recorded that "it was, amongst other matters, resolved at

Table 3.1 Organizational structure of the Toronto County
Orange Lodge, 1875

District	Lodges	Members
Centre	17	527
West	5	457
East	4	231

Table 3.2 Organizational Structure of the Toronto County
Orange Lodge, 1901

District	Members
Centre	1,323
Eastern	704
Western	1,094
Northern	84
Northwestern	122

the annual meeting for 1859 of the County Lodge of York ... that each
electoral division was of right entitled to, and should possess, a County
Lodge of its own for its better internal government." The Order thereby
positioned itself to align its full organizational strength to the geopolitical realities of the day – a strategy that proved to be very successful
in the new Orange county of Toronto, an Orange jurisdiction that was
coterminous with the municipal boundaries of the city.

This same sense of electoral geography dictated a further refinement
of the boundaries of the Toronto County Orange Lodge in 1875. The
county was subdivided into three Orange districts (table 3.1).[6]
The boundaries of each district were to be identical to those established
for the federal parliamentary elections of 1872, and, as the variation
in lodge numbers and membership size indicates, the subdivision was
more anticipatory than reflective of an unmanageable single county
entity. In particular, the new Orange district of West Toronto, which
included the St Andrew, St George, and St Patrick electoral wards, was
well poised to take advantage of the contemporaneous spread of the
city to the west of Spadina Avenue. A further reconfiguration of Orange
districts within the city took place at the turn of the century, with returns
for 1901 indicating the districts as seen in table 3.2.

The parliamentary riding of Toronto North was created two years later and that of Northwestern Toronto did not emerge until 1924. The prior organization of Orange districts in both ridings represented the perceived need to establish a base in all areas of the city, taking account of ongoing suburban expansion and electoral opportunities for municipal elections. By the late 1920s the Northwestern District had been dropped; the Order reverted to its traditional four districts (Centre, Western, Eastern, and Northern), and these remained in place for the next fifty years. In 1979, recognizing the evident attrition in lodge numbers, the County Lodge amalgamated all administrative districts into a single Orange county with jurisdiction over all of the city and its suburbs. Organizational and electoral strength having been dissipated, there was no longer any advantage in shadowing the city's increasingly complex system of parliamentary ridings.

Authenticity of the Order in Canada

The warrant numbering system introduced into British North America in 1830 by the newly formed Grand Lodge of British North America was overseen by the founding grand master, Ogle R. Gowan, a recent immigrant from Co Wexford and proprietor of a local newspaper in Brockville, Ontario. His introduction of a separate warrants system was not without controversy. The newly formed Canadian system developed in parallel, and largely in conformity, with the parent Irish Grand Lodge, but without its expressed permission. In 1825 the Orange Order in Britain and Ireland had been deemed an unlawful society and was banned under the terms of legislation passed in that year.[7] To circumvent the new law, Orangemen in Ulster created the Loyal and Benevolent Orange Institution of Ireland, and for the next three years they operated a system of lodges ostensibly convened for charitable purposes. Presenting himself as grand secretary of this new body, Gowan had travelled throughout Ulster collecting dues and selling warrants, often with duplicated numbers. In 1829, amid allegations of embezzlement, he fled to Canada, where he used his knowledge and contacts to organize a Grand Lodge for the disparate Orange lodges that already existed in the country. Styling himself deputy grand master, Gowan proposed the Duke of Cumberland (titular head of the reconstituted Order in Ireland and Britain) as grand master. The Duke refused to acknowledge either the title or the new body, and Gowan became its *de facto* grand master amid circumstances that would remain controversial for the next two decades.[8] George Nichols, a former member of the Order in Ireland and sometime master of a lodge in Toronto, attacked the idea of such a Grand Lodge and decried its originator, Gowan. In a deposition laid before the Legislative Assembly of Upper Canada in 1841, he alleged that the Order in Canada "is a bastardised Orangeism, professing neither the correct signs or symbols of that in Ireland, nor are they in anyway engaged in the same views or object ... Here it is a purely political institution, introduced and abused for party purposes."[9] Two years earlier, at an official inquiry into political conditions in Canada that had led to the 1837 rebellions, he also presented an unambiguous condemnation of the Orange leadership: "It would seem that their great purpose has been to introduce the machinery, rather than the tenets of Orangeism; and the leaders probably hope to make use of this kind of permanent conspiracy and illegal organization to gain political power for themselves."[10]

The government report did not recognize the important social role performed by the Order in its new environment, but its criticism did point to an abiding issue in cultural transfer and reproduction, i.e., to what extent does a fragment of a transferred culture become universalized into a new identity.[11] Undoubtedly, the Order in Canada had to adjust to an altered set of social, political, and geographical conditions, and in the process its internal configuration and overall *raison d'être* were modified. Some of the rules and rituals popularized in Canada were, however, more the function of a style of leadership than of changed circumstances. For example, the contemporary Irish organization operated a simple system with two degrees, the Orange and the Purple, but the Canadian system, at the insistence of Gowan, created a much more elaborate system of five degrees: Orange, Purple, Royal Blue, Royal Arch Purple, and Scarlet. The Canadian system had some claim to authenticity: it was truer to the more complex system of "old degrees" that had been initially introduced in Ireland in 1795 but which had been reduced and simplified by the Irish Grand Lodge in 1801.[12] Gowan may have been motivated by the desire to create a more hierarchical organization in Canada, one more akin to the ritual complexity of Freemasonry. In addition, he could claim that the Canadian system had roots that extended back into the rituals associated with eighteenth-century Boyne clubs, the precursors of the Orange Order.

Conscious of the value to be derived from maintaining a strong set of linkages within the growing international body of Orangemen, and possibly with the intention of re-establishing himself in the eyes of the Order in Ireland, Gowan suggested in 1853 that the Canadian Order be aligned to an agreed international organization and proposed the opening of dialogue on the matter. Writing to the Rt. Hon. Earl of Enniskillen, grand master of the Irish parent body, he outlined his vision for future strategic development:

> I take the liberty of suggesting to your Lordship the propriety of convening a meeting of Delegates from all the Grand Lodges in the Empire, say at least England, Ireland, Scotland, British North America, Australia, New South Wales, New Zealand to fix upon a Grand Lodge and Grand Master for the whole Empire – to define its duty, power and limits – to declare the fundamental principles of the organization, the number of degrees, establish a perfect uniformity in the Mysteries and Symbols of those Degrees – to secure a more perfect understanding and correspondence in the working of the institution than at present or has hitherto existed.[13]

The approach was rebuffed at the time, but in 1866 the parent body agreed to hold a preliminary meeting of the Imperial Council in Belfast, with Gowan representing Canada. The following year a plenary meeting of the Imperial Grand Orange Council of the World was held in London, and on that occasion the Earl of Enniskillen was elected president and J.H. Cameron of Canada was elected as his deputy. The Council's mission was "To take into consideration the State of Orangeism and Protestantism generally, with the view of devising means for the extension of Orangeism in various parts of the Empire."[14] Significantly, no mention was made of harmonizing the system of degrees, symbols, and ritual. Local autonomy would prevail. The Grand Lodge of Ireland may have had difficulty in accepting the system instigated by Gowan, but it took no official action to halt or revoke it and was content to let it function as long as it did not impact directly on the Order in Ireland. At that time there was little reverse migration between the two countries, and Orangemen initiated in Canada were unlikely to return in numbers to the Order's jurisdictions in Ireland or Britain. Mass migration was unidirectional, and emigrants preparing to sail for Canada were aware of the existence of lodges there and of the willingness of the Grand Orange Lodge of British America to recognize the personal certificates of initiation they carried in their luggage. They were not overly concerned about the minutiae of differences in ritual that were particular to the colonial offshoot. Hereward Senior has perceptibly noted of the Canadian lodges: "Although the Orange lodges preserved an Old World tradition, they were never under Old World control."[15]

The diaspora of Irish Protestants was a central condition for the early and successful transplantation of Orangeism to the colonies of British North America. The substantive and sustained nature of their migration helped create, and sustain, an organization that would attract, in subsequent decades, thousands of Canadian-born adherents as well as recruits from England, Scotland, and Ireland. An emigrant who had been initiated into the Order in the Old World was provided with a signed certificate testifying to his good standing, the degrees into which he had been initiated, and the lodge to which he belonged. The design of the certificates changed little over time. Generally they were simple parchments measuring ten inches by twelve, decorated by the symbols of the Order, and containing the exhortation that the bearer "be recognised as a worthy brother by Orangemen around the globe." On arrival in his new homeland, the Orangeman would present his certificate to the master of the nearest lodge and he would be embraced very quickly within a network of like-minded individuals who could offer support and contacts and facilitate introductions. It was a simple but effective networking system, and it could operate in any milieu in which the organization had been established. It assumed a certain degree of literacy, at least among those officers issuing and receiving the certificate, but that does not appear to have given rise to any recurring difficulties.

Undoubtedly, the earliest lodges were introduced as community support elements, providing comfort, mutual assistance, and solidarity to emigrants isolated on the agricultural and lumber frontiers of the new land. The lives of some of these Orange pioneers were recorded in a series of biographical essays published by the organization's newspaper, the *Sentinel*, in 1899, and although they refer only to a selection of those who had survived and remained in the Order for half a century or more, they do provide many insights into the conditions of earlier days. Marching in his fifty-eighth annual Orange parade, Reuben Switzer, a Palatine born in Adare Co Limerick in 1813, recounted that he had become an Orangeman in 1830 and at the age of thirty-three had arrived in Canada, settling near London, Ontario in 1846. There, despite pioneering duties,

He found time with a number of kindred spirits to plant a branch of the Orange Tree in the wilds of that western country. Our Brother was a charter member of LOL 384 which has met on the Mitchell Road from the early days of the history of the Order in South Perth. In the infancy of the Lodge, our Brother tells us that they met from house to house among the members in that sparsely settled country. Afterwards they met for some time in hotels, until about 1871 when the Lodge built for itself a home, and has continued to own and control its own building ever since.[16]

At Leslieville, now part of the city of Toronto but previously a self-contained village in York County, the early lodge records for LOL 215 reveal in some detail a pattern of social meetings, conviviality, and ritualized celebration of transplanted tradition. The records also reveal a mindset that was unambiguously British and loyal. Founded in 1838 by a small number of immigrant Orangemen and twelve initiates, its opening meeting included this declaration:

> We whose names are undersigned do sincerely promise and declare that we will be faithful and bear true allegiance to Her Majesty, Queen Victoria, as the lawful sovereign of the United Kingdom of Great Britain and Ireland ... That we will steadily maintain the connection between the Colonies of British America and the Mother Country and be ever ready to resist all attempts to weaken the British influence or dismember the British Empire and that we will be aiding and assisting the Civil and Military powers in the just and lawful discharge of their official duties.[17]

The declaration was written in the aftermath of the 1837 Rebellion in the Canadas, but the principles enunciated within it reflected the same defensive mindset then prevailing in contemporary Ireland. Whatever the lofty ideals prefacing its bylaws, the record of the regular monthly meetings indicates that more mundane everyday matters were of recurring interest. The lodge accounts indicate that virtually all the annual receipted income was spent on candles, beer, whiskey, and brown sugar.[18] The monthly meetings were held in a tavern owned by a member, Brother Moffat, and it was to him that the bulk of the income was paid. Lodge dues cost seven and a half pence per member per meeting: initiation into the Order and provision of a personal membership certificate cost two shillings and sixpence, initiation into the Purple Order was one shilling and three pence. The costs of membership were modest, but additional personal adornments and paraphernalia such as sashes, ribbons, and jewels of office cost extra. Lodge equipment was financed from collections from among the members. In August 1841, for example, a special collection for the purchase of a drum was held, but only three-quarters of the total cost of two pounds was raised at the time, for it was an expensive year – a banner was also being purchased at a cost of fifteen shillings for the material, five shillings for a purple fringe, and an additional four pounds for the customized painting of the fabric with a suitable Orange theme. The banner and drum were required for celebration of the Twelfth of July, but these annual festivities also incurred additional expenditure. Hire of a drummer for the day cost ten pence, and a fife and fiddler were two shillings and ten pence.[19] The regular receipted income of that year amounted to £2.11.9 ½ and the expenditure totalled £3.6.7 – an excess of 14.9 ½ that was reconciled by cash in hand and fees for initiation into the Purple degree. Total membership at the time was in the range of twenty men, all of modest means, and attempts to raise the level of fees were stoutly resisted.

The social nature of the early meetings of the lodge was facilitated by the fact that in Leslieville, as in much of Toronto, lodges held their monthly meetings in taverns owned by fellow Orangemen and licensed by like-minded members of the City Council. As the century progressed, not all members were content to support taverns and the tradition of drinking after meetings. In harmony with a growing mood for temperance, LOL 215 voted unanimously in 1856 to become "a temperate lodge from this date," but the same meeting resolved "that Alexander Moffat receive the sum of 3s.9d each night as a remuneration for his room."[20] The social experiment was not a success and eight months later "it was proposed and carried by a majority of the lodge that it be no longer a temperate lodge."[21] The temperance movement did have more success in some other lodges.

As befitted an active community organization, LOL 215 maintained a stance on public morality, and in 1858 it decided that "John Campbell shall be expelled from the Orange Association for life in consequence of a charge of perjury being proven against him."[22] In a similar exercise of social control it was recorded "That the members of 215 have come to a decision that Thomas Truman shall be suspended for the space of six months providing that he gets satisfactory proof by getting a satisfactory sertificate [sic] from a Minister's hand of the Church of England that his wife has renounced the Roman Catholic faith to the satisfactory [sic] of this lodge."[23]

The Leslieville lodge was composed mainly of farmers, labourers, and a small number of merchants, and its overall scale of activities reflected social life in small communities with limited disposable income. Toronto, with a greater degree of social differentiation among its population, was able to support lodges of a more complex social mixture. LOL 301, founded in 1841, was one such lodge. It was from the beginning a temperance lodge and always projected an element of social elitism. Its by-laws, published in 1847 (the year when thirty-eight thousand Irish famine immigrants arrived in the city), were designed to regulate the activities of the thirty-eight men who formed its membership and who were clearly of some substance. Monthly subscriptions cost one shilling and three pence, members arriving late for roll call were fined three pence, and those absent from the whole meeting forfeited seven and a half pence. The distinctive mission of this particular lodge was explicit:

> That this Lodge, having constantly before their eyes the pernicious habit
> of drinking spirituous liquors at the conclusion of their business and dep-
> recating the admission of such custom into this body, do hereby enact, that
> any brother proposing any part of the funds to be expended for such pur-
> pose, shall be suspended for a period not exceeding six months, or receive
> his certificate, as a majority of the lodge may determine.[24]

The by-laws also required the lodge to support members who were unable to work due to illness, providing there was a minimum of twenty pounds in the treasurer's accounts: "Any brother who may be taken sick, and unable to attend to his employment, shall receive the sum of 7s 6d weekly until he recovers, provided such sickness is not brought on by his own misconduct; and should a member die the sum of four pounds shall be paid towards the expenses of his funeral."[25]

Conduct of lodge business was governed in a manner as strict as that of any elite debating society. Offices of treasurer, secretary, chaplain, and tyler (the latter being responsible for controlling admission to the meeting place) were filled by election. Certain duties and committees for investigating prospective members and auditing accounts were established. Conduct of business was regulated by a requirement that each resolution was to be submitted in writing, bearing the names of the proposer and seconder, and "each member, when addressing the Lodge, shall rise in his proper place and commence by saying 'Worship-ful Sir and Brethren' and that at two or more rising at the same time to address the Lodge, the Master shall name who is to speak first; and any member breaking this rule shall be fined 3d." Only those members who had received all "the different degrees of the Orange Institution of B.N.A." were eligible for the positions of master or deputy master, and "no brother shall be eligible to fill the office of Master or Deputy Master whose business leads him from the City, such as sailing on the lakes, driving stages, or trafficking in the country."

Such a requirement was probably designed to maintain the continuity of business and regular attendance of members as emphasized in other by-laws, but it would also have had the effect of removing from consideration members perceived to be transient and socially inferior. The quest for respectability was apparent also in the requirement that "In summer the members shall dress in black coat and hat, white trousers, and white or fancy vest. In winter and at funerals the clothing to be as dark as possible." The order of processing on the Twelfth was determined by the following sequence: tyler with drawn sword, Royal Standard, chaplain with Bible, deputy master with warrant, and master with mace surmounted by a dove. Other officers followed, carrying the symbols of fraternal friendship – a gilded ladder, a mystic cup on a pole – and finally the banner of the lodge and the Union Jack. Such a public manifestation of regulated ceremony, display of the emblematic elements of politics, religion, and mystic ritual, and the marching ranks of its thirty-eight members projected for the lodge an image of civic importance, respectability, and social stability. Whatever the personality of other lodges in the city at the time, LOL 301 was clearly not an unstructured assemblage of immigrant ruffians. It exuded power and position and was a precursor to the status achieved in the city by the Order in general some decades later.

A similar quest for the attainment of respectability and social responsibility may be discerned from the surviving partial records of another contemporary Toronto lodge, LOL 328,[26] founded in 1843. Its original by-laws stated: "The Lodge shall consist of unmarried men, at the time of joining, and shall be called, named and styled, Loyal Orange Virgin Lodge, no. 328." Subsequently, an introductory paragraph in its by-laws of 1872 posited that "This Lodge was originally opened for the purpose of giving unmarried young men, students or mercantile men etc a Lodge where they could assemble together in the folds of our glorious institution."[27] Candidates for admission had to swear that they were not, never had been, nor ever intended to be Roman Catholics. As with LOL 301, monthly membership dues were set at 1s 3d, fines were levied for being late or absent from meetings, and a fee of 7s 6d was required of all initiates. The officers of the lodge were "authorised to examine into all applications for Charity during vacation, and advance any amount in their discretion, not exceeding one pound, from the funds of the Lodge." The charity was directed towards members of the lodge rather than towards society at large and was very much in accordance with the practice of contemporary self-help societies in Britain and Ireland. That sense of mutual aid and fraternal support was enunciated further in the provision that "On the death of a Brother the Worshipful Master shall direct the Secretary to summon a special meeting of the Lodge to attend the funeral, provided the residence of such deceased Brother is within the limits of the city and that the Brother has not died of any infectious diseases, or that his friends object."

The surviving records of LOL 301and LOL 328 do not present a complete picture of the Orange Order in Toronto in the 1840s but they are certainly indicative of attributes that became increasingly clear as the nineteenth century progressed. At the time the total number of lodges in the city did not exceed ten. The register of warrants granted by the Grand Lodge of British America[28] records this number of lodges being authorized prior to 1847, and a deposition given to the Legislative Assembly of Upper Canada in 1841 identified "seven or eight Orange Lodges in the City of Toronto." Given this level of development, Virgin Lodge and Temperance Lodge may have been unique, but they were not insignificant within the contemporary organization and indicate a level of institutional complexity that has been frequently underestimated in historical analyses.

The Order maintained discipline within its ranks by requiring all members to swear an initiation oath to maintain fidelity to the principles of Orangeism and support like-minded brethren. The initiation oath evolved in complexity during the course of the nineteenth century, but the core elements that remained constant included an oath of loyalty to the British Monarch, conditional on the occupant of the throne remaining Protestant; an undertaking to "hold sacred the name of our Glorious Deliverer, King William the Third, Prince of Orange"; a requirement to assemble with the brethren every Twelfth of July; and an affirmation of one's Protestantism and an undertaking never to become, or marry, a Roman Catholic.[29]

Candidates who could produce evidence of having been initiated previously in Ireland were required to affirm their support for the maintenance of links between Canada and the motherland. Strictures on marrying Catholics, or attending Catholic church services, were relaxed during the twentieth century, but it is probable that, even at its peak, the Order in Canada was much more liberal than its Irish counterpart. For example, as recently as 1960 in Ulster, two distinguished politicians were expelled from the Order for attending funerals in Catholic churches, but there is no record of such discipline being imposed in Canada. Indeed, when the Catholic Toronto politician and entrepreneur

Frank Smith died in 1901, a pallbearer at his funeral in St Basil's church in Toronto was Mackenzie Bowell, former prime minister and previous grand master of the Orange Order in Canada.

Strict scrutiny of all applicants precluded the admission of Catholics and, until recently, those married to members of that faith. In 1893, for example, LOL 154 considered a proposal that "Mr Wm Loney, 194 Queen Street W, hotelkeeper, religious denomination Presbyterian, aged 29, is a fit and proper person to become a member of this Lodge." It was a standard application and, in conformity with current practice, it was referred to a standing committee for investigation. At the next meeting the committee reported negatively, "It having come to the ears of the Standing Com. that Mrs Loney did attend the Roman Church." The application was rejected and Mr Loney had his dollar fee refunded.[30] Where an application had been rejected, nothing was left to chance, and other lodges were informed of the outcome. In the same vein, the recording secretary of LOL 621 wrote to the officers and members of LOL 342 in March 1889 giving notice that "Mr Wm H Ashdowne residence no. 96 Church Street, occupation steamfitter, was rejected in LOL 621. Please govern yourselves accordingly."[31] Rejection of applicants was also justified by the increasingly respectable Order taking a critical view on the social reputation and habits of would-be members. In 1918, for example, the Western District Lodge of Toronto circulated all lodges in the city with a notice which it requested be read in open lodge at the earliest opportunity.[32]

Dear Sir and Bro,
The Western District Loyal Orange Lodge of Toronto beg to notify you that it has been notified by E F Clarke LOL no 1684 under the hand of the recording secretary and the seal of the Lodge that one J W Coolhoon, Military Police, 127 Sellars Ave, Birthplace Tottenham Ontario – aged 35 had made application for admission into the Orange Association through said lodge and had been refused admission. The Executive of said lodge reported unsatisfactorily upon his character and habits.

I am
Sir
Yours fraternally
John Robertson
Recording Secretary
Western District LOL of Toronto

The social attractions of membership and the possibility of accessing a route to employment or promotion attracted applications from some whose backgrounds were marginal to the mission of the Protestant body. Professions such as the fire and police services in the city had an exceptionally high proportion of Orangemen in their ranks, and there were instances where unexpected applications were received from co-workers. It was such circumstances that prompted the secretary of the East Toronto District Lodge to circulate lodges in 1913 with the warning that "Mr Lionel G. Gardiner, a police constable of no. 7 division who is a French Roman Catholic has been attempting to connect himself with LOLs no. 913 and 961 but was stopped in both cases."[33] Screening of applicants was thorough, and was enforced by a system of references, local knowledge, and inspection of transfer certificates; where necessary, the originating lodges of those migrating to Toronto were requested to confirm that the departing member was in good standing. Such referencing was necessitated not only by the desire to exercise control over members but also by the wish to project an image of a careful and selective body of some social standing. In the second half of the nineteenth century, this selectivity was motivated further by the actuarial requirements of the medical and fledgling insurance schemes operated initially by local lodges but ultimately taken in hand by the Grand Lodge.

From its inception the Orange Order had inculcated a sense of mutual support among its members and, within a relatively short time, this had evolved into the provision of financial aid or in-kind contributions. Provisions of this kind were codified within the by-laws of individual primary or local lodges and represented an adoption of the provisions for mutual aid that had existed in English self-help and mutual aid societies from the mid-eighteenth century. Aid remained a local responsibility until the incorporation of the Orange Mutual Benefit Fund in 1881 facilitated an insurance fund operated on the principles of contemporary actuarial science. However, the records of individual lodges reveal an increasing sophistication of mutual aid from the 1840s onwards. It is possible that Gowan's experience of operating a system of benevolence within the Irish organization in the 1820s facilitated the early development of this aspect of lodge activity, but the example of contemporary Masonic and other similar groups was probably the primary influence that prompted the emergence of a coherent system of Orange self-help. As early as 1847, LOL 301 had included within its by-laws a provision that

As soon as the funds in the hands of the Treasurer shall amount to the sum of twenty pounds, they will be devoted to benevolent purposes, in the relief of sick brethren and the burial of deceased members. Any brother who may be taken sick, and unable to attend to his employment, shall receive the sum of 7s6d weekly until he recovers, provided such sickness is not brought on by his own misconduct; and should a member die the sum of four pounds shall be paid towards the expense of his funeral. No member shall be entitled to these benefits who may be six months in arrears for contributions, nor for three months after such arrears are paid. Members must be initiated six months before they become entitled to receive any benefits from the funds of the Lodge.[34]

By 1857 LOL 328 was reported as employing its own doctor, W.C. Buchanan of Queen Street, and in the ensuing decades such appointments became commonplace in many lodges. In 1874, LOL 342 defined its mission as the promotion of "the interests of the institution and [to] afford relief to the sick and disabled brethren of this Lodge," specifying in its by-laws the nature of the medical assistance on offer.[35]

Article 7
That this Lodge shall annually elect at their December meeting a duly qualified physician who must have the Royal Arch Purple Degree, whose duty it shall be to examine all candidates wishing to become beneficiary members and report same to the Lodge. Also attend all members of this Lodge in good standing in case of sickness and give a certificate of the nature and duration of such sickness. Any suspended member wishing to become reinstated as a beneficiary member must first procure at his own expense a certificate of health from the Lodge physician.

Article 8
Candidates may at option become Ordinary or Beneficiary members. Those who cannot obtain the necessary certificate of health and others who so desire may become ordinary members. All members in good standing, both Ordinary and Beneficiary, shall in case of illness be entitled to medical attendance and medicine free of charge from the lodge physician.

Article 24
A Beneficiary member during sickness or disability as certified to by Lodge physician or other satisfactory medical authority shall receive assistance from the Lodge for three months according to his advancement in the Order. A Bro of the Royal Arch Purple degree shall receive $3.00 per week

for four weeks and $2.00 per week for eight weeks. Brethren not having their RAP degree shall only receive $2.00 per week.

Article 25
Any brother joining by certificate or otherwise who is fifty years of age or over cannot become a Beneficiary member

Article 26
Upon the death of any benefit member of this Lodge in good standing a sum not exceeding $40.00 shall be appropriated to aid in defraying funeral expenses.

Article 28
Should at any time the funds of this Lodge be reduced by sickness, death or other causes to the sum of $50.00 the members shall be assessed, such assessment not to exceed the sum of 50 cents per month.

Article 29
That on the death of a Brother of this Lodge it shall be the duty of the Rec. Sec to notify the members of this Lodge and the hour of assembling at the lodge room to attend as a body the funeral of deceased Bro and the time and place of the funeral.

The scale of lodge membership, even where it might exceed two hundred, was too small to cope with extended periods of general unemployment or serious illness affecting an aging cohort, and a decision was taken to create a large-scale mutual insurance fund along the lines already implemented by the Independent Order of Odd Fellows. The Orange province of Ontario West, including Toronto, established such a fund in 1881, and the fund was extended into a national scheme after the Order was incorporated by Act of the Canadian Parliament in 1890. However, many individual lodges continued to maintain their own medical assistance, and doctors in Toronto were happy to tender for the lucrative business. In 1888 LOL 342 attracted tenders from three doctors, the general annual charge being $1.25 per member, and the successful applicant, Dr Parry of 592 Queen Street West, eventually became the doctor for two lodges in the city. By 1894 virtually all of the city's fifty-five lodges had formal contracts with doctors; some had their own pharmacists and many of the remainder had some rudimentary system of self-help.[36] In 1903 the Toronto lodges expended $1,050 on sick benefits, $2,067 on lodge doctors and medicine, and $427 on funeral benefits and related expenses – a total of $3,544. The total for the previous year had been $3,872.[37]

The formal system of benefits and medical assistance augmented a more informal system of aid provided by members to brethren in need. Sometimes aid was proffered quietly and unobtrusively in the form of job offers or other assistance; in other instances it was actively sought, as illustrated by a letter sent in January 1890 to the master of LOL 342 by an unemployed member, J.R. Dickson, a recent immigrant. "I have been out of work this past seven or eight weeks and have been up to the present disappointed in receiving a remittance from the Old Country which I expected and which has left me in a bad fix. If yourself or any of the brethren know of any job and would kindly let me know (I do not mind what it is, as I would be willing to go at anything) I would be deeply grateful."[38] The operation of such assistance underpinned the mutuality of the Order and lent substance to its principles of Christian charity. In an era before the state assumed the role of providing for the needy, voluntary societies such as the Orange Order were the bedrock of much local community interaction and to their members they projected a bounded universe of like-minded Protestants determined to protect what they saw as the core principles of the society in which they lived. Their active citizenship was all-encompassing of a particular set of religious and political attitudes, and their defence of them resonated with the old Ulster slogan of "No Surrender." To Catholics, the interwoven fabric of Orangeism and civic culture resonated with an attitude of exclusion; the self-help and mutual aid functions of the inner workings of the lodges were largely hidden from their view.

Conduct of Lodge Business

Lodge meetings were serious affairs, conducted with solemnity in accordance with a prescribed order of business that was heavily imbued with ritual, readings, and symbolism. Printed codes of conduct for the regular meetings and for degree initiation ceremonies were provided by the Grand Lodge of Canada, and all participating groups were expected to comply with the standardized requirements. For the most part the manuals were derivative of those of the Irish parent body and reflected its strident anti-Catholic stance and unswerving loyalty to the Protestant monarchy of Britain. The ritualized proceedings of the organization included a strong sense of the liturgical preferences of the Anglican Church – an outcome of the preponderant role played by Church of Ireland communities in the genesis of Orangeism, and the somewhat later insertion of Presbyterian influences. The procedures whereby a member could progress from the Orange through Purple, Blue, Arch Purple, and Scarlet degrees was a simplified version of the procedures operating within the Masonic Order, and the highest degree, Scarlet, was distinguished further as being a unique creation of Canadian Orangeism. That degree was never introduced into British or Irish Orangeism.

Business in the regular lodge meetings of the city was conducted in a well-regulated manner, overseen by elected and appointed officers. A level of literacy was required both for recording the business and for the ritualized reading of prayers and biblical passages selected mostly from the Old Testament. The average number of officers returned for lodges in the 1894 directory was ten, although the larger and older established lodges could swell this number by the inclusion of up to eight past masters. All proceedings were transacted under the direction of the worshipful master assisted by a deputy master, chaplain, recording secretary, financial secretary, treasurer, director of ceremonies, physician, past masters, and four committeemen – some of whom acted as tylers appointed to secure the doors during meetings. The elaborate deployment of officers, their codified roles, and the solemnity with which they conducted official business were testimony to a highly centralized organization in which middle-class values and attributes were presumed for all, even though there was a majority of artisan and working-class members in most lodges. Late Victorian respectability was a prerequisite for a membership that was self-consciously aware of its assumed responsibility for setting the social and moral tone of the city. It was a tribute to the power and prestige of the organization that it could enforce these behavioural norms, especially given the earlier reputation of the Order, and some of its followers, for riot and mayhem.

In monthly meetings, convened ten or eleven times during the year, local lodges provided social outlets and some colour and ritual to communities that were limited in alternative or competing options. Apart from the obvious camaraderie, the lodges in their formal business adhered to a set of detailed and prescriptive regulations that were codified and printed in Grand Lodge approved procedures and augmented by the by-laws of the individual lodges. Conduct of business was orderly, and minutes, membership lists, and accounts, however rudimentary, were kept in minute books and proposition books that were passed down through generations of officers. The ritual for initiations included memorizing passages from Scripture – usually the Old Testament – and readings from the Bible were part of formal lodge business. A sense of reformed Protestantism infused conduct of business. Given the size of the organization, and the social variety contained within it, there was an inevitable mix of motives and commitment among the brethren. Not infrequently, officials at county, provincial, or national levels exhorted members to be more diligent in their adherence to the underlying religious principles of Orangeism, and this exhortation was sometimes taken up by the organization's supportive newspaper, the *Sentinel and Orange and Protestant Advocate*, founded in 1875.[39] That paper editorialized in 1899 on the idea of the "Lodge as School":

> Many officers of Lodges appear to act on the assumption that the members neither know nor care much about the foundation principles of the Orange Order ... Every lodge should be an active living centre in which the members – especially the new ones – should be taught "line upon line and precept upon precept" the great principles of the Order. A Lodge which faithfully fulfils its mission will be in fact a Protestant school and every member of it will be able to give a clear and intelligible reason for the faith that is in him.[40]

In addition to its proclaimed religious mission, the Order was also a political body of some significance, and its strength in this field was dependent upon the nature and organizational efficiency of the more than two thousand lodges in the country. Local lodges engendered a familiarity with orderly debate, presentation of motions, and voting on resolutions and were, in essence, working examples of participatory democracy. Aspiring politicians, at the municipal level and beyond, put to good effect the experience gleaned in the lodges. Indeed, the Toronto County Lodge provided formal training courses in committee work and operated a Legislation Committee that had the responsibility of tracking impending legislation construed as contrary to the politico-religious principles of the Order. In that manner of operation, the lodge was akin to lobbying groups in modern political environments.

Officers at all levels, particularly those elected to County or Provincial Lodges, invested a huge amount of personal time in the voluntarism required to maintain coherence and some degree of discipline within the organization. In his 1934 report to the Toronto County Lodge, Cecil Armstrong, the county master, outlined in some detail the nature of the activities he pursued in carrying out his duties. During the previous year, he reported:

> Visited 80 Primary Lodges and have attended 60 banquets, socials etc. In addition I have attended 31 executive and committee meetings, and other affairs, making a total of 171 meetings and other gatherings which it has been my pleasure to participate in during my twelve months of office in the Association. I have written 500 communications on your behalf and I thank every member of the Order with whom I have had correspondence for their courtesy and consideration.[41]

It represented an enormous commitment from a voluntary organizer on behalf of his brethren.

The sense of belonging to a community and the assurance of mutual support offered under the auspices of friendship, or in the form of medical or financial aid, attracted many to the Order. The attraction was especially strong for recent immigrants and those dependent upon personal linkages or patronage for access to employment. However, one should not underestimate the religious beliefs and political certitudes that inspired members, focusing them upon the goals of creating and maintaining a civic culture in accordance with the principles of their fraternal body. When Orangemen, bedecked with sashes and banners and accompanied by fife and drums, paraded in strict formation through the principal thoroughfares of Toronto, they were making a public statement of both power and belonging. Toronto was their city, and they were the self-appointed custodians of its culture and defenders of its place in the wider scheme of British imperialism. Their role and importance were affirmed by the inclusion of Orange politicians, dignitaries, city officials, and leading employers among the parading ranks, and certainly, from the 1880s through to the 1950s, they projected an image that resonated favourably with many fellow Protestants outside of the Order. Catholic citizens were understandably less enthusiastic.

Parades, Symbols, and Landscapes of the Order

Their initiation oath required Orangemen to celebrate annually the victory of King William over the Catholic King James at the Battle of the Boyne. They could do so either by private ceremonies conducted within their lodges or by public parades, and, in general, their preference was for a public spectacle. The battle had taken place on 1 July 1690, but with the introduction of the Gregorian calendar, and its eleven-day adjustment, the original date was transformed into the Twelfth of July. Its timing facilitated a summertime celebration (at least in the northern hemisphere), and in rural areas and urban centres alike the day was celebrated in style and with colour. Unsurprisingly, in religiously mixed places the parades were contested public occasions and local tensions were inevitably heightened. Even the descriptive language applied to the celebration differed between Catholics and Protestants. Catholics referred to Orange marches; Protestants referred to parades – the former implied a triumphalist celebration of power and imposed social diminution, while the latter was suggestive of civic festivities. Perceptions differed and so did social behaviour.

Catholics and the Tory elite of the founding fathers of the city – opposite ends of the social spectrum – were united in their criticism of Toronto's early Orange parades, but, notwithstanding, the celebration of the Twelfth became a regular feature of life in the city from 1818. Orangemen themselves were not oblivious to the local impact of the parades, but they rarely conceded the need to curtail this particular ethno-religious manifestation. An early exception, underlining the political significance of the Twelfth, became apparent in 1836 when, conscious of the need to project a more constructive image on the eve of an election, Gowan, the Orange grand master, used his influence to dissuade his brethren from parading that July. But parades resumed the following year. A report in 1838 referred to three hundred men and boys bedecked in Orange ribbons parading the Toronto streets, and afterwards they

Adjourned to the taverns to drink the "Glorious, pious and immortal memory." The procession did not show one man of any weight in the city – but there were such men behind the scenes who deemed it prudent to let their unthinking followers parade and make the demonstration, while they sat over their wine – where they drunk to the Queen, the Prince of Orange.[42]

Clearly, the Order included several social strata within its ranks, and although some early Toronto lodges had by-laws designed to screen initiates and regulate social behaviour, not all lodges had such regulatory mechanisms, and some that did may well have found enforcement difficult. Many of Toronto's seven or eight lodges in the 1840s comprised men of much lower social standing, and through their behaviour, and that of their camp followers, the more contentious and riotous image of the Order was forged. In response to heightened civic tensions, the lieutenant governor, Sir George Arthur, appealed in June 1839 to the "Mayor and Corporation of the city of Toronto" for support in persuading the Orange Order to desist from public parading in the following month. "I would affectionately, yet earnestly, intreat the members of the associations alluded to, to consider seriously the very mischievous tendency of the divisions, by which they thus contribute to the agitation of the community, and to determine that they shall be no longer continued."[43] The appeal had little effect in the city where Orangemen were a growing presence among the elected aldermen. More direct action was required. In 1843 the Party Processions Act banned all parades, although the government did stop short of proscribing the Order in its entirety, an action that had been taken some years earlier in the United Kingdom.

Orange parades remained illegal in Canada until 1851[44] and remained controversial at both community and national levels long after that. Over the course of the next two decades, social tensions persisted, often spilling over into street riots and public brawls, but not all of the protagonists on the Protestant side were members of the Orange Order. Central to many of the civil disturbances were the Order's feeder organizations, the Orange Cadets and the Orange Young Britons. The Orange Cadets, established in 1853 by Gowan,[45] was designed to inculcate Protestant youths with Orange principles and ultimately induct them into the senior lodges. In the 1860s the Cadets evolved into the Orange Young Britons, who, until 1881, acted as an autonomous group, operating independently of the rules and regulations of the parent body. Its members were frequently associated with drunken brawls and attacks on Catholics and their property, and Orangemen in general attracted condemnation for the unruly behaviour of the youths. The Young Britons were ultimately brought under the auspices of the Orange Order as part of its quest for greater respectability within late Victorian Toronto.[46] By then alcohol was banned from all lodge meetings, although it was undoubtedly consumed after formal business had been concluded, and parading members were subject to removal and disciplining if they were obviously inebriated. But, despite the growing sanctimonious nature of the official face of the organization, it proved impossible to maintain complete authority over the celebratory festivities that lasted long into the evenings after the banners, Bible, and emblems had been returned to the lodge chest.

The celebration of the Twelfth commenced with prayer and readings in each local lodge, and, with the Bible remaining open, the lodge meeting was then adjourned as members paraded from their local meeting to the city centre, where they took their allocated place amid the other lodges. Only upon return to their lodge hall after the city-wide parade and celebrations in the Exhibition Grounds was the lodge meeting formally closed. The whole of the public festivities and the traversing of public space were thereby enfolded into the ritualistic proceedings of the Order that symbolically and literally dominated the city, and on that day much of the everyday life of the city was brought to a standstill. Marching bands accompanied individual lodges as they made their way across the city from their local and district halls to the designated assembly point. Along the main thoroughfares of the city the serried ranks of men, all of them wearing Orange sashes, marched to martial airs that had been transplanted from Ireland generations before and which had formed part of the street spectacle of Toronto since the second decade of the nineteenth century. The city's lodges marched in order of seniority, with the lower warrant numbers being accorded precedence along with visiting lodges from the British Isles and the United States. Individual lodges vied for notice, the County Lodge awarded prizes for the best displays, and inter-lodge rivalry was strong. Certainly, from the 1880s onwards a carnival atmosphere permeated the warm summer air. It was a day of public celebration, and the intrinsic centrality of the Orange Order to civic life and culture was emphasized not only by its temporary control of the main thoroughfares but also by the ranks of marching city officials and politicians who proudly displayed their membership to spectators watching and applauding in their tens of thousands from the sidewalks. It was a day when Catholics remained at home or in their workplaces; it was not their day. On that day the Orange Order took control of the public space of the city, and it did so with the consent of the majority of the inhabitants and the active participation of tens of thousands of the citizenry. The geographer Peter Goheen, examining the role of public processions in creating and defining public space in nineteenth-century Toronto, has argued that the processions served to legitimize the role of certain groups in the life of the city where control of public space was a contested issue.[47]

The assembled ranks of Orangemen who took control of the city streets for the annual Twelfth parade were of diverse social, ethnic, and denominational backgrounds, united not by class values but by a shared belief in the supremacy of British Protestantism and the imperial connection. The Order's moral tone was certainly middle-class in emphasis and much of its evangelical purpose was reforming in design, but its composition defied description in simple notions of class; no single denomination dominated its Protestantism, and many, other than the Irish, filled its ranks. Within the organization as a whole, and within individual lodges, the membership transcended class boundaries, and nowhere was this more evident than in the public display of the Twelfth. Marching in unison, with their white shirts, top hats, and frock coats, the members of McKinley Lodge publicly advertised a membership that was largely composed of lawyers. Other lodges had a strong corpus of policemen and firemen in their ranks, and some were prominently linked with manual jobs in the waterworks and transportation industries. No lodge was completely homogeneous in its social composition. The social profile of members was likewise striking. By the closing decade of the nineteenth century, parading members included within their numbers the city's leading social figure, John Ross Robertson, canons from St James' Cathedral, wealthy businessmen who had achieved prominence in politics, and cleaners enjoying a day off from their duties in City Hall. Amid such membership diversity, the appeal of Orangeism provided an amazingly centralizing attraction that facilitated its occupation of the public space of the city for its own celebratory purposes. And it was not merely the city centre parade route that was enveloped in the Orange celebration. Each local lodge made a traverse of its neighbourhood as it wound its way to the designated assembly point for lodges from that district, and they all marched in unison to the city centre starting point for the parade. For example, Enniskillen LOL 711 was directed by the Eastern District Orange Lodge in 1935 to "parade to Gerrard and Jarvis Street (north side) and rest at that point. Eastern district Lodges leaving Riverdale Park at 9.45 A.M. will be proceeding via Gerrard to that station for District assembly. Thence to Wellesley Street for 10.00 A.M."[48] From Wellesley Street the district's Orangemen made their way to Queen's Park, where brethren from throughout the other districts, together with visiting lodges, were gathered. The main parade then processed by way of St Albans, Yonge, Albert, James, Queen, and Dufferin streets to the

Exhibition Grounds. After the festivities and speeches, the lodges, with bands and banners, retraced their route back home, where street parties and hall dinners occupied the rest of the evening. The geography of the day's parades embraced much of the city, including streets where there were significant numbers of Catholic residents: "the right to walk" was an affirmation of the strength and pervasiveness of the Order in the "Belfast of Canada."

Public displays of ritual and colourful processions through the main thoroughfares of Toronto on the commemorative celebration of the Battle of the Boyne were not the only occasions when the Orange Order took control of the social space of the city. On selected Sundays in June and July the District Lodges in the city, and sometimes individual primary lodges, held parades to interdenominational church services where they gave thanks for deliverance from Popery and expressed their appreciation of King William and the defence of civil and religious liberties as enshrined in the Glorious Revolution of the late seventeenth century. A dedication on the Bible presented at a church service to LOL 551 in 1899 captures well the sentiments that motivated the church parades:

> Presented to LOL 551 as a thanks offering for the many great blessings which we of the British Empire have received from the Holy One of Israel by thy Servant King William III, Prince of Orange, of immortal memory who maintained the rights of Civil and Religious Liberty at the Battle of the Boyne July 12th 1690 A.D.[49]

These parades were, in effect, mini "Twelfths," and they brought within their orbit many streets that did not feature in the Twelfth's main parade. The Centre District of the County Lodge paraded through the city centre streets to Cooke's Presbyterian Church at the corner of Queen and Mutual, the Western District along Bloor Street to St Paul's Anglican church, or along College Street to the Lutheran church at the corner of College and Lippincott. Five thousand Orangemen were recorded as marching with "fife and drum" from Queen's Park to St Paul's on Bloor Street in 1930.[50] Eastern District lodges would parade along Queen Street to the Beaches. There was never any doubt in the minds of the organizers as to the value of such parades – a clergyman organizing a service at Bellefaire United church for Sunday 27 June 1936 sought support from Orangemen across the city on the basis that "We are very anxious in the interests of the Orange Order that every possible Orangeman and Orange lady be out at that service. We must make a showing that the East End Protestants may know that Orangeism means business, and to show to any who may be of other beliefs that we are not ashamed to show that for which we stand."[51] On some Sundays the County Orange Lodge, representing all lodges in the city, would take to the streets for a church service that was often held on public property. Minutes of a City Council meeting on 25 June 1900 recorded that "Ald. Loudon, seconded by Ald. Ball, moves that the free use of the pavilion in the Horticultural Gardens be granted to the County Orange Lodge of Toronto, on the afternoon of Sunday 8th July next, for the purpose of holding their annual Church service."[52]

At intervals throughout the year these public processions reminded the citizenry of other significant Orange commemorative dates. Sundays closest to 5 November, the anniversary of the attempted Guy Fawkes coup against the British Parliament and also the birthday of King William, were favoured opportunities for more church parades, and the preceding Saturdays were usually reserved for celebratory lodge suppers at which a mixture of Protestant hymns and Orange ballads would be sung. The calendar was punctuated with a series of special events, many of them designed to raise money for Orange charities, and the net effect was a frequent exhibition of the vitality of the organization locally, and generally, in the city. In 1921 the *Sentinel* reported with some enthusiasm on Imperial Night in Dian Lodge No. 2054 in Rhodes Avenue:

[It] was one of the most interesting, educational, and successful gatherings held under the auspices of the Orange Order in the east end of the city for a long time. It was the anniversary of the beginning of the battle of St Julien six years ago, and was one of the most appropriate dates that Dian Lodge could have selected for a British Imperial night, and a visit of the famous Imperial Lodge No. 2767. Dian Lodge was crowded to the doors with members and visitors ... An unusual toast at an Orange banquet but a most appropriate one was that to the Protestant Church ... Just after the toast was proposed all the Anglicans, Baptists and Presbyterians present joined in singing, Blest be the Ties that Bind.[53]

As early as 1879, the *Globe* reported that the annual parade had attracted large numbers of "the gentler sex, who showed in the colours of their *toilette* sympathy with the cause."[54] As the Order grew in respectability and power, so too did the nature and scale of the celebration. By the early twentieth century, the Toronto parade could rival that of Belfast, and beneath the hot July sun up to one hundred local and visiting lodges and nine thousand Orangemen paraded, watched by twenty-five thousand cheering spectators. The parade took more than two hours to pass a given point, generally wending its way from the downtown City Hall or the provincial Parliament Building on Queen's Park and eventually terminating in the Exhibition Grounds on the lakeshore, five miles to the west. It was a quasi-public holiday, and, until the 1950s, City Hall employees, transit workers, Public School Board personnel, and firemen enjoyed leave of absence with pay in honour of the occasion. Very many other public servants and elected officials strode out bedecked with their Orange sashes and insignia of office in public display of their fraternal association.

The parades were public manifestations of an organization that sometimes has been described as a secret body. But in reality, the nature and extent of its secrets were limited. From its Canadian beginnings in 1830, details of the leadership and organizational structure were reported in the newspapers, and the city directories of Toronto provided information on the place and time of meeting of each local lodge, the names of the officers, and (less frequently) the size of the membership. From the 1860s, the newspapers provided coverage of parades, especially those of the Twelfth of July, to which they sometimes allocated six or more pages of commentary and dozens of photographs. Parading Orangemen, distinguished by either longevity or their social or official standing in the city, were singled out for biographical commentary, and the political speeches delivered at the terminus of the parade in Exhibition Park were reported at length. The *Telegram*, under the partisan editorship of John Ross Robertson, himself an Orangeman, was especially well disposed to covering activities of the Order, and during winter months it sometimes provided by-line comment on those initiated into certain lodges together with the names of the officiating officers. Particularly during the years 1880–1930, the period of its ascendant public respectability and greatest numerical strength, the Order was very much in the public eye. Orangemen took pride in publicly demonstrating their membership on such occasions and, in so doing, they also emphasized the social and political influence attaching to their organization. No other voluntary organization, neither the Masons nor the Odd Fellows, could match the public profile accorded to the Orange Order in the city.

Parading Orangemen carried with them the banners of their lodge, hand-painted sheets of silk fabric up to six feet square on which were depicted images of Orange heroes such as King William, his fallen general

Schomberg, and the Monarch, iconic images such as the *Mountjoy*, the ship which broke the siege of Derry in 1690, and biblical images such as Moses leading the Jews into the promised land. Observant bystanders would have noticed also the identifying inscription of LOL ... followed by a number corresponding to the official registration number for the lodge recorded in the Order's Register of Warrants. The original sashes that were traditionally worn across the chest had, by the early twentieth century, given way to smaller collarets that continued to display the ornamental symbolism associated with the Order from its earliest days. Tin, polished steel, and occasionally silver "jewels" signified whether a member was a worshipful master (WM), past master (PM), or district master (DM), and the LOL number was likewise displayed, together with ribbons signifying the degrees (Orange, Blue, Arch Purple, or Scarlet) into which the bearer had been initiated. Symbols relevant to the initiation ceremonies – a ladder with F, H, and C (Faith, Hope, and Charity) engraved on it, a crown overlying an open Bible, a serpent twisted around a staff, a bucking goat, a miniature coffin – were openly displayed, although their significance was concealed within the printed business and procedural manuals distributed privately to each lodge. It was the existence of such symbols and rituals that projected an image of secrecy, leading informed commentators to describe the Order as an organization with secrets rather than as a secret organization. In reality, many copies of these confidential manuals found their way into archives and public libraries, where they remain available to many who have never sworn the Orange oath.

Toronto's Orange Landscape

The public identity of the Orange Order also found expression in the urban landscape in the form of lodge halls, but unlike rural Canada, where Orange halls were significant and common landscape features, the Order in Toronto was inserted into a landscape that was much more complex and multifunctional.[55] In rural Canada, particularly Ontario, local place names referenced the Orange affiliations of early settlers, commemorating the Order by such names as Orange Corners, Schomberg, Enniskillen, Aughrim, Derry, and the Boyne River, but Toronto provides few statements of this kind. Indeed, the only obvious occurrence was the renaming of Cambridge Street as Nassau Street in the 1870s at the behest of Ogle R. Gowan, who lived on that street and advocated the name in commemoration of King William of Nassau, Prince of Orange. In so doing, the symmetry of Cambridge Street and Oxford Street running parallel to it was destroyed. For some, the diminution of the Oxbridge Colleges in favour of Orange culture may have appeared as an ironic but appropriate development in the social geography of the British colonial city. Within the city, purpose-built Orange edifices were rare, and those that did exist were designed primarily for the higher organizational levels. The earliest hall, home to LOL 4, had existed on Yonge Street for several years prior to the construction of the first County Orange Hall on George Street in 1864. The decision to construct the latter hall was taken soon after the creation of a separate Orange administrative county in 1859, but an additional reason advanced by the organizers was the recent destruction of the Yonge Street hall by an alleged group of "Fenians and Ribbonmen."[56] In 1886 a new County Orange Hall was opened at 55 Queen Street East. Named Victoria Hall, it was an impressive architectural creation, designed by the city's foremost architect, E.J. Lennox, who was a long-standing member of the Order. It provided a base for more than twenty local lodges and operated as both a municipal and national headquarters for the organization. Its design incorporated several small meeting rooms as well as a large hall for plenary sessions, and, in addition, it was equipped with dining facilities and storage lockers for lodge paraphernalia. A resident caretaker and his family lived on the premises in purpose-built accommodation and were required to be members of the Order.

The County Orange Hall derived an income of upwards of $450 per month from the rental of accommodation to voluntary groups and associations – the income being allocated towards the expense of a mortgage held by Knox College in the University of Toronto. In 1912, for example, the Liberal Conservatives held regular executive meetings there at both city and ward levels, and civic employees rented space for their social functions. The Toronto Public School Board paid a monthly rent for singing and drill classes for teachers. The Board also held its prize nights in the lodge meeting rooms. At street level, a number of retail outlets occupied purpose-built accommodation. The printing and business headquarters of the Orange newspaper, the *Sentinel*, was strategically located adjacent to the hall.[57]

On Mutual Street, across the road from the County Orange Hall, stood Cooke's Presbyterian Church, named in honour of Rev. Henry Cooke, prominent leader of mid-nineteenth-century Belfast Presbyterianism and a widely regarded father of Ulster Unionism. Cooke's Church was colloquially referred to as the Irish Presbyterian Church, and, with one exception, its officiating clergy during its first century were drawn exclusively from Irish Protestant stock. It was renowned for the trenchant politico-religious sermons preached within it, and during the Irish Home Rule crisis political rallies supporting the Orange cause in Toronto frequently spilled over from Victoria Hall to find accommodation in the church. On occasion, the Orange crowds simultaneously filled the church, Victoria Hall, and the nearby Massey Hall. The County Orange Hall was strategically placed in the core of downtown Toronto and was close to the locus of urban power and influence, City Hall – another architectural creation of Lennox. Paradoxically, the County Orange Hall was located in a concentrated core of institutional buildings that included also within easy viewing distance the Catholic St Michael's Cathedral and St Michael's Hospital.

Expansion in lodge numbers and memberships in the four decades after the construction of Victoria Hall imposed a strain on the capacity of the building, and, at the peak of its power after the First World War, the Order began to plan for a replacement headquarters. Buoyed up by its popularity among recent immigrants from the British Isles and by a resurgence of interest among soldiers returning from the war, the Order envisaged moving to a building of a scale and significance appropriate to the most powerful fraternity in the city. At the time the most talked about building in Toronto was Casa Loma, an eclectic architectural pile built in the period 1911–14 by millionaire Sir Henry Pellett to a design by Lennox. Casa Loma, located on a five-acre site at the crest of an escarpment at the north end of Spadina Avenue, commanded spectacular views over the city and with ninety-eight rooms was by far the largest private residence in Canada. The building had cost $3.5 million and was incomplete when Pellett went bankrupt in the early 1920s. The Orange Order decided to purchase it as its new and iconic County Orange Hall. In May 1924 the County Lodge instructed its building committee to "get in touch with the owners of the Pellett property and make them an offer of $600,000 for the purchase of the Casa Loma property as follows, $100,000 cash, a mortgage for $200,000 and the present building valued at $300,000."[58] The sale was not concluded, and the opportunity for aggrandizement on this scale never arose again. In the ensuing decades the membership of lodges in the city declined precipitously; many local lodges found it difficult to meet the rental charges imposed for meeting in Victoria Hall, and the building itself faced heavy expenditure for maintenance and conformity to the fire and safety requirements of new building regulations. A distinctive era in the history of Toronto Orangeism crashed to a halt in the midst of the economic depression of the 1930s, and a move from the premises at 55 Queen Street East was contemplated for reasons that were very different from those advanced a decade earlier. The cost of maintaining the 1885 building had become a drag on the finances of the Order. In 1945, LOL 140 requested the county secretary to give "earnest consideration to the disposing of the County Hall and the securing of a suitable site for the erection of a modern up-to-date hall, with first class stores on the ground floor and a bowling alley as a revenue producing investment." A location in the vicinity of the intersection of Bloor and Yonge was suggested.[59] In October 1970 Victoria Hall was sold finally for circa $700,000 and the Order transferred its national organizational and insurance functions to a modest office building on Sheppard Avenue, several miles to the north. The County Lodge moved to separate premises, initially to a church building on Gerrard Street East and then to its present location in the suburb of Scarborough. A proposal by some senior officers at the time that the Order should invest its capital in an office block at Mount Pleasant and Davisville, renting out surplus space to commercial businesses, was rejected as posing too big a risk for an organization that was increasingly conscious of the real limits to its power and viability.[60]

Following its sale, Victoria Hall was demolished to make way for a city centre office building, and today the most striking survival of the Orange landscape of the city is the former Western District Orange Hall located at the intersection of College Street and Euclid Avenue. This extensive hall, opened in 1912, was the culmination of planning and fundraising efforts that dated from the establishment of the emerging western suburbs of Toronto as a separate Orange district in 1870. It had cost $70,000 and its scale and design reflected favourably on the financial standing of its members. There was no mistaking the function of the building, for the figure of King William astride a white horse is prominently displayed on the College Street frontage and the hall's foundation stone on Euclid Avenue records its purpose and original ownership. The hall was designed to accommodate the several lodges in the district, and at its official opening the executive committee expressed the hope that "it would be a comfortable home for the Brethren and a good paying proposition," for it was intended that any spare capacity in room usage should be filled by revenue-paying custom from the wider community.[61] The new hall replaced a smaller district hall that had operated at 273 Euclid Avenue from the early 1890s and, along with the opening in 1886 of the Queen Street County Orange Hall, reflected a growing degree of organizational and financial centralization within the Order at the time.

Local lodges in Toronto, with a few notable exceptions, tended not to construct, purchase, or operate their own halls. In that respect they were very different from their brethren in rural Canada, where Orange halls were prominent components of the landscape and of social and community life. The urban environment of Toronto posed different challenges and offered different opportunities for the organization; property and land prices placed the acquisition of halls beyond the reach of most lodges, but the multiplicity of fraternal and social organizations within the city meant that in combination they constituted a significant market for those who had suitable commercial premises for rent. Originally, the monthly meetings of lodges had been held in a tavern where the proprietor may well have been an Orangeman, and sometimes even the master of the lodge. So common was this relationship that allegations of corruption in the awarding of city licences for taverns were frequently hurled at the City Council. Taverns with names such as the Coleraine Inn were widely known for their Orange linkages and in some cases the symbols of Orangeism were inscribed in the signage hung above the portal. It was claimed, for example, that the General Wolfe Hotel on Church Street, owned by an Orangeman named Irvine, was identified by a sign incorporating a warrior mounted on a grey horse – a symbol instantly recognizable by Orangemen and one that had little to do with General Wolfe.[62] Notwithstanding the rising popularity of temperance movements from the mid-nineteenth century, the links with taverns persisted. In 1856 a total of twenty-one Orange lodges were recorded as operating in the city.[63] Almost half (ten) of them held their meetings in hotels, inns, or saloons, seven met in an Orange hall located at 61 Yonge Street, and of the remainder, two met in McKinlay's hall on Church Street, one met in premises in St Patrick's Market, and one met in a fireman's home on Yonge Street. One such licensed premises, Wilson's saloon on Church Street, was owned by John Wilson, master of LOL 396, and this place, along with other premises such as Marksman's Home Inn and King William's Inn, formed part of a readily recognizable Orange landscape in the city.

The temperance identity of the Order and its mutual aid functions strengthened over the next few years, and the city directory for 1859–60 noted, "There are nineteen Orange Lodges in the city of Toronto; the funds of which are devoted to the maintenance of sick members. Lodge

301 owns the hall they sit in and a splendid library containing 700 volumes."[64] This middle-class lodge was located on George Street and at the time was one of three Orange halls in the city – the others were on Church Street (home to six lodges) and the aforementioned hall on Yonge Street that accommodated seven lodges. In 1860 Wilson's Inn on Church Street had evolved into a confectionery store but it was still home to LOL 396. John Wilson remained master. Only one lodge was recorded as meeting in an inn that year, and even those premises were to be abandoned shortly thereafter as the quest for respectability propelled the organization into a scenario wherein monthly meetings of brethren were scheduled for the more formal environment of halls.

By 1875 all twenty-four lodges within the city were meeting in halls. A building at 209 Yonge Street, described as a District Hall, accommodated fifteen lodges, temperance halls on Brock Street and Queen Street East were each home to three lodges, and premises owned by individual Orangemen provided rented space to three other lodges. Halls such as Bailey's Hall on Huron Street and Foy's Hall on Richmond were essentially speculative building ventures that catered to the needs of local communities and organizations, and it was no disadvantage that the owners were members of the largest fraternal organization in the city. It was an aspect of urban geography that continued to be manifested as Toronto expanded westwards in the decades straddling 1900. Along Queen Street West, for example, much of the contemporary development was piecemeal – the output of small developers such as St Leger from Belfast, who built a shoe store at the corner of Queen and Dennison and in common with current practice had designed the second floor of his commercial building as a hall equipped for public use.[65] The Occident Hall at the corner of Queen and Bathurst was another fine example of this type of development, and in 1885 it was home to six Orange lodges, as well as Masonic and other fraternal bodies. The shared functions of these halls meant that there was limited scope for projecting visible symbols of Orangeism onto the public landscape, and in that respect the Order was somewhat anonymous. An exception to this general pattern, however, was the construction in 1914 of a purpose-built Orange hall on Rhodes Avenue by Dian LOL 2054. The local Orange community in that part of east Toronto constructed a fine two-storey-over-basement hall that had ample space for both Orange meetings and community functions. That hall, now in the midst of a Muslim neighbourhood, still stands, but its function has been completely transformed in keeping with the altered social geography of modern Toronto. In 1991 the hall became the first mosque in the city, and it still operates as such. Its symbolic Orange arches are still discernible in the fenestration, but the crescent and minarets of the mosque now accompany them. Elsewhere in the city, a primary lodge building still functions on Eglinton Avenue near Yonge Street, but at the time of its construction it was a rural lodge located in farmland on the edge of the expanding urban area.

By 1920, when the Order was reaching its peak, a total of seventy-nine lodges operated in the city; twenty-nine of them met in the County Orange Hall and a further twenty-four met in the Western District Hall. However, when analysed at the level of Orange districts within the city, a distinct geographical pattern is discernible. As might be expected, virtually all twenty lodges within the Centre District met in the County Orange Hall on Queen Street East and most of the twenty-seven lodges in the Western District met in the Western District Hall at College and Euclid. The Northern District contained sixteen lodges. With most of the members living in areas of recent urban expansion on the northern and western margins of the city, its pattern of hall usage was much more diffuse. Six of its lodges travelled to either the Western District or the County Halls, but the remainder were spread over nine venues, mostly rented from private proprietors in a pattern reminiscent of that of the Western District thirty years earlier. These communities, at an early stage of development and maturation, lacked the resources to procure their own halls and so they shared space in premises such as Murray's Hall at the intersection of Queen and Northcote, Summerfeldt's Hall on Dovercourt Street, Boon Hall on St Clair Avenue, and Heron's Hall on Wychwood Street. Many of the proprietors were themselves Orangemen, but their halls were essentially speculative developments on an expanding urban frontier. By way of contrast, the sixteen lodges in the Eastern District were the product of long-established Orange communities, and although seven of those lodges did avail themselves of the facilities provided by the County Orange Hall, the majority of them continued to meet in local halls such as Dian Hall on Rhodes Avenue, Playter's Hall on Danforth Avenue, Armstrong's Hall at Pape and Badgerow, the Masonic Hall at Gerrard and Logan, and the Odd Fellows' Hall at Queen and Broadview. Overall that part of the city reflected a very strong sense of community in which the journey to the lodge was short and the meetings were an intrinsic and obvious part of everyday life. The organizer of Dian LOL 2054, Bro James Mayor, publicly proclaimed his belief in the importance of such local lodges, advocating "that it would be advantageous to have lodge meetings in different parts of the city, and thus becoming real community centres."⁶⁶ Social class, tradition, and localism would appear to have operated to distinguish the Eastern District within the overall complexion of Toronto Orangeism. Interestingly, as the Order waned in the city, especially after the Second World War, and as lodges found the rates charged by the County and Western District halls too expensive for their dwindling memberships, many lodge meetings reverted to local halls or even the home of the master, and a pattern of localism began to reassert itself more generally.

Personality of Lodges

It is somewhat misleading to conceive of the Orange Order in Toronto as a homogeneous organization that remained unaltered throughout its history. It was always a complex body and its chameleon-like qualities allowed it to adjust and adapt to its environment, as befitted an organization that perceived itself as being a central and dynamic influence on the social and cultural life of the developing city. From its earliest days, the Order in Toronto had incorporated considerable diversity within its membership, as has been noted elsewhere in the present study's analysis of membership and social class. Most local lodges included a variety of social groupings in their membership, but some lodges such as Virgin Lodge and early Temperance lodges had initially aspired to more restrictive intakes, although few managed to sustain membership individuality beyond the founding generation. Over the years, the original founding missions of individual lodges altered in response to neighbourhood changes, inter-lodge transfers, and patterns of recruitment. Perception of enhanced social attraction, or an anticipated sense of belonging to a particular community, may well have prompted membership transfers between the city's lodges, leading to a considerable degree of mission drift and mobility within the organization. In some instances, lodges that had become dormant were subsequently revived with the same warrant number, but with a membership composition that was very different from that of the original lodge. LOL 551, Toronto True Blues, for example, was first established in 1854 but became dormant in within a decade. In 1870 it was revived, becoming the first lodge to be located in the developing west end of the city, beyond Spadina Avenue. The lodge quickly moved to assert its identity as a body of respectable men; members were directed to turn out for their first Twelfth parade dressed "in black coats, silk hats and white trousers" to accompany the first public display of their expensive new banner.[67] In a similar vein, Gideon's Chosen Few in 1874 adopted the reissued warrant number 342. Altruism informed its founding principles, its mission being defined as "To promote the interests of the institution and afford relief to the sick and disabled brethren of this Lodge."[68]

As the Order increased its profile of respectability, the social particularity of some lodges became much more pronounced. In a spirit of exclusiveness, Imperial LOL 2767 was founded in 1920 "To appeal particularly to business and professional men," and by way of explanation it was argued that the members of the lodge "Do not feel superior to other Orangemen in any way, but they do feel that they can render a distinct service to the Orange Order and the cause of Protestantism by enlisting the support of a large number of business and professional men. To get men of the desired calibre and hold their interest, it is necessary to provide a lodge where they will feel at home."[69] The cultivated social appeal of the lodge met with some success, and within a few months the county master of Toronto, W.H. Elliott, had transferred to it, as had J.O. McCarthy, the former city controller, and G.H. Armstrong, the inspector of public schools for Toronto.[70] Over the next several years, Imperial Lodge acquired a reputation for the elaborate nature of its initiation ceremonies, and it would appear that it was somewhat akin to a Masonic lodge in its social and ritualistic appeal.

It is probable that some lodges were particularly attractive to immigrants, possibly reflecting the social linkages that fuelled the migration process itself. Portadown LOL 919 had been established in 1890 and it projected an image of uncompromising Ulster Protestant political beliefs in its public parades and also in its lodge-based social activities. Describing one such social evening, the *Sentinel* commented that after a fine meal "songs and sweetmeats were the order of the evening – and they were none of the namby-pamby songs either – but the real old Irish songs breathing loyalty to Crown and Constitution, and the brethren of Portadown know how to sing them."[71] Belfast LOL 875, founded in 1876, likewise projected a strong appeal to immigrant Ulstermen and was home to many who transferred from Belfast and Lurgan lodges. It was especially popular among members of the Toronto police force, many of whom had origins in the old Royal Irish Constabulary. City of Derry LOL 2159 emerged in 1910 at the behest of a number of Orangemen from Magherafelt Co Derry, and although its appeal was not confined to immigrants it did continue to provide a special attraction for arrivals from rural Ulster. Canadian migrants, as well as foreign-born immigrants, sometimes projected a distinctive affinity for particular lodges, and of these the most distinctive was LOL 1084, home to large numbers of Newfoundlanders living in Toronto. Many of the Newfoundlanders worked in the construction industry. On celebratory occasions it articulated its distinctive cultural heritage in the form of jigg or salted fish suppers, although these would appear to have had less gastronomic attraction than the dinners hosted by their Italian brethren in Giuseppe Garibaldi LOL 3115. This latter lodge was an outgrowth of Protestant Italian immigrants who came to Toronto in the 1920s, forming their unique lodge in May 1930. Throughout its history its membership has remained almost exclusively Italian and its spaghetti suppers became renowned throughout the city.[72]

Employment niches, often interlaced with social class undertones, formed ready-made nuclei for recruitment into particular lodges, but there does not appear to have existed an exclusive, and persistent, link between particular lodges and specific occupations. It was more a question of relative proportions within the membership. There was some concentration of the political elite in LOL 140, which traditionally was home to many of the officials of City Hall and members of the provincial and federal parliaments. "I saw 140 and knew that business at City Hall was suspended," commented an observer at the 1902 Twelfth parade in Toronto.[73] But even in that lodge, membership was not confined to politicians and it was much more fluid in its recruitment than was, for example, the Orange lodge organized by Sir James Craig, which functioned at the same time in the British Houses of Parliament. LOL 781 had twelve firemen among its membership in 1894, but there were another thirty-five firemen scattered among twenty-one other lodges in the city. By the same token, individual lodges might have contained clusters of brickyard workers or employees of the Grand Trunk Railway, but these men were never limited in their choice of lodge. An intersection of employment, neighbourhood residency, church attendance, and ethnic background all contributed to a complex behavioural matrix that influenced choice of lodge. As a result most lodges tended to contain a range of social classes, reflecting the social complexity of the city itself.

Respectability

As an organization with written rules and regulations, the Orange Order was a self-regulating body to which members voluntarily sought admission, and from which they might be suspended or expelled for infringements of the spirit and purpose of the general body. Rules were comprehensive and detailed, penalties specific, and procedures and processes explicit. Implementation of the regulatory code was at the behest of the officers, but any member could raise matters deemed pertinent to the good name and conduct of the organization. Conduct within the confines of lodge meetings was especially well regulated and the manner in which business could be raised, the method of addressing officers, and even the duration of speeches (in some cases) were subject to by-laws. Unruly behaviour or drunkenness during meetings was frowned upon, especially from the rise of the temperance movement in the mid-nineteenth century, and as parading lodges represented technically the temporary conduct of lodge business in public, the lodges felt entitled to prescribe dress codes and standards of conduct for parades as diverse as funeral processions, church services, and Twelfth commemorations. In 1874, LOL 342, for example, ruled "That any member of this Lodge on any celebration or procession who may be seen intoxicated, smoking or disorderly in the ranks or leaving them without permission of the W.M. may be fined, suspended or expelled as the Lodge may determine."[74] As the Order moved towards a position of greater respectability in the final third of the nineteenth century, its by-laws became increasingly complex, and disciplinary actions transcended the confines of official meetings and public parades to embrace aspects of private behaviour and personal morality. Marrying a Catholic had traditionally been reason for severe censure and expulsion, as were serious criminal convictions. Personal reputations also were evaluated as part of the application process, and matters of sexual morality were sometimes censured in formal proceeding. In 1921, for example, the deputy master of LOL 375 in open lodge made a charge against a member, Bro Ashton, who "Having violated Section 171(sub sec 1) of The Constitution and Laws of the LOA – that is to say during the past summer he has been living in a state of Adultery and Fornication with a Mrs Gibbs 217 Pape Ave of this city and pray that investigation may be had in this matter." The accused refused to appear before the committee appointed to inquire into the matter and expulsion from the Order was recommended.[75]

Private morality was a matter for the Order in so far as the actions of members gave rise to public scandal in a community that was infused by strict and sanctimonious interpretations of church teachings. In the spirit of contemporary Toronto, the life of citizens was regulated by municipal by-laws and Church laws and reinforced by the prescriptions of voluntary societies such as the Orange Order. These regulatory frameworks rarely contradicted each other. Each affirmed an agreed interpretation of what constituted social respectability. Indeed the Order became an important pillar of civic culture, upholding municipal by-laws that regulated the activities of private citizens and businesses, especially in respect of what was deemed proper behaviour on a Sunday. Those by-laws had in turn been enacted by a City Council that was dominated by Orangemen. As the nineteenth century drew to an end, Toronto was a city dominated by robust Protestantism, and, as historians Christopher Armstrong and H.V. Nelles have wryly observed, "Orange lodges kept Protestantism in fighting trim."[76] That heady mixture of politics, religion, and public morality proved to be remarkably long-lasting in "Toronto the Good" and it continued to represent a powerful alliance as the Canadian Orange Order celebrated its first centenary in 1930. In the course of its first century, the Order had moved from the margins of society to the centre of respectability. An unruly body driven by a demand for immigrant democracy had metamorphosed into an organization whose annual celebrations were attended by those closest to the heart of power in the city as well as by a broad social range of the citizenry.

4 Power, Patronage, and Public Employment within the Protestant City, 1850–1920

Patronage exercised publicly and subject to scrutiny and comment is not unique to Canada and is to be found within political systems throughout the world. Appointment to bodies such as the Upper House in Ottawa is a recognized and legally acceptable extension of the power of the prime minister, as is the government's appointment of members and chairs of a designated range of state boards, ambassadorships, and many other representative and administrative positions. Custom and practice of patronage appointments extend far beyond the level of the national government, and, although there may be debate and controversy over the nomination of particular individuals, the process itself is recognized as a legitimate means of rewarding able persons, many of them committed party supporters. It is a process that has operated since the inception of colonization in the territories of the Canadas and was practised in early Toronto by John Graves Simcoe, who rewarded his former military colleagues with administrative offices and established, in the process, a small but powerful nucleus of loyal followers – many of them Irish Protestants from Cork. The early Tory administration was aptly known as the Family Compact, and by its name, practices, and grip on office it epitomized the exercise and benefits of closely controlled patronage. Anglican in religion, Tory in politics, and predominantly English in origin, the Family Compact dominated Upper Canadian politics for some four decades. Its influence was manifest at all levels of administration. Its mission was the reconstruction of a British social structure within the colonial settlement and through its dominance of the Executive and Legislative Councils it was well equipped to pursue that goal.[1] Power in the form of the allocation of resources, sinecures, and employment was wielded in an inherently top-down manner. However, a more horizontal set of distributive relations also functioned in the city, especially during the first century of its municipal history, and arguably this form of patronage, perhaps better described as clientalism, became the dominant allocation model as a semblance of participatory democracy came to predominate in municipal politics after the incorporation of the city in 1834.

The clientalist model was much more community-based and depended heavily upon social linkages and personal contacts for effective operation. It worked best in a city that was larger and more complex than that of the Simcoe era but still small enough to facilitate network linkages, personal endorsements, and introductions. Critical to its success was the existence of link persons or organizations that bridged the gap between the local community and those who controlled municipal office – the conduit through which commodities such as jobs and commercial contracts were distributed. The transactional exchanges intrinsic to this process of clientalism were self-reinforcing, protective of the social equilibrium, and supportive of pre-existing attitudes, divisions, and even local hostilities. Although informal, the system was effective and, despite allegations of cronyism and corruption, it survived for several generations – persisting until growth in the city's scale and political diversity rendered the older machinery of clientalism redundant. Evidence of the existence of a clientalist system in Toronto may be discerned in records of public employment in niche areas such as City Hall, the Custom House, the Post Office, and police and fire services. Local lore and family histories support the allegation that the clientalist system extended also to some of the largest private employers in the city.[2] The persistence and discriminatory effectiveness of the system were widely recognized by contemporaries, including reform candidates who not infrequently stood for election on the platform of eradicating cliques and urban corruption but who had little lasting success until Nathan Phillips's electoral triumph in the mid-twentieth century. His platform explicitly proclaimed a policy of inclusiveness, and he described himself as "Mayor of All the People."[3]

The Orange Order emerged as the main vehicle for the acquisition and distribution of patronage in the city, its effectiveness resting not only on the size and importance of its membership but also on the congruence of its principles with those of the dominant ideology of the predominantly Protestant city. The apparent success of the Order as a conduit of rewards proved to be a self-fulfilling prophecy, attracting very many new recruits, enhancing its power as a political broker, and making it proportionately the largest voluntary organization in the secular life of the city. At its peak, membership of the Order transcended ethnicity and geography – Protestantism was the common denominator. Its organizational structure of lodges and administrative districts, its control of the mayoralty, and its dominance of City Council and powerful positions such as that of city clerk were augmented by a membership that was numbered in the thousands, transcending social class and geographical districts. It was a highly influential organization, but its internal coherence and single-purpose focus were sometimes more apparent than real. Catholics tended to view all power brokers in the Victorian city as being Orange, whether or not they were actually part of the membership, and the Order itself was prone to exaggerate its strength. The very diversity of its membership and its high degree of turnover did not lend itself to a tightly bunched body that blindly followed a single charismatic leader, and in elections for mayor and aldermen alike, it was not uncommon for Orange candidates of different party affiliation to oppose each other. The Order was a much more diffuse machine than that which operated in many contemporary American cities, and beyond its agreed consensus on militant Protestantism it contained all the political diversity expected from a membership that included both radical trade unionists and wealthy employers, recently arrived immigrants and established citizens.

Toronto, with its Orange-dominated politics, was probably the closest Canadian equivalent of the machine politics of American cities. The peak period of Orange power in Toronto (1860–1930) is remarkably coterminous with that of Tammany Hall in New York, and in their patterns of patronage distribution there were many similarities between the two organizations. However, notwithstanding allegations of corruption and several judicial inquiries into the system of municipal governance in Toronto, there is little evidence of the Orange Order ever matching the power, complexity, pervasiveness, and corruption associated with city administrations in either New York or Chicago. The Tammany Hall political machine had originated in New York in 1789 as a fraternal society, the Society of St Tammany. By 1798 its activities had become increasingly politicized, and by the 1830s it was a controlling force in New York municipal politics. Its power base was rooted in the cultivation of immigrant support by means of a network of influence that purported to deliver emergency aid, welfare, employment, accommodation, and an introduction to life in the burgeoning metropolis, together with rapid progression to citizenship. In return, the ward bosses obtained and directed electoral votes. By the 1850s the power of the Tammany ward bosses, allied with the Democratic party and supported by the Irish community, appeared unchallengeable, and leaders such as Tweed and Croker attained national and indeed international notoriety. Tammany Hall remained a formidable force until the social and economic crises of the 1930s weakened its grip on immigrant communities, and although a brief revival followed in the 1950s the organization was by then a spent force.[4] It was a model that was imitated in part by the Orange political machine in Toronto, but the imitation was less effective than the prototype: the context of power in the Canadian city differed greatly from that of the American metropolis. Victoria Hall on Queen Street, home to the County Orange Lodge, accommodated many political meetings and was home to several effective ward bosses who were officers of the Orange Order, but it was no Tammany Hall. The cement of Orangeism was not ethnicity but the more diffuse concepts of Protestantism and monarchism, and it was too democratic in its leadership structures to foster a cult of personality and the ruthlessness of unchallenged power.

Toronto: Context of Patronage

The Family Compact's sense of exclusive power was challenged by the emergence of mass migration in the 1820s, which not only transformed the scale of the colonial settlement but also brought with it political voices of reform and a demand for a model of government that was more participatory in construction and less elitist in tone. The strength of the challenge became very evident in the years following on the elevation, in 1834, of the town of York to the status of an incorporated city, renamed Toronto. In the ensuing political confrontation between the Family Compact and the Reformers led by the elected mayor, William Lyon Mackenzie, the Orange Order, under the leadership of Ogle R. Gowan, operated as a third force – sometimes allying with the Tories, sometimes seeking cause with the Reformers.[5] Gowan's ambition was to win power for the immigrant Order and in the long run he was successful. Immigrant groups that had come from all parts of the British Isles, and especially from Ulster, acquired an early dominance in the city's elected council. By 1847, Irish Protestants, at least half of them Orangemen, filled fifteen of the eighteen seats on Council, and the altered tone of governance was evident to all. Toronto's municipal politics were to be dominated by this group for almost a century, and long after the

Orange Order had ceased to be a purely Irish immigrant organization the political and cultural life of Toronto retained its characteristic flow of Orange patronage to selected individuals, groups, and commercial bodies.

There was general acceptance of a patronage system in Toronto, although the designation of actual beneficiaries might have been questioned. Catholics, and their leaders, were more concerned about their share of the spoils than they were about the principles that underpinned the system. Reformers, when in office, were not immune from resorting to the practice, which grew in complexity and scale as the century progressed. During the 1890s, the Toronto paper the *Week* initiated a campaign for the abolition of the patronage system and its replacement by a public appointments commission – a proposal that was vigorously contested by the *Globe*. That latter paper argued that it was the duty of government to make appointments and it would represent a signal failure if they passed this responsibility over to a commission. Patronage, it argued, was not only well established in Canada at both federal and provincial government levels but also an accepted practice in the English motherland. In both countries, it argued, patronage was exercised under strict conditions for the common good.

> Everyone will agree that incompetent persons ought not to be appointed, or competent persons dismissed for party reasons; that there ought to be no sinecures or overpaid offices to tempt cupidity; that public office ought not be bought and sold for the purpose of raising campaign funds. But when we have eliminated all these there still remains the fact that under party government, the friends of the dominant party will be preferred in making appointments, and to this we say: It is imperfect, show us a better way. Appointments must be made, must be made by somebody, and must be made from some motive, the person appointing and the person appointed never can be other than human, we need never look for perfection.[6]

Thirty years later the issue was still a matter of public debate. In opposition to the introduction of competitive examinations for entry to the Civil Service, trenchant arguments were published in the *Sentinel*.[7] Cheating and theft of papers, it argued, could corrupt the examinations. The argument ignored the widespread corruption that already existed, particularly at the municipal level, but it did reflect the continuing consensus that it was not the principle of patronage that was contentious but rather the allocation of the spoils.

For the system to operate effectively in a self-perpetuating manner, it was a necessary precondition that the citizenry be composed of resilient and clearly identifiable fragments or subgroups. To be successful, the wielders of patronage had to know who their friends were and be in a position to assist them. The specific strength of the Orange Order, operating as a political machine, rested upon a fundamental characteristic of contemporary Canadian society, i.e., that fissure lines were more likely to be defined in terms of religion than class. In a city divided by sectarian animosities, the Order was ideally placed to wield power. Within the city, and in the national overview, religion and national destiny were interlocked in a sense of imperial destiny. There was widespread agreement that the British Empire was, by Divine Providence, an instrument for moral good, and, in the words of a clergyman lecturing in Ontario in 1867, the imperial connection was the means of dispensing "Gospel blessings and liberalizing institutions in every region of the earth."[8] Protestantism was seen as the cornerstone of the British outreach; conversely, Catholicism was viewed with suspicion, not only because of its unreformed tenets of faith but also because it was deemed to be inherently disloyal in its political involvements. In part this suspicion was rooted in power struggles that had aligned Britain against the Catholic powers, Spain and France, for centuries, but for Irish Protestant immigrants to Canada the memory was more immediately informed by the sectarian bloodshed of the 1798 United Irishmen's rebellion and the perceived role of the Orange Order as an effective counter-revolutionary force at that time.

Their marginal position was justified further by the perception that the Catholic community of Toronto was derived from diseased paupers who had been thrown upon the city by the turmoil of the famine and who, by definition, were too impoverished, illiterate, and ill equipped to make a meaningful contribution to urban life. The growth of the Catholic population in mid-nineteenth-century Toronto is a much more complex phenomenon and further analysis of it is still required. Certainly, Toronto had an established Catholic Irish community two decades or more before the famine and its presence was sufficiently strong to warrant the creation of a separate Catholic diocese in 1843. The city became more visibly Catholic during the period 1841–51 – Catholics increased from 2,401 to 7,940 and their share of the city's population increased proportionately from 17 per cent to 25 per cent in those years. We, as yet, know too little about the relative fertility of the two groups of Irish in the city, and more research remains to be done on the numbers of

Catholics who had arrived in the years before the influx of 1847, but it is clear that the Catholic Irish community contained many who were not famine arrivals and some who were of considerable social worth.[9] However, their image has been compressed into a simplified category of alienated "others." To be sure, the Irish Catholic community of Toronto in the middle decades of the nineteenth century did contain within their midst very many who were destitute, hundreds who populated the jail, and numerous prostitutes, drunkards, and shiftless individuals. They harboured supporters of the Fenians during the 1860s and many were known to distrust the police and frequently ignore the rule of law. But very many of them were law-abiding and loyal citizens. A substantial proportion of the Catholic Irish in nineteenth-century Toronto had arrived either before the famine or in the years after it, or had been born in the city. In socio-economic terms they may have borne a closer resemblance to other contemporary immigrants than is generally recognized. Those originating in Ulster were likely to have a background in the domestic textile industry, and others were, like many of their Protestant counterparts, derived from small farming and agricultural labouring backgrounds. Catholics such as Frank Smith, political leader and sometime owner of the Toronto Street Railway, had arrived before the famine with few resources but had flourished in their new home. And in the 1830s and 1840s there was sufficient wealth and leadership within the Catholic community to initiate construction of St Michael's Cathedral and (through the efforts of an English convert) to endow St Michael's College.

The political identity of Catholics was likewise complex. The first Catholic bishop in the city, Michael Power, who died as a result of his exposure to typhus in 1847, was well known for his ultra-loyalist views and his unequivocal support for the imperial connection. There may well have been support among Toronto's Catholics for the Fenian brotherhood and their armed invasion of Canada, but these insurrectionary activities were unambiguously condemned by secular leaders such as Thomas D'Arcy McGee and, eventually, by Archbishop Lynch. The Catholic community was complex. By ascribing a simple descriptor to it, the majority population made it easier to identify and operate the boundaries of what was deemed to be mainstream society. Those boundaries in turn made it easier to define the parameters relevant to the distribution of patronage.

As Toronto's Catholic community matured and grew in numbers during the 1850s and 1860s, its leaders, lay as well as clerical, articulated a sense of grievance, coupled with a demand for parity of esteem, and a request that equal space be afforded them in the distribution of power and privileges. Given the fact that Catholics constituted upwards of a quarter of the city's population in both the 1851 and 1861 censuses, there was indeed some apparent merit in their argument, but then, as later, it proved difficult to translate their demographic strength into political influence. To be sure, during the episcopacy of Bishop Charbonnel the principle of separate schools for Catholics in Ontario had been conceded, and the Scott Act of 1864 extended that principle further. It was a concession of fundamental importance, for it consolidated the principle of segregated education for Catholics in schools paid for by Catholic taxpayers and ensured the survival of a distinctive ethnoreligious group identity. But other advances on the political front were negligible, with attainment of elected office at municipal or parliamentary level being a rarity. Newly appointed, and politically astute, Archbishop Lynch threw his weight behind the Conservative party in the 1861 election, and it would appear that the Irish Catholic vote was, for a time, marshalled effectively. In return, Lynch claimed an entitlement of some degree of patronage and was rewarded by being asked to nominate a suitable person for the position of inspector of penitentiaries. He did so in the person of T.J. O'Neill. Historian Michael Cottrell has observed that "O'Neill's appointment also carried with it a great deal of patronage and this would work to the benefit of ordinary Irish Catholics, by effecting their structural integration into Canadian society."[10] O'Neill was succeeded in turn by two other Irish Catholics, J.G. Moylan and Thomas McCrossan, but there is no evidence that these individual appointments had any long-term systemic effect. The penitentiary service did not become a significant employer of Irish Catholics. Nonetheless, the appointments helped establish the credentials of the archbishop as a power broker. The newly appointed governor-general, Lord Dufferin, observed in 1872 that "my most obsequious courtier is a Paddy Roman Catholic Archbishop" – an obvious reference to Lynch.[11] But concessions of patronage were slow in coming, and Lynch became progressively disillusioned. In February 1872 the archbishop confided in Frank Smith, "Railroad companies are generally Masonic, the municipalities Orange and the Government employees are for the most part of both camps."[12] Overall, the allocation of official patronage to Catholics remained small compared to that retained for the majority population, and, until his death in 1888, Lynch continued to fight for a more favourable allocation to his co-religionists.

Archbishop Lynch was probably correct in attributing the small share of patronage to the paucity of Catholic representatives in the provincial parliament and the municipal councils of Ontario. It was, he argued, a very different situation from that in Quebec. In 1876 the archbishop published an open letter in the *Irish Canadian* refuting allegations made by Sir A.T. Galt about the disadvantaged position of Protestants in the province of Quebec and asserted:

> [Protestants in Quebec] have a number of Protestant constituencies almost secured to them, and have a Protestant representative always in the parliament of Quebec. In fact, the Protestants of the province of Quebec are like all petted children when they grow up. They live on the memories of past Protestant ascendancy and legislation, when Catholics had no rights to speak of. When the Catholics wished to be represented in the Cabinet of Ontario, and to have a few members in the local House, their pretensions as Catholics were considered as quite out of place.[13]

The Catholic community was conscious of its position at the margins of civic society, and, as its leader and spokesman, Archbishop Lynch was especially adroit in promising bloc votes at election times. At the provincial level he switched his support from the Conservatives to the Liberals and was a key factor in the prolonged period of Liberal dominance during the last third of the nineteenth century and especially the premiership of Oliver Mowat, 1872–96. Mowat, himself a pragmatic politician, managed to successfully disguise his earlier anti-Catholic image in order to avail himself of the support. Lynch was equally pragmatic, and he had to be, for his political options were circumscribed within the context of two parties, neither of which was a natural ally – the traditionally anti-Catholic Liberals founded by George Brown of the *Globe* or the Orange Tories. He rode both horses with considerable skill and he saw no contradiction in supporting the Liberal administration in Ontario while offering support at the federal level to John A. Macdonald's Conservatives. Patronage was sought, and won, from both. In 1869 Macdonald wrote to the archbishop, stating, "I am doing all I can in order to give the Catholics their fair share of public employment," but he went on to qualify his actions by arguing that, although Catholics were capable of holding their own in middle and lower offices, their low educational standards limited their suitability for higher offices.[14] Lynch's interventions were in the tradition of caring for the temporal as well as spiritual well-being of his flock and he was acutely conscious of his self-assigned role as leader of the Catholic Irish in the city. Towards the end of his episcopacy he faced an internal challenge from an ambitious lay leadership, but his role as a vital link, connecting the needs of his community to the reservoirs of patronage controlled by political leaders, exemplified perfectly the hierarchical nature of the distributive system. Through his efforts, the principle of sharing patronage had been won by the 1870s, but the extent and nature of it remained contested.[15] The advances did not go unnoticed by the majority population, and in 1879 the *Telegram*, a pro-Orange Toronto paper, acerbically editorialized that "the Mowat cabinet performs as Archbishop Lynch pulls the strings."[16] Lynch himself was self-congratulatory in his assessment of progress and noted in a personal letter to Bishop Gibbons of Baltimore that the "Protestant ascendancy is pretty well down in Toronto. The Catholic Archbishop ranks first after the Governor or representative of Her Majesty there."[17]

Lay Catholic leaders were less content with the extent of progress, and, under the political leadership of entrepreneur Frank Smith and barrister John O'Donohoe, the Ontario Catholic League was formed in 1869. The League, closely affiliated with the Ontario Liberal party, aspired to harnessing the Catholic vote for that party and its federal counterpart. The League's mission paralleled that of Archbishop Lynch – both lay and clerical leadership were united in a common perception that Catholics were discriminated against in many walks of public life. To prove this assertion, J.L.P. O'Hanly, Ottawa city engineer, former Fenian sympathizer, and self-confessed Liberal, produced a statistical analysis of denominational representation in public life in 1872. He presented his report to the League as proof of the anti-Catholic behaviour of the Conservatives.[18] Whatever his introductory political hyperbole, there was a strong evidence-based aspect to O'Hanly's analysis of the actual number and level of public offices held by Catholics. Office holders were benchmarked against a proportionality projected from the 1861 census figures, the 1871 census data being unavailable at the time of his writing.[19] In short, it was O'Hanly's contention that the proportion of jobs held by Catholics in public employment should be reflective of their relative strength in the overall population – a stance common to many advocates of the time, including Archbishop Lynch. It was an interesting presentation of the argument "Representation by Population." Factors such as levels of educational attainment, duration of residence in the province, and overall aptitude for public- as opposed to private-sector employment were not incorporated into his analysis. The

Table 4.1 Religious affiliation of public service employees in Ontario, 1872

	Catholics	Protestants
Provincial civil service	9	180
Administration of justice	29	753
Legislative employees	1	7
Federal government	64	872
Total	103	1,812

Source: O'Hanly, *The Political Standing of Irish Catholics in Ontario*

demonstrated result was explained solely in terms of the Conservative party's anti-Catholic stance. Notwithstanding the inferred causality, it is very evident from his data that Catholics were underprivileged in contemporary civic society and that while some Catholic individuals may have prospered in the field of private business, their co-religionists had met with less success in public employment, at either municipal, provincial, or federal levels (see table 4.1).

The claim for Catholic parity in public appointments was based on the argument that their share should be equivalent to their percentage of the taxpayers in the jurisdiction. Whatever the quantum of taxes contributed by Catholics, the fact that they occupied less than 6 per cent of the offices analysed by O'Hanly would appear to substantiate his claim of systematic under-representation. Were salary levels to have been included in O'Hanly's analysis, the data would have been even more extreme, for many of the Catholics were employed at levels of messengers and clerks. Unfortunately, O'Hanly did not include Toronto in a separate analysis, but the overall pattern for the province does provide a context within which the city may be measured using data for subsequent years.

Michael Cottrell has argued that, in the quarter-century after Confederation, "Irish Catholics evolved from a despised and virtually powerless minority into a cohesive and influential ethno-religious pressure group."[20] Likewise Mark G. McGowan, a specialist on Toronto's Irish community, has argued for the sustained and quantifiable improvement of the position of Catholics and their integration into mainstream Canadian society during these decades.[21] Yet by the yardstick of demographic parity, it is clear that Catholics had less than what might have been an expected share of public employment, and leaders, religious as well as lay, demanded further progress. In certain districts in rural Ontario, Irish Catholic political leverage was comparatively strong, but in the provincial capital, where the proportion of Catholics in the urban population was steadily declining, old orders still held sway. The "Belfast of Canada" exhibited a firm and restrictive Protestant identity for several generations after national confederation, and a distinctive, and exclusive, status quo was maintained through the exercise of power, patronage, and employment networks.

Employment in publicly funded posts in Toronto was highly prized. It was comparatively well paid, more secure than the private sector, and managerial posts especially conferred considerable social status. It offered also the opportunity and means to exercise power and further patronage in a myriad of preferential ways, including control of procurement, allocation of service contracts, and promotion of like-minded individuals. The office of the city clerk, for example, controlled the award of commercial contracts in fields as varied as construction, maintenance, and repair of street surfaces, fuel supplies for city offices, food for the municipal gaol, hospital and care facilities, and fodder and equipment for the horses in the city stables. Annual municipal expenditure was considerable, and public representatives took a keen interest in its disbursement. There was some truth in the *Irish Canadian*'s allegation "that the fabulous sums wantonly expended by that Council, manipulated as it is and has been for years by that faction, have found their way into the pockets of Orange heelers and wire-pullers."[22] The paper was specific in its allegations of malpractice in procurement of goods and services for the city and identified Brother James Craig, clerk in the city's Engineers' Office, as being especially complicit. It alleged that Craig opened sealed tenders and, having informed his favoured contractors of the contents, resealed them.[23] Renovations of the City Hall and police and fire stations, together with the construction of a morgue and drill shed, cost the city $45,000 in 1880, and it was alleged that the contracts were awarded "so that ex-aldermen Gearing, Wagner and Withrow might supply materials to the contractors thereof, contrary to the provisions of what was known as the Mowat by-law No. 504." The Board of Water Commissioners and "the Orange Brethren thereon" were accused of squandering half a million dollars on defective materials, incompetent repairs, and unwarranted salaries for "superfluous officials of the Orange persuasion, as appointed by Brothers Bell, Medcalf and Morrison of that Board."[24] Allegations of corrupt practices were frequent and the explanations varied from the expected Catholic

response that such practices were the inevitable outcome of the dominance of municipal politics by the Orange Order to a more reflective
socio-political analysis by the *Globe*. That paper argued in 1894:

> Despite the warnings of the press the electors have persisted in sending
> men of doubtful public record to the City Hall to decide contracts involv-
> ing in the aggregate millions of dollars and dispose of franchises of enor-
> mous value. Now that the civic corruption, that is the natural outcome of
> this state of affairs, is shown to exist there may be an awakening of the
> citizens and a real effort towards raising the Aldermanic standard.[25]

The evidence of specific corruption referred to by the paper related
to a scandal over the awarding of a contract for street lighting. Amid a
public outcry following allegations that certain aldermen had sought a
bribe of $13,000 from the Toronto Electric Light Company for renewal
of its current contract, the City Council had agreed to set up a judicial
inquiry under Judge Joseph E. McDougall, County Court judge of the
County of York. An interim report provided a guilty verdict on William
T. Stewart, chairman of the Fire and Light Committee of Council. Alderman Stewart was a past master of LOL 455 and a manufacturer of roof-
ing material in the city. With the assent of Council, Judge McDougall
widened his inquiry and established a *prima facie* case for the involvement of aldermen in the demand for a $4,000 bribe from the Edison
Company, which had tendered in 1891 for the installation of motors
for the Street Railway. Aldermen Bailey, Gowanlock, Hall, Hewitt, and
Thompson were investigated, and the first two were charged with "corrupt practices." Hewitt and Thompson resigned from Council. Apart
from their common role as aldermen, the four representatives were also
prominent members of the Orange Order in the city, and although that
organization certainly did not endorse political corruption, the practice of the machine politics it orchestrated did facilitate opportunities
for personal aggrandizement and corruption in municipal affairs. It
was the dark side of patronage as operated in late nineteenth-century
Toronto.[26]

More than anything else, however, it was the recurring issue of access
to jobs that defined the debate about patronage in nineteenth- and early
twentieth-century Toronto. From its inception as a colonial town, public
employment had been a prized attribute of the local economy, and even
as it developed into a major industrial and commercial metropolis in the
latter part of the nineteenth century, Toronto remained home to a wide

variety of jobs in what might nowadays be described as the public sector. The burgeoning city required a number of municipal services, ranging from architects to waterworks engineers, firemen, and policemen. Its status as a provincial capital required a civil service, and its role as a lake port and pivot in the national urban system necessitated a federal Customs House, a branch of the Inland Revenue, and a well-resourced Post Office. Hundreds were employed in these niches by the end of the century, and inevitably they were overwhelmingly male, of British origin, and Protestant. Their skill levels ranged from those of street labourers to medical inspectors. Middle classes and unskilled labourers alike benefited from the all-pervasive operation of the patronage system. Access to employment was carefully controlled, and in keeping with the highly personal nature of contemporary society: most appointments were made from pools of local applicants whose personal credentials were known. Political influence was of major importance in the selection of candidates, and the ward organization of the predominant party played a central role. It did so within a national context that perceived no moral difficulty in cabinet ministers interfering in a wide range of appointments. Even while serving as prime minister, Sir John A. Macdonald was reputed to have intervened personally in the filling of postal clerkships in his home constituency of Kingston, and it has been suggested that Mackenzie Bowell, grand master of the Orange Lodge, future prime minister, and minister of customs, 1878–91, was preoccupied with the operation of patronage throughout his career.[27] Four parliamentary commissions investigated complaints about the operation of the system in the years 1880–1912 but to little immediate effect. The Civil Service Commission did not materialize until after the First World War, and even then municipal bodies could continue with their established practices.

Effective operation of the patronage system required a combination of hierarchical conduits of power, link persons who would forward the names of recommended individuals, and a horizontal network that operated knowledgeably within the local community. A complex local machine filtered supplicants, processed their nomination if deemed worthy, and forwarded specific recommendations to those with the power to hire. Within the otherwise clandestine system, elements of transparency did sometimes emerge in the form of patronage lists for specific ridings.[28] Political representatives, in general, had a keen sense of territoriality; they jealously sought to advance the prospects of the constituents of their own electoral areas and promoted localism over open competition. The Report of the Civil Service Commission, 1907–8, noted that in respect of the Inland Revenue Department, "Political appointments, as in other branches of the public service, prevail and as a rule the officers in one district are confined to that one district."[29] Whatever its adverse effect on the evolution of a progressive system of administration, the system certainly ensured stability within the public service. The system was widespread in both English and French Canada, but the intrinsic sense of localism that underpinned it facilitated the development of nuanced manifestations within particular areas. Toronto was, therefore, not unique in its employment of a complex patronage system, but it was unusual in that the nature of the city, and its long-established religious divisions, supported a system that considered religious affiliation as a valid indicator of suitability for public employment. Ward aldermen in the city, and the executive officers of ridings held by the Liberal Conservative party, were strongly influenced by the Orange Order, and the organization was not slow to exert its influence on the patronage process. It was evident to all in Toronto that employment in publicly funded posts at municipal, provincial, and federal levels was not a random event. Operating to greatest effect within a social landscape where personal relations were paramount, recommendations for vacancies epitomized a fluid and regulated system of "who do you know." It was a system of some complexity, requiring mechanism for selection and prioritizing of individuals, and it was capable of operating both vertically and horizontally within a web of meshed levels and interests.

The functioning of the patronage system in Toronto has been analysed in some detail by Alan Gordon in his study of Edmund Bristol, who represented the federal Toronto Centre riding as a Conservative from 1905 until 1926. Bristol was an undistinguished parliamentarian, but he survived the vicissitudes of successive electoral contests through an adroit distribution of patronage that kept his supporters content; what was more, he recorded his decisions in a systematic manner that reveals the inner workings of the process.[30] A well-connected Tory lawyer, Bristol moved easily within the echelons of Toronto's elite, but he was also very conscious of the need to accommodate his more humble constituents. To aid him in his tasks he had recourse to a patronage committee that filtered applications for employment, forwarding advice from officers of the party organization at the local or ward level. "Members of Parliament [he explained] do not make appointments off their own bat – in the first place they take the advice of the officers of the Ward Associations in which the candidate for the position lives, and the general organiser of the Party is better aware than anyone of the vacancies that are apt to occur and the possibility of getting a particular position for a particular candidate."[31] Those with the power to make recommendations acted as gatekeepers and they were effective and systematic in their processing. They had an obvious, and powerful, opportunity to impose their own value system on the process and they did not hesitate to do so. Party loyalty was an especial key prerequisite for selection, and, given the nature of the Liberal Conservative party, such loyalty was to a large degree synonymous in Toronto with Protestantism, Britishness, and Orangeism. Correspondence from Bristol to relevant ministers in Ottawa seeking appointments for named individuals often referred to the supplicant as being "one of our friends," and as an additional persuasive overture, Bristol frequently referred to his success in winning a marginal seat for the Conservatives in the previous election and to the necessity to distribute jobs to constituents in order that he might secure that seat in future elections.[32] In particular, the Liberal Conservative party secretary, Hilly Birmingham, was exceedingly powerful in filtering the names of those seeking employment, Bristol himself noting, "Mr. A.H. Birmingham acts as a sort of clearing house in these matters."[33]

Gordon's analysis does not discern the role of the Orange Order in what he terms "the science of connection," but that role may be understood by fuller analysis of Bristol's correspondence, as well as the construction of linkages revealed by supporting data. The same Hilly Birmingham had succeeded his father, Robert Birmingham, to the position of party secretary in the city and he came of impeccable Orange stock. Robert, a native of Ireland, had been master of LOL 613 and in his day he had risen beyond ward politics to become secretary-treasurer of the Liberal Conservatives in Ontario. An Anglican by religion, he had spent his early years as a salesman in the city before scaling the heights of the local and provincial party organization, and he was sufficiently powerful to have his son succeed him in party headquarters. In 1889, Robert had corresponded directly with Sir John A. Macdonald, enclosing "the names of a few legal friends who rendered us special service in the recent campaign in the hope that you might be able to repay them with the much sought after QC." Contained in the list was Emerson Coatsworth, described as "a rising young barrister, pillar of the Methodist Church, a strong temperance advocate, President of the Liberal Conservative Association for his ward."[34] Coatsworth was a member of one of the most prominent Orange families in the city; his father had sat as a member of Parliament and he himself became a QC and city commissioner shortly after Robert Birmingham's letter to Macdonald. Hilly Birmingham proved to be as successful as his father in the operation of the patronage machine in the city and he was quite open about combining his roles as ward boss, party organizer, and Orange official. Fellow members of the Orange Order could reasonably expect favourable consideration when seeking a public service position.

Bristol himself was an Orangeman – a long-time member and past master of McKinley LOL 275 wherein he and Mayor E.F. Clarke had been contemporaries. Ward meetings of the Liberal Conservative party were held in the County Orange Hall on Queen Street with Birmingham and Bristol officiating, and a seamless web linked all interests. Requested appointments ranged from that of sub-postmaster on Queen Street West to a variety of jobs in the Postal Service, Customs House, and Civil Service. "Mr T.M. Stead, a member of Cameron Lodge" was advanced for a Civil Service position. John Brown, a carpenter, was proposed for public employment on the basis that "He is a Conservative and has also worked for the Party. He also belongs to McKinley Lodge." Bristol advised D.G. Lorsch, a prominent Toronto stock broker seeking employment for a friend, "I would be glad to have Mr. Kingsmill call on Mr. Birmingham and talk the matter over with him, as he has a better idea than anyone I know of any possible situations that are, or might be vacant, for which Mr. Kingsmill would be fitted. The class of appointments we usually have, of course, is in the Custom House or in the Post Office." Of the dozens of applications for employment contained among the Bristol Papers, most were treated cordially. An exception was Charles O'Leary of Markham Street. Birmingham rejected O'Leary, a Canadian-born Catholic of Irish ancestry, on the basis that "I do not know whether or not he is a Conservative, and I certainly think no time should be wasted on the gentleman in question."[35]

The activities of Edmund Bristol, MP were not unique, but he was exceptional in that he kept detailed written records of the exercise of clientalism and the use of public posts to reward party stalwarts. Members of the Provincial Legislature in Toronto were equally concerned to advance the cases of their constituents, although few written records survive. William Mack, MPP for Cornwall, for example, managed, with the consent of the secretary to the provincial government, to place an applicant in employment in the Mimico Institution on the outskirts of Toronto. The applicant, Mr Warner, was a farmer but was employed as

a gardener on the basis that the government secretary presumed that
"Mr. Warner would have sufficient knowledge of vegetable gardening
to be fairly successful in taking this position. It is nothing more than
what most farmers have to do, only that it would be done on a much
larger scale. Probably 30 or 40 acres will have to be utilized and the
main thing will be to show willingness in utilizing and taking charge
of the labour of patients."[36] The secretary also indicated his willingness
to seek an alteration in the Book of Estimates in order that the newly
appointed gardener, notwithstanding his lack of specific qualifications,
might be better remunerated. By such means, the impersonal nature of
official structures was mediated, and even in a fast-growing city such
as Toronto there persisted an intimacy that is not often recognized.
That intimacy was especially obvious at the municipal level, where the
Orange Order, acting as a powerful political machine in City Hall, was
able to inject a particular tone to the conduct of affairs and the construction of civic culture.

The partisan Catholic newspaper the *Irish Canadian* published a series
of condemnatory editorials and feature articles in 1884 outlining the
apparent disadvantages under which Catholics operated in Toronto,
especially in the field of municipal employment. Although hyperbole
was to the fore, there was, nonetheless, sufficient factual material to
lend credence to its argument. In response to a counter-attack from
the *Sentinel*, the Catholic paper further denigrated the activities of the
Orange Order in unflinching language:

> Whether conspiring against the interests of Catholics in the secrecy
> of their Lodge, or pelting them with stones on the public streets, the
> objective of the Orange Order is the same – the exclusion of the Papist
> from honour and emolument, and the elevation of the Brethren to place
> and power. The corporate affairs of this city have been in their grip for
> many years; and the consequence is that nearly all the civic officials are
> Orangemen, and the Corporation itself is simply an Orange Lodge. Can
> this be denied? Look for proof to the City Hall, to the firemen and to
> the police. In any city outside Belfast was ever witnessed anything so
> intensely mean and contemptible as this Orange influence, which bars
> the Catholic from every position to which his ability and good citizen-
> ship fairly entitle him.[37]

The following year, 1885, the *Irish Canadian* returned to the theme of
job discrimination, providing a detailed account of the employment

Table 4.2 Religious characteristics of municipal employees, Toronto, 1885

	No. of employees	Protestant	Catholic
City treasurer	7	7	0
City clerk	7	7	0
Auditor	2	2	0
Engineers	7	7	0
City solicitors	2	2	0
Health inspectors	3	3	0
Weigh master	4	4	0
Licence inspector	1	1	0
Police court	4	4	0
Miscellaneous	7	7	0
Assessors	14	13	1
Tax collectors	11	10	1
Bell ringers	2	2	0
Water works	36	33	3
Total	107	102	5

Source: *Irish Canadian*, 7 and 12 November 1885

pattern in the municipal offices.[38] The data were provided and analysed by post, salary level, religion, and name, and the result clearly vindicated the proposition that Catholics were represented in numbers far below what might have been expected, given the fact that they constituted 18 per cent of the city's population in the census of 1881 and that the range of jobs enumerated was not confined to any single skill set. The City Council consisted of the mayor, Alexander Manning, and thirty-six aldermen, three of whom at the time were Catholic, and this weakness in representative power was reflected directly in the employment structure of the various departments in City Hall (see table 4.2). Of the 107 employees in City Hall, five were Catholic: three of these were in the Water Works, where two were lowly turnkeys and the third was a skilled distribution foreman, hired originally when the Water Works had been under the control of a private company. The two Catholics in the tax collection and assessment departments were part-time employees. No other Catholics had secured permanent municipal employment. By any standards, City Hall presented a cold environment for Catholics.

The position was only slightly better in the firehalls of the city, where four out of seventy-three firemen were Catholic, but among the police the position, at least on the surface, appeared to be more equitable as almost 10 per cent were Catholic. Many of these were direct recruits from the Royal Irish Constabulary, which included a large number of loyal Catholics in its ranks at that time. However, no Catholic held the rank of either officer or non-commissioned officer in the Toronto police force of more than one hundred and fifty men.[39] Geographer William Jenkins has argued that the relative paucity of Catholics in the force reflected a sense of community avoidance, as "working-class Irish Catholics in Toronto had far less interest in policing and other public employment than in Buffalo."[40] The argument for career avoidance has little credence. The evidence is much more indicative of the operation of a prevailing practice of exclusion and a sophisticated practice of patronage.

Toronto police and firemen had long been recognized as Protestant and Orange in their employment characteristics, and this identity proved to be remarkably durable, transcending organizational reforms of both services in the second half of the nineteenth century. As early as the 1840s, more than half of the police force was reckoned to be Orange, as was the police chief, George Allen. At the same time, half of the city's aldermen were also reckoned to be Orangemen, and the two facts were not unrelated. Riotous behaviour in which the police themselves were partisan participants had generated an official demand in the 1850s for professional reform. However, attempts to exclude Orangemen and other members of secret societies from the force failed to find the necessary political support, and, as a compromise, policemen were allowed to maintain Orange affiliation providing they did not allow it to impinge upon their professional work. Oversight of the force was delegated to a three-person commission – the mayor, a police magistrate, and the city recorder. At the outset, two of the three commissioners were Orange, and, in 1859, at least twenty of the fifty-strong force were members of Orange lodges.[41] Power, partisanship, and patronage in the force proved to be remarkably enduring. In the 1930s, allegations akin to those made by the *Irish Canadian* in 1885 were repeated.

The nature and scale of public employment in Toronto, as outlined by the *Irish Canadian*, may be refined and objectively tested for the following decade by reference to relevant manuscript censuses and street directories and to the nominal data that are available for the Orange Order in the city in 1894. At the time Toronto had emerged as the leading city in

English-speaking Canada, its metropolitan position being increasingly evident in its power and influence over the resource frontiers of both the Canadian west and the northern shield. For more than two decades the city had been evolving as a major industrial centre, and, although commercial and service activities still predominated, it was home to more than two thousand manufacturing firms – some of which, such as Massey, Gooderham and Worts, and Inglis, employed several hundred workers. It had a published census population of 144,023 and was not inconsiderable in its ranking among North American urban centres in general. As a metropolitan centre of national importance, Toronto had a complex employment profile in which industry, natural resource exploitation, and banking activities took their place alongside commercial activities and public service occupations. This latter sector, like its private sector counterpart, was expanding rapidly in size and complexity as the nineteenth century drew to a close.

Public Employment, 1894

In post-Confederation Canada, the federal government emerged as a major employer. Parliament, the civil service, and most organs of government were located primarily in the national capital, Ottawa, but regional centres also benefited from an inescapable decentralization of service activities. Toronto's population of federal employees was strongly concentrated in the postal, customs, and revenue services located in the city. The largest of these was the postal service, which, in the 1890s, employed almost three hundred persons, ranging from messengers, letter carriers, and clerks to managers of branch post offices, inspectors, and superintendents. It was a complex, highly structured organization. Letter carriers enjoyed steady and reasonably remunerated employment, and, although they were exposed to the vagaries of weather as they carried their sacks of mail through residential neighbourhoods and commercial districts, their positions were much sought after. Clerks enjoyed an enviable social status, their appointment requiring a level of basic education somewhat higher than that demanded of the carriers, and, in many respects, they typified the essence of lower middle-class Toronto. They were overseen by a small but influential group of inspectors and superintendents who enjoyed both high social status and power. In combination the postal workers represented a significant and recognized portion of "official Toronto," and their religious and ethnic characteristics expressed, and confirmed, a distinct set of civic norms. They were complemented at the interface of public and private services by the managers of branch post offices, where the postal franchise was normally combined with other retail activities such as grocers, jewellers, and hardware merchants, and, uniquely within a federal service staffed almost exclusively by males, women, especially widows, did enjoy a strong representation among this group.

The employment characteristics displayed in table 4.3 for those employed in the Custom House, City Hall, or Post Office are striking. Random chance might have been expected to generate an employment pattern somewhat akin to the demographic characteristics of the city in general – assuming that no one group possessed characteristics that rendered them totally, or partially, unfit to perform the tasks assigned. There is no evidence to suggest that Irish Catholics were inherently unsuitable by virtue of physical or educational abilities for the range of jobs on offer. Irish Catholics were represented among the postal clerks in numbers almost proportionate to their demographic strength, but in all other sectors they were significantly under-represented. In niche occupations requiring little education (letter carriers, messengers, packers, porters, and manual workers) Catholics filled only 9 out of a total of 141 positions. Among the heads of the fourteen departments of the city administration, the ten departments in the Custom House and the eight sections attached to the Post Office, Catholics were not represented at all. The highest-ranked Catholic was the second-in-command in the gas inspector's office – a man of English parentage.

City Hall, another significant employer, would have been responsible for hiring several hundred part-time labourers on a seasonal basis as well as a large cohort of permanent employees. Catholics accounted for 5 per cent of identified full-time municipal employment – a figure that was somewhat akin to that pertaining in Belfast City Hall at that time. The records indicate that this pattern was amended only slightly over the next forty years. Overall, it is evident from the data that, as the nineteenth century drew to a close, contemporary official Toronto had done little to facilitate the employment of Catholics, the overwhelming majority of whom were Irish; by way of contrast, there was a very clear and supportive identification with their Protestant countrymen.

The employment data that form the basis of table 4.3 were developed from a number of sources. Data for the Custom House, Revenue, and Post Office were obtained from the city directory, 1894. Data for municipal employees were obtained from the city directory, augmented

Table 4.3 Religious characteristics of public employees, Toronto, 1894

Grade	Anglican	Meth	Presb	Bapt	Catholic	Other	Total
Post Office							
Manual/unskilled	1	2	2	–	–	–	5
Clerical/skilled	102	52	51	7	22	6	240
Professional	5	4	4	–	–	–	13
Branch PO	9	5	2	1	–	–	17
Total	117	63	59	8	22	6	275
%	43	23	21	3	8	2	100
Customs House/Revenue							
Manual/unskilled	9	5	2	2	2	–	20
Clerical/skilled	36	21	13	2	6	3	81
Professional	12	3	7	2	1	–	25
Total	57	29	22	6	9	3	126
%	45	23	18	5	7	2	100
Municipal							
Clerical/skilled	39	26	18	5	5	4	97
Professional	24	16	10	–	1	1	52
Total	77	50	38	7	9	8	189
%	41	27	20	4	5	4	100
Firemen	38	35	24	5	3	8	113
%	34	31	21	4	3	7	100
Policemen	85	60	52	6	10	3	216
%	39	28	24	3	5	1	100

Source: *City Directory*, 1894; City Council minutes, 1894, 1907; census of population, 1891; *Directory of Orange Lodges*, 1894

by information from the Orange directory, and cross-tabulated with the 1891 and 1901 censuses. The data for firemen were obtained from City Council minutes, and the police force was reconstructed from a 1907 nominal roll of policemen, adjusted for those recorded as having joined the force in or before 1894. This information was also augmented by reference to the Orange register and linked to available manuscript census material. The figure of 216 policemen represents about 80 per cent of the force at that time.[42] In total, the number of identified public employees amounts to almost one thousand. There is no reason to assume that the assembled data are skewed in their derivation, and in combination they provide a detailed reflection of the operation of public policy in the city in the 1890s.

The data for municipal employees presented in table 4.3 are an aggregate of those employed full time by the main departments in the civic administration, including employees based in the City Clerk's Office, the City Solicitor's Office, the City Treasurer's Office, the Licensing Inspectorate, the Medical Health Office, the Fire Department, the Engineer's Department, the City Commissioner's Office, the Assessment Office, and the Water Works. The employment profile was very similar to that demonstrated for the federal services located in the city. In terms of religion the workforce was overwhelmingly Protestant, with Catholics constituting 5 per cent. Only nine Catholics were employed in these city departments, and of those, three were turnkeys, two were assessors, three were clerks, and one was a health inspector. Invariably the head of each department was Protestant, and it would appear that opportunities for promotion were carefully regulated in a manner that did not upset the status quo, for the pattern altered little over the next several decades.

Toronto's firehalls had long been regarded as providing particularly poor opportunities for Catholics, and there were many recorded incidents where the behaviour of firemen was partisan and disruptive of community peace. The small scale of most firehalls, the fact that firemen on call could sleep on site in purpose-built accommodation, and the prevalence of family ties among the firemen engendered sets of close-knit relationships. Firehalls represented a series of micro-communities, and feelings of mutual support were very obvious. The "otherness" of Catholics could not be easily accommodated, and, unsurprisingly, few found employment as firemen. In 1894, out of a total of 113 firemen, only 3 were Catholic, the smallest proportion of any of the five employment sectors analysed in table 4.3. Indeed, their relative position had deteriorated in the decade since the *Irish Canadian* had first published its data. In 1885 there had been 4 Catholics among a total of 73 firemen, and although the number of firemen in the city had increased by more than 60 per cent by 1894, the number of Catholics had declined by one person. This same trend was apparent within the police, where the proportion of Catholics had declined by 2 per cent, 1885–94, despite a marked expansion of the force. Growth in employment opportunities did not facilitate catch-up by Catholics.

Table 4.4 Religious characteristics: City of Toronto and its public employment, 1891, 1894

	Anglican	Meth	Presb	Bapt	Catholic	Other	Total
City of Toronto							
1891	46,804	32,505	27,409	6,909	21,830	6,164	144,023
%	33	23	19	5	15	5	100
Public employees	374	237	195	32	53	28	919
%	41	26	21	3	6	3	100

Source: *City Directory*, 1894; City Council minutes, 1894, 1907; census of population, 1891; *Directory of Orange Lodges*, 1894.

In summary, out of a total of 919 public employees identified in table 4.3, a total of 53, 6 per cent, were Catholic. Ninety professionals were identified within the matrix of employment; one of them was Catholic. Furthermore, it was not simply a case of Catholics being relegated to the ranks of the unskilled – only 2 out of 64 unskilled workers were Catholic. The majority population was privileged over all employment grades. Patronage was not confined to jobs for the elite. The 1891 census had recorded 21,830 Catholics living in the city, 15 per cent of the total population, and it is difficult to envisage a set of random forces that would produce such consistent under-representation of Catholics across such a wide range of occupations.

Protestants were a privileged group within the field of public employment, but within that group further nuances may be discerned. The religious groups that were most advantaged were the Anglicans and Methodists (table 4.4). Presbyterians were about on par with their proportion of the city's population, and Catholics, as noted already, were the most disadvantaged. Toronto's Anglicans and Methodists reflected the legacy of both English and Irish immigration to the city. The Irish arrivals also contained large numbers of Methodists from the more industrialized parts of eastern Ulster; however, the majority of Methodists probably emanated from the ranks of industrial workers from northern England. Presbyterians accounted for less than one-fifth of the city's citizenry, and their relative position reflected the comparative weakness of the contemporary Scottish migration stream to Toronto. Constituting more than half the population of the city, Anglicans and Methodists were the primary influencers of its civic culture – a culture that retained a legacy of distrust of Catholics for reasons that transcended theology to include ethnicity and social class. Catholics were the only major religious group identified with a single nationality, the vast majority of them being Irish by birth or ethnicity. Protestants contained a greater ethnic plurality derived, in the main, from the English, Scottish, Welsh, and Irish regions of the British Isles, although by modern standards they reflected quite a homogeneous cultural background. As the nineteenth century drew to a close, the proportion of immigrants in Toronto's population diminished, and by 1901 more than 70 per cent of the inhabitants had been born in Canada. Yet within that new cohort old values and biases persisted, and preferential patterns denominated earlier in the century survived with surprising vitality.

In 1891, 68 per cent of Torontonians had been born in either Canada or Newfoundland; virtually all of the remainder were natives of the British Isles – England and Wales (16 per cent), Ireland (9 per cent), and Scotland (4 per cent). Only 3 per cent of the citizens had been born elsewhere, mostly in the United States. The city contained little challenge to a culture that was very much British and Irish in derivation. Comparison between its overall demography and that of its public employment (table 4.5) indicates that slightly less than half (49 per cent) of identified public employees in the city were Canadian-born; persons born in Ireland or Britain held 47 per cent of the jobs, although they amounted to only 29 per cent of the overall population. By this analysis, immigrants from the imperial motherland were over-represented by more than half in the allocation of highly desirable full-time posts at municipal or federal levels. The preferential status enjoyed by those born in the imperial motherland was, in part, a by-product of the colonial relationship that channelled those with specific vocational qualifications into specialist niches such as leadership of the police, senior customs officers, and health inspectors. However, unskilled and clerical posts constituted the bulk of the public employment, and, in theory, they should have been equally available to a wide field of applicants, including the Canadian-born. It was patently not the case, and the data indicate that the Irish-born were the most over-represented of all groups, holding a quarter of all jobs although they constituted only 9 per cent of the city's population. Notwithstanding the image of Toronto as "a British city on American soil," there is no evidence of the English acquiring a greater than expected share of public employment. Likewise, being Scottish imparted no general advantage. Toronto was Irish Protestant in its preference for public sector workers.

Table 4.5 Place of birth, Toronto, 1891, and its public employees, 1894

	Ireland	England	Scotland	Canada	Other	Total
Toronto						
1891	13,252	22,801	6,347	93,753	7,870	144,023
%	9	16	4	68	3	100
Public employment						
1894	231	152	45	452	39	919
%	25	17	5	49	4	100

Source: *City Directory*, 1894; City Council minutes, 1894, 1907; census of population, 1891; *Directory of Orange Lodges*, 1894.

Table 4.6 Place of birth of identified public employees, Toronto, 1894

	Ireland	England	Scotland	Canada	Other	Total
Toronto (1891)	13,252	22,801	6,347	93,753	7,850	144,023
%	9	16	4	68	3	100
Post Office	47	52	11	146	19	275
%	17	19	4	53	7	100
Customs/Revenue	30	15	10	63	9	127
%	24	12	8	48	8	100
Municipal	43	46	11	79	9	188
%	32	12	6	42	4	100
Firemen	24	16	2	70	1	113
%	21	14	2	62	1	100
Policemen	87	23	11	94	1	216
%	40	11	5	44	–	100
Total	231	152	45	452	39	919

Source: *City Directory*, 1894; City Council minutes, 1894, 1907; census of population, 1891; *Directory of Orange Lodges*, 1894

The greatest over-representation of the Irish Protestants was to be found among the police, where they amounted to 40 per cent of the force, more than four times their expected proportion (table 4.6). But in all other sectors they were over-represented by factors of between two

Table 4.7 Nativity of parents of identified public employees, Toronto, 1894

	Ireland	England	Scotland	Canada	Other	Total
Toronto (1891)	24%	31%	11%	26%	8%	100%
Customs/Revenue	43%	25%	18%	9%	5%	100%
Post Office	44%	28%	12%	12%	4%	100%
City Hall	44%	36%	11%	5%	4%	100%

Source: *City Directory*, 1894; City Council minutes, 1894, 1907; census of population, 1891; *Directory of Orange Lodges*, 1894.

and three. In the Post Office and City Hall the English outnumbered the Irish in absolute numbers, but proportionate to their numbers in the city the Irish were significantly more over-represented than their English-born fellow citizens. Scots were proportionately over-represented only in the Custom House, where they were very evident at the rank of superintendent. They were strikingly under-represented among the firemen. To have accessed these posts in such disproportionately large numbers, the immigrants, especially the Irish, must have been able to avail themselves of the mechanisms that informed and directed the operation of patronage in the city. Recent arrivals were not disadvantaged by the clientalist system. On the contrary, they would appear to have been advantaged by it.

When the nativity of the parents of the employees is considered (table 4.7), the relatively recent origins of the public sector employees become even more apparent.

In the Post Office, 88 per cent of the employees were either immigrants or the children of immigrants, and the figures for the Custom House and City Hall were 91 per cent and 95 per cent respectively. Furthermore, those of recent Irish origin, i.e., those born in Ireland or having at least one parent born in Ireland, held more than 40 per cent of the jobs in these three sectors, and with almost half of all the jobs they were the overall predominant ethnic group. An Irish accent and Irish attitudes were never far beneath the surface. The under-representation in public employment of those whose parents or previous ancestors had been born in Canada is an unexpected occurrence and one which merits further analysis in another study. It is possible that the preference for private employment exhibited by this population reveals a propensity for greater risk taking, but the hypothesis is unproven. In many ways the easy insertion of British and Irish immigrants into public sector jobs is a demonstration of the colonial nature of the city at the time, and the most apparent filter in operation among them was that of religion, as shown previously in table 4.4.That religion was a factor of public note in City Hall employment is beyond doubt, for not only was it a topic regularly discussed in the newspapers of the day but also data on religious affiliation were officially recorded for specific categories of employment. Nominal records for the police included information on the place of birth and religion of all members from the mid-nineteenth century. Employment records of firemen did not contain such details. However, and especially for the period 1917–34, detailed personnel information was collected annually for the influential City Clerk's Department. That department was, *inter alia*, responsible for attending and writing minutes for all committees of Council, preparing the voters' lists, appointing election officials, and overseeing the counting of votes and scrutinizing all petitions for local improvements. It was the formal repository of the city's records and traditions and was well positioned to ensure continuity of those same traditions. It was a powerful and politically sensitive organ of municipal governance. Personnel records for the department listed all its employees, giving name, marital status, occupation, salary, religion (whether Protestant or Roman Catholic), and British subject status. It was a unique data collection exercise. Table 4.8 has been constructed from data for sample years in the early twentieth century, and, for comparative purposes, it is presented with data for 1884 and 1894. In 1884 the city clerk's department was quite small, consisting of six or seven personnel, but, reflecting the growing scale, complexity, and importance of the city, it doubled in size from nineteen to thirty-nine employees during the period 1917–34.[43] Throughout the period 1884–1934, the management and supervisory positions remained the exclusive prerogative of Protestants, many of them Orangemen. Catholics were very much a minority, and occupied positions of lesser rank. In 1884 there was one Catholic clerk out of a total staff of six. A decade later no Catholics were listed. By 1920 a total of three Catholics were employed out of an expanded staff of twenty-two, and, noticeably, these were all women, employed as telephone operators at salaries equivalent to, or below, that of the (Protestant) office messenger boy. The following year the list was amended to exclude the post of telephone operator from the enumeration – an administrative exclusion prompted by the concerns of those opposed to the employment of Catholics. However, this reclassification of posts within the

Table 4.8 Religious characteristics of the City Clerk's Office, Toronto, 1884, 1894, 1920, and 1930

	1884	1894	1920	1930
City clerk	P	P	P	P
Asst city clerk	P	P	P	P
Sec board	–	–	–	P
Chief clerk	–	–	P	P
Clerk	3 P	5 P	11 P	22 P
	1 RC			
Stenographer	–	–	3 P	P
Tel operator	–	–	3 RC	–
messenger			P	P

Source: *Irish Canadian*, 7 and 12 November 1885; *Toronto City Clerk's Department, Employee Salaries 1917–1934*
Notes: P = Protestant; RC = Catholic

department did not appease all critics, and the mayor received a formal letter of complaint from the worshipful master of Royal George LOL 2340 in June 1925 stating, "We desire to place ourselves on record as being absolutely opposed to the Knights of Columbus' female proté-gés controlling the telephone switchboard at the City Hall and consider that the Protestant majority of this City are entitled to some explanation from the Mayor and Council as to the reason of these anomalies."[44] The same letter complained about the appointment of "Mr. Claude Pearce, Papist and member of The Knights of Columbus, to represent Council on the Board of The Children's Aid Society, said institution being Prot-estant."[45] Notwithstanding this partisan opposition, some clerical posts in the department were allocated, from 1923 onwards, to Catholics, but their numbers remained small – four out of a staff of thirty-five – and their average annual salary remained consistently lower than that of their Protestant colleagues.

Continuity of practice and tradition within the City Clerk's Depart-ment was ensured by the remarkable longevity of the serving city clerks. Only eight men had held the office in the first century of Toron-to's history, creating a powerful institutional memory. Some of the city clerks held office for remarkably long periods of time; most had spent their whole career in City Hall. Arguably this permanent civil service was even more important than elected officials in operating the system of civic governance and ensuring a continuity of tradition within it. Between 1884 and 1948, three men – John Blevins, W.A. Littlejohn, and J.W. Somers – covered the sixty-four-year period. Littlejohn may have been an Orangeman; Blevins and Somers certainly were. When he died in office at the age of eighty-four in 1948, J.W. Somers merited an unprecedented four-page obituary in the minutes of City Council, in which it was formally recorded:

> He has been the mentor of every Mayor and every member who has sat in City Council. His long experience in Municipal Office since 1884, extending as it did over the term of office of 27 Mayors, had given him a wealth of knowledge of parliamentary procedure and of municipal etiquette, second to none in Canada ... Blest with a retentive memory, Mr. Somers could recall with consummate ease, the established tradition and custom of former City Councils. From his encyclopaedic storehouse of memory, he was able to advise and enlighten the members of Council on many perplexing municipal matters, and sometimes to suggest the correct procedure and practice in dealing with municipal problems of great political import.[46]

The relative insignificance of Catholics in the City Clerk's Office, and their total absence in some years, do not convey a convincing picture of advancement and acceptance of Catholics. By any standard, they were still located at the margins of "official Toronto." This, together with the analysis of public employment presented earlier in this chapter, calls into question the degree to which the Catholic population of the city were successfully integrating into the mainstream of civic culture. It is possible that there was greater integration in the worlds of private business and the professions, where Catholics may have faced fewer obstacles than they did in the realm of public employment. Data for support of this possibility, however, remain somewhat sparse and are sometimes contradictory.

Quantitative analysis of the 1871 manuscript census by historians Gordon A. Darroch and Michael D. Ornstein has shown that Irish Catholics were represented in Canadian society at all levels, and, although they were unquestionably over-represented among the labouring class, they were present in large numbers in the skilled and business classes. In general Darroch and Ornstein's analysis reflects for Irish Catholics a much more complex social profile than that of an impoverished urban proletariat.[47] In urban centres of more than thirty thousand population, the Irish Catholics were found to be particularly evident among the manufacturing/merchant grouping and among artisans and the semi-skilled, and in all of these categories their percentage representation was very similar to that of Irish Protestants. However, Irish Protestants were twice as likely to engage in professional and white-collar occupations as their Catholic counterparts. The Darroch and Ornstein study is specific to the 1871 census and does not purport to indicate social mobility over time. No similar study currently exists for later census years. Neither does their study contain specific reference to Toronto. Fortunately, McGowan has provided a detailed longitudinal analysis of Irish Catholics in Toronto and he makes a number of challenging statements about social change within that cohort.

The data published by Darroch and Ornstein for 1871 and those produced by McGowan for 1890, 1910, and 1920 are not precisely comparable, but they are useful as indicators of broad trends. The 1871 data were generated from a structured sampling of the manuscript census of that year, and the information presented in table 4.9 refers to the position of Catholic Irish in urban Canada in general. It is neither province- nor city-specific, but the authors did enter the caveat that the degree of provincial variance was considered to be small and, by implication, Toronto was not judged to be unique. On the other hand, McGowan's study is specific to Toronto and is focused on the Catholic Irish as a distinctive group. It does not allow for comparisons with other ethnic or religious groups. His data are derived from a careful and detailed analysis of heads of households recorded in the assessment rolls for selected Catholic parishes in Toronto. Further refining the data through the employment of surnames, he reconstructed a Catholic population that was Irish in origin and not distorted by recent immigration, particularly from southern Europe. His data set excludes family members who were not the head of household, although otherwise they may have been active participants in the workforce, but the extent to which this causes a generational bias in the observed data is indeterminate.

The data generated by McGowan have been adjusted in the present study to exclude persons with no registered occupation, e.g., heads of households who were recorded as pensioners, widowed, and gentlemen, and those for whom no data were available. The size of this excluded group is not inconsiderable – in 1920 it ranged between 12 per cent and 28 per cent of the parish heads of household. In some parishes it was a group that expanded more rapidly than the employed population. In Our Lady of Lourdes parish, for example, the percentage of heads of household described as widowed or spinsters increased from 12.5 in 1890 to 23.1 in 1920, probably a reflection of the aging profile of heads of households recorded in the assessment rolls. Exclusion of these non-occupational categories makes analysis of occupational trends more obvious and allows for more relevant comparisons with the model established in the Darroch and Ornstein study.

There is a broad sense of agreement between the Darroch and Ornstein depiction of the national occupational characteristics of the Catholic Irish in 1871 and that produced by McGowan for Toronto in 1890. Occupational groups follow the same rank ordering, with the exception of the skilled and semi-skilled groups, where differences in definition may account for much of the variance. McGowan has identified the period 1887–1922 as a period of great occupational and residential change among Toronto's Catholic Irish, but it may be argued that when his data are adjusted to remove heads of household with no declared occupation a somewhat static picture of Catholic Irish social mobility emerges. In 1890 approximately 62 per cent of the Catholic Irish group could be described as unskilled or semi-skilled. Some modest improvement was evident over the next thirty years, but by 1920, 50 per cent of the group could be placed in these two occupational categories. The marginal occupational status still attributable to half of the Catholic Irish in 1920 was reminiscent of the national position identified for the 1860s by Darroch and Ornstein, on which they commented, "the Irish Catholics did stand out as the one distinctly different nationality group, with 60 percent remaining labourers over a decade [1861–71] compared to just 23 percent of Irish Protestants and 42 percent of Germans."[48]

Those classified in table 4.9 as belonging to skilled or artisanal categories registered virtually no change in the period 1890–1920. The only category to display a significant improvement over the period of McGowan's study was the white collar/clerical group. The growth in the clerical profession must be interpreted in the context of a city that was rapidly developing as a commercial centre of national importance. This major structural shift in urban function generated an ever-increasing demand for clerical workers, and the Catholic Irish were able to take advantage of the new possibilities. However, as will be demonstrated later, there is reason to believe that the expansion of this occupational category was even more pronounced among the majority Protestant population in the city.McGowan's adjusted data reveal stagnation in the relative position of Catholics among the professional elite in the city – the teaching profession excepted. Catholics would appear to have made little progress in fields such as architecture, civil engineering, medicine,

Table 4.9 Percentage distribution of occupations of Irish Catholics in Canada, 1871, and Toronto (some parishes), 1890, 1910, and 1920

	Manufacturer/ merchant	Professional	White collar	Artisan	Semi- skilled	Unskilled labourer
Darroch & Ornstein (1871)	11.3	3.9	6.0	33.8	10.7	34.3
McGowan (1890)	13.5	1.4	9.5	13.9	20.4	41.3
McGowan (1910)	12.4	1.1	15.8	15.4	21.3	34.1
McGowan (1920)	12.1	2.3	20.6	14.4	22.2	28.4

Source: Darroch and Ornstein, "Ethnicity and Occupational Structure," 324; McGowan, *The Waning of the Green*, 34
Note: The percentage (2.3) recorded as farmers by Darroch and Ornstein has been subsumed into the labouring/unskilled category to align with the classification employed by McGowan. Servants have also been subsumed into this category for the same reason.
Note: McGowan's data have been adjusted to exclude pensioners, gentlemen, and widowed and those without employment, as these groups are not apparent in the Darroch and Ornstein study.

and the university. On the other hand, they had established an early strength in the merchant/manufacturing group, and they retained but did not build on this over the period 1890–1920. This characteristic has been identified also by Brian P. Clarke, who noted that in the 1860s and 1870s the Irish Catholics garnered an evident strength among the businesses of the city, excelling in particular as owners of taverns and hotels, small building contractors, and service providers. "Petty capitalism, rather than the professions or white-collar occupations, was the main avenue for Irish-Catholic mobility out of the working class,"[49] and in the process, the community of co-religionists developed an apparent degree of self-reliance. The strength of the Catholics in the business professions may reveal two distinct processes – one reflecting integrative forces, the other reflecting the direct opposite. Entrepreneurs such as the Co Armagh–born Catholic immigrant Frank Smith did emerge from the Irish community, and his achievements were of national significance. Socially and politically, men such as Smith were part of Canada's Anglo elite, counting men of all religions among their friends and business colleagues. But their numbers were small. Much more common in the Catholic world of business were the shopkeepers, cab owners, undertakers, tavern keepers, and boarding-house owners who drew much of their trade from within their own community and who were introspective rather than integrative in outlook.

Geographically, Toronto Catholics did not retreat to residential ghettoes, and, although a few small clusters did emerge, their overall distribution pattern was one of high dispersion and their propensity for home ownership remained above average. However, as Clarke has remarked, the "Irish-Catholic ghetto was less a place than a state of mind."[50] Arguably that state of mind reflected a vibrant self-conscious ethnic population that was distinguished and nurtured by a deep religious faith and a separate school system – institutions that they guarded passionately.

But the strength of their distinctive self-identity was not unrelated to the attitude of the Protestant majority that was conscious of the "otherness" of their Catholic neighbours and often hesitant about making space for them in their lives and in the official structures that they controlled and operated. The relative weakness of Irish Catholics within the Toronto elite in the late 1880s was obvious to contemporaries and was specifically commented upon by Timothy Warren Anglin, a Catholic, and a recent migrant to the city. His status as former speaker of the legislature in New Brunswick warranted his inclusion within the higher echelons of Toronto society, but he found few co-religionists among his fellow guests at the elite social gatherings.[51] Two parallel universes, two solitudes, operated at a number of geographical and social scales in contemporary Canada. In many ways, the Irish Catholic community was beset by a garrison mentality that was a mirror image of that of the Protestant community. The often-expressed political aspiration of religious and secular leaders of the Catholic community was to achieve a percentage of patronage posts and public service employment commensurate with their percentage share of the total population. They did not seek to exceed the boundaries suggested by demography. In both communities, maintenance of the divide was codified not in law but in a matrix of a learned behaviour informed by history, rooted in distrust, and ever fearful of the unknowns that might follow from a more integrative approach. Within Toronto, people knew full well which employers operated a restricted hiring policy, which taverns attracted a clientele of like-minded citizens, and which undertaker was most in sympathy with the religious mores of the community. Irish and British immigrants, coming from a narrow range of geographical sources, found the civic culture of Toronto to be resoundingly familiar, and the tools and skills needed to navigate it were virtually innate. They could read and navigate the social geography of the city with consummate ease. The community profile suggested by table 4.9 raises many questions about the nature of civic culture in Toronto in the two generations before 1920, and more than anything else it is one that was reflected in the pattern of public employment in Toronto. The processes that generated and perpetuated that pattern are more complex and less discernible.

Perpetuation of the system was facilitated by provision of a constant stream of rewards to loyal voters and also by a mindset that saw no ethical problem in identifying certain jobs and board positions as being reserved for the brethren. An example of such practice was detailed in the hostile columns of the *Irish Canadian* in respect of leading Orangeman William Bell, an Englishman by birth. Bell served as an alderman for St Stephen's Ward, 1881–3, and during his last year on council he was appointed tax collector for the same ward. In the following year he secured election as a school board trustee for St Mark's Ward but held on to the tax collector post until his son was able to succeed him. During these years, it was alleged that he was able to secure a road improvement costing $5,280 along the frontage of his property.[52] This trickle-down effect of patronage helped create a web-like sphere of influence that was mutually reinforcing and self-sustaining, as long as the dominance of the group in charge was not undermined by either external threat or internal change. It created a civic culture that was most evidently Protestant, heavily infused with Orangeism, and recognized for its sectional inclusiveness. Its corollary was the construction of an environment within which Catholics had only a weak grip on power, either formal or informal. A desire to look after one's own kind underpinned the culture, and, although a strident anti-Catholicism did inform the actions of some, the overall culture was more reflective of a common consensus that Catholics were different, imbued with a sense of otherness, and preferment was owed in the first instance to those who were deemed to share in the common majority culture. The prevailing system of patronage allocation, operated through a sophisticated and effective mechanism of personal contacts, directed introductions, and selective information, was self-fulfilling and supportive of the maintenance of the status quo. Catholics, as well as Protestants, recognized the checks and balances that operated within this regulated system. Indeed it is striking that when the civic culture was finally challenged in its entirety, and successfully reformed by a new City Hall administration, the agent of change was not a Catholic but a Jew, Nathan Phillips, who campaigned on the slogan that he would be mayor for "all the people," not a representative of a minority that had won the right to share space at the font of municipal power. The population of Catholics was, and remains, much greater than that of Jews in the city, but they have singularly failed to elect one of their co-religionists to the office of mayor. Today, so much change has been wrought in Toronto that the issue of the religion of a candidate for mayor is devoid of significance, and in that rests the strongest evidence of the demise of the older culture of sectarian divisiveness. The reform of municipal politics, and its attendant power over patronage, created a new dynamic in which the old divisions of Catholics versus Protestants were minimized and became increasingly redundant in defining power blocs within the city. Furthermore, by the second half of the twentieth century the traditional ethnic homogeneity of Catholics had been eroded by the influx of immigrants from a plurality of regions and cultures. Italian, Portuguese, Hungarian, and later Caribbean and Asian Catholics altered beyond recognition the nature of the Catholic community in Toronto. Episcopal power remained in the hands of the Irish somewhat longer, but the sense of a distinctive ethno-religious power bloc no longer existed. Space at the table of civic power and culture would be claimed and allocated on different premises thereafter.

5 The Emergence of a New Order: Toronto's Orangemen at the Close of the Nineteenth Century

As the nineteenth century drew to a close, Toronto reflected with pride on a century of urban growth and achievement. It had prospered through the hard work and ingenuity of its people and a fortuitous geographical location that had allowed it to tap into a diverse array of British and American capital, while simultaneously developing a controlling grip on the regional economies of central Canada and the emerging west. By 1900 more than two hundred thousand people lived within its urban boundary, and with its growing industrial, commercial, wholesaling, and administrative power it merited the title of "the nearly national metropolis."[1] It was a city of continental significance. Yet beneath its economic success, and its relentless drive for progress, it remained at heart a conservative place whose preoccupation with public morality, temperance, and maintenance of the sanctity of the Lord's Day had generated the epithet "Toronto the Good." The city was as renowned for its display of church spires as for its business streetscapes.[2] The coexistence of these two ideologies, unfettered private and corporate entrepreneurship and suffocating public morality, lent a distinctive personality to the city – simultaneously driving economic expansion and underpinning a dour tone of municipal governance. Coincidentally, the city's most powerful voluntary society, the Orange Order, also celebrated its first century of existence in the 1890s, and, like the city with which it was closely associated, the Order too had experienced a prolonged process of rapid growth, development, and transformation of status and identity. On the cusp of a new century it was obvious to most citizens that the identity of Toronto and that of the Order were intimately entwined.

In 1884 Toronto had celebrated, with some style, its first fifty years of city status. It was a year of economic depression, but the city fathers, nonetheless, managed to produce an appropriate array of celebratory functions and pageantry, including an elaborate procession of officials and organizations deemed to be authentically reflective of life in the metropolis.[3] Chaired by a former mayor, eleven committees with a combined membership of 272 designed and managed the city's anniversary celebrations. Friday 4 July was designated "The Benevolent Societies' Day" and it was marked by a parade of "Uniformed and un-uniformed Lodges of Masons, Odd Fellows, Knights of Pythias, Knights of Malta, Foresters; National Societies, Orange Societies, Emerald and Irish Catholic Benevolent Societies, etc., etc."[4] Further evidence of the official recognition of the Orange Order was demonstrated a week later when, on the occasion of the annual celebration of the Twelfth of July, national flags were hoisted from St Lawrence Hall, the Queen's Park legislative building, and all the firehalls in the city.[5]

The Orange Order was an omnipresent and highly visible component of city life. Its public parades and the political utterances of its leaders attracted detailed and increasingly favourable newspaper coverage. The role of the organization in the governance of the city was obvious to all. Public perception of the Order had changed. The raw confrontational image of earlier times had diminished and there was certainly no shame in declaring one's Orange credentials. In keeping with the Order's confidence and social standing, it published a directory of its officers and more than three thousand members in 1894. Supported by dozens of business advertisements, ranging from barristers to regalia suppliers, the directory provides an invaluable insight into the life of the city and the standing of the members whose names and addresses were recorded within it.

The Register and Directory of the Loyal Orange Association of the City of Toronto 1894 [6] contains the names and addresses of the officers of the County Orange Lodge of Toronto, the five District Lodges, and fifty-five local or primary lodges within the city. A complete list of members and their addresses for forty-five local lodges, a total of 3,094 Orangemen, was published together with details of a further 130 officers attached to the other ten lodges. Some duplication of names arose, owing to the fact that officers might be listed in more than one capacity, or were returned as both officers and members.[7] After adjustment for duplications, a final population of 3,168 Orangemen may be identified. In its report on the Twelfth of July parade of the previous year, the *Sentinel* had published the numbers parading in each lodge, and from that source one can determine that at least 702 members belonged to the ten lodges for which the directory had published incomplete information. Many others, wearing their sashes, stood on the sidewalks that Twelfth – having been deterred from parading by the inclement weather.[8] A projected total population of about 4,000 Orangemen in Toronto at the time is therefore reasonable. In the present analysis, the names in the Orange directory have been cross-referenced to the Toronto city directories for the period 1892–5 and also to the manuscript censuses of 1881, 1891, and 1901. In some instances the roll books and proposition books of local lodges have been used to further develop a profile of the Order in the contemporary city. Of the 3,168 members, 92 per cent have been identified in the supporting records, 1 per cent had moved to specified locations outside the city, and almost 7 per cent could not be identified with any degree of certainty – probably due to a combination of geographical mobility, death, and inaccurate recording at the outset. The data were then assembled in a database that included a wealth of information including name, lodge number, lodge rank/office, address, marital status, age, occupation, religion, place of birth, place of father's birth, place of mother's birth, and literacy status.

Unquestionably, the database represents a unique source for interrogating the nuances of both the Order and contemporary Toronto. By implication, it provides fresh light on the evolution of Canadian society in general.

The occupational and social background of the Orange Order in Toronto has been the subject of considerable comment and debate, but for the most part the analyses have been based on comparatively small sample populations. Cecil J. Houston and William J. Smyth selected a sample of 246 Orangemen from the directory for their 1980 analysis, and from that they demonstrated the complexities of the occupational characteristics of the organization.[9] At the time of their analysis, the 1891 manuscript census records were not available and it was impossible to determine additional variables such as place of birth, ethnicity, denominational affiliation, and age. In a separate study, Gregory S. Kealey analysed a larger population of 657 members, but his names were garnered not from a single unified sample but from the membership lists of four lodges ranging over a twenty-year period, 1872–92.[10] The changing nature of the city, the questionable representational character of the four lodges, and the evident evolution of the Order during that twenty-year period did not feature in his analysis. The present study, specific to 1894, involves at least 80 per cent of all Orangemen in the city at the time, and is unprecedented for the scale and comprehensiveness of its social data. Confidence in the general applicability of the findings is warranted.

The organizational complexity of the Order is clearly discernible from the directory. The County Lodge, which had responsibility for the overall coordination of Orange activities in the city, met quarterly in the County

Table 5.1 Orange District Lodge structure, Toronto, 1894

Centre District
Dates of meeting: fourth Wednesday of March, June, September, and December
Place of meeting: County Orange Hall, 59 Queen Street East
Local lodges: 22
West Toronto District
Dates of meeting: first Tuesday of January, April, July, and October
Place of meeting: Orange Hall, Euclid Avenue
Local lodges: 15
East Toronto District
Dates of meeting: second Tuesday of January, April, July, and October
Place of meeting: St George's Hall, corner of Queen and Berkeley Streets
Local lodges: 8
North Toronto District
Dates of meeting: fifth Thursday in each quarter
Place of meeting: Jackson's Hall, Yonge Street
Local lodges: 6
North-West District
Dates of meeting: second Tuesday in each quarter
Place of meeting: Dawe's Hall, Bloor Street West
Local lodges: 4

Source: *Register and Directory of the Loyal Orange Association of Toronto*, 1894.

Orange Hall at 59 Queen Street East on the fourth Wednesday in January, April, July, and October. In addition, an annual general meeting was convened on the first Tuesday in February. Membership of the County Lodge consisted of three *ex officio* members, the county master, secretary, and chaplain together with the masters of five District Lodges. The District Lodges, whose spatial positioning was designed to keep pace with the expanding limits of the city and the boundaries of federal parliamentary ridings, provided a vehicle for disseminating policies of the County Lodge to the fifty-five local lodges in the county jurisdiction and were composed of representatives of all subsidiary lodges. The five District Lodges met on a quarterly basis, on prescribed days that did not conflict with the schedule of either each other or the County Lodge, thereby facilitating visits of officers within the organization (table 5.1).

The fifty-five local lodges were grouped into the five districts, but the location of their meetings was determined by the availability of suitable accommodation and by local community tradition. Twenty-one lodges in the Centre District met in the County Orange Hall on Queen Street East; the remaining lodge met in Chosen Friends Hall at the corner of Yonge Street and Yorkville Avenue – a venue close to the residence of its past master, John F. Loudon, then current director of ceremonies in the County Lodge and, by day, a municipal inspector of drains. The Western District, serving the growing middle-class communities to the west of Spadina Avenue, accommodated eleven of its lodges in its own hall on Euclid Avenue; the remainder met in a variety of halls and privately owned facilities along College Street and Queen Street West. Local community-based halls were the preferred meeting place for the lodges of the Eastern District, and only two of its lodges met in the County Orange Lodge. The two most recent districts – North Toronto and North-West Toronto – drew their membership from the geographical margins of the city and tended to use privately owned halls in more established locations such as Yonge and Bloor, College and Spadina, Bathurst and Bloor, and Lisgar and Queen, as well as the centrally located County Orange Hall. Meetings of all local lodges were scheduled for one night per month, but special events such as preparing to march on the Twelfth, an annual church parade, or arranging to process at the funeral of a deceased member, necessitated additional meetings. As a general rule, all meetings were held in the evening on a Monday to Friday basis. In the event that the Twelfth of July fell on a Sunday, the annual parade was held on either the previous Saturday or the following Monday. However, ceremonial church parades, with Orangemen parading in full regalia along the main arteries of the city, did take place on the Sabbath.

The order of business at a monthly meeting was conducted in accordance with the organization's constitution: "Lodge to be opened with prayer. Lecture to be read. Minutes of former meeting read. Members to be proposed. Candidates to be initiated. Public business concerned with principles, honour and prosperity of the Association discussed. Roll called and dues collected. Lecture repeated. Lodge closed with prayers."[11] Only the processing of names of initiates and those against whom disciplinary proceedings had been commenced provided a local variation on a most standardized template. However, in the nature of things it would have been surprising if socializing, alliance formation, and the pursuit of opportunities for patronage did not occur in the comfort of the hall and amid the camaraderie of like-minded men. In an era when socially acceptable gatherings tended to be limited to church services, private clubs, and fraternal societies, the Orange Order filled an important niche. The relative importance of that niche was, of course, a reflection of the significance attached to politico-religious sentiment in a city that had been shaped by a distinctive set of historical and geographical forces.

Lodge meetings were an opportunity for conviviality and socializing in familiar company, and while few members would have attended all scheduled meetings, a residual group did provide continuity and organizational stability. The 1894 directory indicates that lodge size varied enormously within the city, ranging from the smallest with 19 members to the largest with 213, providing an average membership of 72 members. Three-quarters of the lodges were in the range of 19–50 members, and, within such a scale, it would have been comparatively easy to make and maintain friendships. It is difficult to determine the factors that dictated lodge size, but newer suburban lodges in the early stages of formation were understandably smallest. Personal factors, such as the quality of the leadership provided by the master, disagreements over internal election results, and the aging profile of some long-established lodges could also lead to stagnation or the emergence of breakaway groups who might request authority to establish a new lodge in the neighbourhood. Constraints imposed by the size of available halls suggested an optimum membership of about fifty; anything in excess of that meant that the meetings would have to be held in the County Hall or in other large city centre venues that were not necessarily convenient to the residential neighbourhood of the membership.

Each primary lodge in the city was identifiable by a number that related to its registration in the *Register of Warrants*, which recorded all warrants that had been issued with the authority of the Grand Lodge of British America since its inception in 1830.[12] No primary lodge could be formed without such a sealed warrant, properly authenticated by the signature of a number of established Orangemen, one of whom would become the master of the new primary lodge. LOL 4, the oldest lodge in Toronto, was the proud bearer of a warrant number issued in 1831, and the most recent lodge, LOL 1388, derived its authority from a warrant issued two years earlier, in 1892. In addition to their warrant number, the primary lodges were free to add a title of their choice. The titles chosen by the individual lodges were generally reflective of the history of the organization either in Canada or in Ireland: epic figures and events were the most common choices, although, given the immigrant background of many members, the place names of Ulster were also popular. With the exception of four very recent establishments, all lodges in the city had adopted a name as an extension to their warrant number. The names may be classified as in table 5.2.

Table 5.2   Classification of Orange lodge names

Historic Orange figures and places
Nassau LOL 4
Prince of Orange LOL 111
William Johnston LOL 127
William LOL 140
Schomberg LOL 212
Torbay LOL 361
Duke of York LOL 396
Cumberland True Blues LOL 621
Rev George Walker LOL 791
Lord Erne LOL 804

Canadian Orange figures and places
Armstrong LOL 173
Parkdale True Blue LOL 207
Brockton LOL 255
McKinley LOL 275
York LOL 375
Maple Leaf LOL 455
West End True Blues LOL 551
Cameron LOL 613
D'Arcy Boulton LOL 657
Northern Star LOL 778
Medcalf LOL 781
Toronto LOL 800
McLeod LOL 821
Queen City LOL 875
Beaver LOL 911
Dalton McCarthy LOL 1084

Others
Temperance LOL 301
Virgin LOL 328
Luther Pioneer LOL 479
Sentinel LOL 506
Wycliffe LOL 585

Irish Orange places
Boyne LOL 127
Enniskillen LOL 387
Ulster Heroes LOL 675
Enniskillen Purple Star LOL 711
Magherafelt Purple Star LOL 864
Belfast Purple Star LOL 875
Sons of Portadown LOL 919

Biblical
Joshua LOL 154
Ebenezer LOL 157
Gideon's Chosen Few LOL 342
Star of the East
Occident LOL 954

British Royal Family and peerage
Eldon LOL 136
Brunswick LOL 404
Lansdowne LOL 469
Prince Alfred LOL 50l
Stanley LOL 560
Victoria LOL 588
Royal Oak LOL 966
Britannia LOL 1388

Source: *Register and Directory of the Orange Association of the City of Toronto*, 1894.

Almost a quarter of the adopted lodge names referred to Canadian places or Canadian Orangemen such as Medcalf (a former mayor of Toronto), Cameron (a previous national leader of the organization), and Dalton McCarthy (a prominent member of Parliament and leading anti-Catholic activist of the day). The preponderance of Canadian nomenclature was a revealing indication of the established strength and accrued history of Orangeism within the city. Understandably, figures and places intrinsic to the original iconography of the Orange Order were also to the fore, with King William's landing at Torbay and his subsequent victories in battles at Enniskillen and the Boyne being prominent. Iconic figures in the development of Protestantism – Luther and Wycliffe – together with members of the Royal Family (Queen Victoria and Prince Alfred) were commemorated, as were prominent lords of the realm such as the Duke of Cumberland (heir to the throne and the grand master of the Irish and British Orange Order in the early nineteenth century), and Lord Lansdowne (governor-general, 1883–8) and his successor, Lord Stanley (governor-general, 1888–93). Given the dependence of Orange ritual upon Old Testament writings, the inclusion of names such as Joshua, Gideon, Ebenezer, and Occident were common not only to the Toronto lodges but also in Ireland, Scotland, England, Australia, and wherever else the Order existed. Many of these biblical names were common also to Masonic lodges of the time. Other names referred to the membership requirements of specific lodges; e.g., Temperance Lodge prohibited the use of alcohol and Virgin Lodge comprised young unmarried men. Unsurprisingly, Ulster places such as Belfast, Magherafelt, and Portadown were also to the fore. In 1894 the membership of these three lodges included many recent arrivals from Ireland, and they were known in the city for lending a particular stridency to the Orange voice. Scrutiny of the forty-eight members of Portadown LOL reveals that twenty-two were immigrants from Ireland, fifteen were from Canada, and the remainder were drawn from England and Scotland. It was not exclusively linked with Ulster settlers in the city but the Irish were the dominant group (see figure 5.1).

In a similar vein, migrants from Newfoundland lent a particular identity to a lodge in the western suburbs of the city. LOL 966 met each month in the Western District Hall on Euclid Avenue and had a total of thirty-three members, eighteen of whom were migrants from Newfoundland and five of whom bore the distinctive family name Le Drew. In part the lodge represented a classic case of kin-based migration from a peripheral region, and the social activities and networking

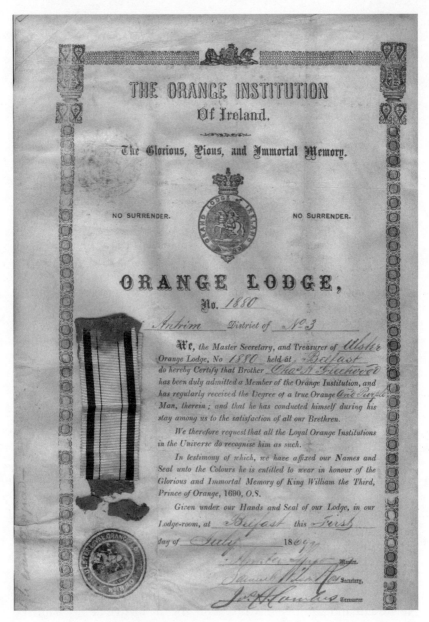

5.1 Orange certificate, Belfast, 1869

opportunities would have been extremely useful for the group, many of whom worked as carpenters and builders. However, LOL 966 was not restricted to Newfoundlanders – eight Ontarians and six Englishmen were also members. Furthermore, not all Orange Newfoundlanders belonged to it, for, in total, there were fifty-nine Newfoundland Orangemen in Toronto and forty-one of them were scattered across half a dozen lodges other than LOL 966. In general, the conviviality of lodge evenings attracted, and retained, the support of hundreds of recent arrivals in the city, but while some of their songs may have been tinged with emigrant nostalgia, their repertoire also included "The Maple Leaf Forever," a distinctive Canadian ode that was particularly popular given its composition by the master of a local lodge. The shaping of a Canadian future as well as commemoration of a romanticized past were celebrated in the Orange festivities.

Individual lodges, through their particular configurations of occupational, social, and ethnic profiles and specific missions, constructed distinctive organizational personalities and identities for themselves, but their images and identities were neither exclusive nor fixed. They tended to alter over time, and after a decade or more the original intent of the founding officers would have been diluted. New recruits, the requirements of a new generation, and neighbourhood transformations all brought about change in the local community lodges. Lodge identities, however, were sufficiently distinctive within the overarching homogeneity of the organization to engender friendly rivalries, competition in public parades, and distinctive lodge hospitality on festive occasions. Recruitment drives by individual lodges, targeting the workplace, church communities, and personal friendship networks, created a fluidity in membership patterns and precluded any narrow association of geographical neighbourhood and lodge membership. Despite its rapid population growth and an expansion of municipal limits through annexation of adjoining suburbs, Toronto remained a city of modest scale with a total of 144,023 inhabitants being recorded in the 1891 census. In the mid-1880s the city stretched no more than six kilometres by three and even after the boundary changes of 1883–93 the city limits extended to no more than twelve kilometres from east to west and four kilometres from north to south.[13] In 1894 electric streetcars, replacing their horse-drawn predecessors, made movement within the city even easier. Commuting to work, or commuting to lodge, did not require a huge investment of time, and although the city was home to several distinctive neighbourhoods such as the working-class communities of the Ward adjacent to the commercial core, Cabbagetown along the Don Valley in the east, and the middle-class suburb of Parkdale to the west, there would appear to have been less rigid demarcation of residential districts than was the case in contemporary Belfast or the American industrial cities to the south. The social composition of the Orange lodges in the city reflected this fluidity. In very many ways the lodges were a microcosm of the city at work and at play.

Occupational Characteristics

The occupational background of Orangemen has been the subject of frequent comment, but less frequent analysis. In the decades before Confederation, the Order attracted public condemnation from Tories and Reformers alike, and in public depictions Orangemen were most usually portrayed as low-class immigrants, responsible for introducing Irish bigotry and sectarianism to the New World. Orangemen were perceived as marginal to the growing bourgeois respectability of the colonial settlements. In part, the image was derived from those occasions when the Order entered the public eye – parades, riots, and rancorous debates – and, arising from the associated disturbances, the epithet "Orange" was applied indiscriminately to all protagonists, many of whom were never members of the organization. With its ascent to municipal power, especially after the 1864 mayoralty victory of Francis Henry Medcalf, the social complexity of the Order became more recognizable and more recognized. Houston and Smyth have emphasized this evolving complexity in their analysis of sample lodge data for the last third of the nineteenth century,[14] and, while accepting that the majority of members belonged to skilled, semi-skilled, and unskilled categories, they took issue with the class interpretation implicit in Kealey's description of the contemporary Order as being "An organization largely composed of plebeians."[15] Class-consciousness is, of course, not synonymous with occupational classification; each is susceptible to the subjectivities of the analytical method. Within the present study the classification of occupational categories is similar to that devised by Peter Goheen for his 1970 study of Toronto and subsequently replicated by Mark G. McGowan in his 1999 study of Toronto's Irish Catholic community.[16] A minor adjustment has been made in the present study by the inclusion of five farmers as members of the business class on the basis that they were supplying milk and vegetable products to the urban market. Furthermore, twenty-one gardeners were included among the

Table 5.3 Occupational classification of Toronto Orangemen, 1894

Occupation	Number	Percentage
Professional	170	5.8
Business	368	12.6
Clerical	514	17.6
Skilled	401	13.7
Semi-skilled	815	27.8
Unskilled	658	22.5
Total	2,926	100.0

Source: *Register and Directory of the Loyal Orange Association of the City of Toronto*, 1894.
Note: Some Orangemen within the data set were retired and did not return an occupation.

semi-skilled rather than among the unskilled. Undoubtedly a sense of arbitrary judgment underpins any such classificatory system,[17] but the logic intrinsic to that devised by Goheen is acceptable, and especially so in the present instance where a static analysis rather than an evaluation of social mobility through time is being attempted.[18]

The occupational structure of the Orange Order, table 5.3, was broadly, but not precisely, reflective of that of the city in general. Toronto in 1894 was a city in transition. Its industrial base had expanded considerably in the previous decade and a half with the range of industries increasing and the nature of individual enterprises developing in both size and complexity. An older structure of workshops and small producers remained, but industrialists such as Massey, who employed seven hundred in his agricultural machinery plant in 1891, and the Ontario Bolt Company with five hundred workers represented the future.[19] In general, however, even the largest enterprises could not rival the scale of enterprises in contemporary Belfast. Orangemen were to be found across the range of industries, but concentrations within individual enterprises are discernible. Eight were identified as case-makers in the American Watch Company, six were recorded as working for Taylor Safes, eleven were returned as cigar makers, and many of the fifty-one described as machinists were employed in Massey's. Forty-four Orangemen were identified as printers, but their employers included a range of publishers such as the *Globe*, the *Telegram*, the *Sentinel*, and a number of church-related publications. Orangemen were not limited to any single industrial enterprise and they certainly did not exercise a monopoly in any skilled or semi-skilled niches.

About half of the Orangemen could be described as semi-skilled or unskilled, and in that respect Kealey's identification of a strong proletarian element is accurate. However, the other half of the membership covered a very wide range of occupations, and, strikingly, the number who may be described as clerical exceeded by a considerable margin those involved in skilled manual trades. The prominence of the former was a reflection of the patronage that had directed many to the Customs House, the Post Office, and City Hall, and it was a critical component in the growing sense of respectability projected by the Order. The lower-middle-class component of clerical workers took its place in an organization where there was also an established cohort of business owners and a sizeable cohort of professionals, including many doctors and barristers. The number of businessmen was almost as large as that of skilled workers and was composed mostly of the proprietors of modest-sized enterprises such as contractors, cab owners, and retail and wholesale merchants. The elite of the city's entrepreneurial class, Eaton, Massey, and Gooderham, were not members.

Employing McGowan's 1890 data, adjusted to remove retired persons, and the 1894 County Lodge Directory, it is possible to construct a comparative occupational analysis for Orangemen and their nemesis, Irish Catholics. The data presented in table 5.4 demonstrate that, in comparison with the Orange brethren, Catholics were twice as likely to belong to unskilled occupations. They were also less likely to be occupied in semi-skilled jobs, but, strikingly, skilled employment was equally common in both communities – a fact that reflected the high demand for craftsmen in the burgeoning construction industry as well as more traditional occupations such as shoemakers and tailors. Notwithstanding the fact that clerical work was a recognized avenue for social mobility among Catholics in a city that was developing a strong commercial sector, their relative participation in this area was much lower than that of the Orangemen, who were twice as likely to find employment in this niche. The strength of the Orange presence amid Toronto's white-collar workers was mostly a reflection of the avenues of patronage open to them in public sector employment, but it is suggestive also of a pattern of preference in private sector employment. Notwithstanding the fact that Catholics were slightly over-represented among the business owners, it is probable that their enterprises were

Table 5.4 Toronto Catholics and Orangemen: An occupational comparison, 1890 and 1894

Occupation	Orangemen (%)	Catholics (%)
Professional	5.8	1.4
Business	12.6	13.5
Clerical	17.6	9.5
Skilled	13.7	13.9
Semi-skilled	27.8	20.4
Unskilled	22.5	41.3

Note: Data for the Catholic population is based on McGowan's figures for 1890 (*The Waning of the Green*, 297–301), which have been adjusted to exclude persons with no recorded occupation.

more likely to offer a smaller scale of employment. Certainly, no Catholic business could rival the opportunities for clerical employment provided by retailers such as Eatons and Simpsons, the commercial banks and trust companies, and the rapidly growing Stock Exchange. Catholic businesses were less likely to feature among the large-scale enterprises of "establishment Toronto" and were more likely to be small and medium-sized enterprises, many of them serving the Catholic community itself. Professionals, especially those engaged in legal, medical, teaching, and architectural specialties, accounted for almost 6 per cent of the Orangemen – a proportion that was four times greater than that to be found among the Catholic community. Very many of the professional class who had joined the Order were immigrants to the city, others were the privileged sons of established Torontonians, and together they were well able to avail themselves of the networking opportunities associated with the largest fraternal organization in the city.

Almost two-thirds of Toronto's Orangemen were employed in unskilled, semi-skilled, and skilled jobs, and, as befitted a city in which no single type dominated the tapestry of industry, no single occupation predominated. They straddled a range of employment niches in a city that continued to retain many of its more traditional characteristics as it underwent a major industrial transformation. There was no equivalent of the large cohorts of linen workers or shipbuilders in Belfast, but there was no doubting the strong working-class complexion of the Order in both cities. Toronto's largest concentrations were in the unskilled categories of labourer and teamster and the semi-skilled category of carpenter, all three of which contained more than one hundred members. The remainder of the working-class membership (1,297) was distributed over more than 180 other occupations, only twenty of which contained more than twenty registered Orangemen. The common unifying factors within this diversity were personal commitment to the resolutely Protestant and monarchical principles of Orangeism, and access to networking and patronage preferment. A sense of working-class camaraderie may have coexisted, but it is difficult to envisage how that might have been translated into a sense of transcendent class solidarity. There was too much variety, fluidity, and smallness of scale attaching to the occupational background of the majority of brethren to allow for the forging of a strong class identity, but in some niche areas there may have been some alignment of interests. Kealey has pointed to the role of Orange leaders in leading a strike of printers in contemporary Toronto and has evaluated their role in developing a coherent set of demands for improvement of work conditions.[20] Certainly, there was a recognizable cohort of forty-four Orange printers in the city in 1894, but the population of those working in the printing industry exceeded two thousand at the time. Undoubtedly, some of the most prominent trade unionists and leaders of the impassioned printers' strike of the early 1870s were Orangemen, and activists such as E.F. Clarke, later mayor of the city, and John Hewitt were among the most influential labour leaders of their day.[21] Both men went on to become owners and editors of the *Sentinel*, a paper more renowned for its strident anti-Catholicism than for its defence of workers' rights. At the same time, the Order also included wealthy owners of printing presses and newspapers, the most famous of whom was John Ross Robertson, the owner of the *Telegram*. Orangeism appeared able to contain, and subsume, a polarity of social views, and, at most, the inferred class solidarity among printers was exceptional within a mass organization of men who were more identifiable as supporters of King William than disciples of Karl Marx. The voluntary fraternal organization included hundreds of members from white-collar and professional occupations, including very many who were the employers of the working-class members, and within the structure of individual lodges a mixture of social groups and occupational classes coexisted.

Table 5.5, listing the five most common occupations in each of the skilled, semi-skilled, and unskilled categories, reflects well the diversity of the Orangemen. Labouring provided the single most common source of employment, with almost 10 per cent of members being so classified

Table 5.5 Most common occupations for Orangemen in skilled, semi-skilled, and unskilled categories, 1894

Skilled		Semi-skilled		Unskilled	
Plumber	32	Carpenter	182	Labourer	268
Shoemaker	39	Painter	63	Teamster	117
Tailor	30	Machinist	51	Porter	30
Moulder	26	Fireman	47	Caretaker	29
Plasterer	25	Blacksmith	44	Conductor	27
Category total	391		815		658

Source: *Register and Directory of the Loyal Orange Association of the City of Toronto*, 1894; various city directories and census of population, 1891.

in a spread of activities ranging from unskilled factory labour to construction, railways, drains, and road making. Carpenters, classified as semi-skilled in accordance with Goheen's system, were the second largest category. Their prominence reflected not only the rapid pace of construction in the growing city but also the reality that virtually every manufacturer, as well as the streetcar company, the railways, and retail outlets, had a need for people with a modicum of skill in carpentry and no single employer dominated the sector. It was an occupation that also facilitated personal mobility and development, as illustrated by the fact that men described as carpenters in directories and censuses might well be listed as interior decorators or builders in subsequent records. Others dropped down to become labourers. Carpenter would appear to have been a more fluid category than plasterer or plumber, both of which contained twenty-five and thirty-two Orangemen respectively.

The third most common category of employment was that of teamster, an occupation requiring little skill, other than the ability to handle horses, and very little capital, most being employees not proprietors of haulage enterprises. It was a manual niche that suited recent migrants to the city, especially those coming from rural Ontario or Ireland. Employment requiring some degree of ability in the management of horses was extensive within the city and included blacksmiths, hostlers, grooms, cab companies, and delivery men; the city, which had just introduced electric streetcars, was still very much dependent upon traditional modes of transport. Even the firemen were reliant on horses to draw their equipment, and mounted police were common on the city's streets. Cartage firms were vital to servicing commerce and industry, and while many of them were very small, some did maintain elaborate stables and employed several dozen teamsters. In that respect William Boyd, resident of Sherbourne Street, member of LOL 140, and employer of forty men, many of them fellow Orangemen, was not unique.

The range of skilled workers was also broad and was not specific to Toronto in any way. Immigrants and Canadian-born men alike had specific skills honed by apprenticeship and they filled occupations as diverse as plastering and bookbinding. A transitional sense of bridging old and new modes of production was apparent in trades such as shoe-making and tailoring, where some of the operatives continued a tradition of artisanal self-employment and others worked within the rapidly expanding garment and shoemaking factories of the city. Additional to those identified as employee tailors in table 5.5, there were at least five Orangemen, enumerated as merchant tailors, employing between two and ten operatives and being well established within the business community of the city. Some of them specialized in the manufacture of regalia for the Orange Order and the dozen or more other smaller local fraternities.

Somewhat more than one-third of Toronto's Orangemen belonged to the clerical, business, or professional categories. Their range of occupations was small, and distinct patterns of clustering were evident (see table 5.6).

The clerical occupations were dominated by clerks, many of whom worked in the Post Office, the Custom House, or businesses such as Eatons and bank outlets. They were the solid backbone of the Orange Order, bringing to it a sense of respectability and community solidity. Commercial travellers, representative of the new consumer market for factory-produced goods in a city that was becoming the most important wholesale distribution centre in the country, were also prominent, and for them the Order provided a sense of belonging as well as a network of business contacts. Policemen, letter carriers, and municipal inspectors completed a profile that represented emerging lower-middle-class Toronto. Two-thirds of all categorized in the white-collar professions were clustered in these five occupations; the remainder were scattered across some fifty others, including bookkeepers, managers, salesmen, journalists, custom officers, and supervisory foremen.

The business class was associated mostly with small-scale enterprises, many of them family-owned, limited in financial turnover and with few

Table 5.6 Most common occupations in clerical, business, and professional categories, 1894

Clerical		Business		Professional	
Clerk	168	Grocer	41	Physician	56
Commercial traveller	53	Agent	35	Barrister	32
Policeman	45	Hotel keeper	23	Teacher	22
Letter carrier	31	Contractor	14	Architect	6
Inspector	30	Undertaker	11	Clergyman	6
Category total	514		368		170

Source: *Register and Directory of the Loyal Orange Association of the City of Toronto,* 1894; various city directories and census of population, 1891.

employees. Grocers and agents, selling anything from steamboat and railway tickets to real estate and life insurance, and hotel and tavern keepers were most common. Real estate agents, of whom thirteen were Orangemen, were offshoots of the same housing boom that sustained so many carpenters, plasterers, and plumbers in the city. Contractors, some employed directly by the city for the laying of paving stones, and others engaged in excavation and construction activities were likewise reflective of the rapidly growing city. John Page, for example, a native of England and member of LOL 778, employed forty-five men in his excavation business and was heavily involved in laying sewers and water pipes for the city. Another common business was that of undertaker, and these businessmen, representing every major Protestant denomination in the city, had a commercial advantage as members of a fraternal body that placed much store on Orange funerals and elaborate burial ceremonies. A scattering of other small businesses complemented these more common enterprises. W.G. Simpson employed nine men in his lumber mill, Elijah Westman was responsible for four workers in his hardware store, and William Teskey employed four in his coal and wood business. Only John Ross Robertson, owner of the *Evening Telegram* with eighty recorded employees, could be described as an employer of major significance. Missing from the list were the owners of the major industrial plants of the city. To be sure, many of these might have had a hidden sympathy with the principles espoused by the Orange Order, and their managerial and supervisory staff did hire many Orangemen as employees, but the leading citizens preferred the social networks of the

Masonic Order to the somewhat strife-ridden history of the Orange. The elite exercised power within civic life in many different ways; the *petite bourgeoisie* of Orangeism sought to construct it upon the social linkages and patronage-laden opportunities provided under the auspices of the most numerically strong voluntary organization in the city.

One hundred and seventy professionals, representing 6 per cent of the city's Orangemen, lent considerable respectability to the Order. Their presence was significant in the city's social complexion, especially so in three professions – medicine, law, and teaching – which, in combination, contained two-thirds of the total number of Orange professionals. The predominance of doctors reflected a commercial as well as an ideological link with the Order. An Orange Mutual Insurance Society scheme had operated in Ontario since 1881, evolving by 1890 into a national scheme founded upon solid actuarial principles.[22] From the early decades of the century, many Toronto lodges had provided mutual benefit schemes for their members, and all participating bodies had employed doctors to vet applicants and certify sickness claims. Some doctors were registered as members of more than one lodge in order to attain a critical mass for their services; larger lodges sometimes had two physicians on their rolls, and by 1894 every lodge in the city had access to a designated physician. The total number of physicians identified as members was almost exactly the same as the number of lodges in the city.[23] Many of these physicians would appear to have been recent entrants to the profession, or at least recent migrants to the city. A surprising number of those identified from the city directories for the period 1892–5 were not recorded in the 1891 census for the city, and it would appear that joining a lodge was a reliable means for a newly qualified physician to acquire a clientele and establish a professional reputation. Appointment of physicians was governed by lodge by-laws, and some, such as LOL 342, required an annual review of the appointment: "This Lodge shall annually elect at their December meeting a duly qualified physician who must have the Royal Arch Degree."[24] When the lodge sought tenders for medical services in 1888, it received three applications. W.T. Parry, son of a Welsh immigrant, was successful. In his letter of application he agreed to "Undertake the duties of Surgeon, supplying all medicines and examine all candidates for admission into the order for one dollar and twenty five cents per annum. I feel since if the brethren honour me by electing me to the position I can discharge the duties of the office with credit to myself as well as for the welfare of the Lodge."[25]

In lodges with one hundred or more members, the contract could be quite remunerative.

The number of barristers within the order is more difficult to explain, for no obvious, or direct, fiduciary relationship bound them to the organization. A social network that included thousands of members and their families would have provided them with access to potential clients, not all of whom would have been arraigned for street disturbances and misdemeanours. But a more likely attraction was the pathway provided for political patronage and preferential advancement. The historian Gordon T. Stewart has noted, "County judgeships and the earning of the title Queen's Counsel (QC) were sought-after plums in the legal profession and were at the disposal of the party in power."[26] The papers of Prime Minister John A. Macdonald contain several listings of barristers together with their political affiliations and recommendations for appointment. Being an Orangeman would have opened up avenues of access within a fraternal body that was well used to processing applications for patronage. Nineteen separate lodges accommodated the thirty-two barristers, with the largest concentration (five) being members of LOL 613, a lodge that had been founded in 1878 by Robert Birmingham, secretary of the Liberal-Conservative party in the city. This particular lodge continued to attract barristers well into the twentieth century, and it was highly regarded for the top hats and formal black coats worn by members in the annual Twelfth parades.

The teaching profession was much more obviously linked to the machinery of local politics and was, therefore, immediately open to the influence of the Order. Within the educational system of Ontario, the policy of separate schools for Catholics left open the possibility that public school boards would become *de facto* Protestant school boards, and in the city of Toronto this was precisely what happened. The elected school trustees were often aspiring politicians, and the board was viewed as a launching pad for future City Hall elections. The board was an extremely powerful body and had responsibility for curriculum design, provision of school buildings, and the hiring of staff ranging from inspector through principals and teachers to caretakers. J.L. Hughes, school superintendent, founder of the kindergarten movement in Canada, and prominent Orange provincial leader, was an especially strong influence on the education policies enunciated by the trustees. There were sixty public schools in the city in the mid-1890s; the principals in one-fifth of them were members of the Orange Order. Notable among them was Scottish-born Alexander Muir, past master of LOL 142 and principal of Gladstone Public School. His composition "The Maple Leaf Forever" was written in 1867 at the time of Canadian Confederation and was championed by fellow Orangemen, and many others beside, as an unofficial national anthem. Its stirring words asserted the centrality of the British connection in defining Canada's identity and its invocation of British ethnicity was perfectly aligned to the central tenets of Orangeism.

> In days of yore, from Britain's shore,
> Wolfe, the dauntless hero, came
> And planted firm Britannia's flag
> On Canada's fair domain.
> Here may it wave, our boast and pride
> And, joined in love together,
> The thistle, shamrock, rose entwine
> The Maple Leaf forever![27]

Board patronage was not confined to the teaching profession. Caretakers in at least 10 per cent of the schools were members of the Order; the sinecure of their posts acquired added value in that they included residential accommodation and heating for the incumbent.

Among the professionals within the Order were a number of influential figures within the municipal administration of the city. The chief clerk in City Hall, his equivalent in the Post Office, the city treasurer, the chief inspector of the Water Works, the assistant chief of the Fire Department, the assistant city solicitor, and the chief inspector in revenue were all recorded as Orangemen in 1894. Among other professionals, the most numerous were architects, the most famous of whom was E.J. Lennox, designer of three of the most significant edifices in the city – City Hall, the nearby County Orange Hall, and the eclectic Casa Loma. Absent from the list, however, was the intelligentsia of the city; apart from the dean of Wycliffe College, no professors were identified, but a gardener and a janitor in the university were listed. However, the 1888 Twelfth celebrations in Toronto had featured the leading public intellectual of the day, Goldwin Smith. Addressing the assembled Orangemen and their families in Exhibition Park at the conclusion of the annual parade, Smith, who earlier in his career had denounced the Orange Order, acknowledged the political value and growing respectability of the organization and was willing to contribute to its profile, although he did not take out membership. His appearance on the Orange platform was encouraged also by a generous honorarium paid by the County Lodge.[28]

Surprisingly few clergymen were identified in the membership rolls of 1894, and although each lodge had a chaplain who performed a liturgical function at the commencement of meetings, that office-holder was usually a layman. Religion was central to the organization – Orange parades to designated churches were regularly held, and all members were expected to declare a personal commitment to organized religion – but the linkage to the personnel of the major Protestant churches remained tenuous. There were, of course, exceptions, and in the early twentieth century the vicar of St Albans Cathedral in England, Rev. F.C. Ward-Whate, retired to Toronto, becoming honorary grand chaplain of the Orange Council of the World, and he officiated frequently at County Lodge functions.[29]

Membership in the Order was not a complete subset of the population of the city, but it was remarkably inclusive of a wide range of occupations and social groups. Working-class members certainly predominated, taking their place alongside persons from very different social backgrounds, and a complex set of relations permeated the local and district lodges and also the County Lodge. The officers of the County Lodge (table 5.7) were by definition the most powerful figures in the organization and would be expected to be politically astute as well as possessed of leadership qualities. Election to these positions was via prior office holding in the local and district lodges, and all were therefore long-serving and experienced Orangemen.

The master and deputy master had both served as aldermen in City Hall, and McMillan had unsuccessfully stood in the mayoralty election of 1890. Both were consummate municipal politicians, and McMillan owed his position in the gaol to political patronage. Dixon served as chaplain, as befitted his position as a leading clergyman in the city; Lee's position was *ex officio* as he was a full-time salaried officer in the provincial organization and was based in Victoria Hall, the powerhouse of Orange officialdom. Lloyd and Louden were officials in the Customs House and City Hall respectively, and Edward Scott, a coal merchant, salesman, and employer of several men, was a long-serving member of LOL 380. Collectively the officers were reflective of middle-class Toronto, distinguished more by their connections and links with officialdom than by any high social status or possession of great personal wealth. They may have been an elite within the Order but they were by no means an elite within the city. There was a sense of ordinariness about them, an abiding

Table 5.7 Officers of the County Lodge of Toronto, 1894

Office	Name	Occupation
County master	John McMillan	Manager of Don Gaol
Deputy master	John Bailey	Carpenter
Chaplain	Rev. H.C. Dixon	Clergyman
Record. secretary	Wm Lee	Secretary, Grand Lodge, Ontario West
Treasurer	Frank E. Lloyd	Landing waiter, Customs House
Dir. of ceremonies	John Louden	Inspector of drains
Lecturer	Edward Scott	Salesman

Source: *Register and Directory of the Loyal Orange Association of the City of Toronto*, 1894.

sense of respectability. All seven officers were immigrants – five of the seven officers had been born in Ireland, Bailey had been born in England, and McMillan had been born in Scotland. In this predominance of Irish-born officers, the County Lodge was at variance with the nature of the membership at large, as Canadian-born men and migrants from elsewhere in the United Kingdom formed the majority of members. All County Lodge officers belonged to professional, business, or clerical groups.

The pattern of occupational status and place of birth characteristics evident in the County Lodge differed also from that of the leadership of local lodges, a group that was very similar to the background of Orangemen in the city in general. District Lodge leaders represented a somewhat intermediate state between the two extremes – not surprisingly, as they formed the corpus out of which the county officers were elected. Table 5.8 indicates that almost two-thirds of the district officers belonged to the three more prestigious occupational groups in contrast to about one-third among the local leaders and general membership. Interestingly, the occupational background of district officers in Toronto in 1894 was quite similar to that of Belfast's district officers in 1901; the same rank ordering applied to both cities.[30]

Middle-class confidence, greater levels of literacy, and perhaps more flexibility in working hours may all have contributed to the inversion of the occupational pyramids of the County Lodge and the five District Lodges as compared to the general membership. But the relationship

Table 5.8 Occupational characteristics of District Lodge officers and Primary Lodge masters, Toronto, 1894

	District officers		Lodge masters		Toronto membership	
Professional	7	10.6%	2	7.7%	170	5.8%
Business	16	24.2%	5	9.6%	368	12.6%
Clerical	18	27.3%	10	19.2%	514	17.6%
Skilled	7	10.6%	11	21.0%	401	13.7%
Semi-skilled	10	15.2%	9	17.3%	815	27.8%
Unskilled	8	12.1%	13	25.0%	658	22.5%
Total	66		50		2,926	

Source: *Register and Directory of the Loyal Orange Association of the City of Toronto, 1894*; various city directories and census of population, 1891.

was never simple. Centre District had a builder for its master, although its other officers included a schoolteacher and John McMillan, manager of the gaol. The West Toronto District, chaired by a blacksmith, included among its officers the principal of a school and three coal merchants. North-West District, with a teacher and two printers, a horse dealer, and a letter carrier as officers, had elected a physician to the position of master; nearby North Toronto District, comprising a barrister, four clerks, and letter carriers from the Post Office, was under the direction of a baker. East Toronto District included a school principal, a school caretaker, several clerks, and two grocers and had a stenographer for its master. Personal qualities, not occupational backgrounds, were to the fore in the election of officers, but the complexity of the pattern points to a broad level of democracy and egalitarianism within the middle leadership of the Order in the city.

Of the sixty-six district officers, half were immigrants (eighteen had been born in Ireland and thirteen in England), thirty were Canadian-born, and one was from the United States. None of those born in England were recorded as having parents who had been born in Ireland. Leadership at the local lodge level was predominantly working class and most were Canadian-born. All officers in the organization could read and write, but this was not in itself a determining factor in the choice of officer, as, with the exception of two individuals, all of the more than three thousand Orangemen listed in the 1894 directory claimed to be literate. Surviving manuscript records of individual lodges do reveal marked differences in the quality of penmanship and composition, but all were able to competently perform their assigned tasks as officers of the organization.

At the local level, the occupational characteristics of lodges were neither fixed nor all-embracing; they altered with the passage of years, and, with the possible exception of the Garibaldi lodge, which catered specifically to Italian Protestants, the lodge memberships were not defined by exclusive social, ethnic, or occupational backgrounds. It was by emphasis, rather than exclusiveness, that some lodges managed to maintain a distinctive identity – a trend that continued well into the first two decades of the twentieth century. Many members joined through the influence of workplace colleagues, and the 1894 Directory contains several examples of brethren returning their work address in lieu of residential details. The Customs House, Post Office, City Hall, and several firehalls were provided as contact addresses. There was no doubting the prominence of the workplace influence. The work addresses referred not only to public sector places of employment but included also private bodies such as the Women's Medical College, the Freehold Loan Building, the St Lawrence Foundry, and the offices of the *Mail* and the *Telegram*. Men of high status were just as likely to resort to this type of contact address as those in more menial occupations. Former alderman and mayoralty candidate John McMillan returned the Toronto Gaol as his address, and Charles Matthews, an accountant in the Engineering Department, identified City Hall in his details, as did R. McIntyre, a messenger in the same place.

At least forty-nine firemen were members of the Order; eleven of these were concentrated in LOL 781. Five who were based in Firehall No.15 were members of LOL 207, but the remainder were scattered across twenty-two other lodges. In no lodge did they form anything approaching a majority of the membership. Clearly the relationship between lodge identity and occupational characteristics of membership was complex, and while there is truth in Kealey's assertion that "Each Toronto lodge, then, possessed its own history and some articulated specific idiosyncratic aims,"[31] there was also a great deal of social variety within each lodge. Kealey's chosen example of a working-class lodge, Enniskillen Purple Star LOL 711, which he described as originating among brewery workers in 1872, retained demonstrable links with that industry twenty-two years later, but its much-expanded membership now included John Blevins, city clerk and one of the most influential men in municipal affairs, several firemen and policemen, and the principal of a school. LOL 711 had a total of 145 members in 1894, and while three-quarters of them belonged to skilled, semi-skilled, and unskilled occupational groups, not all of those were linked to the brewing industry. Its twelve businessmen and the five professionals were likewise devoid of links to the brewing industry. Similarly, LOL 173, described by Kealey as originating among transportation workers, had modified its identity within two decades of its inception with one-third of its membership classified as professional, business, and clerical in 1894. It would appear that the identity of lodges altered as they matured and expanded, with the effect that, ultimately, they each contained several social nuclei, all accommodated within a body united by its adherence to Orange principles. Analysis of membership suggests also that the sense of social and occupational identity was quite fluid in the late nineteenth-century city; the chief city clerk shared his lodge with a foreman, a labourer, and an inspector who were also on the payroll of the city, and this situation may not have been anomalous in the conditions of the time.

Membership: Nativity and Ethnicity

The conventional view of the membership of the Orange Order in Canada is that it was a uniquely Irish immigrant insertion into the cultural mosaic of the new country, the resultant social tensions that frequently spilled over into street violence being imported versions of ritual antagonisms between Irish Catholics and their Protestant countrymen. Houston and Smyth's analysis of lodge memberships effectively challenged that view,[32] and the present study further refines their argument, demonstrating that the identity of the Order had become increasingly complex by the closing decade of the nineteenth century. Using nominal census information, it is possible to establish not only the birthplaces of the Orangemen but also their family background as revealed in the nativity data for their parents. The diversity of background that emerges from the analysis reveals a voluntary organization more concerned with its role in Canadian society than with a simple perpetuation of Irish immigrant culture.

The Order in 1894 (table 5.9) was not a purely immigrant body, but neither did it exhibit the deep roots that might have been expected of an organization that was well into its third generation of existence in the city. Slightly less than half of its membership had been born in Canada; the overwhelming majority of these were Ontarians, with

Table 5.9 Place of birth: City of Toronto, 1891, and Orangemen, 1894

Toronto	Canada	Ireland	England	Scotland	USA	Other
N = 144,023	93,753	13,252	22,801	6,347	5,086	2,794
%	65.1	9.2	15.8	4.4	3.5	1.9
Orange Order						
N = 2,755	1,315	666	556	147	55	16
%	47.7	24.2	20.2	5.3	2.0	0.6

Source: *Register and Directory of the Loyal Orange Association of the City of Toronto,*
1894; census of population, 1891.
Note: The place of birth of all members cannot be established.

Newfoundland (fifty-nine) and Quebec (thirty-five) accounting for most of the remainder. Surprisingly few had migrated from Nova Scotia and New Brunswick. At that time, two-thirds of the city's population were Canadian-born. Less than a quarter of Toronto's Orangemen had been born in Ireland, their numbers being exceeded by the combined totals of those born elsewhere in the British Isles; England was just as likely to be the source of adherents as Ulster. Fifty-five members had been born in the USA, often the sons of immigrants passing through that country prior to settling in Canada, and the remainder had backgrounds as diverse as Gibraltar, Malta, Germany, Brazil, and Italy.

However, the extent to which the Order had become a pan-British and Canadian organization is qualified when one examines the birthplace data for parents of the members. Notwithstanding the fact that almost half of Toronto's Orangemen had been born in Canada, the generational roots of the organization remained surprisingly shallow. An analysis of parentage (table 5.10) indicates that only 12 per cent of Orangemen were the sons of Canadian-born fathers, compared with almost double that proportion for Torontonians as a whole. Eighty-five per cent of the fathers had been born in the British Isles; the equivalent figure for the city was 69 per cent. In the case of both the Order and the city, the preponderance of British ethnic origins was paramount. However, the roots of the brethren were much more recent than those of their fellow citizens; the longer one's family had been in Canada the less likelihood there was of the next generation of sons being attracted to the Orange Order.

The Orange Order was an organization that was heavily dependent upon immigrants and the sons of immigrants for recruits – 88 per cent

Table 5.10 Place of birth of fathers: Toronto, 1891, and the Orange Order, 1894

Toronto	Canada	Ireland	England	Scotland	USA	Other
N = 144,023	33,240	35,459	46,472	16,904	5,137	6,808
%	23.1	24.6	32.3	11.7	3.6	4.7
Orange Order						
N = 2,755	338	1,154	902	295	43	23
%	12.3	41.8	32.7	10.7	1.6	0.8

Note: The place of birth of all fathers cannot be established.

of its membership was derived from these two groups, and both cohorts had a relative strength much greater than would have been suggested by the city's norms. Canadians of second generation or longer provided 12 per cent of the membership, yet their relative share of the city's population was almost double that figure. The sons of Irish-born fathers (41.8 per cent) were almost twice as numerous as would have been expected, given their relative strength (24.6 per cent) in the urban demography, but their share of the membership was marginally less than that of the combined numbers of the sons of English and Scottish fathers. These were represented by almost precisely the same percentage in both the urban population and lodge membership, and there is no evidence to suggest that they had been enticed to join the Order by reason of an extended Irish lineage. They were not the sons of a previous generation who had migrated from Ireland to England or Scotland. Of the 556 Orangemen in Toronto who had been born in England, only 6 had Irish-born fathers; of the 147 Scottish-born Orangemen, 8 had Irish fathers. The figures for maternal lineage were of similar proportions. Qualitative analysis of the family names of the English members further supports the contention that an Irish ethnic background was of little significance. The presence of so many English and Scottish immigrants and their sons in the Order conformed to the general pattern of recent British migration into the city. But the questions remain: why did this group consider it appropriate, or advantageous, to select Orange lodges as an expression of their fraternal interests, and why did so many of them rise to become officers in those same lodges? The Order was not hidebound by the narrow ethnic geography of its Irish origins; it had emerged as a successful organization that projected an especial appeal to those in the early generational stages of integration into life in the city.

APPLICATION FOR ADMISSION

To the W. M. of Brunswick L. O. L. No. 404 :

SIR,—It is my desire to become a member of the LOYAL ORANGE ASSOCIATION by joining L. O. L, No. 404.   I herewith enclose $...................., part fee of admission, and am vouched for by two members of said Lodge.

Proposer ....*J. H. Burch*...........................

Seconder ...*G. B. Sweet*...........................

Signature.....*J. Hopkins*.........................

Residence....*11 Boustead ave*...................

Age...*5-7*..... Profession or Occupation...*carpenter*....

Religious Denomination....*church of England*....

Where Born...*England*...............................

Dated.....*11*.............day of....*Nov*............191..*3*..

Your Committee, to whom was referred the above Proposition, having carefully considered the same, beg respectfully to recommend that the applicant be initiated.

All of which is respectfully submitted.

Senior Com......*G. R. Sweeney*...........

2nd Com. ....4th Com............*J. Collins*............

3rd Com...........................5th Com......*G. Collins*..........

Obligat

5.2 Application for admission, 1913

Membership of the Orange Order was perceived as offering not only fraternal camaraderie but also access to power, patronage, and preferment in the new environment.

At the end of the nineteenth century, 58 per cent of Orangemen in Toronto had no direct Irish lineage, either through their own generation or the generation of their parents, and while Irishmen may have retained organizational power at the level of the County Lodge and to a lesser extent in the District Lodges, they were demonstrably not in control of many of the local lodges. Forty of the fifty-five lodges in the city in 1894 were led by men who had not been born in Ireland; England and Scotland were just as likely as Ireland to produce a master of a Toronto lodge. Irish lore, tales of heroic battles, and partisan songs had been assimilated into the commemorative traditions of members, many of whom must have had only a vague notion of the specificities of their antecedents. The appeal of the Order in Toronto was not narrowly directed towards those who had a family or personal exposure to the sectarian life of contemporary Ireland: rather it appealed to a broad swathe of immigrant men from throughout the British Isles, reflecting an appeal of Orange principles and practices that transcended narrow ethnic origins. An outcome of this ethnic mix was that Orangeism in Toronto was defined in terms of its British, monarchical, and Protestant heritage and lacked the intensity of sectarian hatred that characterized the organization in Belfast. The social geography of a New World experience had modified the stance of the Order, and its resultant flexibility facilitated longevity and power in the changing dynamic of late nineteenth-century Toronto.

Age Profile

Toronto had a relatively young population structure in 1891, as might be expected from a city that was growing by a combination of high rates of natural increase and large-scale immigration of persons of working age. About 70 per cent of the male population at that time belonged to the productive age group of twenty to fifty years. The total male population aged fifteen years and above totalled 47,193 persons, and the number of male Protestants eligible for membership of the Orange Order was probably in the region of 40,000. Ten per cent of these were members in 1894 and at least a further 10–20 per cent may have been lapsed members. The Order had always experienced a high turnover of membership, and suspensions for non-payments of dues were numbered in

Table 5.11 Comparative demographic characteristics of adult males in Toronto, 1891, and
Orangemen, 1894

Age	Toronto	%	Orange Order	%
15–19	6,956	14.3	164	5.9
20–4	8,072	17.1	411	14.9
25–9	7,426	15.7	504	18.3
30–4	5,820	12.3	443	16.1
35–9	4,542	9.6	345	12.5
40–4	3,861	8.2	309	11.2
45–9	3,016	6.4	211	7.6
50–4	2,577	5.8	165	5.9
55–9	1,578	3.3	98	3.6
60–4	1,420	3.0	66	2.4
65–9	783	1.7	26	0.9
70+	1,142	2.4	13	0.5
Total	47,193		2,755	

Source: *Register and Directory of the Loyal Orange Association of the City of Toronto,*
1894; various city directories and census of population, 1891.

the thousands. This coterie of active and suspended members, together
with their families, represented a powerful influence in the construction
of the cultural identity of Toronto.

Membership, apart from its obvious exclusion of Catholics, was representative of the mainstream population; its ethnic, religious, occupational, and residential characteristics were not, in any way, unique. In
addition, the age profile of the Order in 1894 reflected the strong presence of those who had a stake in the community, and an earlier image
of an assemblage of rebellious youths and unruly adults was no longer
relevant.

Table 5.11 depicts the relevant age cohorts of the membership in
the context of the adult male population for the city as a whole. In
the age grouping fifteen to nineteen years, the Order contained a
much smaller percentage than might have been expected, but this
was most likely due to the fact that youths below the age of eighteen
were formally enrolled as Orange Young Britons, joining the senior
body on maturity. The Order was especially strong among men
aged twenty-five to forty-nine years, with 80 per cent of members

belonging to this category compared with 69 per cent in the control population of adult males. This active age group was one likely to benefit most from the social networking opportunities provided by an organization of like-minded individuals. These men, and their families, were the mainstay of the urban community and were not irresponsible youths seeking rambunctious social diversions. Neither was the Order dominated by a coterie of aging members drawn together by an abundance of social time and enthused by reminiscences of former glory days. Only a handful of members were over seventy years of age. Seventy per cent of members were heads of household and at least 30 per cent were homeowners.[33] Fifteen per cent were described as sons living in the household of their parents with a small number of brothers and nephews complementing this family grouping. Slightly more than four hundred men (15 per cent of the total) were returned as lodgers, mostly labourers, teamsters, and travelling salesmen who had yet to establish more permanent roots in the city. Sixty-six per cent of the members were married. Likewise, virtually all members were recorded as being in employment in the census of 1891, an attribute that may have been somewhat self-selecting in that members who became unemployed were unlikely to continue to pay their monthly dues and would automatically have been suspended from the Order.

In every way, the members were an authentic cross-section of Protestant Toronto. The typical Orangeman was a householder of English, Scottish, or Irish background, most likely married and unlikely to be unemployed. He was equally unlikely to be very wealthy. Orangemen were to be found in virtually every residential neighbourhood of Toronto, including older communities along the Don River, the impoverished area of the Ward in the city centre, and the new suburbs on the western and northern fringes of the city. Indeed, the lack of residential distinctiveness was shown by several instances where census data revealed that young Orangemen and Catholics sharing the same occupation sometimes lived as lodgers in the same multiple dwelling. No ghetto was evident. Toronto was not Belfast and neither was it Glasgow or Liverpool.[34] There was nothing aberrant about the Order or its members by the end of the nineteenth century. A sense of sameness made the Order very appealing to a wide spectrum of citizens, allowing it to outstrip in size every other voluntary organization, including the Masons and Odd Fellows, and exceeding also the appeal of trade unions. The Knights of Labour, an American-inspired trades union body, had acquired a membership of five thousand in Toronto in the late 1880s,[35] a period when the city's Orangemen numbered about four thousand, but its eclipse of the Order was temporary. Within a decade that labour body had faded away, and correspondingly the Order, which had pre-dated the union movement by many decades, continued on a course of growth and development. The survival and vitality of the Orange Order over many decades is itself a reflection of the centrality of Orangeism to mainstream life in the burgeoning city.

Religion

Known variously as "the city of churches" and "the city of homes," late nineteenth-century Toronto was a place where religion was not only a matter for one's private conscience but also a social determinant of some public significance. In common with most Torontonians of the time, Orangemen were regular churchgoers, and on application for membership they were required to be affiliated with a Protestant church. Catholics were explicitly excluded from membership; marriage to a Catholic was punishable by expulsion from the Order. Jews were also ineligible for membership.[36] It was scarcely surprising, therefore, that almost all members identified themselves with an organized church in their returns to the census takers, and their wives and children were likewise returned as members of a Protestant denomination – though not necessarily the same as that to which the head of household belonged.[37]

In the census of 1891, some 83 per cent of Torontonians were affiliated to Protestant churches, the most popular of which were the Anglican (Church of England), the Methodist, the Presbyterian, and the Baptist. A similar alignment, and the same rank ordering, pertained within the Orange Order, but minor differences were discernible. Anglicans and Methodists were over-represented and Presbyterians were slightly under-represented within the Order, and evangelical groups such as the Plymouth Brethren and the Salvation Army had less of a following among Orangemen. Only two Quakers but forty-five Congregationalists (mostly American-born) were members of the Order. Place of birth explains much of the variance.

As table 5.13 clearly demonstrates, the relative strength of Presbyterians among immigrant Orangemen was not only due to their overwhelming preponderance among the relatively small Scottish

Table 5.12 Denominational characteristics, Toronto, 1891, and Orangemen, 1894

	Anglican	Methodist	Presbyterian	Baptist	Other	Total
Orangemen	973	819	642	111	210	2,755
1894	35.2%	30.0%	23.3%	4.0%	7.5%	100%
Toronto						
Protestants	46,084	32,505	27,499	6,909	27,821	140,768
1891	32.7%	23.1%	19.5%	4.9%	19.8%	100%

Source: *Register and Directory of the Loyal Orange Association of the City of Toronto*, 1894; various city directories and census of population, 1891.

Table 5.13 Denominational characteristics of Irish, English, and Scottish immigrants in the Orange Order, 1894

	Anglican	Methodist	Presbyterian	Baptist	Other	Total
Irish	46.1%	20.7%	30.5%	1.2%	1.5%	666
English	56.3%	27.7%	4.1%	6.5%	5.4%	556
Scottish	2.7%	4.8%	87.1%	0.7%	4.8%	147

Source: *Register and Directory of the Loyal Orange Association of the City of Toronto*, 1894; various city directories and census of population, 1891.

component but also reflected the fact that almost one-third of the Irish belonged to that church. Almost half of the Irish immigrant members were Anglican and, together with the English-born Anglicans, created a preponderance of Anglicans in the Order. The primacy of Anglicans was at variance with the traditional image of Ulster Scots that has been applied generally to Irish Protestant immigrants in Canada and elsewhere. Appropriate as a descriptor of Ulster settlers in colonial America, the appellation "Ulster Scot" has little meaning in Canada, where the earliest frontier settlers included large numbers of Anglicans drawn from throughout Ireland, including south and mid-Ulster. Notwithstanding the fact that Presbyterians were the largest Protestant denomination in Ulster in the mid-nineteenth century, they were ranked behind the Anglicans on a nationwide basis and the geography of emigration was accurately reflected in the outcome depicted in table 5.13. The elite leadership of the Irish Grand Lodge remained mostly Anglican throughout the nineteenth century. A similar position was evident in the Canadian lodges. The subject of the sectarian attitudes of Anglicans warrants further research, but there is no doubt that the Church harboured many who had little time for Catholics and who found within Orangeism an ideology with which they could comfortably coexist.

The strength of the Methodist community within the Toronto lodges was an outcome of two mutually reinforcing factors. That denomination was especially strong among both Irish and English immigrants, and its relative position reflected the source regions and social backgrounds of urban working-class immigrants. The industrial cities of England and Ulster generated many emigrants to Canada, especially in the second half of the nineteenth century, and they brought with them a reformed faith that was most supportive of restrictions on social and commercial activities on the Sabbath. Irish Methodists included also within their numbers members of the Palatine settlements of the Limerick region who had converted to Methodism in the 1780s and migrated in the 1820s and 1830s to the farming frontier of southern Ontario.[38] In Canada the immigrant Methodists were augmented also by conversions from other denominations. Timothy Eaton, born into a Presbyterian family in Ulster, was probably the most famous of the Irish converts to Methodism. By the closing years of the nineteenth century, the Methodists of Toronto were seen as a powerful community in setting the tone of civic life, embodying within their religious beliefs a strong commitment to hard work and the pursuit of worldly success.

The Toronto lodges included a scattering of several minority Protestant denominations, their presence being roughly proportionate to their share of the city's population. Salvation Army members were almost invariably the product of migrations from Newfoundland, augmented by a few from London. They took their place in lodges alongside other minority groupings such as Baptists and Congregationalists, who were mostly American in origin, Lutherans, who reflected the presence of a small number of Germans, and Plymouth Brethren, who were primarily immigrants from England. In Ireland, and also in Canada, more liberal denominations such as the Quakers had scant empathy with the sectarian principles of the Order and were noticeable by their absence. As befitted a fraternal organization that prided itself on its defence of Protestantism, virtually all members identified in the 1894 Directory returned a religious affiliation in their census returns. Only two members recorded that they were atheists (a belief contrary to membership rules), and no more than a handful opted for the general description of "Christian."

The Public Profile of the Order

The public presence of the Order in the city in 1894 was manifested in a number of ways, and there was no doubting the fact that it was a central part of civic life. On the occasion of the annual Twelfth parade, the city administration ground to a halt: officials and employees in City Hall took the day off work to participate in a parade that would bring the main thoroughfares of the city to a standstill for several hours. Spectators in their tens of thousands – family members, neighbours, and curious citizens – turned out to watch and applaud. The parade of marching bands, floating banners, mounted horsemen, and lines of men bedecked in their best attire and Orange sashes was an acknowledged highlight of the summer season. The mayor, members of the federal and provincial parliaments, city dignitaries, and elected aldermen marched behind the banners of their own lodges and were proud to be recognized and applauded for their Orange affiliation. There was nothing secretive or socially repugnant about the public demonstration except in the eyes of Catholic citizens, who generally ignored, or avoided, the spectacle of partisan power. The annual parade, augmented throughout the year by smaller parades on occasions such as Guy Fawkes Day, church commemorative services, and funerals of deceased brethren, were significant public statements of territorial control of streets, neighbourhoods, and city parks. Most emphatically they were not confined to ghettos or minority areas in the city.

The public persona of Orangeism in 1894 was exemplified clearly and unambiguously also in the elected offices of the city and in the social pattern of public remunerated employment. The year had begun in customary fashion with municipal elections held on 3 January, and although candidates did not campaign on party tickets, it was clear where their allegiances lay. Liberal Conservatism was the underlying alignment of most of those who would be elected: Liberals, and especially Catholics, returned few representatives. Elections to the office of mayor, Council aldermen, and public school trustees were the business of the day, and the electorate, enfranchised on the basis of a property qualification, had included since 1884 widows and unmarried women.[39] Turnout of voters was rarely large. Throughout the 1890s it rarely exceeded 25,000 – a figure that was very susceptible to the coordinated inputs of organized bodies such as the Orange Order. In 1894, for example, Robert J. Fleming and Warring Kennedy contested the position of mayor. Kennedy with 13,830 votes triumphed over outgoing Mayor Fleming, who received 9,306 votes. A prominent businessman and dry goods wholesaler in the city, Ulster-born Kennedy was a long-time Orangeman, Methodist, and active in many church-related activities. Twelve months later Kennedy managed to hold off another challenge from Fleming by the slender margin of 14 votes.[40] The margin of his victory illustrated clearly how even small numbers of well-organized votes had the potential to decide outcomes, and it was noted that, in respect of that specific electoral contest, Kennedy's vulnerability was due in no small measure to a loss of support in Ward 5, "home of Orange and PPA [Protestant Protective Association] stalwarts." This was interpreted somewhat prematurely by the *Globe* as an indication of the "waning powers of partyism in civic politics."[41]

The mayor headed a city administration of twenty-four aldermen – each of six wards elected four representatives. In 1894 every ward returned at least two Orangemen. Ward 5 in the west of the city returned three, and it is possible that other successful candidates had Orange credentials but were not listed in the contemporary register of brethren. Orange halls were widely used for electioneering meetings during the brief week-long electoral campaign, and the Orange vote was generally acknowledged as significant.

That same partisan vote was effective in determining the outcome of the vote for twelve public school trustees, two elected from each ward. At least eight Orangemen were returned as trustees in that election and they constituted a school board that already had responsibility for several Orangemen in remunerated supervisory positions. Catholics met with limited success in the municipal elections. The office of mayor was invariably in the hands of a Protestant, and, prior to the twentieth century, the aldermen elected annually to City Council did not include more than two or three Catholics at any one time. In 1894, for example, no Catholics were returned. It was difficult for Catholics to assemble sufficient votes to guarantee success. As a community, they were spread throughout the city and did not control any ward or even parts of wards. Their weakness in attaining elected municipal offices translated also into a weak grip on the allocation of patronage – a fruit of office exercised by those in power to solidify electoral support and reward loyalty. It was scarcely surprising, therefore, that the solid Protestant, and obviously Orange, municipal representatives should preside over an administration that was composed of kindred spirits.

The municipal administration in 1894 was divided into eleven departments of which one, the police, was administered by ex-officio commissioners including the mayor and the county judge. The remaining ten departments were led by nineteen principal officers, all of them Protestant, half of whom were Orangemen. They included:

Treasury Department: R.T. Coady, treasurer, LOL 404
John Patterson, deputy treasurer, LOL 140
Audit Department: W.W Jones, auditor, LOL 778
Clerk's Department: John Blevins, clerk, LOL 711
Solicitor's Department: Thomas Caswell, city solicitor, LOL 127
Engineer's Department: John Jones, street commissioner, LOL 857
Fire Department: Thomas Graham, chief engineer, LOL 140
Property and Markets Department: Emerson Coatsworth, LOL 781
Assessment Department: J.C. Forman, LOL 212

These nine officials were members of eight different lodges, and although some held officer positions in the Order, most did not. They were an impressive and influential group of mandarins whose influence extended into virtually every corner of municipal government. They led a municipal administration that employed hundreds of permanent and seasonal workers, allocated work, and awarded supply contracts, and was, in effect, a permanent civil service, maintaining continuity within a system that elected its mayor and aldermen annually.

Using city directories, the Orange register, and linked census data, the names of 188 permanent municipal employees have been identified for 1894. At least 113, or 60 per cent, were members of the Orange Order. The Orangemen were employed at all levels and, apart from the principal officers identified above, were particularly numerous among the inspectors of pavements, sewers, water works, and public works. The city stables employed eleven brethren as drivers and stable hands, and many more were employed as clerks and foremen in various departments. Labourers were certainly on the list, but it is impossible to establish the full number of manual workers as they were hired mostly on a seasonal basis. The range of occupations was a good representation of the social diversity inherent in the fraternal body in its entirety. No corner of municipal employment was beyond access.

A similar Orange dimension was present among both police and firemen. The police force in the city numbered 269 in 1894, and of these it has been possible to identify 216 men by name. At least 76 Orangemen were included in the force, ranging from inspector through detective and down to constable; more than half of them were natives of Ireland. The pattern was repeated with the 121 firemen employed by the city, of whom 113 have been identified in the nominal records. Forty-six of these were Orangemen, including the assistant chief of the department and a variety of foremen, hosemen, and drivers (table 5.14). Most firehalls had two or more Orangemen, but in the hall at the corner of Cowan Avenue and Queen Street all five firemen were members of the Order, four of them in LOL 207.

Within the sphere of municipal employment, Orangemen were significantly over-represented. The best estimate for the total number of active Orangemen in the city at the time was 4,000, or about 8.5 per cent of the total adult male population. Catholics were probably 15 per cent of that population cohort. Table 5.14 presents an analysis of more than five hundred municipal employees, a population sufficiently large to warrant a comparative social analysis. From it one may discern that the likelihood of employment was increased by a factor of between five and seven by virtue of one's Orange affiliation. The data set does not permit an evaluation of whether membership of the Order was a prerequisite for employment or was attained subsequently, but either way there was an undeniable link between the Order and employment funded by the city: the brethren enjoyed privileged access to employment opportunities, and, conversely, Catholics were least likely to attain such employment. The number of Catholics in the active age group of males was almost double that of the Orangemen, but while 235 jobs were occupied by Orangemen only 20 were held by Catholics, and, with few exceptions, those posts were of low rank. The sheer scale of its membership, its insertion into the most senior ranks of the municipal administration, and its evident success in delivering patronage conveyed on the Orange Order the status of power broker and directive influence on the creation and projection of civic culture. In a report on Toronto's annual celebration of King William's victory at the Boyne, the *Globe* captured imaginatively the centrality of Orangeism and the civic culture of the intensely British city:

Table 5.14 Comparative strength of the Orange Order among identified municipal employees, 1894

	City Hall	Police	Firemen
Total employees	188	168	113
Total Protestants	180	159	110
Total Catholics	8	9	3
Total Orangemen	113	76	46
Orange as % employees	60%	45%	41%
Catholics as % employees	4%	5%	3%
Total Orangemen			4,000
Orangemen as % adult male population of more than 15 years			8.5%
Catholics as % adult male population of more than 15 years			15.0%

Source: The employees were identified from a variety of sources, including city directories, censuses of populations, and Orange Records

Very little business was transacted at the [City] Hall yesterday morning. Quite a number of the younger officials had obtained leave of absence on account of "the twelfth" and those who remained talked over the prospects of rain or sunshine for the parade. The Mayor spent a couple of hours in his office and left at 11.45 to join his lodge. His only decoration was the jewelled star presented to him by the County Lodge in 1883 on the occasion of his third term as master. Ald. McMillan wearing his Royal Scarlet sash dropped into the Mayor's office for a few minutes and accompanied his Worship to the Orange Hall. Alderman Hallam brought the Mayor yesterday a splendid bunch of Orange blossoms that he raised on his Rosedale reservation. Some of the blossoms were distributed among the faithful while the remainder were carefully preserved by his Worship.[42]

There was nothing subversive or secretive about the transplanted organization that now stood at the centre of municipal power in the city. The Orange Order in Toronto, at the end of the nineteenth century, was a complex organization that defied easy stereotyping. It was chameleon-like in its ability to accommodate large numbers of men drawn from diverse social, ethnic, and religious backgrounds while still maintaining a strong centralizing focus – factors that unquestionably allowed it to maintain and exert authority as the most powerful voluntary organization in the contemporary city. It exuded a sense of power that attracted both recent migrants to Toronto and second- or third-generation Canadian-born. The Order and its lodges were part of a very dynamic system, and the changes associated with its evolving identity were the foundations of its success in successfully adapting to a rapidly changing metropolis.

6 The Climax and Onset of Decline of the Orange Order, 1900–1940

The attainment of numerical strength, social respectability, and power, evident by the close of the nineteenth century, continued apace for another three decades, during which the profile of the Order reached its zenith and also commenced its ultimate decline. In the 1920s, membership peaked at a figure of about ten thousand men, and upwards of a thousand joined annually. A similar number left. Patronage continued to be dispensed through the channels of Orange power brokers, and Toronto retained its overwhelming Protestant and British identity. Catholics made but limited progress in the field of public employment in the city and they were still distrusted by the Order. In turn, Catholics maintained their social dislike and political opposition to what they perceived as an outmoded sectarian organization, but the days of riotous behaviour and public brawling were a thing of the past. Within the Catholic community there was a tacit, if unpalatable, acceptance of the centrality of Orangeism in the life of the city, and cordial relations were maintained, notwithstanding the extremism of some public utterances by Orange leaders on occasions such as the Twelfth of July celebrations. To a considerable extent, the polarity of Catholic and Orange attitudes and social positions was codified within a demographic and political reality in which the minority position of the former was acknowledged and recognized by an accepted proportionality in the disbursement of patronage in public offices. Catholics continued to be ignored for senior positions in City Hall, the police, and the fire service, but they were to be found, albeit in small numbers, in the elected positions of aldermen and Board of Control members, in the judiciary, and, increasingly, in the workforce of firms such as the Eaton retailing empire. In private, leaders of the Order could communicate respectfully with the Catholic

Archbishop of Toronto, but in public their stances remained much more polarized.[1] Toronto continued to be a city in which the divide between Catholics and Protestants remained significant; consensus maintained good order, but a lingering undercurrent of mistrust and perception of social differences persisted. Archbishop McEvay, newly appointed to the Catholic Archdiocese of Toronto in 1908, was under no illusions about the complexity of life in the city, and in a personal communication to the Canadian prime minister, Sir Wilfrid Laurier, he observed, "Toronto is a difficult city to manage both for Church and State, and while I hope to be conciliatory no doubt there will be local religious storms sometimes."[2]

One such religious storm erupted little more than a decade later, and it illustrated not only the social tensions that lay close to the surface in Toronto but also the ethno-religious elements which distinguished the civic culture of Toronto from that of contemporary American cities. In the summer of 1920 a convention of American fire chiefs met in Toronto at the invitation of the local fire chief. John Kenyon, fire chief of New York City, was president of the convention, and in that capacity he invited the Catholic Archbishop of Toronto, Neil McNeil, to open proceedings with a prayer. Rev. H.J. Cody, a leading Anglican and later president of the University of Toronto, was invited to deliver an oration. Kenyon, a Catholic and leader of New York City's largely Irish Catholic fire service, saw no problem in issuing the invitations. Uproar ensued. Toronto city aldermen demanded that the invitation to the Catholic archbishop be rescinded. The matter was resolved by the resignation of Kenyon and Archbishop McNeil's withdrawal of his previous acceptance to conduct the opening prayers. Kenyon recorded that the row arose from the fact that "Toronto was a very large Orange City, that it was always referred to as the Belfast of Canada," and alleged that the objections had arisen from "a bigoted, intolerant cabal that happens to be at present in control of the local government of this city."[3]

The experience of the fire chiefs' convention demonstrated clearly the chasm that separated Irish experiences in Toronto and New York – an ephemeral public expression of the deep fissures that characterized the Canadian city. Away from the glare of such publicity, in the daily management of the city, cognizance continued to be taken of the religion of public employees, and, with few parallels elsewhere in North America, official records listed not only the age and place of birth of policemen, firemen, and staff in the City Clerk's Office but also details of their religious

Table 6.1 Return of employees in the City Clerk's Department, 1920 and 1930

Year	Office	Employees	Median salary	Gender	Religion
1920	City clerk	1	$5,750	M	P
1930	City clerk	1	$7,012	M	P
1920	Asst c clerk	1	$4,500	M	P
1930	Asst c clerk	1	$4,750	M	P
1920	n/a				
1930	Sec Board Control	1	$4,687	M	P
1920	Chief clerk	1	$4,000	M	P
1930	Chief clerk	1	$3,554	M	P
1920	Clerk	11	$2,175	M	P
1930	Clerk	18	$2,164	M	P
1930	Clerk	4	$1,928	M	RC
1920	Stenographer	4	$1,450	F	P
1930	Stenographer	3	$1,900	F	P
1920	Messenger	1	$1,689	M	P
1930	Messenger	1	$1,700	M	P
1920	Tel operator	3	$1,490	F	RC
1930	n/a				

Notes: P = Protestant; RC = Catholic
Source: City Clerk's Department, Employees Salaries 1917–1934, Toronto City Archives.

affiliation. Records pertaining to municipal administrative staff for the period 1917–34 indicate that during these years the bureaucracy of the city clerk's office doubled in size from nineteen to thirty-nine, a reflection of the growing scale, complexity, and importance of the metropolitan centre.[4] As in the past, the employees were overwhelmingly male; women were relegated to newly established posts such as stenographer or telephone operator. Religion was enumerated by a simple binary system – Protestant and Catholic – with no differentiation of the denominations of Protestantism. The pattern identified for 1894 persisted – Protestants, many of them Orangemen, occupied all senior positions. Catholics were very much a minority and were most likely to occupy marginal positions. In 1920, for example, a total of three Catholics were employed out of twenty-two staff in the city clerk's office (table 6.1).

They were all women and employed as telephone operators at salaries equivalent to, or below, that of the office messenger boy. From 1923 onwards a limited number of clerical posts in the City Clerk's Office were filled by Catholics, but the numbers remained small and somewhat below the level to be expected from their proportionate strength in the city's overall population. Their average annual salary remained lower than that of their Protestant colleagues in equivalent grades.

Expansion of public employment continued apace with the rapid development of the city, and opportunities for members of the Orange Order abounded, especially in the department headed by a city clerk who was a prominent member of the Order. Commenting that the Twelfth of July was a semi-holiday in City Hall, the *Telegram*, in 1920, reported that participants in the annual parade included the city architect and two of his staff, the city's relief officer, the county crown attorney, and members of the city's district judiciary. They took their place alongside hundreds of other employees, manual, clerical, and professional. All were proud to openly affirm their membership of the Orange Order.[5]

The police and fire services of the city likewise remained as objects for the disposition of patronage, and, unsurprisingly, these two services remained overwhelmingly Protestant in composition. Despite a growing percentage of Canadians within their ranks, their religious profile had altered little since 1894. As with the staff of the City Clerk's Office, the religious composition of the police force was considered to be of public significance, and the city's annual report published this information in some detail. The report of 1907 is especially detailed, containing information on religion, place of birth, marital status, height, date of joining the service, and relevant prior experience (table 6.2).[6]

The British-born share of Toronto's population in 1911 was 28 per cent, but they held 56 per cent of the policing jobs in the city, and the immigrant character of the force remained strikingly evident. Within that particular demography, the Irish were very much over-represented; constituting one-third of the entire force, they outnumbered the English and Scots combined, although the English had dominated migration to the city for decades. At the senior level, four out of five inspectors were Irish, and their relative strength was evident also at the lower ranks of sergeant, constable, and operator. Canadian-born men, many of them of Irish ethnic origin, dominated detective ranks. Surprisingly, men of Scottish and English birth were very much under-represented in the force, and while there may be some merit in the argument postulated by

Table 6.2 Descriptive roll of the Toronto Police Force, 1907

Rank	Place of birth					Religion	
	Ireland	Scotland	England	Canada	Other	Protestant	Catholic
Chief constb	0	0	0	1	0	1	0
Dept chief	0	0	0	1	0	1	0
Inspector	4	1	0	0	0	5	0
Detective	15	4	7	50	0	71	5
Sergeant	15	3	6	8	0	30	2
Constable	31	20	21	36	2	97	13
Operator	36	7	17	58	1	109	10
Clerk	11	1	3	4	0	19	0
Total	112	36	54	156	3	331	30

Source: City Council minutes, 1907.

Stephan Thernstrom that Irish immigrants in North America tended to be risk-averse, preferring public service employment to the uncertainties of the private sector, it is more likely that patronage and personal connections tended to support an ethnically self-reinforcing employment pattern.[7] In that respect there was little difference between the Irish Catholic dominance of the police force in American cities and the preponderance of Protestant Irish in the Toronto equivalent. Out of an operating force of 361, there were only 30 Catholics, one-eighth of the total, and only seven of those had been born in Ireland. The remainder were Canadian-born with the exception of two who had come from England. Protestant Irish immigrants contributed 105 men in the force and were well represented at all levels. Considering that Catholics constituted 14 per cent of the city's population in 1911, their 8 per cent representation in the police force, the bulk of them at the lower ranks of constable and operator, does not suggest that they had successfully transcended their historically marginal position in civic society, and it would appear that Jenkins's conclusion that the under-representation of Catholics "was gradually pared away after the turn of the century" may have been somewhat anticipatory.[8] For the ordinary citizenry, and for arriving immigrants, there was no ambiguity about the identity of the police, and the chances of employment within the force were adjudged accordingly.

It is impossible to ascertain the number of serving policemen in 1907 who were members of the Orange Order, but we do know that at least seventy-six of them had been Orangemen fourteen years earlier and many more would have joined the Order in the interim. Some lodges such as Belfast Purple Star contained an unusually high number of policemen within their membership, but most lodges in the city contained some members of the force. Officers and constables took their appointed places in lodge meetings, irrespective of their ranking in the work situation. Certainly, fraternal bonds would not have impeded either hiring or promotion prospects. By 1923 the force had doubled to 750 men and the opportunities for preferment increased accordingly.[9] Indeed, policemen became so numerous within the Order that, uniquely, members of the force were permitted to constitute their own degree team; it travelled among the lodges of the city and officiated at the initiation and ceremonial progression of fellow policemen through the Orange, Blue, Purple, and Scarlet degrees. Such degree ceremonies were the social and ceremonial highlights of lodge meetings, and it is noteworthy that no other profession was sufficiently numerous, or privileged, to selectively oversee advancement of its co-workers within the fraternity. These degree teams continued to function well into the second half of the century, and in 1954, for example, the *Sentinel* recorded

Belfast Purple Star LOL 875 were hosts to the Toronto City Police department on Nov 3rd in the Western District Hall when a Police and Remembrance night was held. A police degree team under p/s Barney Sithes, PM of LOL 2793 had the pleasure of initiating six members of the police department in a manner which thrilled all who witnessed it ... His Worship, Mayor Leslie Saunders, Deputy Grand Master of British America and Chairman of the Honourable Board of Police Commissioners, was the speaker of the evening.[10]

Also participating as a member of the Orange degree team on that occasion was Inspector John Cobb of no. 1 Division. It is inconceivable that, given such a close alliance of the Order, senior elements within the police force and police commissioners would not have facilitated the preferential recruitment of like-minded men. The vibrant Orange presence in the police force had its equivalent among the firemen of the city. Reporting on the Twelfth of July parade of 1920, the *Telegram* noted that "Included in the procession were 250 firemen consisting of those on night duty and others who got non-members of the Order to take their shift."[11]

Table 6.3 Personal characteristics of dead firemen, Toronto, 1902

Name	Firehall	Age	M. status	Service (years)	Origin	Rel	LOL
W. Collard	Rose Ave	32	Married	11	Toronto	Presb	857
W. Clarke	Lombard St	27	Married	3	Toronto	Cong	455
A. Kerr	Lombard St	28	Single	2	Ireland	Presb	875
F. Russell	Yonge St	32	Married	7	England	Bapt	1084
D. See	Lombard St	29	Single	5	Gananoque	Presb	140

Source: *Sentinel*, 27 July 1902.

At that time there were fewer than 600 firemen employed in the city,[12] and although the size of the fire service had increased fourfold since the 1890s, the number of Orangemen within it had increased at a comparable rate. The entrenched Orange presence in the firehalls of the city may be exemplified with some poignancy by a tragic event that had occurred in the city a few years previous.

In the early hours of the morning of Thursday 10 July 1902, a large multi-storied flour and feed store in downtown Toronto was reported to be ablaze. McIntosh's premises at the corner of Front and George streets had a large quantity of hay and straw stored in its loft to feed the teams of delivery horses, and, fuelled by this, the conflagration erupted. For a time it appeared to threaten the destruction of the entire core of the city. The fire was successfully contained, but not before five firemen were killed and another seriously injured in what was the greatest single loss of life in the history of the fire service in Toronto. Apart from the scale of the tragedy, other noteworthy details of the event were the subject of extensive media and public comment. All five dead firemen were members of the Orange Order, as was their injured colleague. Their family and personal profiles reflected accurately the contemporary nature, composition, and status of the fraternal organization in the life of the city (table 6.3).

The victims had been stationed at three different firehalls: William Clarke, Adam Kerr, and David See had been attached to the Lombard Street Hall, Walter Collard was from the Rose Avenue Hall, and Frederick Russell was from the Yonge Street Hall. Collard's father, Joseph, was the caretaker of the hall in which his son was employed and was probably an ex-fireman. See's brother was also employed in the Lombard

Street Hall, and his father worked for the city's gas works; none of the other three had any discernible family links with the fire service or municipal employment. All five firemen were members of different lodges, as was the injured Charles Toplis, a member of LOL 207.

The five firemen had little in common other than their occupation, membership of the Orange Order, and the fact that they were all in the prime of their active years. Two were natives of the city, one had been born in Gananoque near Kingston, and the remaining two had been born in England and Ireland respectively. Three of them were Presbyterians but were members of three different congregations; one was a Baptist. The fifth man was a Congregationalist. All lived on different streets in the city and, with the exception of Adam Kerr, would appear to have been established members of their local neighbourhoods, where they were waked and mourned for a day after their deaths. Kerr, although living in the city for the previous nine years, appeared to have been less settled. He lived in lodgings and was buried from his aunt's house on King Street West. Their employment as firemen represented secondary career development; all had been employed previously in occupations such as wood turner, butcher, piano polisher, warden in an asylum, and grocer's assistant before obtaining the apparent security of work in the fire service. Their diversity of background was by no means unusual in Toronto at the time and their aspiration to attain the sinecure of municipal employment would have been shared with many.

What did unite them was their membership of the Orange Order, but even there they had elected to join different local lodges. Kerr, for example, had joined Belfast Purple Star LOL 875, a lodge whose membership included many Irish immigrants, and it was his brethren who paid for and erected the simple stone, replete with Orange insignia, that marks his grave in Mount Pleasant cemetery. Russell was a past master and charter member of Dalton McCarthy LOL 1084. David See's father and two brothers shared membership of LOL 140 with him, and his youngest brother was due to be initiated shortly into that same lodge. All five were committed members of the Order. Virtually all of them had marched with their lodges in the annual County Orange Lodge church parade on the previous Sunday, and they would all have been planning their participation in the Twelfth parade that was held two days after their tragic deaths. Indeed by dint of cruel irony, Walter Collard had not been scheduled to work on the fateful morning of 10 July but had exchanged hours with a colleague so that he would be free to parade on the Twelfth. Their deaths were random accidents in the cause of duty, but the commonality of their membership of the Orange Order, albeit in different local lodges, represented anything but randomness in the implied linkage between the Order and the fire service. Over a period of more than half a century, carefully directed patronage and personal contact networks had supported the numerically strong presence of Orangemen in this particular employment niche, and that relationship would be continued for many years to come. The statistical probability of any sub-group of Toronto firemen being coincidentally members of the Orange Order was high.

The funerals of the five victims were held on Sunday 13 July. They provided an occasion not only for an outpouring of grief and support from the citizens of Toronto but also for a public endorsement of the role of the role and social standing of the Order within the city. Rev. H.G. Dixon, grand chaplain of the Orange Order in Ontario West, conducted the funeral service in the packed St James' Cathedral. Family and friends of the deceased were seated in the reserved front pews, followed by members of the City Council, civic officials, representatives of the fire brigade, and members of the Orange Order – the latter group being so large as to preclude the possibility of additional space being found for members of the public. A reported seventy-five thousand people thronged Yonge Street from King Street northwards to Mount Pleasant cemetery, muted observers of what was the largest funeral procession ever seen in the city. The procession took an hour to pass a given point, and as it wound its way along the five-kilometre route, no one present could have been unaware of the significance of the choreography attached to the public spectacle. Commenting on the procession, the *Globe and Mail* noted:

> First were the Orangemen, not in regalia or by lodge, but a solid column four abreast, reaching from Richmond Street to King, and wearing bits of Orange ribbons and crepe. At their head was the Toronto piccolo band, 22 strong led by C. Smith, followed by the York naval brigade, the Orange Young Britons and the Prentice Boys. The Orangemen were marshalled by W.J. Parkhill of Midland, PGM, John McMillan, GM of Ontario West, Wm Lee Grand secretary and Robert Burns Imperial Grand Director of Ceremonies.[13]

The Orangemen were followed in the procession by ethnic associations and trade unions reflective of the origins and previous occupations of the young men. The Toronto Railway Employees' Union (150 members), Sons of Scotland (65), Mayflower Assembly (50), Knights of Labour, Toronto Safe Workers Benefit Society (70), and Umberto Prime Society (50) were followed by the South African Association (60), which was showing respect to See, a veteran of the Boer War, the Musical Protective Association (300 band), the Royal Grenadiers (50), and the police (20). Ten hearses followed, one for each of the deceased and another for his floral tributes. The processional order was allocated on the basis of length of service in the fire brigade. Family mourners and members of City Council, civic officials, members of the Board of Trade, and Fire Underwriters processed in a long line of carriages, and general citizens followed the cortege. The Hon. Israel Tarte, minister of public works, and a Catholic, represented the federal government. When they reached Mount Pleasant cemetery, the Orange Order's burial service was used for the interment. Following on from the Twelfth parade, which had taken place on the previous day, there was no doubt but that, in paying homage to the bravery of its members who had lost their lives in the line of duty, the Orange Order was also imprinting its signature on the city's tribute to the dead firemen. What is equally significant is the fact that no one commented adversely on the arrangements. The funeral incorporated Catholics in the procession and among the observers, but no rancour was displayed; to do otherwise would have been to dishonour those who had died in the service of the city. In the funeral procession and in civic life, the Order had transcended the marginalizing controversies of its history, moving to the centre of political and social life.

The centrality of the Order in civic culture was reinforced by the continuation of a pattern of political dominance that had been developing over previous decades. E.C. Hocken, MP, former mayor of Toronto, Orangeman, and previously the editor of the *Sentinel*, writing in 1923, described the state of municipal governance with some precision.

The municipal council of twenty-nine members has in 1923, only four aldermen who are not connected with the association. The administration of the Public School System has, from its inception, been carried on by elected trustees, the great majority of whom have been Orangemen. James L. Hughes LLD, for a generation the Chief Inspector, was a Grand Master of the Orange Association and an ardent imperialist ... The spirit of this institution has been stamped upon the Public Schools, through the men who have directed the primary education of the population, either as trustees or officials.[14]

Indicative of the close involvement of the Order in the management of the public school system in the city are the manuscript minutes of a meeting of Magherafelt Purple Star LOL 868 in November 1939, which recorded, "The W.M. called on Rt. W. Bro. Carrie, Past Grand Master of the Grand Lodge of Ontario West and member of the Board of Education, who had another meeting to attend for a few words. Bro. Carrie spoke on the work of the Board of Education in Toronto and through Ontario."[15] Through their influence on the school board, Orangemen sought to ensure that the ethos of the educational system and the engagement of schools in community concerts and other public events remained unambiguously Protestant and British in tone.

It has been demonstrated in chapter 4 that there was a well-established tradition of providing Orangemen with employment as postal clerks, letter carriers, and higher administrative officers. That tradition persisted well into the twentieth century, as illustrated by the intervention by the Order in seeking a resolution to a strike of postal workers in 1924. In that year the Toronto County Lodge wrote to both the prime minister and the postmaster-general, urging a resolution of the ongoing strike among postal workers, "as we believe their requests are reasonable and just ... [and that] ... the said employees have proved themselves faithful and efficient public servants."[16] Clearly not all postal workers were members of the Order, but the majority of them were Protestant, and there was a sufficiently large coterie of Orangemen as to warrant the political overtures made by the Order.

A similar employment pattern was apparent in the urban transportation system – especially since the city had taken charge of the street railway in 1894. Its regulatory and supervisory body, the Toronto Transportation Commission, was presided over for many years by a leading Orangeman, William C. McBrien, whose name is memorialized in the current headquarters of the TTC at Yonge and Davisville. Over a twenty-year period, 1934–54, he laid the foundations of Toronto's modern transit system, overseeing plans for the construction of the subway network. At the time of his unexpected death in office in 1954, he was one of the best-paid public appointees in the city. During McBrien's chairmanship it had become customary for streetcar workers to be granted leave of absence (often with pay) to parade with their lodge on the Twelfth, and paid leave was granted also to employees who were required, as lodge officers, to attend Provincial and Grand Lodge meetings elsewhere in Canada. The Commission in 1938, for example, wrote to the County Orange Lodge "acknowledging the request of the County

Lodge to allow employees off and divert Yonge and Queen cars on July 12th and stating they would cooperate in every possible way."[17] The preferential treatment confirmed not only the strength of Orangemen within the workforce but also the strength of the social network that facilitated the Order's public display.

Opportunities for employment in more menial jobs as cleaners, groundsmen, park attendants, and street cleaners continued to be susceptible to the influence of fraternal brethren who might be foremen or others in positions capable of influencing hiring practices. Such practices were well known, and it was with a certain sense of pride that the *Sentinel* boasted in its review of the Twelfth parade in 1914 that "All the cleaners who shine the marble walls of the city Hall were in the procession with the exception of three [who] were unavoidably absent."[18] A certain familiarity with personalities and individuals would have been required for the official Orange organ to substantiate that report. Apart from its permanent workforce of manual workers, the city also hired several hundred unskilled seasonal labourers. In 1923, for example, the street-cleaning service, which was under the direction of the property commissioner, employed 1,200 men and had an annual budget of $1,600,000.[19] Hiring for these positions, as well as for so many others, was not a random process.

In the private sector there were similar employment niches for those who had signed up to Orange principles, and although the image of effectiveness of preferential treatment may have been greater than the reality, nonetheless, there were well-known pathways to gaining employment. The Eaton Company had a reputation for hiring Protestants – especially Orangemen – and during the 1930s when the company employed some eleven thousand workers, more than 80 per cent of them were Protestants of British stock. Catholics represented 7.6 per cent of its workforce, and Toronto folk memory recalls that Irish Catholic immigrants were usually restricted in their direct contact with the customers lest their accents should prove difficult to understand. Jews were even less likely to find employment, with only twenty being employed.[20] The Eaton family were never members of the Orange Order, but Sir John Eaton, Timothy's son and heir, often watched the annual Orange parade from an upstairs window in his city centre store.[21] Other smaller firms often projected a partisan image in their hiring practices, and at all times, but especially during economic downturns, the Order openly sought to secure employment for its members. In the winter of 1914 the County Lodge, for example,

opened an Orange Employment Bureau to "reduce the unemployment and distress among our brethren" and appealed for assistance
from all Orangemen both employers and employees.

> This work which is a very noble one cannot be carried on successfully
> without the co-operation of every member of our Association; and as the
> County Lodge is bearing the entire expense of this bureau, we feel, that
> it should be the duty of every member of our Order who is an employer
> of labour or who is directly or indirectly responsible for the employment
> of men, to see that any vacancies under his control shall be filled as far as
> possible by the members of the Loyal Orange Association. There is also
> good work to be done by our members who are employees by keeping
> this office informed of any vacancies that occur in connection with the
> Office, the Factory, the Building Trades, or any other work in which they
> are themselves employed: then our members could be the first to apply
> for the same.[22]

The secretary of the committee overseeing this networking function
within the County Lodge was William C. McBrien, later chairman of
the Toronto Transportation Commission. In a similar vein, during the
economic depression of the 1930s, the Toronto County Lodge instructed
the secretaries of all local lodges within its jurisdiction to "Send to the
County Secretary right away, the names of members of your lodge who
are employers, or who hold key positions in firms where employment
might be given, and the names of firms with which they are connected ...
If you know a Protestant friend who is likely to give an Orangeman a
chance, let us have his name, and we will do our utmost to get his cooperation in this matter."[23]

The Order sought proactively to encourage its members to patron-
ize Protestant establishments and, conversely, to avoid Catholic firms
where possible. Illustrative of this was the compilation and publication
of a list of Toronto business establishments that assigned all, or part, of
their assessed municipal taxes to the support of Catholic schools rather
than public schools. Since 1886, businesses in Ontario had assigned
their assessment taxes to Catholic schools on the basis of a formula that
reflected the Catholic ownership of the enterprise.[24] It was a cumber-
some instrument and it became increasingly difficult to operate when
corporations and multiple ownerships became common. Nevertheless,
at a reductionist level the tax assignment could be interpreted as a surrogate measure of the Catholic identity of business establishments, and

it was on this basis that the Orange Order constructed what was in effect a blacklist of Toronto firms. The list was first circulated in 1936 at a time of political controversy over the extension of financial support to the separate school board, but a decade later it was still being updated and was made available in bulk to lodges for distribution to members at a cost of a dollar for one hundred copies.[25] More than 170 businesses were ranked according to the percentage allocation of the taxes designated for the support of Catholic separate schools, and it is a striking illustration of how, even in the worlds of manufacturing, commerce, and services, fissure lines determined by religious affiliation were deemed significant. Sixty-nine firms allocated 100 per cent of their school taxes to the Catholic schools, and included among that number was Laura Secord Candy Shops, a firm owned by the prominent Catholic leader Senator Frank O'Connor. Construction companies such as Swansea Construction and Daniels Construction were listed together with newer businesses such as Maynard Film Distribution, Canada Law Book Company, and Roach Pharmacy. Twenty-six hotels and taverns were defined as Catholic, including the Wheat Sheaf tavern, founded in 1849. But in acknowledgment of the religious pluralism of their ownership, almost one hundred businesses allocated a pro rata share of their taxes to Catholic schools, the relative apportionment being determined with some precision. Thus the Toronto Stock Exchange allocated 3.09 per cent of its taxes, the Albany Club allocated 0.945 per cent, and, surprisingly, the O'Keefe Brewing Company allocated only 15 per cent to the separate school board. Such allocations were of public significance and, in the eyes of some, of political importance.

As in the nineteenth century, Catholic Irish newspapers such as the *Irish Canadian* continued to monitor the percentage of public service jobs held by Catholics. Municipal and provincial authorities were frequently chastised for what was perceived as a lack of generosity when vacancies arose. Such comments and analysis belied an unwritten but established practice of allocating a certain amount of patronage in publicly funded employment to the minority group. When the percentage of Catholics in the city's population fell in the opening decades of the twentieth century, there was evidence of an enhanced vigilance and sensitivity in the analyses published in the *Irish Canadian*, political point scoring being very much to the fore. Claiming that the relative position of Catholics in the civil service was the worst in more than a decade, the paper editorialized in 1901 that when a vacancy was due to be filled by a Catholic it was dangled before the community for an inordinately long time and was used to foment division within its ranks. It purported to illustrate its case by reference to three vacant licence inspector posts in Toronto: "The three positions were vacated simultaneously. Two were to go to Protestants and the third (of course the third, not the first) to a Catholic. The two Protestants were appointed immediately and without any difficulties. The Catholic appointment was kept open for a considerable time ... At last when the Ministers thought they had obtained sufficient advertisement and notoriety for their proposed Catholic appointment it was made."[26]

Appointments to the Toronto-based provincial civil service were especially distrusted when the Conservatives were in power, for the Orange credentials of that party were well known. Little had changed since the previous century, and overall the complexion of employment, public and private, in Toronto in the inter-war years continued to be not only Protestant and British, as might be expected given the demographic composition of the city, but also restrictive in terms of the inclusion of Catholics. It was the comfortable and wide-ranging presence of Orangeism in a diversity of occupations from the unskilled jobs through skilled and professional positions that confirmed the image of the city as the "Belfast of Canada." Nowhere outside of the Ulster metropolis did the Orange Order maintain such a tight grip on public elected office and dispense effective patronage through public and private employment. Immigrants and long-term residents were aware of this aspect of the civic culture. For Protestants it represented opportunity and access; for Catholics it was confirmation that they remained somewhat on the periphery, although the older among them might contend that at least the aggravated sectarianism of the previous century was no longer visible.

Public Profile of the Orange Order in the City

The public profile of the Orange Order continued to be manifested in the composition of the elected representatives in City Hall, and especially in the office of mayor. Almost without exception, the mayors of the city in the first half of the twentieth century were Orangemen. The prevalence of aldermen with an Orange affiliation and the virtual monopoly on the mayoralty exercised by the Order during this period was certainly not accidental. Electoral strategies first employed in the previous century evolved in line with the growth of the organization and the ongoing rapid expansion of the city, whose population now exceeded half a million. Personal contact, endorsement of ward bosses who were officials in the Order, and the use of Orange halls as electioneering supports remained vital strategic components, but a more formal and overt strategy was also designed and implemented. In the 1920s and 1930s the County Orange Lodge of Toronto, through its Legislation Committee, reviewed and publicly endorsed slates of candidates standing in the annual municipal elections, commandeering the considerable strength of the fraternity on polling day to assist in their success. The 1925 municipal elections, for example, endorsed a slate for mayor (one candidate), Board of Control (four candidates), aldermen (seventeen candidates), and school board (eleven candidates), and the level of success was striking. Leading Orangeman Thomas Foster was elected mayor, three of the four controller posts went to Orange candidates, and fourteen Orange aldermen and seven Orange school board trustees were also successful. It was noteworthy that the Order fielded candidates in every one of the city's eight wards, and only Ward Four, which included the former St Patrick's Ward, failed to return an Orangeman on this occasion as either alderman or school trustee. The electoral strategy of the Order was not confined to sub-districts within the city; Toronto in its entirety was envisaged as being potentially an Orange fiefdom.[27]

The pattern was repeated at other levels of elected representation. In the twenty years prior to its electoral districts being reorganized in 1924, Toronto had been represented in the national Parliament by five members, and at various elections in 1911, 1917, and 1921 four ridings had returned Orangemen in the persons of Edmund Bristol (Toronto Centre), Albert Kemp (Toronto East), Thomas Church (Toronto North), and Horatio Hocken (Toronto West). The fifth riding (Toronto South) returned an Orangeman, George Geary, in the 1925 election. All were members of the Conservative party. No federal Liberal was returned for the city of Toronto during the 1920s, and organized labour failed to elect even one candidate from a city that had a strong industrial presence. Politics in the metropolis continued along lines that were derivative of nineteenth-century patterns; Toryism continued to reign supreme, and within that ideology Orangeism was a comfortable and, at times, guiding partner.[28] The electoral appeal of a political philosophy within which Orangeism was a comfortable bedfellow was equally apparent at the level of provincial politics. The Ontario Liberal party under Oliver Mowat had dominated Ontario politics for thirty years after Confederation, but in 1905 the Conservatives gained power and, with the

County Orange Lodge of Toronto

Legislation Committee

Dear Sir and Brother,

The Legislation Committee of the Orange County Lodge has decided to conduct a SLATE in the coming Municipal Election, similar to that of last year.

The Slate will be chosen by popular ballot at a Convention to be held the night following the City Nominations.

The Committee is desirous of having a full representation of every Lodge in the City. You are therefore requested to appoint an additional Delegate to represent your Lodge at Convention, and forward his name and address at once to the Secretary.

answered
Dec 13. 1925

Fraternally yours,

R. OULLAHAN

Secretary

174 Grace Street—Trinity 8793

6.1 Slate for municipal elections, 1925

exception of the period 1934–43, remained in government until 1985. No other democracy in the western world, other than Northern Ireland, returned a single party for such a prolonged period in the twentieth century: coincidentally, both the Ulster Unionist party and the Ontario Conservative party had access to the political machinery of the Orange Order especially during the first half of the century.

Indicative of the strength of Orangeism within the Ontario Conservatives was the government led by G. Howard Ferguson. Ferguson became premier of Ontario in 1923, his party winning 75 out of a total of 111 seats in the Legislature. Forty-one of the elected Conservatives were Orangemen. Only 10 elected representatives, all Liberals, were Catholic. Ferguson's Tories won all seats in Toronto and continued to dominate that political scene for several decades. The Ontario Legislature at the time has been described as resembling more "the style and manner of an over-sized county council than it did the federal House of Commons," and Ferguson was "well suited to the rough exchanges and partisan manoeuvres which characterized the politics of pre-war Ontario."[29] He held office from 1923 to 1930, at which point he was appointed Canadian high commissioner in London. He was a lifelong member of the Orange Order and, while premier, he wore his Orange sash and past master jewels proudly in Toronto's Twelfth processions. His reputation as a strident Orangeman extended throughout Ontario and also abroad. When he was preparing for a visit to the newly established state of Northern Ireland in 1925, a leading Toronto Orangeman wrote to Sir James Craig, the prime minister in Belfast, advising him that Ferguson was "one of our own sort in every way."[30] The Unionist government of Northern Ireland responded warmly to their brother Orangeman and hosted his visit in a manner befitting the imperial, demographic, and fraternal ties common to the two jurisdictions.

The accepted social and political prominence of the Order was reflected in the increasingly supportive and comprehensive coverage in the press of the day. Coverage by the *Sentinel* and the *Telegram* was to be expected, but less partisan papers also provided favourable reviews of Orange celebrations. The *Telegram* devoted nine pages of text and photographs to the Twelfth parade in its issue of Monday, 12 July 1920, noting that 8,300 had marched, including members of the ladies' affiliated body, the Loyal Orange Benevolent Association, and the Orange Young Britons. Lodges from across Ontario and elsewhere had joined their Toronto brethren in a massive public display of Orange fervour. It was reported that 117 lodges, 51 bands, 300 cars, 15 floats, and 46 mounted men participated in the five-mile-long parade that took two hours to pass a given point en route to the Exhibition Grounds, where twenty-five thousand supporters and members were to gather to listen to political and religious speeches and enjoy the bonhomie of a community picnic. Prominent among the marchers were Mayor Thomas Church, former Mayor Oliver, and dozens of public figures including officials, aldermen, and controllers from City Hall. Among the marching lodges, King William 111 LOL 140 was especially proud of the fact that federal and provincial parliaments were both represented among its ranks.[31] The *Globe and Mail* and the *Star* also carried extensive coverage of the event. There was a certain respect and even pride in the reporting; in no way was it implied that the Orange Order was anything other than an acceptable element in mainstream civic life and culture. It could scarcely be otherwise, given the status of some of those in the parade.

In July 1930 the Orange Order, celebrating its Canadian centenary, organized a series of local and citywide parades in the weeks preceding the Twelfth. On 6 July, some five thousand Orangemen in full regalia paraded from Queen's Park along University Avenue and Bloor Street to St Paul's Anglican Church for a religious service, and one week later the largest Orange parade in the city's history took place. Fifteen thousand Orangemen paraded, including visiting lodges from Rochester, Chicago, and Detroit, and the parade took four hours to wend its way to Exhibition Park. Tens of thousands of Torontonians watched and applauded family and friends as they paraded in the centenary celebration of the foundation of the Grand Lodge of British America, and they would have recognized many public figures in line behind the banners, fifes, and drums. Premier G. Howard Ferguson, who had marched in all but two Twelfths during his thirty-five-year membership of the Order,[32] and Ashmore Kidd, grand master of British America and then speaker of the Ontario Legislature, were there, as was Mayor Wemp, members of the House of Commons, public representatives from every part of the city, and senior municipal officials. It was a public display of power, prestige, and Protestantism: the open Bible, the Crown, and the symbols and colours of the seventeenth-century Irish Battle of the Boyne reflected a civic culture that was manifest in identical form on the same day on the streets of Belfast, where the Northern Ireland prime minister, speaker of the House, and members of the Belfast and Westminster Parliaments accompanied the lord mayor and thousands of fellow Orangemen to the picnic grounds on the outskirts of the Ulster city.

Annual Church Service

OF THE

Loyal Orange District Lodge
OF

Centre Toronto.

will be held in

Cooke's Church, Cor. Queen & Mutual Sts.
Sunday, May 30th, 1926 at 3 p. m.

Rev. Bro. L. Gibson, B. D., Ph. D., will officiate
Collection in aid of True Blue and Orange Orphanage.

It is desired that every member if possible turn out on this occasion, so that the Centre District may be able to make a creditable showing.

Brethren will assemble at Allan Gardens at 2.15.

Band in attendance.

ALL ORANGEMEN WELCOME.

W. CREECH,   W. F. McKELL, Recording Secretary
District Master   17 Arundel Ave.

6.2 Annual church parade and service, 1926

The Organizational and Numerical Strength of
the Orange Order, 1920–1940

A reciprocal relationship between the number of lodges, size of membership, and social and political power created a positive environment for the development of the Orange Order within the city, and, measured by any of these factors, it is clear that the organization attained unprecedented heights during the first three decades of the twentieth century. Thereafter, it maintained a brief period of stability before commencing a process of inexorable decline that continues up to the present day. The centrality of Toronto in the overall dynamic of the Canadian Order had been long recognized by the senior officers of the organization, and when the Grand Orange Lodge of British America met in the city in the spring of 1906, T.S. Sproule, grand master and member of the House of Commons, proclaimed, "From an Orange point of view, Toronto might well be designated the Hub of the Empire. It may justly be proud of its 53 primary lodges (without counting those in the suburbs) each with a large membership of enthusiastic and loyal brethren composed of men of all classes and ranks and recognised as excellent citizens."[33]

The organizational strength of the Order has traditionally been measured by numerical analysis of the number and distribution of local or primary lodges that were in good standing with the national and provincial Grand Lodges,[34] a technique that is especially useful in developing an understanding of the geographical extent and spread of the organization. Employing this approach, Houston and Smyth explored the dynamic relationship that existed between the settlement history of Canada, the nature of its expanding frontier, and the growth of the Order in the decades after 1830. The normal size range for an established Canadian lodge was determined as being of thirty to sixty members, and a close correlation between the scale of local communities in small-town and rural Canada and the distribution of lodges was demonstrated. Where distances became too great for social travel on dark winter evenings, new lodges would be formed among adjacent evolving communities, and through this process the Order demonstrated, in form, function, and location, a vibrant organic relationship with community development in general.[35]

However, in large urban centres such as Toronto, where a combination of higher population densities and greater geographical accessibility pertained, the number and distribution of lodges is a less sensitive indicator of organizational vitality. During the closing years

Table 6.4 Orange lodges in Canada, Ontario, and Toronto, 1900–40

	1900	1910	1920	1930	1940
Canada	1,469	1,837	2,205	2,168	1,847
Ontario	988	1,056	1,167	1,108	1,004
Toronto	55	59	82	96	69

Source: various Grand Lodge reports and Toronto County Lodge reports.

of the nineteenth century and the opening decades of the twentieth, the number of lodges in Toronto grew at a steady pace, almost doubling between 1900 and 1930 (table 6.4), but in the same period the number of registered Orangemen increased threefold. The explanation lies in the greater elasticity of individual lodge memberships in the metropolis, where a higher population threshold, greater accessibility, and larger halls meant that greater variation in lodge size could be tolerated. In 1894 lodges had, on average, about seventy members, but by 1922 average membership had swollen to one hundred and twenty. The range of lodge size was great: one lodge had more than four hundred men on its books, ten lodges had more than two hundred members. In such circumstances an analysis based on the number of functioning lodges requires supplementation by a more detailed review of actual membership numbers and a longitudinal analysis of the balance between initiations and suspensions within the organization. At any given time, the membership of the Order was quite dynamic – the inflow of initiates being balanced, and sometimes exceeded, by suspensions and withdrawals.

The network of local or primary lodges within Canada peaked in the early 1920s, by which time the Order had managed to spread into every province and had colonized a variety of settlement niches, ranging from the fishing and resource centres of the Atlantic provinces to the English-speaking enclaves in Quebec, and onwards through rural and urban Ontario to farming communities on the prairies and mining towns in British Columbia. It was an impressive and unrivalled geography for a voluntary organization, representing a century of continuous expansion. The Order was, by far, the most successful of all contemporary fraternal bodies. Toronto's developmental pattern was broadly in keeping with the national and Ontario trends, but its growth dynamic lasted a decade longer, with decline in the number of lodges becoming apparent only in the 1930s.

6.3 Orange parade, Toronto, 12 July 1930

The pattern of historical development demonstrated by the Order in Toronto reflected the ongoing demographic expansion of the city, the popularity of fraternalism in general, and the unique, but endemic, local politico-religious environment. Undoubtedly, the Order also derived tremendous momentum from its widely recognized grip on the conduits for dispersal of patronage. Notwithstanding the rapid expansion of jobs in the commercial and industrial spheres, the attractions of publicly funded employment remained strong throughout the 1920s, and the sector continued to expand as the range of services increased in line with an increasingly complex municipal government. Federal, provincial, and municipal jobs, part time and full time, were numbered in the thousands and included a range of skill requirements and salaries that extended from seasonal labourer to city architect. It was this spectrum of employment niches, and the fact that filling them was amenable to political influence, that made the Order so attractive to a wide social range, although it continued to be numerically dominated by skilled, semi-skilled, and manual workers. H.C. Hocken, then a federal MP and a former mayor of the city, noted in 1917: "In the City of Toronto, where we have 20,000 Orangemen, they are in great proportion working men. This is true of every city in Canada."[36] However, the Order was conscious of the advantage of attracting and retaining men of influence and social standing. In 1920, for example, Imperial LOL 2767 was established specifically to cater for business and professional men; the initiation fee was $12 and the collars for officers cost $180 each. As a justification for the creation of the new lodge, the Order pointed out, "The members ... do not feel superior to other Orangemen in any way but they feel they can render a distinct service to the Orange Order and the cause of Protestantism by enlisting the support of a large number of business and professional men. To get men of the desired calibre and hold their interest, it is necessary to provide a lodge where they will feel at home."[37] The lodge was an initial success: seven past masters of other lodges were members of the founding group and on the opening night all officers appeared in formal attire. To them, and to the members in general, the utility of Orange membership within the city was more than a perception: it was a well-used mechanism for accessing employment, conducting business, and ensuring electoral support. This innate attractiveness of the Order fuelled the growth of an extensive and elaborate lodge network that was sufficiently flexible to facilitate absorption of growth in membership from Canadian-born and immigrants alike. Only Belfast and Liverpool could rival the strength of this organizational characteristic of Toronto, and nowhere, other than in the Ulster heartland, did the Order command such power and centrality within civic culture.

At the beginning of the twentieth century, the Order, with slightly more than three thousand members, appeared somewhat smaller than it had been a decade earlier. In part, this was due to the lag between the evolving jurisdictional boundaries of the Order and the rapidly developing suburbs to which many members were migrating. The next ten years were to witness a tripling of its strength. The dynamic for growth drew upon the traditional Orange community as sons followed their fathers into the lodges in an affirmation of traditional values and civic culture, but the contemporaneous growth of the city through in-migration from rural and small-town Ontario and immigration from the British Isles provided an additional and invigorating supply of new recruits. The number of Orangemen in the city peaked at the commencement of the First World War, and although peacetime did bring about a renewal of interest, the numbers never exceeded those of the previous decade (table 6.5). Nonetheless, membership did maintain a corps

Table 6.5 Orangemen and population growth, Toronto, 1901–41

	1901	1911	1921	1931	1941
Population	208,040	356,538	521,893	631,207	667,457
Orangemen	3,282	10,117	9,891	9,048	5,500 (est)

Source: Census of population and annual returns of the County Orange Lodge of Toronto.

slightly in excess of nine thousand men from 1921 through to 1931. In that period the number of lodges actually increased as some members reorganized themselves in new lodge groupings based on friendships and networks established during the war. Others established new lodges in the suburbs of the city. The war was to prove to be a defining moment for the Order and for Canada. Given the strong imperial sentiment that permeated the ideology of Orangeism, it was scarcely surprising that recruitment for the military should have proven particularly fruitful among the brethren. The minister of defence at the time was Sam Hughes, a somewhat controversial figure and a lifelong Orangeman. His brother John had served as grand master of Ontario East and another brother, James, had been grand master of Ontario West. He himself was a past master of LOL 557. Orange halls across Canada were deployed as recruiting stations during the war, and the Order claimed that 50,000 members joined the Canadian Expeditionary Force. Toronto lodges provided 3,061 recruits – almost one-third of the total membership and probably half of those in the age group eighteen to forty-five. A total of 338 members were killed in action. In 1917, for example, Joshua LOL returned a total membership of 52, of whom 26 were soldiers currently serving overseas. Since the beginning of the war, 37 members of that lodge had served overseas and a total of 8 had been killed.[38] In the immediate aftermath of the war it appeared as though the Order might revert to its previous pattern of dynamic expansion, and the 1921 annual parade included 2,300 returned servicemen who had resumed their place in the local lodges – more than 80 per cent of those who had survived the combat.[39] War deaths, therefore, did not of themselves prompt the onset of decline in Toronto's membership, but within the post-war environment many Canadians began to question the value of their commitment to the Empire, and over the next decade a drift of members away from the organization became gradually apparent.

Growth within the Order was traditionally dependent upon the initiation of new members and the recruitment of a smaller number joining "on certificate," i.e., by transfers from other lodges, based either elsewhere in Canada or abroad. Recruitment of new initiates initially proved robust in the years immediately after the war: upwards of one thousand new members joined the Toronto lodges each year during the 1920s and their numbers were augmented further by hundreds of established Orangemen migrating to the city. In 1921, for example, 942 men were initiated into the Toronto lodges and a further 441 transferred on certificate from external lodges – a total of 1,383 new members. They did not amount to an overall increase in the strength of the Order, however, for in the same year 1,368 members were suspended for non-payment of dues and 96 others died. Five years later one thousand initiates joined and 436 transfers were also added, but 1,138 current members were suspended. Suspension for non-payment of dues was really a barometer of waning interest; members simply drifted away from the regular meetings and eventually ceased to include membership fees within their discretionary expenditure.

The intake of new members during the 1920s was striking – probably more than ten thousand men joined in the course of that decade (table 6.6). These figures represented a potential 10 per cent rate of growth per annum, but the counterbalancing exodus from the lodges meant that the overall membership figures remained more or less in equilibrium. The fundamental membership flux was initially camouflaged, only being revealed in the 1930s.[40] The scale of the recruitment was a positive indicator of the continued appeal of the Order, especially for those who were newcomers to the city; conversely, the level of suspensions reflected the short-term interests of many who had joined only a few years earlier. The Order failed to capitalize on the strong influx of recruits during these years, and the exceptionally poor retention rate exhibited during the decade of its most prolific recruitment was a function of a devastating combination of internal and external factors. The instability that ensued was ultimately to lead to a reduction in power and, inevitably, the marginalization of the Order in the civic politics and culture of the city. Many members dropped their affiliation after a few years, and although there was a greater degree of stability among the ranks of lodge officers, prolonged periods of high-volume membership turnover removed a fundamental element of long-term organizational constancy in a body whose ideology enshrined a belief that the seventeenth-century Irish Williamite wars were of relevance to the politics of religion in contemporary Toronto society. Amid the socio-economic stress of the Great Depression, the collapse of the Orange Order became obvious (table 6.7).

Table 6.6 Components of growth of the Orange Order in Toronto, 1920–30

Year	Joined by initiations	Joined by certificate	Total membership
1920			10,117
1921	942	441	9,891
1922	931	332	9,627
1923	1,001	388	9,779
1924	n/a	n/a	9,725
1925	1,000	436	9,725
1926	798	377	9,654
1927	692	305	9,356
1928	637	353	9,152
1929	657	424	9,230
1930	674	399	9,048

Source: Annual returns of the County Orange Lodge of Toronto.

Table 6.7 Components of membership change, Toronto lodges, 1930–6

Year	Initiations	Transfers in	Suspensions	Transfers out	Total membership
1930	674	399	1096	168	9,048
1932	268	151	886	69	6,740
1934	269	115	931	66	6,999
1936	242	140	696	70	5,941

Source: Annual returns of the County Orange Lodge of Toronto.

The economic depression of the 1930s severely tested the fraternal organization's ability to provide access to employment and welfare assistance, traditionally two of the main attractions of membership. Likewise, the precipitous decline in both municipal and corporate fortunes caused by the international crash had a profound impact on life in the city. By 1931, 17 per cent of the city's workforce was unemployed; two years later this had increased to 30 per cent. In the private sector, manufacturing and construction were worst hit; in the public sector, expenditure reductions had to be imposed on public works and the police, both of which traditionally employed hundreds of Orangemen.[41] Attempts within the Order to contain the worst impact of the economic crisis proved ineffective. Despite the exemption from capitation tax granted by the County Lodge for certified unemployed members, and the valiant effort made by many local lodges to carry the unemployed on the books for several years, the problem was inescapable. In 1932 five city lodges, LOL 136, LOL 154, LOL 212, LOL 396, and LOL 657, reported "fully two-thirds of the membership being unemployed and the lodge income depleted by this cause." High levels of distress were evident also in many other lodges.[42] Suspensions could not be deferred indefinitely. The Eastern District reported in 1937, for example, decreases "caused by several of the larger lodges suspending members for non-payment of dues who had previously been carried by the lodges for a period of up to five years with no sign of financial returns from such members."[43] With dwindling household budgets and wage reductions of 40 per cent, many men were no longer willing or able to allocate a couple of dollars per month for membership, and with higher demands on their welfare and sickness benefit schemes, many lodges simply could not maintain these once-attractive programs. The district master of the Eastern Toronto reported in 1937:

> Many of the members who have been in good positions for years, and in a good many cases, got what they wanted out of the organisation, either directly or indirectly, now apparently do not wish to continue with membership ... we find that in most cases the suspensions are not unemployed members (these being carried by their respective lodges) but is just a case of most of the lodges getting rid of a lot of "dead wood" which they have been carrying for the last few years in the hopes of the members in question fulfilling their obligations.[44]

The decline of almost 50 per cent in membership of the Toronto lodges during the 1930s was a blow from which the Order never recovered. Initiations remained constant at a modest level after a precipitous drop at the beginning of the decade, and transfers into the lodges were stabilized for a while at a low level, but the key determinant of decline was the very large number being suspended from membership: their scale exceeded the intake by a factor of three or more. Relatively few transferred out with their certificates, indicating that the attrition was an abandonment of membership entirely, rather than a temporary cessation of participation.

The Changing Identity of Toronto Orangeism

The County Orange Lodge did not maintain a centralized register of recruits – such records were properly the business of each individual local lodge. However, from the surviving manuscript rolls of four large lodges it has been possible to construct a data set of relevance for the ten-year period 1919–28, the period of most rapid growth of the Order in Toronto. There is no reason to believe that the pattern revealed is at variance with the overall norms of the time. Records for a cohort of 258 initiates (about 2.5 per cent of all initiates in those years) provide insight into their age, occupational characteristics, birthplace, and religious affiliation. Only in a few instances are there gaps in the lodge data. All initiates were under sixty years of age, more than half of them being under thirty. As with the 1894 population, the recruits were young men in their active years; they were not in the senior years of their life, looking for camaraderie amid a convivial fraternal environment of aged men. Rather, the age profile is very similar to that of the total population of migrants and immigrants at the time – young males looking for employment and a fresh start in life. Others were the sons of established Orangemen who were joining the Order on coming of age.

About one-third of the initiates were natives of the city; the remainder were from a diversity of source regions within the realm of Orangeism (table 6.8). The Canadian-born originated primarily in Ontario. Forty-six per cent were from the British Isles, but, strikingly, Ireland was the least favoured source by a very large margin indeed. In contrast to the 1894 data set, Scotland had strengthened as a source area and England had also increased its share – it had contributed about 20 per cent of members in 1894, but by the 1920s this had expanded to 30 per cent. Both England and Scotland were, at the time, home to a large number of indigenous Orange lodges, especially in Glasgow, Liverpool, and the industrial cities of the midlands and northeast, and it is most likely that those immigrants who subsequently joined lodges in Toronto would have been very familiar with Orangeism and all it stood for. But these men had not joined the Order in their homeland; their initiation into lodges in Toronto was in accordance with the organization's provision for interested Protestant males who had never previously taken the Orange oath. They were new recruits, and as English and Scottish immigrants in a new land their decision to join the Orange Order was a deliberate personal choice and one that was unlikely to have been influenced by family tradition. Why should a teacher from London, a glass

Table 6.8 Place of birth: Orange initiates, 1919–28

Ireland	England	Scotland	Toronto	Canada	Other	Total
11	76	31	72	61	7	258
4.3%	29.5%	12.1%	28.0%	23.6%	2.7%	

Source: Miscellaneous file, Country Orange Lodge of Toronto.

engraver from Birmingham, and a printer from Surrey join the Orange fraternity in Toronto? A commonality of Protestant faith and a set of kindred political values derived from an early immersion in British culture provided the immigrants with the prerequisites for Orange membership, but other voluntary fraternal bodies such as the Masonic Order and the Foresters could also offer a supportive environment for such beliefs and without the additional ideological baggage of the Battle of the Boyne or the Siege of Derry. Yet thousands of the British immigrants choose to join the Orange Order.

Many of the immigrants may have joined more than one fraternal body, but their specific identification with Orangeism placed them within the largest voluntary and most powerful organization in their adopted city and aligned them with a set of influences and opportunities that were of central relevance in their quest for employment, social standing, and networking in the new environment. Analysis of clustering in initiation ceremonies in each of the four lodges reveals no overriding pattern, but it is clear that at certain lodge meetings initiates might include a cluster of four or five men from England, united in their Anglicism but distinguished by a diversity of occupations. On other occasions, family and business background overlapped; e.g., in 1907 the Price brothers from Greenwood Avenue, owners of a brickyard, were initiated in the same meeting of LOL 711, and several other brickmakers joined that lodge in the following months. There were many other recorded instances of persons living on the same street or working in the same trade, e.g., printers, being initiated at the same lodge meeting. In 1922, for instance, five motormen were initiated into the same lodge within a few weeks of each other – two shared an address on Chesholme Street, and the remainder were from adjoining streets. The lodges were microcosms of sub-communities within the city, and the initiative for joining may well have been prompted by a mixture of factors such as the influence of neighbours or fellow church-goers, employment niches,

Table 6.9 Religion, initiates, 1919–28

	Anglican	Methodist	Presbyterian	Baptist	Other	Total
Initiates	134	29	61	13	14	234
	53.9%	11.4%	24.1%	5.1%	5.5%	
City of Toronto						421,167
Protestants	41.1%	20.2%	26.9%	6.7%	5.6%	

Source: Miscellaneous file, Country Orange Lodge of Toronto.

or ethnic background. But to all there must have been some perceived utility value. The fact that the English were the largest single grouping was a reflection of the fact that they were the largest immigrant stream in Toronto in the 1920s and does not necessarily indicate a greater pre-disposition on their part.

In 1921, somewhat more than 80 per cent of Toronto's population was Protestant with Anglicans composing the largest denomination. Pres-byterians were about one-quarter of the Protestant cohort and Method-ists were ranked in third place. The rank ordering among the Orange initiates of the time followed the same pattern (see table 6.9), but, sig-nificantly, Anglicans were strongly over-represented and, conversely, Methodists composed only about half of the expected share. Presbyteri-ans and Baptists mirrored the city pattern quite closely, as did the com-ponent described as "other." Congregationalists, Plymouth Brethren, and Salvation Army members dominated this latter category, but their combined relative strength indicated clearly that evangelical groups were not overly susceptible to the appeal of the Orange lodges. All the Orange initiates professed affiliation to Protestantism and they were very much drawn from the mainstream churches, although the regu-larity of their worship is difficult to ascertain. Indeed, compared with the 1894 profile of the Order, the representation of the "other" churches within the membership had diminished by a third – a demographic feature that was reflective of overall changes within the city, where the three major denominations (Anglicans, Presbyterians, and Methodists) had increased their presence within the Protestant community from 75 per cent to 88 per cent. In the inter-censal period, 1891–1921, Toronto had become a more Anglican city, with 41.1 per cent of all Protestants identifying with that church compared with 32.7 per cent thirty years earlier. During that period Anglicans had increased their relative pres-ence among Orange initiates to 53.9 per cent – evidence, *inter alia*, of the growing centrality of the Order within the urban community. It was also a reflection of the numerical significance of Anglican members recruited from the city's population of English immigrants.

The Toronto lodges, home to a large number of immigrants who were initiated into the organization within their adopted city, were further strengthened by an inflow of committed Orangemen who joined by transfer certificates issued by lodges in their homeland. Those joining the Order by means of transfer certificates amounted to about 30 per cent of all entrants. The majority of these came from Ulster. Unlike their English and Scottish counterparts, most Irish Protestant immigrants who were predisposed to joining the Order had done so prior to immigration, and they easily transferred their membership certificates to Toronto lodges on their arrival in the city. Consequently, few Irish men were initiated into lodges in Toronto, but their numbers were expectedly higher among those bearing certificates of prior initiation. As with initiations, no centralized record of the names of those transferring by certificate was maintained by the Order, but a surviving cache of certificates retained by Cameron LOL 613 does provide insight into the background of more than two hundred Orangemen who transferred into that lodge in the years 1900–20.[45] In Cameron Lodge very few transfers originated in Canadian regions outside of Ontario; other Toronto lodges contributed forty-three members – men who for personal, family, or other reasons now wished to transfer to LOL 613. Immigrants from Ireland, primarily Ulster, were the largest component, composing more than two-thirds of those transferring (table 6.10). One-third (thirty-six men) of the Ulster contingent came via Belfast lodges and a similar number (thirty-five men) were from Antrim and Down, the two counties which contained the urban district of Belfast.

In Cameron LOL 613, these Belfast Orangemen formed a significant component of a lodge that, with about 350 members, was one of the largest in the city; they would certainly have lent a very distinctive tone to the proceedings of that particular unit of Toronto Orangeism. Other contemporary Toronto lodges that contained a strong Ulster immigrant component included Belfast Purple Star LOL 875, Magherafelt Purple Star LOL 864, North of Ireland Defenders LOL 3082, Aughrim Rose of Derry LOL 2159, and Sons of Portadown LOL 919. But it is probable that most Toronto lodges included some Ulstermen among their members, and it was their presence throughout the 1920s, and later, that continued to refresh the image of the city as the "Belfast of Canada." Indicative of this strong presence of Ulster Orangemen in Toronto is

Table 6.10 Source of transfers by certificate into LOL 613, 1900–20

Ireland	Toronto	Canada	England	Scotland	USA	Other	Total
156	43	22	0	2	4	1	228
68.4%	18.8%	9.7%	0	0.9%	1.8%	0.4%	100%

Source: Miscellaneous file, Country Orange Lodge of Toronto.

a 1923 description of the voyage of *SS Doric*, which had sailed from Belfast with four hundred Ulstermen aboard en route for Canada. In the mid-Atlantic, "a regular Orange Lodge meeting was held, over 27 [Ulster] primary lodges being represented in the smoke room."[46] In the middle of a transoceanic migration, social connections of future value were being forged under the auspices of the fraternal organization.

The selective data on source regions for initiates and transferees in these specific lodges suggests that the organizational pattern evident in 1894 had continued to predominate. About half of those joining Toronto lodges in the first three decades of the twentieth century were recent immigrants. The immigrant identity of the Order was thus perpetuated, but, while neophytes of English and Scottish origin composed the bulk of the initiates, a strong and recognizable stream of established Orangemen transferring from Irish lodges augmented them. These seasoned brethren may have constituted as much as 20 per cent of the annual recruitment, and their presence does much to explain the informed and passionate interest in Irish political developments exhibited by the Order in Toronto during this pivotal period of Irish political history. In recognition of this close and immediate contact with Ireland and Britain, some Toronto lodges selected names honouring the leaders and bodies central to the Irish political crisis; e.g., LOL 2488, founded in 1913, was named "Sir Edward Carson," LOL 2799, founded in 1920, was named "Castle Dawson Ballyclair-Ulster Volunteer," and LOL 3082, founded in 1929, was named "North of Ireland Defenders." Others recalled contemporary imperial warfare developments, with LOL 954 taking the name "Dreadnought" in 1907 and LOL 880 choosing "Men of the Empire" in 1920. In tone and in content the utterances of the Orange lodges of Toronto revealed an enduring intimacy with the Irish, British, and imperial worlds. As such, the Order in Toronto exhibited a progressive estrangement from the social and political values of small-town and rural Canadian lodges that had evolved over several generations and whose experience remained Canadian and local rather than transnational. In many respects it would seem that the Toronto lodges maintained greater links with the original Irish and British fonts of Orangeism than they did with their confrères in Bonavista, Gaspé, or Brockville, and they were continually reborn in the baptism of imported attitudes and values.

The Order reached the apex of its political power in Toronto around 1930 at a point when internal organizational dynamics were beginning to weaken its stability and connectedness with mainstream Toronto. In 1931 immigrants from the British Isles constituted a quarter of the city's population; a further two-thirds had been born in Canada, and the remainder were mostly from the USA, Russia, and Poland. The Orange Order, which had existed in the city for more than a century, straddled this demographic mixture of British immigrants and Canadian-born and drew support from both. However, compared with the city in general, immigrants were proportionally over-represented within the Order, notwithstanding its long-established Canadian presence. By the 1930s probably half of its members were immigrants; among them, the English and Scots were as numerous as the Irish. Immigration, a source of renewal and recruitment, was also potentially a marginalizing force. When the British source regions of Toronto's immigration wave altered to include a much more ethnically and religiously diverse set of immigrants, the potential for support of Orangeism was diminished. The civic culture and governance of the city ultimately evolved to reflect a much-reduced British identity. Immigration, for long a positive influence for the Order, was to emerge as a potential threat. Leaders of the organization were simultaneously faced with the reality that the attraction of the Orange Order for the Canadian-born residents of the city was not as entrenched as they might have hoped. The changing demographic identity of the city and its associated impact on recruitment for the Orange Order would eventually expose an inherent ecological instability within the organization. Coincidentally, the debilitating effects of the economic depression of the 1930s adversely affected retention of current members.

The Demographic Context

The First World War had a profound effect on the emerging identity of Canada, and in the aftermath of the wholesale slaughter of thousands of its young men in the cause of imperial defence, the country began to reassess its relationship with the mother country. Contemporaneously, Britain was also redefining its relationship with its former colonies, and the concept of Empire and imperialism began to evolve into a more benign sense of a Commonwealth in which parity of esteem moved to the fore. That process of imperial transformation had been hastened by the Irish War of Independence, which had challenged the integral unity of the United Kingdom and led to the creation of an independent Free State for twenty-six of the thirty-two Irish counties. Ireland, birthplace of the Orange Order, was perceived as carrying a special responsibility for the weakening of the Empire, and the separatist campaign of Sinn Fein was interpreted by Orangemen, and many others, as an assault on the whole concept of imperial unity. Orangemen projected a fear that Catholics would dominate an independent Irish Parliament into the Canadian context, where, they posited, the ongoing demographic transformation might someday lead to a political domination by Catholics.

A Canadian demographic transformation had been apparent since the end of the nineteenth century when central Europeans had begun to flock to the "Last Best West" of the Canadian prairies in numbers that augmented, and eventually surpassed, the traditional migration streams of Irish, Scottish, and English settlers. In the years following upon the First World War, Canadian immigration included a growing number of Mediterranean Catholics as well as Central Europeans among the new arrivals. As the fastest-growing Canadian city, Toronto was very much part of this demographic change, and with it there emerged a concomitant drive towards redefining the civic culture of the Queen City. The rapidly changing national demography was at variance with the ideological position of an Orange Order that was passionately committed to the preservation of a British, Protestant, and monarchical culture and a vibrant imperial sentiment. To Canadian Orangemen it appeared that their worst fears were being realized. Canada's growing sense of nationhood, a loosening of imperial ties, and an infusion of mass immigration from non-traditional source regions were coalescing to construct a new set of geopolitical relations for the loyal colony. The dynamics of global geopolitical change, expressed in the peace arrangements that emerged in the aftermath of the First World War, had the effect of creating a new international order, and older certitudes attaching to Empire were weakened beyond recall. Orangemen at national levels, in both the British heartland and the former colonies, reacted angrily and defiantly to the weakening of imperial sentiment – a view that they expressed collectively through their aptly named Imperial

Grand Orange Council of the Loyal Orange Association of the World. In addition, from the perspective of the Order, the emergent stream of non-British migrants, many of them Catholic, represented a threat to both the traditional identity of Canada and the future membership recruitment of the organization.

At its annual general meeting in 1927, the Grand Orange Lodge of British America announced: "The Orange Order has taken the definite stand that Canada's energies should be directed mainly to supplementing our population from the surplus of the Motherland."[47] It was a repetition of a position that had been frequently articulated in the previous decades, but it was now uttered with a new urgency. In rural Canada, particularly the prairie provinces, the non-British immigrants were sufficiently numerous to provide local majorities in large swathes of territory, while in cities such as Toronto and the industrial centres of southwest Ontario there were many examples of immigrant neighbourhood concentrations that were very much at variance with the perceived cultural norms of the established population. Visible minorities were becoming apparent, and the Order did not like it. Orange political networks were called into operation to influence immigration policy and also to recruit immigrants from the "old country." With a network of lodges that spanned Canada and strong organizational linkages to Britain and Ireland, the Orange Order was potentially in a strong position to influence the composition of the migration stream, and it tried to do so by establishing, in 1928, an "Immigration Department" under the auspices of the Grand Orange Lodge of British America. All Canadian lodges were circulated with an appeal entitled "How Many Britishers Can Your Lodge Place in 1929?" Stating that it had twenty-one families and an indeterminate number of single men, boys, and girls ready to sail, the Grand Lodge sought placements for them on farms and in domestic service. It claimed to have placed over five hundred in 1928, and requested each lodge to nominate a dependable man to find suitable placements on the basis of yearly contracts that would include winter employment. "We have been TALKING 'Keep Canada British'. Here is your opportunity to 'Make Canada British' by providing employment with a farmer in your locality. He will join your Lodge as scores have done this year and in this way you swell your membership."[48] Although it may have met with some success in its opening year, the scheme did not prosper: its launch coincided with the onset of the Great Depression, and over the next several years unemployment among existing Canadian residents rose inexorably. But even under more benign economic conditions the scheme would not have been sufficiently powerful to alter the character of the flow of migrants who were crossing the Atlantic in tens of thousands annually. Ireland's population, ravaged by seventy years of post-Famine emigration, lacked the base for supporting very large-scale migration, and, in any event, the USA provided a very powerful counter-attraction for migrants from all quarters of the British Isles. Even in a niche area such as Toronto, with its long-standing links to Ulster, the impact of Orange immigration policies was insignificant.

Religion and cultural differences informed the Order's opposition to the migration stream pouring into Canada, and in the immediate aftermath of the Second World War an additional objection was publicized – lack of democratic credentials among the immigrants. In 1946 the Provincial Grand Lodge of Ontario West passed a resolution demanding a new national immigration policy. "The people from lands who have possessed for some time a democratic form of government are the type we require, not a motley throng who have no knowledge of what democracy means. They can be secured in the British Isles, the United States of America and north-western Europe."[49] There was no doubting the preference for the Lutheran and Calvinist immigrants and an explicit avoidance of Catholics or Jews. No reference to colour was made, but in any event the black population of Canada was numerically low during the first half of the twentieth century.

Catholics were perceived as the main threat to the established and cherished way of life. Growth in Catholic numbers was carefully monitored, enrolments in separate schools were tracked, and local and regional patterns of demographic change were commented upon. Catholic population growth was a function of natural increase – especially among the existing Canadian population – internal migration, and changes in immigration patterns. French Canadians and Irish Catholics were the groups that were most closely monitored, and it was French Canada that was deemed to pose the greatest threat. A rural French Canadian population had been spilling into eastern Ontario from the 1840s, and the traditional Orange enclaves of Prescott and Russell counties, and other districts near Ottawa, had felt increasing pressure from settlements that were not only Catholic but also French-speaking. The movement of the French into this region was part of a wider colonization movement that was supported by the Catholic Church and led by priests seeking land for parishioners whose rural Quebec homeland was overcrowded and lacking in opportunity. New settlements across the Ottawa River in eastern Ontario and in the clay belt in the north of the province were identified, and a landscape replete with Catholic churches, crucifixes at road intersections, and a long-lot farming landscape reminiscent of the lower St Lawrence Valley was created. It was anathema to "les Orangistes" who were building lodges and Protestant churches and implanting British values in the same regions.[50] In an open letter to all lodges in 1946, the provincial grand master of Ontario West identified the scale of the perceived threat, drawing attention to the growth of separate schools in the bilingual districts of eastern and northern Ontario, and proclaimed, "Ontario must be kept Protestant and English speaking if we are to remain a truly democratic Province."[51] Toronto Orangemen monitored the provincial trends with concern and frequently commented upon them, but within their own city the presence of French Canadians was not a major issue. Prior to 1950, French Canadians constituted less than 2 per cent of the city's population, and even in the second half of the twentieth century their demographic growth remained modest. Toronto's French population was exceeded by that of the Jews as early as 1900, and the latter group attracted many adverse Orange comments, especially in relation to its increasing share of the business and property of the city.

The traditional adversaries of Orange Toronto were Irish Catholics, who, as a group, were distrusted by the Order, although many individual Catholics did enjoy good relations with their Orange neighbours. The proportion of Catholics in the city had never been dominant, and it had declined over the opening decades of the twentieth century. Published census returns do not provide cross-tabulations between religion and ethnicity, but it may be assumed, with some confidence, that in 1900 the Irish composed at least 80 per cent of the city's Catholic population.[52] As a percentage of the urban population, Catholics had fallen from a peak of 27 per cent in 1861 to 12.3 per cent in 1911, before rising to 14.6 per cent in 1941 (table 6.11).

Notwithstanding an increase in absolute numbers, the proportionate diminution of the Irish Catholic presence did alter perception of their political strength; their claim for a share of public patronage was correspondingly reduced. When a modest increase in the relative strength of the Catholic population became apparent in the 1930s, the Irish could claim only limited responsibility for it, as much of the increase arose from the immigration of French, Italian, Hungarian, Polish, and Ukrainian Catholics. The Irish continued to be pre-eminent in the administrative structure of the Catholic Church in the city, but their demographic

Table 6.11 Comparative population strength: Catholics and Jews, Toronto, 1901–41

	1901	1911	1921	1931	1941
Catholics	15.0%	12.3%	12.4%	14.3%	14.6%
Jews	2.0%	4.8%	6.6%	7.2%	7.3%

Source: Census of population

base was weakened both in the Church and in the city. Throughout the remainder of the twentieth century, their relative position continued to diminish against a backdrop of an overall surge in the multi-ethnic Catholic population of the city. The implication of this set of changes for the Orange Order is difficult to assess definitively, but the certitude of a single identifiable opponent was eliminated. The religious, linguistic, and ethnic landscape had become much more complex mid-century; Catholicism and "foreign" immigrants became twin pillars for Orange condemnation, but that stance appeared increasingly irrelevant in a Canada that was well on the way to projecting itself as a multicultural nation. The Orange Order faced the new set of challenges with a weakened membership, a diminished leadership capacity, and reduced political influence. Its perceived enemies were more diverse than ever and its friends were increasingly scarce. An organization that had successfully spanned the Atlantic throughout almost a century and a half now faltered, becoming irrelevant in a city and a nation that was no longer willing to define itself in the narrow context of British Protestantism and imperialism.

The new pattern of Canadian immigration provided little demographic potential for Orange recruitment. Protestant immigrants from outside of the British Isles had no awareness of the history of the Order and little commitment to its proclaimed values. A notable exception to this general pattern did, however, emerge within Toronto's Italian Protestant community. In an intriguing example of religion transcending ethnicity, Giuseppe Garibaldi LOL 3115 was founded in 1930 as an exclusively Italian lodge. The Elm Street Mission, a Methodist outreach to Protestant immigrants, was the conduit that led to the inclusion of the Italian Protestants, and under its first master, Carlo Lamberti, LOL 3115 marched in the 1930 Twelfth parade behind an Italian flag and a Union Jack. Its new banner, acquired a few months later, bore a depiction of Giuseppe Garibaldi on the front and King William on the back.[53] The lodge became renowned in Orange circles for its hosting of

6.4 Giuseppe Garibaldi LOL 3115

spaghetti suppers on special occasions, and throughout its history its membership has remained almost exclusively Italian. One of its members, Dominic DiStasi, became grand master of the Order at the national level in the 1980s, and the lodge remains as a small but distinctive element in Toronto's Orange community up to the present day. To eliminate any ambiguity about its loyalty, the lodge mounted its own church parade in Toronto on 17 September 1939. The parade may well have had a subscript of affirming national loyalty at the commencement of the Second World War, but it was held ostensibly to commemorate the sixty-ninth anniversary of the downfall of the Pope's temporal power in Italy in 1870. The parade route led from Queen's Park along College Street to St Paul's Italian United Church on Lippincott Street, and the master, Bro. Di Stassi, appealed for "the cooperation of all members of the Orange Order in Toronto to help make this one of the largest Orange Church parades ever to be held in this city as this is our first attempt to bring to the attention of the Italian Roman Catholics the fact that the Italian Orangemen are strong in Protestant faith."[54] The inclusion of this distinctive group proved to be the exception rather than the rule in the rapidly changing social, religious, and political realities of modernizing Toronto.

Internal Political Tensions within the Order in the Inter-War Years

The 1920s were a golden decade for the Orange Order in Toronto. Endowed by a flood of initiates and transferred members joining by certificate, and augmented by hundreds of returning servicemen, the Toronto lodges reached their historical peak in membership. The Order's political influence and control of patronage in the city peaked also. There was no doubting the fact that Toronto was a recognizable facsimile of Belfast, and to very many citizens that was a source of pride. The Order was well able to maintain its position as the largest voluntary association in the city and it projected its image accordingly. Its position of power and influence, built up over more than a century, had considerable intrinsic durability, and its leadership was well able to continue to project an image of power, influence, and demonstrable success. It was a long-established fact that success in the arena of Toronto politics required an alignment of interest with the Order, and membership was deemed a necessary support for aspiring politicians.

The following decade, dominated by the global economic depression, saw both a rapid reversal of the trajectory of growth of the Order and a clear diminution of its power, as well as growing internal tensions that became increasingly apparent and, not infrequently, spilled over into the public gaze. The *raison d'être* of the Order was openly questioned in the Orange publication, the *Sentinel*, and also at lodge meetings. The politicization of the Order had been a cause of concern for many years to purists within the organization who viewed it primarily as a socio-religious not a religio-political body, but their views did not hold sway at a time when the Order was delivering tangible benefits to its members. For example, in 1899 a regular columnist in the *Sentinel* had campaigned repeatedly for greater scrutiny of the motives of those seeking to become Orangemen:

> The Orange Order has suffered more from the presence of designing men who have connected themselves with the Association for selfish purposes than any other organization that I know of. These men – few in number – have traded upon the earnestness and enthusiasm of the rank and file of the Order, and have allied themselves with it not because of their belief in the principles which they had pledged themselves to uphold, but because of their expectation that their connection with the Order would be for their personal profit.[55]

The advice was ignored and the Order continued to develop its local political identity, albeit continuing to articulate a national perspective infused with strident Protestantism and imperial sentiment. Political successes in Toronto were applauded by the brethren across the country, and at its annual meeting in 1916 the Grand Orange Lodge of British America noted, "The Orange Association views the growth and development of Toronto with pride and satisfaction because Toronto is the greatest Orange centre on the American continent, and for generations leading members of the Orange Order have been leaders in the civic and public life of the city."[56]

By the 1930s the external environment of the growing complexity of municipal governance required for a rapidly growing city together with internal disenchantment among Orangemen was generating obvious tensions. A growing divergence between the Orange electorate and their elected representatives materialized. Traditionally, municipal politics had operated within an environment of convention. The allocation of jobs and commercial contracts continued to be handled in the time-honoured fashion of clientialism: the favouring of Protestants had become the norm and a modest share of patronage was reserved for Catholics. There was an apparent acceptance of the status quo. However, in the early 1930s, the Catholic School Board's claims for increased public funding and its request to have Board elections conducted in the same polling stations as the regular municipal elections threatened to disturb the equilibrium. The mayor, Sam McBride, himself a leading Orangeman, supported the proposed reform of the election procedure, and his apparent conferring of official recognition on the Catholic School Board was the occasion of a major internal row in the Order. McBride openly proclaimed his Orange credentials and asserted that, while he would adhere to his obligations, he would not be dictated to by the brethren. LOL 857 sought the views of the Grand Lodge of Canada, but the grand master refused to censor the mayor and responded:

> A member of the Orange Order is not curtailed in the exercise of his rights and privileges as a citizen. Similarly, if elected by popular choice to public office, he must be free to serve his constituents according to his own conception of duty. If his course, in any particular, is disapproved by individuals who he represents, they may refuse to re-elect him. The only qualification to this general freedom of action is that, having subscribed to a certain line of conduct as a member of the Order, he exposes himself to discipline if he commits a breach of his undertaking. That breach, however, must be tangible and to be found within the four walls of his obligation or the constitution. His delinquency must be such as is defined as an offence against Orange law. There is no such situation in the complaint alleged and the brother against whom resentment is directed has not exposed himself to any particular charge upon which discipline can be imposed.[57]

Legal advice had undoubtedly been sought in formulating the reply and it revealed a recognition that the political space within which the Order traditionally operated was undergoing fundamental challenge. The four Orange aldermen and the mayor, who had supported the separate schools' position in City Council, stood for re-election the following year, and, despite the condemnation of their stance by the Orange brethren, they were returned with increased majorities.[58] Central to this new reality were the changing demographic identity of the city and the contemporaneous pattern of an evolving national identity. Municipal politics could no longer be viewed simply as an extension of Orange behaviour. Compromise was required, and that requirement became very apparent in the post-war era. Returning Orange servicemen did not emulate the example of the previous generation. Very many of them declined to rejoin their lodges and a new era took shape. For the Orange Order, the twentieth century was indeed a period of two halves.

7 The Faded Sash: Toronto and Orangeism, 1940–c. 1950

During the inter-war decades, Toronto engaged in a process of political, social, and cultural change that would have far-reaching consequences for the city's identity and personality. Ultimately, the sense of place that defined the city was transformed. Toronto ceased to be regarded as dull and sanctimonious and acquired a new persona as a vibrant multicultural centre of modernity. Change was cumulative. Its trajectory, clearly discernible in hindsight, was evident to only the most perceptive of contemporary observers in the 1920s and 1930s, but in the years following the Second World War it became obvious to most. Central to the process of change was the acceptance of a burgeoning immigration flow from central and southern Europe, a growing interconnectedness with the economy and value system of the USA, and a proportionate weakening of trade and demographic links with Britain. Continentalism replaced an Atlantic colonial perspective as Canada in general, and Toronto in particular, underwent a fundamental reorientation. The indicators of change were plentiful. Alterations in patterns of stock market trading, transport linkages, and export dependencies affirmed a commercial realignment within an urban system that bound Toronto to major centres in the northeastern and midwestern United States, and they had their equivalencies in less obviously economic fields such as the touring circuits of dance bands, movie distribution, and sporting leagues. Internally, Toronto's political and cultural values adjusted to the new realities; old certitudes were challenged, abandoned, and replaced with new thinking and new ways of conducting civic affairs. City Hall, now accommodated within a new modernist architecture, was an appropriate metaphor for a fresh approach to municipal politics. The Orange Order, established icon of "The Belfast of Canada," yielded power, and its nemesis, the Catholic Church, assumed a new prominence. The starkness of old-fashioned sectarianism was replaced by the dynamic complexity of a new multiculturalism that irrevocably expanded horizons once bounded by attitudes transferred from an introspective corner of the British Isles.

Arriving in Toronto in 1929 from New Brunswick, Northrop Frye, Methodist clergyman, academic, and future distinguished scholar of Canadian culture, was struck by the uses to which religion was deployed in the public life of the city. He described a world wherein evangelical lay preachers commandeered street corners on Saturday evenings, threatening Hell and eternal damnation for those who choose not to see the light of the Lord's Word, and promising eternal reward for the "Saved." It was an authentic replication of life in contemporary Belfast, and, even for a man as religious as Frye, the public display was disturbing, conjuring up a sense of social introspection, community divisiveness, and a stifling civic culture.

> Toronto's spiritual life began on Saturday evening, where many downtown corners had a preaching evangelist, and continued through Sunday, a day of rest of a type I have never seen paralleled except in Israeli Sabbaths. One could then learn from a celebrated preacher that God was in his heaven and that the only events that bothered Him were produced by the machinations of the Roman Catholic hierarchy. The Orange Order kept a firm grip on municipal government.[1]

In Frye's view there was a reciprocal link between municipal governance and civic culture, and the presence of Orangeism was common to both. Sabbatarianism, a convergence between politics and religious like-mindedness, an underlying anti-Catholic ethos, and an inflexible public morality were well-established features of life in what was probably the most cohesively British city in the whole of North America at the time. Any immigrant arriving from Belfast would have sensed a familiar environment.

Central to that sense of familiarity were common threads of imperial sentiment, monarchical values, and Protestant supremacy. Strikingly, those values were not exclusive possessions of the elite but rather were the lynchpins of mass popular culture. The Canadian columnist Randall White has parodied this sentiment, suggesting that late nineteenth- and early twentieth-century Toronto was in denial of its North American geography and spiritually envisaged itself as part of Europe, especially

Britain and its imperial outreach. He describes Toronto of the 1920s as "a world where the Orange Parade on the 12th of July was still a big annual event. Swaggering British Protestant young men marched around the downtown streets, banging ominous drums to reaffirm the message that the real Toronto belonged to them, and no one else."[2] That populist culture was supported and sustained with the able assistance of dozens of Orange lodges and newspapers such as the *Telegram* and the Order's own organ, the *Sentinel*, and had infused municipal politics with a distinctive hue over many generations. In the mid-1920s not only was the mayor a member of the Orange Order but so also were twenty-five of the twenty-nine elected members of the city council.[3] Belfast contemporaries would have been impressed.

It was a world vision that had endured for at least a century, but by the Second World War that world was in decline. Discerning the green shoots of cultural change, Northrop Frye commented astutely, "By 1929 the loyalty to the British Connection in Ontario began to have a suspiciously vociferous quality to it; obviously it masked the fact that Canada was rapidly ceasing to be a British colony and was becoming an American one."[4] A new regional culture was emerging, he argued, and within it the logic of North America's geography would imply a diminution of the older European and especially British ties. In consequence, the props that supported a "Belfast of Canada" culture in Toronto would be challenged and face inevitable decay.

In the post-war period, the journalist Allan Anderson commented upon the process of cultural change within the city in an article that generated considerable controversy in City Hall. Writing in the monthly magazine *Mayfair* in March 1949, he entitled his essay "Toronto Is Growing Up" and proclaimed, "There's a metamorphosis going on in this city. The old, traditional, self-centred, self-righteous Tory Toronto is changing into a lusty, progressive, modern city."[5] In his view, Toronto was becoming less stuffy; its attitudes were now more liberal, and the city's old guard, who

> had accepted the inherent bigotry of many of its own beliefs with enthusiastic innocence [was being replaced by] a new generation of the thirties and forties [which had] never really accepted the rabid imperialism of their fathers ... Nevertheless, it is a sour reminder of Toronto's past that it is still impossible on Sundays in the city to go to a movie, buy a drink or even get a packet of cigarettes! It is equally a reminder of the past that, because the upheaval going on in the city hasn't yet caught up with them,

great masses of Torontonians still go about their daily business wearing that bleak gloomy look that freezes the marrow in the bones of strangers.

Illustrating his argument by reference to the impressive streetscape of University Avenue, the efficient public transit system, the striking growth in restaurants and theatres, and the high quality of its university, Anderson maintained that Toronto was now emerging as "a first-rate centre of Canadian culture," with a definite and invigorating personality. Unlike the Toronto of the recent past, where the culture had been "rabidly imperialistic, anti-Catholic and anti-French," the new image was one of vibrant cosmopolitanism. Indicative of that, he suggested, was a new reality in which "the archiepiscopal of Toronto is occupied by a Cardinal, and the Orangemen's parade has become rather moth-eaten and pathetic."

Anderson's essay captured the essence of a city undergoing fundamental cultural change, and if proof was required for his thesis it soon appeared in the form of an official condemnation. Executive power within the municipal government of Toronto at the time was vested in the mayor and a four-person Board of Control. Leslie Saunders, the senior member of the Board, took it upon himself to circulate the *Mayfair* article to every elected member of the Council, drawing specific attention to the references to anti-Catholicism and inner-circle Orangemen, and the derogatory description of the Orange parade as "moth-eaten." He sought their support in condemning what he regarded as a baseless attack on the good name of the city. Saunders, a future mayor, was a prominent Orange leader at the time, and few were surprised by his response. However, the City Council agreed with him and expressed its official regret at the perceived inaccuracy of the article. Writing on official Board of Control notepaper, Saunders informed the *Mayfair* manager, Bertram Tate: "as one who knows something about the Orange Movement in this city and country, I can see no point in Mr. Anderson's statement or reason for his deduction." The manager offered a very qualified apology, stating, "I would like to assure you, on behalf of your Orange brethren, that I am sorry that we published a remark that offended them without accomplishing any useful purpose," but he went on to defend the journalist, whose "references to the Orangemen's parade were prompted, I believe, not so much by the physical appearance of the parade, as by the writer's feeling that narrowness of all kinds is prospering less and less in Toronto as time goes on."[6] In contradistinction to the official protest by the Council, the manager pointed to considerable popular support for the views expressed in the article, and in the following month's issue contained the editorial comment:

> It is not always pleasant to see ourselves as others see us. An official protest was made by the Board of Control of the City of Toronto against opinions which Allan Anderson expressed in an article about Toronto in Mayfair of last March. Yet the Toronto newspapers, and an overwhelming majority of those citizens who commented, agreed that Mr. Anderson's observations were reasonable and fair. And newspapers all over Canada poked fun at the fuss which the Toronto City Hall made about the Mayfair article.[7]

The exchange of correspondence captures well the sense of a city in the midst of change, and, if anything, the response from City Hall illustrated just how much "official" Toronto remained entrenched in an outmoded mindset – defensive as ever against the prospect of a more open society. That Controller Saunders should have expressed such trenchant views was scarcely surprising, for he was well known for his hard-line attitudes, but the fact that he was able to carry the remainder of the Board and a majority of elected members of Council with him was a salutary reminder of the entrenched and pervasive nature of an Orange mentality within the civic culture. Yet even Saunders conceded that some change was discernible, and in his letter to the editor he admitted that, although recent parades had been fine, they nonetheless "were not as large as those held twenty years ago. Many factors contribute to this, but they were colourful, orderly and a patriotic observance of a great event in British history."[8] The attitude of the City Council was echoed in the correspondence of Orange lodges within the city. In response to the public criticism expressed in the press, the County Orange Lodge refused to insert advertisements for its annual church parade in any of the local newspapers.[9] The boycott of all newspapers was a telling admission that public opinion in general was in favour of the cultural changes then enveloping the city, the attitudes of the elected representatives notwithstanding.

In the midst of change, Toronto continued to celebrate in style the victory of King William over King James at the Battle of the Boyne in 1690. In keeping with established practice, the mayor, a majority of aldermen, and senior officials paraded the city thoroughfares in the company of thousands of their brethren, very many of whom were public employees facilitated by a day's leave with pay. The public spectacle of Orange banners, sashes, and marching bands still held an attraction for many Torontonians. In July 1949, William Irwin, who had been initiated into the Order in Belfast in 1894, marched in his fifty-fifth parade, joining some 6,500 Orangemen en route from City Hall to the Exhibition Grounds. Three thousand family members joined them there, a figure much reduced from that habitually present in the 1920s. The *Globe and Mail* carried its usual description of the parade, but its copy of that day included also a feature article on a Gaelic hurling match that had taken place in High Park together with an account of the death of the first president of the Irish Republic, the Protestant scholar and statesman Douglas Hyde.[10] Old certitudes were everywhere changing. An opinion piece in that same paper had intoned earlier that year, "That Toronto is changing rapidly is apparent to anybody who was born here and who has lived here all his life."[11]

Rising Profile of the Catholic Church

The metamorphosis of Toronto's civic culture was characterized not only by a greater sense of openness and rising cosmopolitanism but also by a radical transformation of the fortunes of the Catholic Church, long seen as the nemesis of militant Protestantism. By the 1950s the Church, augmented by new waves of immigrants, had commenced a period of sustained growth that would make it the largest denomination in the city by the end of the twentieth century. Italian, Portuguese, Spanish, Hungarian, and Polish nationals were now the backbone of the Catholic Church in the multicultural city. It would be enlarged later by immigrants from the Caribbean, Latin America, and Asia. Its increasing prominence, public recognition, and general acceptability in the life of the city were supported not only by changing local demographic conditions but also by a contemporaneous recognition and acceptance of Catholic Church leaders in both Canada and the United States.

The rise in the profile of Catholics in the city not only was acknowledged locally but also attracted approval at the level of the universal Church. At a special consistory in February 1946, Pope Pius XII consecrated thirty-two new cardinals, and, in an obvious departure from tradition, he selected bishops from a wide geopolitical spectrum to augment the largely Italian-dominated Curia. English-speaking archbishops from Canada, the United States, Australia, and England were proposed as new cardinals. Cardinals McGuigan of Toronto, Gilroy of Sidney, and Griffen of Westminster, dubbed the Empire Cardinals, were all of Irish ethnic stock, as was Cardinal Spellman of New York. The social and educational attainments and religious fidelity of the sons of the diaspora were thus recognized at the highest level in the Church. Nationally, and internationally, these men were accorded the respect due to intellectual and religious leaders, but provincialism and its still dominant public Protestantism challenged Toronto's official response. It rose to that challenge, thereby confirming the fundamental changes then transforming the culture of the city.

James Charles McGuigan, a native of Prince Edward Island, had been ordained Archbishop of Toronto in 1934, and with his elevation to the College of Cardinals he became the first such representative of the English-speaking Church in Canada. Returning from Rome, Cardinal McGuigan was fêted on disembarkation in Halifax and again in Montreal, and a civic reception was planned for his archdiocesan see, Toronto. Never before had a Catholic prelate been accorded such an honour by the city, and the proposal generated some controversy among the traditionalists in City Hall. In the tenets of Orangeism, the Pope was conventionally described as the Antichrist, and his bishops and cardinals were viewed with suspicion and, on occasion, with ill-concealed dislike. On joining the Orange Order, the mayor and a majority of aldermen had taken an oath to oppose any temporal advances of what was described as Romanism, but as civic representatives they were challenged by the international recognition that had been accorded to their city at the elevation of its pre-eminent Catholic citizen. Robert Hood Saunders, later to be chairman of Ontario Hydro, was mayor of the city at the time and, although a long-serving member of the Orange Order, decided on pragmatism as the best course of action and proceeded with plans for the reception. Cardinal McGuigan could not have been unaware of the challenges facing the mayor, but as leader of a large and growing community of Catholics in Toronto he was bound by protocol and politico-religious realities to accept the offer of a civic reception. The day was carefully choreographed, a balance of views and positions was maintained, and the city fathers, or most of them anyway, extended a courteous and generous welcome to the returning Prince of the Catholic Church. The cardinal, for his part, balanced with care and sensitivity both a salute to his Catholic flock and the meeting with civic leaders who numbered only one Catholic among their elected ranks.

On the morning of 27 March 1946, the cardinal was met at Union Station by leading Catholic laymen; most of them were in attendance as members of the Holy Name Society and were dressed in the ceremonial regalia of their fraternity. After greeting these lay leaders from his archdiocese, the cardinal inspected a uniformed and sword-bedecked guard of honour drawn from the Fourth Degree Knights of Columbus, and escorted by both groups his cavalcade made its way to City Hall. There, his first action was to lay a wreath at the cenotaph in honour of all Canadians who had given their lives in war – a gesture that affirmed his credentials as a loyal Canadian and one that would have had a particular and reassuring resonance for Orangemen, who traditionally commenced their annual Twelfth of July parade with a similar ceremony. From there the cardinal moved to the steps of City Hall, where he was officially greeted by Mayor Saunders and Controller Balfour, the latter being the only elected Catholic in the civic administration. Before proceeding indoors Mayor Saunders introduced his distinguished visitor to Bernard Gloster, a Catholic and well-known society photographer from the *Telegram* who was covering the occasion, and in a friendly banter designed to defuse any residual tensions he commented, "This man is rather famous, your Eminence. The last time I saw him he was taking photographs at the Twelfth of July parade." In reply the cardinal suggested, "Apparently he is all things to all sides," to which the photographer replied, "Your Eminence, we'll make a left-hander out of His Worship yet."[12] The casual banter, so carefully crafted, informally recognized the religio-political realities of the occasion, affirming the delicate context within which the mayor was operating.

In recognition of his Catholic identity, Controller Balfour was chosen to escort the cardinal from City Hall to his next appointment, an official reception in the provincial legislature at Queen's Park. Later that evening Cardinal McGuigan preached in St Michael's Cathedral, where he emphasized loyalty and inclusive nationhood, stating, "In union with all loyal Canadians, Catholics of Canada may be relied on to do their full share in the arduous tasks which lie in the future."[13] It was a bold statement designed to dispel any lingering doubts that the Catholics of the city, and indeed the nation, were conditional in their nationhood. The majority of Torontonians were of one mind with the cardinal on the matter. Tens of thousands of citizens, Protestants and Catholics alike, greeted the returning dignitary from the sidewalks of the city, and even the usually anti-Catholic *Telegram* editorialized, "The spirit we should like to see prevail in this matter is the spirit in which the plug hat which marches resplendent on the Glorious Twelfth is freely lent to decorate the march of the Ancient Order of Hibernians on March 17."[14]

Four Orange aldermen publicly boycotted the official reception,[15] and a Toronto lodge demanded to know what words Mayor Saunders had exchanged with the cardinal. But the County Orange Lodge ignored the protests and remained silent on the matter.[16] The action of Mayor Robert Saunders was a clear demonstration of the growing sense of compromise then pervading the civic culture. His behaviour would have been unthinkable a generation or two earlier, but for him to have done otherwise, in the face of the public support for Cardinal McGuigan, would have been politically untenable. That public mood of acceptance was captured also by Premier Drew's hosting of a reception for the cardinal in the legislature building, notwithstanding the fact that his government contained no Catholics and numbered several prominent Orangemen among its Cabinet ranks. In the emergent culture of post-war Toronto, tolerance was now perceived as a public virtue – whatever individuals might think, or say, in private.

Decline of the Public Persona of the Order

From the inception of the Toronto County Lodge in 1859, the organizational structure of the Order had been sensitive to the advantages accruing from an alignment of Orange county and district boundaries with those of parliamentary ridings.[17] The county had been subdivided with this in mind over the years, but, conscious of their declining strength on the ground, a group of Orangemen petitioned the County Lodge in 1947 for the replacement of the district arrangement by a single county structure. On grounds of improving efficiency, they argued that "the present system results generally in a duplication of effort [and] there are other times when the multiplicity of meetings called by the various lodges results in but a meagre attendance and matters of great importance to our association are passed with but scant consideration being given to them."[18] The plea, motivated by a need to harness efficiently the declining organizational resources, revealed also a resource weakness that had hitherto been compensated for by an ever-growing and active membership. Now an aging cohort with many other demands on their time was less able or willing to provide the level of engagement that had sustained the political dynamic of Orangeism in the past.

At the level of municipal politics, Orangemen had always stood for election on platforms wider than the defence of a Protestant ethos within the city, and, following from the public stance taken by Mayor Sam McBride in the 1930s, they no longer felt hide-bound by the views of their Orange constituents – their availing themselves of the electoral machinery of the lodges notwithstanding. Some lodge officers voiced criticism of the elected representatives, observing that "some of the Aldermen and Controllers who were Orangemen were pretty luke-warm Orangemen when the time came to prove themselves."[19] But the complexity of governing a rapidly growing, and increasingly diverse, city required considerable political agility. Flexibility and compromise were the essence of pragmatic leadership in Canada's second largest city. To ignore this reality would have resulted in public derision and electoral defeat. Indeed this was to prove the case when Leslie Saunders (no relation to Robert Saunders) succeeded to the mayoralty in 1954.

English immigrant Leslie Saunders was an Orangeman of the old school, and through hard work, dedication, and shrewd judgment he had established a reputation as the most outspoken Orange loyalist of post-war Canada. In time he was to become worshipful master of LOL 137, owner of the Britannia Printers (an Orange in-house publisher), and eventually grand master of the Order in Canada. A long-time alderman and controller, he succeeded to the mayoralty when a mid-term vacancy occurred in 1954 with the resignation of Mayor Alan Lamport. In a particularly insensitive gesture, and within a few weeks of assuming office, the new mayor issued a public message to the citizens of Toronto on the occasion of the Twelfth of July celebrations. Oblivious to the difference between his role as a leading Orangeman and his duties as first citizen of the city, he published, on stationery bearing the crest of the mayor's office, a statement that was at the very least partisan and improper. To many it was inflammatory and a harking back to an era that many believed was now long gone.

> The victorious Battle of the Boyne is of interest to all who value freedom. Wherever men have struggled to be free they could gain inspiration and courage by turning their eyes to the Glorious Revolution. The "Liberties of England," which William of Orange pledged to maintain, have long since become the liberties of a large scale of the civilized world. Orangemen traditionally celebrate this day, but the success of that struggle – as, in fact, with many similar contests in world history – benefited millions in other lands. We do well, therefore, to remind ourselves of the struggle of our forefathers down the centuries for a minimum of justice. Each protest brought the day of freedom nearer. These blessings were enjoyed far beyond the scene of the conflict, just as victory against the Hun, the Nazi and the Fascist gave others hope that they would be saved the ordeal of blood, sweat and tears. Every lover of liberty – men and women of every faith – thank God for those whose courage against wrong hastened the

dawn of freedom. Because of the Glorious Revolution and under the aegis of the Union Jack, a wide measure of civil and religious liberty is enjoyed by countless millions in every part of the Globe in and outside the Empire and Commonwealth. This day, then, while being observed by Orangemen, will be recalled by all who cherish the dearly bought heritage which this important 17th century event secured – civil and religious liberty for all.[20]

While few citizens of Toronto in 1954 would have questioned the value of civil and religious liberty, especially in the aftermath of the recent world war, many were outraged that the mayor's office should be used to articulate a message that linked universal freedoms with the partisan politics of Orangeism. More than Catholics were loud in their objections; many liberal Protestants were likewise outraged by what appeared as an attempt to "set the clock back in Toronto and return to the days of religious animosity."[21] A citizenry drawn increasingly from diverse ethnic backgrounds was ill at ease with the definition of their political freedoms as a legacy of an Irish battle 264 years previously and were unwilling to see the future of modernizing Toronto prescribed in such terms. The glory days of Empire that resonated throughout the message were also seen as old fashioned, a legacy of a world that was fast disappearing. In the eyes of many, Toronto's first citizen should not have privileged a partisan organization of which he himself was a leading member and whose local history, at best, had been less than inclusive. Saunders was adamant about the correctness of his action. "It is certainly no crime to be a Protestant in the Protestant city of Toronto," he declared, recalling that "Toronto has had many Orange Mayors through the years and many of them made strong pronouncements … I am not only proud of my Orange membership, but proud to issue the statement I did on one of the great days of world history."[22] The fact that the civic culture had altered over the years did not register with him. The reaction to his telescoping of history and his perceived abuse of power was to prove significant in the mayoralty elections of the following year.

When Leslie Saunders had become interim mayor in June 1954, he had displayed many qualifications for the post. He was a long-serving alderman and senior member of the Board of Control, and in a gesture of goodwill the Catholic alderman, David Balfour, had nominated him. The *Globe and Mail* enthused: "He has been active in committees and in recent years has supervised the assembling of the civic budget. Few mayors have had the grasp of the civic machinery which Mr Saunders now commands."[23] However, the circumstances of his appointment as mayor and his subsequent behaviour were to evoke a series of responses that concentrated media and political attention on the patronage and privileged expenditure of the old style of Toronto politics. Within six months, Torontonians would elect a new mayor and endorse a public crusade for reform of the civic administration. Those closing months of 1954, more than any other period in the history of Toronto, are identifiable as a fundamental break with the civic culture of the past.

Saunders's interim mayoralty had arisen from the resignation of the serving mayor, Alan Lamport, another Orangeman. Lamport had resigned mid-term in order to place himself as the leading contender to succeed William C. McBrien – Orangeman and chairman of the Toronto Transit Commission for the previous twenty years – who had died unexpectedly in early June. The position of chairman of the TTC was one of the most desired public appointments in the city at the time, carrying with it an annual salary of $15,000. The filling of the vacancy rested with the Board of the TTC, itself a politically appointed body and one that was susceptible to the influence and direction of City Hall. McBrien had been a self-made businessman, and following service in the First World War he had entered municipal politics, becoming in time chairman of the Board of Education. Like many municipal politicians of his day, he was heavily engaged with numerous fraternal organizations and would have been well positioned to avail himself of public patronage. At the time of his death it was noted, "He was a member of the Masonic Order, an Orangeman, a Shriner, and a member of the Sportsmen's Patriotic Association. He was also a member of the United Church."[24] His ability as a businessman stood him in good stead and his career in the TTC was highly successful, with its crowning achievement being the initiation of the Toronto subway system. His unexpected death precluded the grooming of an obvious successor, and it was with some sense of opportunism that Mayor Lamport, considering his own candidature, resigned. City Council proposed him as the sole candidate for the vacancy on the Board of the TTC, and from that position he contended the vacant chairmanship. In the event Lamport only succeeded in being appointed vice-chairman, having been defeated by a long-serving member of the Board. In large measure his defeat reflected a growing public disenchantment with the style of excessive patronage and clientalism he had practised as mayor, and within a few months of his departure from City Hall a number of hostile articles appeared in the Toronto press. A court conviction and a fine of $40,000, which he later appealed, established that he had been guilty of libelling a taxi firm after it had accused him of illicit dealing in taxi licences.[25]

Some weeks later, on the run-up to the scheduled election for the new term as mayor, a story purporting to identify an unprecedented scale of municipal corruption made headlines in all the local papers. Room 1735, a luxury suite on the seventeenth floor of the grandiose Royal York Hotel, was identified as a venue for private dinners, receptions, and meetings hosted at public expense by the City Hall elite. After much filibustering by interim Mayor Leslie Saunders, the accounts in City Hall were opened to public scrutiny. It became apparent that over the previous two years $48,000 had been spent, from public funds, for entertainment in the suite at the request of Mayor Lamport and with the authority of the city clerk. Some expenditure had been incurred even while the mayor was abroad. It was alleged that an inner group of elected officials had unimpeded access to the public purse. A subsequent revelation that no rent for the room had been charged by the Royal York raised unproven suspicions that the hotel was in receipt of generous treatment of its municipal taxes. A judicial inquiry was promised, but in the aftermath of the municipal elections, and following evidence that previous mayors had entertained generously in the King Edward Hotel, the matter was quietly dropped.[26] It did, however, raise in the public consciousness a sense that a self-serving clique of long standing governed the city. An agenda of reform was accelerated by the rejection of the electoral defeat of Saunders and the election of Nathan Phillips, a Jew who was elected with the promise to clean out "the backroom crowd of ex mayors and officials" who were governing the city.[27]

Leslie Saunders had not been implicated personally in the scandal of providing hospitality in Room 1735. Indeed, as an advocate of temperance and a staunch sabbatarian, he was very much opposed to lavish entertainment, the use of alcohol, or the undocumented use of city taxes. A few weeks before the election, in a gesture that was oblivious to public sentiment, he had refused to maintain the tradition of hosting a drinks reception on the weekend of the Grey Cup game in Toronto. In the event of his expected electoral victory, he had arranged a celebratory feast of coffee and biscuits.[28] But his assumed entitlement to the mayoralty was firmly rejected by the electorate, who were increasingly disillusioned by the dictatorial style he employed during his few months in office, his apparent connivance in the departure of Lamport for an expected sinecure in the TTC, and his public espousal of the political views of the Orange Order.

In common with the tradition set by many of his predecessors, Saunders commenced his brief election campaign in the County Orange Hall on Queen Street East, where it was proclaimed that, with him as mayor, "matters of Protestantism will be well looked after."[29] His next address was in the Western District Orange Hall on Euclid Avenue, and throughout the campaign he depended upon Orangemen to publicize his cause, claiming that the traditional press were in a conspiracy against him. The *Globe and Mail*, supportive of him in June, had turned completely against him by November – describing his five-month rule as being one of missed opportunities, arrogance, secrecy, and discourtesy. He was portrayed as "A militant Protestant who publishes and edits *Protestant Action*, a monthly newspaper founded to fight the separate school system and champion public school education. Now 18 years later the publication devotes itself largely to violent attacks on Roman Catholic influence."[30] A generation earlier, Leslie Saunders's stand would have raised few questions and would probably have ensured victory, but in a changing Toronto, his behaviour, attitudes, and ideology allowed him to rescue defeat from the jaws of victory and permit Nathan Phillips, whom many had regarded as least likely to succeed in the three-person contest, to triumph.[31]

His having been an elected member of the city's government for almost three decades strengthened Nathan Phillips's candidature for mayor, and although he had not served on the most influential committees he was nonetheless warmly regarded as "the Dean of city council." The intellectual strength he had displayed as a lawyer was augmented by his deeply held desire to reform and modernize the city in all aspects of its life, and, although a Jew and a member of a minority group, he was by no means isolated from the social networks of the city's elite. His social profile was supported by membership of the Masonic Order, within which he was master of his own lodge and district deputy grand master for the city. In addition he was a charter member of the Canadian Progress Club, a member of the Canadian Club, curator and executive member of the York County Law Association, and a member of the Progressive Conservatives. It has even been alleged by some leading Orangemen that he used frequently to drink coffee in the County Orange Hall on Queen Street East, a few hundred metres from City Hall, and that there he cultivated support from members who were opposed to the trenchant leadership style of Saunders.[32] As such, Phillips was an ideal bridge within the evolving civic culture of Toronto. He was sufficiently connected with past and current elites that he could envisage a framework for the future that would distance itself from the incestuous networking and patronage of earlier times. His Jewish faith was an emblem of the change; it was not an impenetrable obstacle.

Rabbi Feinberg of Holy Blossom Temple, the oldest synagogue in Toronto and usual place of worship for Phillips, summarized well the significance of the outcome of the election.

> The election of a Jew as mayor of Canada's greatest city is a tribute to the greatness of Canada's people. But even more noteworthy is the fact that religion was not an issue in the contest. Undisciplined religious absolutism, with all due respect to a man's sincerity, can become dangerous in the mayor's office. It was even more important, however, that the religious question be kept out of the political battle. Such an issue, even when right in motive, leads only to confusion and bitterness. Furthermore the assumption that a Jewish or Catholic or Protestant vote exists in Toronto would be fatal to the political judgement and maturity of its citizens. Toronto has grown up. The day of political-religious venom has vanished, I hope forever, from our city.[33]

In his reference to Toronto growing up, the rabbi echoed the description that had first appeared in the controversial *Mayfair* article of 1949, thereby reiterating the belief that the political-religious culture which had characterized the city in its earlier history had now been transcended and that a narrow set of values that had once permeated virtually every facet of civic culture had been eliminated. This stirring political message had much truth within it, but civic culture is rarely transformed so abruptly or so completely. The new mayor served seven years. Two years after his tenure ended, an Orangeman, William Dennison, was elected to the position. His term of office (1966–72) was the last time the Orange Order successfully laid claim to the mayoralty.

Nathan Phillips was dubbed "Mayor of all the People," a reflection not only of his popularity, which continued to expand during his time in office, but also of his non-partisan approach to governance. In keeping with his belief in reform, Phillips was determined to transform not only the social but also the physical landscape of Toronto. "The time has come to lead Toronto architecture out of the dark ages," he asserted, and announced that he would initiate a worldwide architectural competition for a cultural and convention centre.[34] His initial action to transform the public architecture was controversial – he agreed to accept funding from the brewing magnate O'Keefe's towards the construction

254 Toronto, the Belfast of Canada

of an auditorium. His old rival, the teetotaller Saunders, and many other Orangemen were incensed that profit from alcohol should be used for such a purpose, and, to make matters worse, the corporate funding was being provided by a firm that had endowed a Catholic seminary in the city a generation earlier. Undaunted, the mayor continued with his plans to transform the image of the city. The O'Keefe Hall was constructed, and, in September 1956, he announced the commencement of a competition for the design of a civic square and city hall on a thirteen-acre site in the centre of the city. It was reckoned to be the biggest architectural competition ever held, with 510 entries being received from forty-two different countries, and in keeping with its international flavour the winning entry was that of a team from Finland led by Viljo Revell. His design was decidedly modernist and very different from the nearby old City Hall, originally designed by the celebrated architect and Orangeman E.J. Lennox. Half a century later Revell's design is still regarded as one of the finest contributions to modern Toronto, and the city hall building has achieved and retained iconic status. In conjunction with the election of Toronto's first Jewish mayor, the city hall represents a benchmark of fundamental significance in the evolutionary trajectory of Toronto civic culture.

Following upon Phillips's election as mayor, the new civic administration initiated a survey of the social and religious characteristics of the recently elected office holders. The list itemized the name, marital status, religious denomination, and political affiliation of the mayor, four controllers, and eighteen aldermen. In addition, members were identified with reference to their status as veterans of the First and Second World Wars and whether or not they were members of either the Masonic Order or the Orange Order. It is a unique and fascinating document; its compilation and construction reveals much about Toronto at the time and also suggests that the disclosures were but part of an overall transformation of the city's governance. Few other cities in the world, with the probable exception of Belfast, would have warranted such a compilation of the politico-religious characteristics of elected officials, and contemporary Belfast would certainly not have supported such openness.[35] Twenty-three elected representatives – twenty-one men and two women – governed Toronto in 1956. All were married. All members of City Council professed membership of an organized religion; two-thirds were associated with various Protestant denominations, of which the largest was Anglicanism. Four Jews and an equal number of Catholics completed the group. The religious homogeneity of earlier generations of municipal representatives had been firmly breached, and Protestants now held only about two-thirds of the seats, a figure that was in conformity with their demographic strength in the city. At the time, Protestants would have constituted about 70 per cent of the population, Catholics probably in excess of 25 per cent, and Jews about 5 per cent. Strikingly, the impetus for change had not emerged solely from the Catholic community. The Jewish community had driven much of the transformation.

In terms of political party alignment in the city, the official listing revealed the dominance of the Progressive Conservatives, who held fifteen positions, including that of mayor. Four Liberals, three members of the CCF, and one independent completed the picture. No correlation between religion and political party was evident. Catholic members were identified as two Progressive Conservatives, one Liberal, and one Independent. Moreover, contrary to the often-voiced Orange propaganda that Catholics were less than fully committed in their national loyalty, the list demonstrated that all four Catholics were veterans of the Second World War; only one of the four Jews and five of the fifteen Protestants were registered as war veterans. There was a clear distinction between the propaganda image and the reality of the situation.

The list demonstrated also the continuing significance of fraternal organizations in public life. Twelve of the elected representatives, including Mayor Phillips, were returned as being members of the Masonic Order, and seven were returned as members of the Orange Order – five of whom were also Masons. As might be expected, Catholics were not included among the membership of either body. The numerical weakness of the Orange Order in comparison with the Masonic Order reflected a diminution of old-style politico-religious values in City Hall and the rise to prominence of an organization that was more clearly identified with the commercial and business interests in the city. The Masonic Order had long been associated with public life in Toronto, and its membership had traditionally included many who were also Orangemen, but for several generations it was the latter group who had been numerically superior and to the fore in municipal politics. But by 1956, with control of fewer than half the aldermanic seats and having lost control of the position of mayor, the Orange Order was at a political disadvantage, and seven of the twelve Masons saw no advantage in maintaining dual membership with the Orange.

Lingering Opposition to Change

Toronto entered the second half of the twentieth century with a new confidence in its social and economic future, a growing multicultural demography, and a sense of merited international standing. Yet old views and attitudes lingered, fed by a trickle of immigrants from Ulster and other parts of Britain who had been attracted to the city by their perception of its economic potential and its British and imperial past. An Orange Order that could still number several thousand among its ranks in the city was an obvious repository of such trenchant attitudes, but it was not alone. Many other overlapping militant Protestant groups continued to articulate a set of values that were more reminiscent of Belfast than the increasingly diverse Canadian metropolis. However, it was apparent to most that the potency of these traditional groupings was very much reduced from their earlier glory days, and the mainstream media largely ceased to report the outbursts and speeches of the proponents of unyielding anti-Catholic rhetoric. The Orange house organ, the *Sentinel*, niche monthly pamphlets such as Leslie Saunders's *Protestant Action*, and the *Gospel Witness and Protestant Advocate* were the main outlets for anti-Catholic propaganda, but many outbursts never proceeded further than the recorded minutes of the local, county, provincial, and national lodges of the Orange Order. Nonetheless, the continuation of attitudes and tradition that had generated such a powerful earlier identity for the city remained a fervent, if much reduced, component of political utterances.

The Orange Order, for example, continued to operate its Legislation Committees at several levels throughout the second half of the century. These committees, originating in the nineteenth century, had been established to maintain a watching brief on any proposed legislation – municipal, provincial, or national – that might be deemed contrary to the interests of Protestants. On occasion these committees raised funds to oppose, by legal action or political tactics, impending legislation. On other occasions they resolved to block the offending initiatives through private appeals to like-minded school trustees, aldermen, or members of Parliament. The County Orange Lodge of Toronto maintained a particularly assiduous Legislation Committee that held regular meetings at which all of the city's lodges were represented. Executive committee meetings preceded the plenary meetings. Both were convened on a monthly schedule. The recorded minutes of these bodies reveal the pettiness of the issues that constituted the focus of debate. In April 1942, for example, "the attention of those present was drawn to the fact that some Roman Catholic churches were running Saturday night dances and charging admission. Also that if one knew the right answer beer could be purchased at some of them."[36] The following month, concern was expressed at the apparent inclusion of a Catholic hymn in a Festival of Song publication issued by the Public School Board. It was resolved that the County Officers would speak with Orange school trustees with a view to having the hymn removed. At its November meeting of 1942 the committee ordered inquiries into allegations that an Orange lodge was meeting in a hall rented from a Catholic and likewise into the allegation that "Roman Catholics were meeting in an Orange Hall in Orillia." Other regular business included statistical reports on the relative numerical strength of Catholics and Protestants on school registers in the city, and concern was also generated by the growing population of Jews, many of them displaced from war-torn Europe. It was alleged that "*Tip Top Tailors* was a nest of foreigners, some of them very recent," and concern was expressed at the reported fact that Jews now owned many downtown offices and businesses.[37] Vigilance was also urged lest the existing national flag be replaced by one of a new design, thus affording an opportunity for "Papists [who] would do their utmost somehow and some way to have a Papist emblem in it."[38]

The defensive vigilance of the Order was augmented by the concerns of others, including private individuals, clergymen, and organizations not all of which were formally linked with the lodge structure in the city. Increasingly, these extreme viewpoints were marginal to the perspectives of the majority of Torontonians, but they did, nonetheless, attract a recognizable body of support. In large measure the views that emanated from all of these sources represented a call for the preservation of an unreconstructed societal ethos in which Protestantism was placed as the defining element in all aspects of civic life. The Rev. Dr Campbell, a Presbyterian clergyman in the city, petitioned the Legislation Committee to have the Order sponsor an annual "Protestant Week" in the city as a means of combating "the stranglehold being taken on Canada by the R.C. Church [and] the failure of Protestants to grasp the situation, and the seeming lack of concern for the future of this great Dominion."[39] Similar concerns about the apparent growth in Catholic influence were articulated by the editor of the *Sentinel*, who warned that the Catholic Church was "buying up newspapers in the West to be in a still better position to advance their cause" and pointed out that coincidentally the Church was also sponsoring radio stations in those provinces. Fearful of the erosion of their traditional values, the Ladies' Orange Benevolent Association advised "that a vigilance committee be set up to look after our Protestant interests at City Hall, Queen's Park and Ottawa."[40] At the same meeting, opposition to the sale of public lands to the Catholic Church in Scarborough was urged.

The purchase of land by the Catholic Church was of special concern to the Orange Order and related interest groups because the geographical landscape of Catholicism might become more visible. New separate schools, expanded parishes, and church building programs were evidence in the landscape of a shift in cultural power. Catholics, as they increased in affluence, confidence, and proportionate strength, were no longer content with low visibility in the new Toronto.

The scale of their institutional buildings testified to their growing self-confidence, capitalizing on the local, national, and international recognition accorded them and their spiritual leader, Cardinal McGuigan. Conversely, militant Protestants were openly opposed to any such territorial or landscape enhancements of the presence of the Catholic Church in the Queen City and observed with dismay every purchase that removed land from public or Protestant hands. In keeping with this mentality, the *Gospel Witness and Protestant Advocate*, an extremist publication of limited circulation in the city, published a "Special Cardinal Edition" to commemorate the return of the Catholic prelate. Appropriately emblazoned in red, the paper published a vitriolic rant about the cardinal and, interestingly, distilled its opposition into an illustrated analysis of the changing geography of the city. A detailed map listed by lot and date all the land purchases made over the previous decade by the Catholic Church in the downtown vicinity of St Michael's College, a Catholic institution within the federated University of Toronto. In the vicinity of the college, and adjacent to the provincial legislature in Queen's Park, the Catholic Church authorities had assembled several blocks of land during the 1930s and 1940s. The land bank was to be used to support the expansion of St Michael's and its teaching and administrative functions. Militant Protestants construed these property dealings as evidence of a cleverly conceived scheme to create a site for a palace to accommodate the new cardinal, thereby constructing a geography of power in which the buildings of the provincial government would be dwarfed by the symbols of Romanism. "Has this buying-up of this choice area been in anticipation of the recent appointment of a Toronto man as Cardinal? Within a few hours of the announcement that Archbishop McGuigan had received the red hat it was being openly

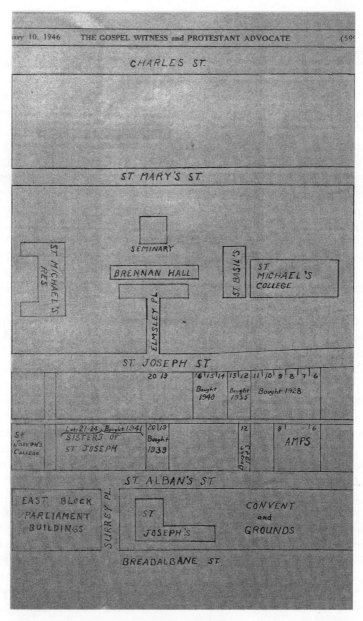

ary 10, 1946   THE GOSPEL WITNESS and PROTESTANT ADVOCATE   (59

7.1 Purchase of Church property, 1928–40

avowed that the place for his palace had already been selected and that the site would dominate both the Ontario Legislative Buildings and the University of Toronto."[41] In the event, the land was never used for a palace for the cardinal, and the landscape of power, already established in Queen's Park, was not compromised by the modest institutional buildings constructed for the Catholic college. The paranoia expressed in the publication did, however, convey in unambiguous terms the residual fears about change that lingered within contemporary Toronto.

Clearly, social change was being observed and opposed, but the waning power of Orangeism could no longer guarantee success through opposition. In a previous era when the Order and the majority culture of Torontonians were *ad idem*, limits to the public display of the presence and power of Catholic institutions and associated groupings were more easily imposed; now there was no longer such an implicitly agreed and effective civic consensus. Old certitudes were under threat from many different sources. In its defensive strategy, the Orange Order reiterated the vigilance role of its Legislation Committee and established formal contact with "authorised sources of information at Ottawa, Queen's Park and City Council."[42] But in many ways the creation of such a formal communication strategy revealed the diminution of the informal power base of the organization. Matters would have been handled differently in the past.

Notwithstanding its diminished power, especially on the national and provincial stage, the Orange Order continued into the second half of the twentieth century with its efforts to influence the outcome of municipal elections in Toronto and to publicize to its membership the preferred Orange candidates. Newspapers published the Orange affiliation of candidates, and District and County lodge meetings continued to be used as electioneering stomping grounds and indeed may have acted as a screening mechanism for those seeking to advance in public life. As late as 1946, the incumbent mayor, who was an Orangeman, and several serving Orange aldermen attended a meeting of the County Lodge's legislation committee that recorded: "Bro Hodgins was presented to the meeting as a candidate for Ward 8 Board of Education. Best wishes were extended to the Brother who is an officer of Eastern District LOL and Past Master of Beaches LOL."[43] Also in attendance were the mayor, Bro R.H. Saunders OBE, KC, and the guest speaker was Controller McCallum, vice president, Board of Control, and aldermen Innis, Frost, Murdoch, Walton, and Shannon. The meeting also recognized Bro Leslie Saunders, candidate Ward 1, Bro Hodgins, candidate Ward 8, Bro

T. Murphy, MPP, and Bro Earl Hunt, county master. Mayor Saunders "congratulated the members for their interest in setting one night aside in the interest of Civic Government."[44] Such civic nights were annual occurrences at this level in the organization and were part of a tradition of carefully cultivated interfaces between the Order and municipal politics that stretched back to the second quarter of the nineteenth century. The influence of the Order remained in evidence throughout the · 1950s, but when William Dennison was elected as Toronto's last Orange mayor in 1966, his success owed as much to his public profile outside of the Order as it did to his reputation as a long-serving Orangeman.

At the level of provincial government, the Orange tradition still retained a considerable presence in a legislature that in the mid-twentieth century was still overwhelmingly Protestant. The 1943 Progressive Conservative government led by George Drew was elected on a platform of a strong pro-British emphasis in immigration and a publicly stated preference for the maintenance of an older established value system. That party won sixty-six of the ninety seats in the legislature and was applauded by *Protestant Action*, which noted, with satisfaction, that all members of the new government were Protestant and that among the opposition benches there were only ten Catholics. Even more striking was the fact that more than one-third (twenty-five members) of the government were active members of the Orange Order.[45] The Progressive Conservatives continued to dominate Ontario politics until the early 1980s, and, although the party by then included many members of non-British ancestry, the "Big Blue Machine" that powered the governments of Premier Bill Davis was generally recognized as retaining some political legacies of a very different past. In 1981 the *Maclean's* columnist Allan Fotheringham asserted, "Bill Davis knows he has the last remnants of the Orange bigots. Ontario is one of the last places where they still have King Billy parades. It is all demeaning."[46]

Toronto and Ulster: The Enduring Connection

The persistence of a recognizable Orange culture in mid-twentieth-century Toronto was apparent to many, including not only citizens of the city but also potential migrants from Ulster and elsewhere in the British Isles. Migration flows, albeit at a relatively low level, continued to inject vitality into the transferred culture, and Irish political events deemed pertinent to the cause of Orangeism featured in lodge circles on both sides of the Atlantic. Toronto's innate attraction for visitors from

Ulster was illustrated in some detail by the visit to the city in 1950 by the prime minister of Northern Ireland, Sir Basil Brooke.[47] Brooke was at the time a somewhat controversial figure in Irish politics and was widely known for his public anti-Catholic statements and the politico-religious discrimination over which his government presided in Northern Ireland. Anxious to establish a positive international profile for the Northern Ireland jurisdiction, Brooke led a propaganda and trade mission to North America in the early summer of 1950. In the United States he was boycotted by figures such as the Irish Catholic mayor of New York and confined his speeches to private gatherings of Scotch-Irish societies and the restricted audiences of accommodating civic leaders. The second part of his tour encompassed visits to Ottawa and Toronto, and it was on Canadian soil that he was to find the most open welcome of his North American sojourn. A fishing holiday with his old friend and former neighbour from Ulster, Lord Alexander, the governor-general, set a tone of sociability and conviviality, but it was in Toronto that he delivered public addresses to audiences of several thousand and engaged in the rhetoric for which he was renowned in Belfast.

In both the preparations for the trip and the design of its itinerary, there was an abiding perception that Toronto would be a welcoming destination. Two weeks before the arrival of his party, the *Globe and Mail* published an opinion piece that set the tone for much of the press coverage that was to follow.

> When Sir Basil Brooke and Lady Brooke come to Toronto early in May there will be a special emphasis in their welcome. The citizens will feel that they have something to make up to the Brookes because of what happened in New York. There they were treated with considerable boorishness by the Mayor who was born in the south of Ireland and there drank with his mother's milk a hatred of the British. The Brookes met the affront with practised imperturbability. In Toronto they will be made to feel that they are amongst their own people. Indeed in times past this city has been compared to Belfast largely because it is one of the great cities which continue to observe the Battle of the Boyne.[48]

The schedule for his Toronto visit was by far the busiest of any part of his tour. A hectic round of meetings and public functions extended over three days, and many invitations had to be declined owing to the pressures of the busy schedule. At official functions, public meetings, and private gatherings, Brooke was fêted as a distinguished visitor and, in the eyes of some, as a defender of Ulster. Diplomatically, he avoided any specific public engagement with the Orange Order, of which he was a member, but his whole visit was punctuated with meetings organized by Orangemen acting in other capacities. Most of the logistical details of the Toronto visit, for example, had been organized by Loftus Reid, then chairman of Ontario Hydro, sometime officer of the Irish Protestant Benevolent Association, and serving secretary and treasurer of the Grand Orange Lodge of British America. The *Globe and Mail* carried a prominent notice from the officers and members of the Loyal Orange County Lodge of Toronto, welcoming him to "Toronto, the Queen City, the Belfast of Canada," and all the city's newspapers carried extensive coverage of the visit, although it was pushed off the front pages by the horrendous floods then threatening Winnipeg.

As befitted the reputation of the city, Mayor McCallum, himself an Orangeman, hosted an official reception in City Hall on the opening day of the visit and assured Sir Basil that "he was by no means a stranger in a strange land ... people from Ireland are the backbone of Toronto."[49] Unexpectedly, the City Hall visit was disrupted by the discovery of an unexploded smoke bomb on the grounds, but it was quickly dealt with. The following day the lieutenant governor of Ontario hosted a reception, and Premier Leslie Frost, a fellow Orangeman, presided at a formal dinner in the legislature in Queen's Park. The elite of Protestant Ontario attended the functions, and flowers, supplied by the appropriately named Ballymena gardens in Oakville, decorated the building. Whether by accident or design, the floral arrangements – golden forsythia in the hallway, purple amaryllis lilies in the purple drawing room, and scarlet tulips in the tea room – were indicative of the orange, purple, and scarlet degrees of Canadian Orangeism. A banquet hosted by the Irish Protestant Benevolent Society, a tour of Upper Canada College, where the principal was an Irish Protestant from Dublin, and a visit to Eaton's store were predictable inclusions in the Brooke itinerary. But in Toronto an additional element appeared for the first time in a North American tour. On the evening of 17 May, Brooke addressed a crowd of some 2,500 in Cooke's Presbyterian Church directly across the road from the County Orange Hall. Most of the crowd were probably linked in one way or another to the Order, and Brooke was not reticent in his defence of Protestant Ulster. It was the only public political rally with which he had engaged throughout the entire trip, and the partisan Toronto *Telegram* captured the spirit of that encounter the next day. "Into the Royal Orange heart of Toronto's Ulsterdom last night strode the spirit of the Six Counties personified in suave sober-suited Sir Basil Brooke, Prime Minister of Northern Ireland. The 2,500 who packed Cooke's Presbyterian Church – for 99 years 'a temple of fighting Irish Protestantism' – expected Sir Basil as a member of the fighting Brookes of County Fermanagh to take a few good clips at the southerners and sure and he did." In many ways Brooke felt at home and he relished the atmosphere and people he met in Toronto. Writing later of the visit, he confessed, "Of our entire tour in the United States and Canada, I feel that Toronto has been the place which most warmed our hearts ... The meeting in Cooke's Church, as I told you at the time, was one of the most touching experiences I have ever been fortunate enough to have."[50] When he returned to Belfast, Brooke was accorded the freedom of that city, and, in his address to the more than fifty thousand supporters who came out to greet him, the Northern Ireland prime minister again singled out for special mention his time in Toronto and his meeting of compatriots who had left Ulster thirty or forty years previously. To him, and to the assembled fellow Orangemen who had pulled him in a flag-bedecked carriage through the streets of Belfast, the Canadian city of Toronto was still unambiguously the Belfast of Canada, notwithstanding the cultural shift that was already underway in the Canadian metropolis. In that same year a Unionist senator in the Northern Ireland parliament was also invited to Toronto, and with pride he reported leading "the [Twelfth] Procession with the Mayor of Toronto ... and address[ing] the Toronto brethren. I also feel very proud to possess a certificate declaring me an Honorary Member of North of Ireland Defenders LOL No. 3082, Loyal Orange Association, British America, dated 9th July 1951, for services rendered."[51] By such linkages, public and private, some level of sustenance continued to be provided for a process of cultural transfer and organic development stretching back in an unbroken line over a century and a half.

Fading Orangeism

The golden era of Orangeism in Toronto in the 1920s was never replicated. By 1960 there were about three thousand Orangemen in the city – less than one-third of the peak four decades earlier – and they were dwarfed in a city that now contained almost seven hundred thousand inhabitants. The decline in lodge numbers was less precipitous than that of membership, for lodges prolonged their institutional existence by means of a much-reduced cohort of members. Many lodges, however,

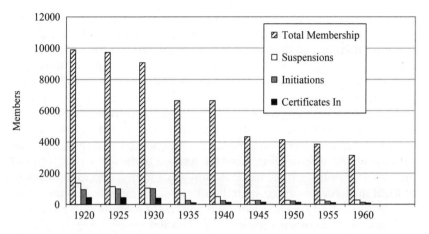

7.2 Components of membership change, 1920–60

found it increasingly difficult to remain viable in the face of an aging and dwindling membership and a commensurate reduction in lodge funds. During the 1960s, several lodges handed back their warrants to the County Lodge, formally ceasing operation. The decline in membership was the inevitable and cumulative outcome of four decades of reduced recruitment and persistent withdrawals. In the peak year of growth, 1925, more than 1,400 men had joined the Toronto lodges, but by 1960 only 129 initiates and 81 transfers into the Order were recorded. In that same year, 300 members were suspended for non-payment of dues, and 75 members died.

Figure 7.2 displays the stark reality of the organization's decline. A statistical profile for the years of the Second World War is somewhat unreliable, owing to the numbers who were carried on the books while serving in the armed forces, but a short-lived return to apparent equilibrium in the years immediately after the war is discernible from the graph. This was in large measure due to the immigration of Orangemen, mostly from Ulster, together with a few from Scotland, who transferred their certificates to the Toronto lodges at the rate of about 130 per annum. They accounted for more than one-third of all new members at the time. Simultaneously, the Canadian-born sons of current members displayed waning interest in inheriting the sashes their fathers wore. Indeed the rate of organizational decline was even greater than that suggested by the recruitment data, for the death rate among the aging cohort of Orangemen increased as the century progressed. What had once been a minor cause of membership attrition in an Order dominated by men of less than forty-five years of age now became a major concern in an organization whose membership had aged significantly. In 1920, for example, the number of deaths was equivalent to 7 per cent of recruitment, but by 1960 this had increased fivefold to 36 per cent. The trajectory of recruitment was pointing to an inevitable outcome where a small number of faithful members, augmented by handfuls of recent immigrants from Ulster and Scotland, would find themselves as the custodians of an organization that refused to die, yet which tottered on the verge of insignificance. For a few decades the retention of a core of loyal members, coupled with their personal longevity, disguised the inherent instability arising from the pattern of recruitment, but inevitably the aged members died or simply became unable to attend regular lodge meetings. The ecology of the organization would never again return to a state of equilibrium.

In this concluding era of organizational decline, the number of immigrants joining by certificate was large enough to skew the overall identity of the Order. Its immigrant complexion became more and more apparent, and gradually the Orange Order in Toronto reverted to an image of an immigrant institution fuelled by anachronistic causes from another place, another time. It became increasingly ineffective as an interest group within the city. It ended the twentieth century with no Orangemen in elected office in either City Hall or the Ontario legislature in Queen's Park. In a cycle of development spanning two centuries, the Ulster-born organization that had been transplanted so successfully to Canada, becoming in the process a national movement of major significance, had lost its New World identity. Indicative of the attenuation of its acquired Canadian heritage is the fact that of the surviving lodges in the city only one, Belfast LOL 875, can trace its continuous existence back to the nineteenth century. One other lodge dates back to 1912, but the remainder have all been established after the golden era of the 1920s, and no new lodges have been established in the city since 1944. As the new millennium commenced, the number of active Orangemen in Toronto was probably no more than three hundred, and in 2010 when the Order celebrated the 190th anniversary of the first Orange parade in the city there were only five lodges remaining in what would have been the original jurisdiction of the County Orange Lodge of Toronto (table 7.1). One of these, Giuseppe Garibaldi LOL 3115, met only twice a year, and its still predominantly Italian membership appeared to be

Table 7.1 Numerical strength of the Orange Order, Toronto, 1935–2010

	1935	1945	1950	1955	1960	2010
Members	6,641	4,331	4,131	3,854	3,134	150 (est)
Lodges	93	77	69	60	58	5

Source: *Toronto County Orange Lodge, Annual Returns, 1935–1960.*
The 2010 figure is derived from the web-published report of the County Lodge.
Note: The five lodges of 2010 were identified as belonging to the Orange jurisdiction previously designated Toronto County. Three additional lodges now in the Toronto metropolitan area were previously part of the adjoining Orange counties of York East and Ontario South.

virtually inactive. Total membership for the five lodges was no more than 150 men.

Membership data spanning almost a century has been reconstructed for Enniskillen LOL 711 – historically, one of the largest in the city – and Gideon's Chosen Few LOL 342, a medium-sized lodge which was a pioneer in designing a self-help and mutual benefits scheme. Both were founded in the 1870s; LOL 342 closed in 1969 and LOL 711 in 2006. The trajectory of membership growth and decline for both lodges in the period 1872–1960 is remarkably similar, notwithstanding differences in their social profiles over the years. LOL 342 had commenced operation in 1874 with some ambition for the future. It commissioned a subcommittee immediately to "secure a hall for this lodge to meet in," and at its second meeting it agreed to pay a member, Brother Bailey, a stipend of twenty-five dollars per annum for the use of a hall he owned. The founding mission was "to promote the interests of the institution and afford relief to the sick and disabled brethren of this lodge." In common with most lodges in the city, LOL 342's membership peaked 1910–25, declined precipitously in the 1930s, and experienced a minor flip in the late 1940s before entering a period of terminal decline. The lodge minutes for May 1955 capture well the process of institutional decay. There were then twenty members on the rolls, but of these, one had recently died in hospital, and seven others were too ill to attend meetings. Another was spending the winter in California. In spite of this precarious position, the lodge was determined to maintain appearances, and in its June meeting it instructed all members able to parade on the Twelfth "to wear dark trousers and white shirts." By 1961 the lodge was finding the rent of the County Orange Hall prohibitive and, in 1966, it transferred the monthly meetings of its remaining nine members to the

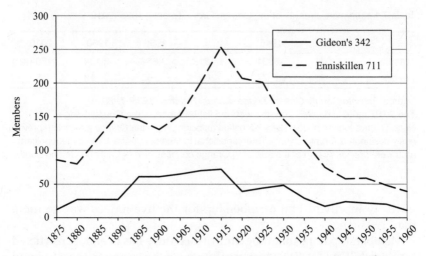

7.3 Membership of Enniskillen and Gideon's Chosen Few LOLs, 1875–1960

home of the master. At its final meeting on 11 December 1969, the lodge resolved to arrange for the transfer, in an orderly fashion, of members to other lodges and to donate regalia and banner to designated fellow lodges, and "The lodge was closed in due form for the last time. God Save The Queen."[52] Over a period of almost a century, members of the lodge had been custodians of a tradition and a centre of community activity, but there was no future in an environment that no longer provided sufficient recruits to carry on that tradition. In ecological terms, the lodge, deprived of sustenance, had withered and died.

Similarly, LOL 711, established on 1 October 1872 with a charter group of thirteen members, grew to a peak of almost three hundred members before it faced eventual decline. In the second half of the twentieth century it was sustained for some years by the acquisition of members transferring from dormant lodges in the city, but eventually it too was to cease operation in the face of an inability to attract a cohort of fresh members.[53] The sense of an evaporating tradition is palpable in the concluding minutes of this and other lodges – none more poignant than Brunswick LOL 404, which recorded in the minutes of its final meeting on 12 December 1963, "That in the best interests of the Association we hand in the warrant of Brunswick Lodge, founded in 1854 and the members join William III, LOL 140. It is with great sadness that we have come to this conclusion."[54] Five elderly members attended that closing meeting of a lodge that had contained more than a hundred members only a generation earlier.

The aging membership of the Order was the result of a generational shift in attitudes towards the organization. There had always been a cohort of older members, but their numbers were proportionately small as they were normally dwarfed by the sustained influx of young men in the active age groups. In the 1930s the influx of the young had dropped to a quarter of what it had been twenty years earlier. A new generation was simply not attracted to the Order in the way that its fathers were, and the sense of a family tradition of Orangeism was fractured and eventually broken. Distinguished Torontonian James Hughes, former grand master of Ontario West and brother of Sir Sam, the minister of defence, was openly critical of the generation of Canadians who reached adulthood in the aftermath of the First World War, and he scathingly remarked, "The Canadians born of British stock in Ontario have little to boast about. The grandsons of the men I walked with on the 12th of July in my young days are most of them degenerates."[55] Hughes's embitterment may have emanated in part from the loss of his son in action during the war, but his comments were very pertinent for an organization that was increasingly dependent upon immigrants from the British Isles for initiates and transfers. The weakened commitment of the generation coming of age in the inter-war years was demonstrated further by the instability of membership as evidenced in the growing number of suspensions. There was a lack of long-term commitment among many. Eventually this ecological instability resulted in the attenuation of generational spread, the relict members being increasingly deprived of successors to take over the organizational duties and responsibilities that were necessary to maintain vibrancy in the institution.

In Toronto, by the mid-1960s, the weakened state of the Order was apparent not only in the ranks of its members but also in its diminished presence in the urban landscape. The Western District Hall on Euclid Avenue had become an Asian dance club, its gable-end emblem of King William on a white horse incomprehensible to the weekend patrons. The County Orange Hall on Queen Street had been sold to a developer and torn down, and a similar fate had befallen Cooke's Presbyterian church, located across the road at Queen and Mutual streets. The "temple of fighting Irish Protestantism" and the organizational headquarters of the Order had been obliterated from the landscape of downtown Toronto at a time when the belief system they represented was also retreating from its central position within the civic culture of the city,

7.4 Fatih Mosque, formerly Dian LOL

now classified as an urban centre of international significance. The fate of Dian Hall on Rhodes Avenue in the east of the city illustrates well the challenges posed by demographic transformation. Named in honour of the first Orange lodge in Ireland, the Dian lodge was one of the very few halls ever built in the city by a primary lodge. Erected in 1912 with a capacity for 250 members, the hall still stands, and the Orange arches that decorate its original fenestration are clearly visible. A porch, added more recently, bears the title "Fatih Mosque," and it has functioned as an Islamic centre for more than twenty-five years.

Unlike rural and small-town Ontario, where former lodges have sometimes been preserved as local museums, there is no record of heritage designation for Toronto's Orange halls; interestingly, Black Creek Pioneer Village on the edge of the city preserves many artefacts of the past, including a Masonic Hall, but it omits any reference to the Orange Order from its inventory of historic buildings. That aspect of Toronto's past has been largely ignored.

Twelfth of July parades still attract some limited attention, but the parades have become smaller, and the designated routes shortened in deference to the cohort of elderly members. Sub-components of recent parades have included "blood and thunder bands" directly imported from Ulster, and their repertoire of sectarian tunes, complete with swaggering youthful followers, has constructed a social scene more typical of contemporary Belfast than commemorative of a subset of almost two centuries of Toronto's history. The Orange Order that had helped make Toronto the "Belfast of Canada" is now more expressive of "Belfast in Canada." The degree of change has been so all-encompassing that most Torontonians would be puzzled by any reference to the previous appellation.

Conclusion

Creations of the Victorian era of industrial and commercial progress, the cities of Belfast and Toronto were united by a shared inheritance of cultural and political traditions. Migrants from rural Ulster and trans-oceanic emigrants from the same region were common demographic components in the two rapidly growing cities that came to share several common features. Many of the similarities were the product of directly imported Orange traditions. Descriptions of sea voyages in the 1820s and again in the 1920s are almost identical in their portrayal of Orangemen from diverse Irish lodges coming together in mid-Atlantic to celebrate their shared traditions at an impromptu lodge meeting. On arrival in Canada, they would have found themselves in a social environment that they could navigate with confidence, aided by the mutual support of members of the Order who had preceded them. Few towns in English-speaking Canada lacked an Orange lodge, and in Toronto their fraternal brethren were evident in all walks of life. The Queen City of Ontario, with its Orange-dominated City Hall and associated networks of power and patronage, presented a familiar social landscape to the newly arrived. Catholics and Protestants alike recognized the coded hierarchies and opportunities for preference, or lack thereof, contained in the transplanted geography. A plethora of church buildings and patterns of church attendance confirmed a set of social attitudes that were as much political as religious badges of identity. The city's school system, organized, as in Belfast, on lines of religious division, and the confessional collegiate structures of the University of Toronto reflected the social realities of a community in which religion was not merely a matter of private morality but also a public indicator of a set of secular beliefs and behavioural attributes. Street preachers on a Saturday evening, threatening fire and brimstone to non-believers and Catholics alike, made an indelible impression on Northrop Frye, who arrived in the city in 1929. A few years previously, Ernest Hemingway, newly arrived from Paris, had complained vociferously about the claustrophobic atmosphere of the city of churchgoers. A distinguished professor of anthropology in the University of Toronto remembered how he and his expectant wife sat anxiously in a traffic jam on 12 July 1930, their emergency route to the downtown maternity hospital blocked by thousands of parading Orangemen.[1] Their journey would not have been any different had it taken place on the same day in contemporary Belfast.

In both cities the civic culture was resoundingly Protestant, Orange, and, officially at any rate, dedicated to preserving the Sabbath as a day for family and church activity, uninterrupted by boisterous recreation in public playgrounds where team games were prohibited by bylaw, and, in the case of Belfast, the swings and roundabouts were immobilized by padlocks and chains. On Sundays also, theatres were shuttered, few restaurants were open, and sales of alcohol were prohibited. Downtown stores had their window blinds drawn and doors firmly locked. Many Catholics perceived themselves to be at the margins of power, peripheral to the main thrust of official civic culture. But there were significant differences too between Toronto and Belfast. Sectarian rioting and street violence were part of life in both places, but the scale, intensity, and duration of public violence were much less in Toronto. Sectarian murders, aggregated for the whole of the nineteenth century in the Canadian city, were considerably fewer than those arising from a bad weekend in Belfast. The appellation "Belfast of Canada" projected an image that was always more all-embracing than records of civil disturbance. It suggested a civic culture that was affirmative of a particular British and Protestant mindset, filtered and refined by the machinery and machinations of Orangeism. In many ways, the Order defined the concept of loyalty and British heritage for Toronto's majority Protestant community. It was a barometer of political correctness, albeit a somewhat vociferous one, and its contribution was not entirely negative. Very many Torontonians, perhaps a majority, were comfortable with its unflinching views and sameness, and, over the years, thousands benefited from the power and patronage channelled through its lodges. A succession of city mayors and several provincial premiers were proud to display their Orange credentials. In Belfast similar conditions prevailed in a city that was not always at war. In both cities, Catholics found it difficult to win official affirmation of their citizenry, and there was a general unwillingness to make space for them in the design and operation of civic culture. A cold environment for Catholics persisted over several generations in Toronto and Belfast. They were regarded with a sense of "otherness."

Toronto civic culture during the period 1850–1950 was referenced to a complex set of geopolitical realities and scaled in harmony with the particular demands, opportunities, and perceived necessities of life in the city, in Canada, and in the British Empire. Overall, the culture celebrated the civil and religious liberties guaranteed within British constitutional monarchism and it took enormous pride in the worldly and moral achievements of an imperial power that controlled one-quarter of the global land mass. It was not a uniquely Irish Protestant culture; Scots, English, and Canadian-born men all endorsed the principles of Orangeism, and it was this ethnic plurality that permitted their fraternal association to set the tone and standards of the wider civic culture. At its peak in the 1920s, not only did the Order include a diverse group of men who were British and Canadian by birth, but these men also numerically dominated it. Men of Irish birth were in the minority. The pan-British ethnic background of the ascendant Order and its centrality to mainstream life in the city were nowhere better demonstrated than by the annual Twelfth parades of the 1920s and 1930s, which took control of the city core, including among the ten thousand participants not only the mayor of the city, many aldermen, civic officials, judges, and representatives of every social class but also the premier of the province of Ontario and several members of the legislative assembly. Only in contemporary Belfast was the Order capable of producing such a public manifestation of social standing and concentration of those who controlled the levers of power.

The centrality of the Order to power in Toronto and its diverse pan-British membership suggest that the organization was not simply a vehicle for the advancement and social integration of Irish immigrants. It was, in reality, a political machine that could harness the support of immigrants from all parts of the British Isles, successfully linking them to the social, economic, and political controls then operating within municipal structures. Recruitment of members, whether new arrivals or the sons of earlier settlers, was encouraged in large measure through the exer- . cise of patronage distribution and employment provision, facilitated by formal and informal procedures for the filling of vacancies in both the public sector and private businesses. To some extent the perception of preferment was as powerful an incentive as the actual acquisition of the prizes of patronage; only in the midst of the economic depression of the 1930s did the inherent weakness of the system become apparent, and membership declined dramatically as a result. In that respect the role and power of the Orange Order was very akin to that exercised by it in Ulster and was very much at variance with that described by MacRaild in his seminal study of the Orange Order in England.[2] The Orangemen of northern England, predominantly immigrant and primarily working class, represented a much narrower profile of their urban communities than was the case in Toronto, and their lodges were small (about thirty members) and organized to facilitate camaraderie along with a modicum of mutual self-help. Liverpool, with 197 lodges in 1915, had about five thousand Orangemen; Toronto, at the same time, had about half as many lodges but at least twice as many members as the Merseyside city. Lodges in Toronto tended to be larger than their English equivalents, and with some of them returning between two hundred and four hundred members it is hard to see how camaraderie would have been their primary *raison d'être*. Connectedness, networking, and identification with the operation of municipal power were the attractions that drew many, especially recent English and Scottish immigrants, to the Order. In that respect the Orange Order in Toronto represented a form of social capital that was available to all except Catholics. The collective ideology of Toronto's Orangemen was undoubtedly rooted in a defensive interpretation of British, monarchical, and Protestant values, but the functioning of their Order transcended its historical origins and operated with some efficiency within the *realpolitik* of a complex and wealthy Canadian metropolis. The collective action of that Orange community may have appeared loosely organized and entirely voluntary, but its effectiveness may be measured in the tight grip that was maintained on City Hall and on the distribution of patronage within the city. Over a period of at least a century, Orangeism was unquestionably a primary arbiter in Toronto's civic life and politics.

That social networking and access to patronage were primary reasons for the extensive and prolonged success of Orangeism in Toronto may be demonstrated by reference to the ultimate decline of the organization. Recruitment and retention dropped precipitously within a few years of the onset of the economic depression of the 1930s. But the Order did not retrieve its former power and prestige in the prosperity of the post-war period. Economic resurgence, driven by rapid expansion of the private sector, generated a scale of industrial operation that rendered older traditions of filtering applicants through a fraternal network system obsolete. Correspondingly, in the public sector a requirement for greater accountability and scrutiny in the expenditure of munici-pal and government budgets led to the creation of a more systematic and objective system of appointments. The reputed patronage power of the Order became redundant. Old-fashioned clientalism had simply become outmoded and the utility value of the Order had been dimin-ished accordingly.

The Orange Order would remain powerful in Belfast for another half-century after it had ceased to be a political force in Toronto, but during the century of its common success, the Order displayed an ability to span several generations and cross class and occupational boundaries with ease. Only Catholics remained incapable of being accommodated by the elasticity of its appeal. Their exclusion remained a defining and ubiquitous organizational characteristic in both places. When William Dennison stepped down from the mayoralty of Toronto in 1972, he was the last of a long line of Orangemen who had held the position, and never again would the Orange Order fill that office. Under its watch, stretching back to the foundation of the city in 1834, no Catholic had ever been elected mayor, but relations with Catholics had improved dramatically in the twentieth century, and certainly they were no longer perceived to be on the margins of society. Their social inclusion had pro-ceeded at a pace much greater than their political accommodation. The last major outbreak of sectarian rioting in Toronto occurred in 1879, and although there were episodic outbreaks through the 1890s, the spectacle of major street violence ceased. In Belfast it remained otherwise, and the 1970s and 1980s recorded the largest number of sectarian deaths in the history of the city. The pragmatism that had characterized Orange politics in Toronto remained subservient to the persisting raw hatreds in Belfast.

The International Context of Institutional Decline

Economic, demographic, and political changes have radically trans-formed Toronto, creating in the process an environment wherein Orangeism simply could not flourish. These changes, particular to the fortunes of the Orange Order in Toronto, were augmented by a more general set of causative social changes that were transforming advanced industrial societies in the western world. Robert D. Putnam's masterly work *Bowling Alone*[3] presents an insightful and invigorating analysis of American society in the closing third of the twentieth century. In it, he

identifies the emergence of behavioural changes that favour the individual and the private, at the expense of community-based social structures. His analysis of membership in a range of voluntary organizations
displays patterns that are strikingly similar to the trajectory of change
applicable to the Orange Order in Canada, in general, and Toronto in
particular. In the United States, the Knights of Columbus, the Masons,
the Shriners, and the Odd Fellows all exhibited precipitous membership
declines in the 1930s, and although some did experience a brief revival
in the decade immediately after the Second World War, all appeared to
be locked into a pattern of long-term decline that extended throughout the remainder of the century. Other, more recent bodies such as the
Lions, Rotary, Optimists, and Parent-Teacher Associations displayed
a pattern in which long-term decline commenced later, usually in the
1960s. Putnam has attributed this collapse of community organizations
partially to changing patterns of work and greater suburbanization, and
partially to generational change. Advances in personal entertainment,
especially television, more families with two parents working, and less
time for shared community recreation have, he argues, created a civic
culture in which participation assumes much less significance than it
did for previous generations. Americans have apparently "Stopped
doing committee work, stopped serving as officers, and stopped going
to meetings ... In short, Americans have been dropping out in droves,
not merely from political life, but from organized community life more
generally."[4] This fundamental transformation of American civic society would appear to have had its counterpart north of the border, and
may do much to explain the fortunes of the Orange Order and other
voluntary bodies in Canada during the second half of the twentieth century. The altered nature of civic society weakened many of the support
structures that had sustained the older system. Generational abandonment was not specific to the Orange Order, but it did increase for that
organization the impact of other threats more specific to the tenets and
practices of the brethren.

Indeed the validity of this generational approach may be further
exemplified by the fortunes of the Orange Order in its Ulster homeland.
Despite the persistence of sectarian tensions, and a political system that
remains highly sensitive to the religious composition of society, the
Orange Order in Ulster has also suffered a decline in recent years. Peaking in 1969, the Order in Ulster has declined for the past forty years,
and, although the rate of decline has been more gradual than that which
affected Toronto a generation earlier, there does appear to be a broad

278 Toronto, the Belfast of Canada

level of coincidence in fortunes.[5] In both post-modernist Canada and post–Peace Process Ulster, the organic vitality of the Orange Order has waned; it has been abandoned, or ignored, by younger generations whose views of civic engagement are at variance with those of their parents and grandparents. Ultimately, the rise and decline of the Orange Order in Toronto is an appropriate surrogate measure for an analysis of the forces of cultural change which reoriented the governance and civic culture of an Ulster outpost in the Canadian heartland.

Notes

Introduction

1 J.M.S. Careless, *Toronto to 1918: An Illustrated History* (Toronto: Lorimer, 1984), 41.

2 For a fuller analysis of the origins and spread of the Orange Order in Canada, see Cecil J. Houston and William J. Smyth, *The Sash Canada Wore: A Historical Geography of the Orange Order in Canada* (Toronto: University of Toronto Press, 1980).

3 Carl Berger, *The Sense of Power: Studies in the Ideas of Canadian Imperialism 1867–1914* (Toronto: University of Toronto Press, 1970), 128–52 makes the point that belief in imperial unity was really a form of Canadian nationalism, not a negation of national identity.

4 In his acceptance speech at the Nobel Peace Prize ceremony in Oslo, December 1998, David Trimble, Unionist leader and first minister in the Northern Ireland administration, acknowledged: "Ulster Unionists, fearful of being isolated on the island, built a solid house, but it was a cold house for Catholics. And northern nationalists, although they had a roof over their heads, seemed to us as though they meant to burn the house down." Nobelprize.org. The official web site of the Nobel Prize. This mindset of distrust and its associated garrison mentality is central to the present interpretation of the epithet "Toronto, the Belfast of Canada."

5 See, for example, Mark G. McGowan, *The Waning of the Green: Catholics, the Irish, and Identity in Toronto, 1887–1922* (Kingston: McGill-Queen's University Press, 1999).

6 Robert D. Putnam, *Bowling Alone: The Collapse and Revival of American Community* (New York: Simon and Schuster, 1999).

7 Eric P. Kaufman, *The Orange Order: A Contemporary Northern Irish History* (Oxford: Oxford University Press, 2007).
8 Houston and Smyth, *The Sash.*

1. Canada and Ireland: The Imperial Context

1 For a stimulating analysis of Ireland and the Empire see Stephen Howe, "Questioning the (Bad) Question: Was Ireland a Colony?" *Irish Historical Studies* 142 (2008): 138–53. See also Terence McDonough, ed., *Was Ireland a Colony? Economics, Politics and Culture in Nineteenth Century Ireland* (Dublin: Irish Academic Press, 2005); Kevin Kenny, ed., *Ireland and the British Empire* (Oxford: Oxford University Press, 2004); and Stephen Howe, *Ireland and Empire: Colonial Legacies in Irish History and Culture* (Oxford: Oxford University Press, 2000).
2 Linda Colley, *Britons: Forging the Nation, 1707–1837* (New Haven: Yale University Press, 1992), 8.
3 Jacob M. Price, "The Imperial Economy," in P.J. Marshall, ed., *The Eighteenth Century: The Oxford History of the British Empire* (Oxford: Oxford University Press, 1998), 100.
4 David N. Doyle, *Ireland, Irishmen and Revolutionary America, 1760–1820* (Dublin: Mercier Press, 1981)
5 Stephen Constadine, "Migrants and Settlers," in Judith M. Brown and Wm. Roger Louis, eds., *The Twentieth Century: The Oxford History of the British Empire* (Oxford: Oxford University Press 1998), 163–97.
6 Cecil J. Houston and William J. Smyth, *Irish Emigration and Canadian Settlement: Patterns, Links and Letters* (Toronto: University of Toronto Press, 1990).
7 R. Louis Gentilcore, ed., *Historical Atlas of Canada*, vol. 2 (Toronto: University of Toronto Press, 1993), 22.
8 Cole Harris, *The Reluctant Land: Society, Space and Environment in Canada before Confederation* (Vancouver: University of British Columbia Press, 2008), 231.
9 The term "Imagined Communities" was coined by Benedict Anderson, *Imagined Communities: Reflections on the Origin and Spread of Nationalism* (London: Verso, 1983).
10 Colley, *Britons*, 12.
11 George M. Grant, *Picturesque Canada: The Country As It Was and Is* (Toronto, 1902), 182.
12 For a discussion of the filtration effect see Cecil J. Houston and William J. Smyth, "The Irish Diaspora," in Brian Graham and L.J. Proudfoot, eds.,

An Historical Geography of Ireland (London: Academic Press, 1993), 338–66. Bruce S. Elliott, *Irish Migrants in the Canadas* (Kingston and Montreal: McGill-Queen's University Press, 1988), provides a good analysis of Protestant chain migration from Tipperary.

13 R. Cole Harris, Pauline Roulston, and Chris De Freitas, "The Settlement of Mono Township," *Canadian Geographer* 19.1 (1975): 1–17.

14 For a discussion of the mindset of early Ontario see Alan Smith, "Old Ontario and the Emergence of a National Frame of Mind," in F.H. Armstrong, H.A. Stevenson, and J.D. Wilson, eds., *Aspects of Nineteenth Century Ontario: Essays Presented to James J. Talman* (Toronto: University of Toronto Press, 1974), 194–221.

15 For a fuller discussion of the social and geographical dimensions of the Orange Order see Cecil J. Houston and William J. Smyth, *The Sash Canada Wore: A Historical Geography of the Orange Order in Canada* (Toronto: University of Toronto Press, 1980).

16 A good account of the political dimensions of Canadian Orangeism is contained in Hereward Senior, *Orangeism: The Canadian Phase* (Toronto: McGraw-Hill, 1974).

17 Ian Radforth, *Royal Spectacle: The 1860 Visit of the Prince of Wales to Canada and the United States* (Toronto: University of Toronto Press, 2004), 205.

18 An excellent summary of these developments is to be found in Jonathan Bardon, *A History of Ulster* (Belfast: Blackstaff Press, 1992), 354–466.

19 For a discussion of the origins and significance of the Canada First movement see Carl Berger, *The Sense of Power: Studies in the Ideas of Canadian Imperialism, 1867–1914* (Toronto: University of Toronto Press, 1970), 109–52.

20 *Resolution of the County Orange Lodge of Toronto, 26th April 1893*, Orange Archives, Toronto.

21 Report of a meeting held in Clifton Street Orange Hall, Belfast, 12 July 1891, Public Records Office of Northern Ireland, Belfast, D/880/7/4A.

22 *Sentinel*, 14 May 1914.

23 Address of the grand master to the Provincial Orange Lodge of Canada West, 13 March 1912, Orange Archives, Toronto.

24 Robert McLaughlin, "Orange-Canadian Unionists and the Irish Home Rule Crisis, 1912–1914," *Ontario History* 1 (2006): 69–101.

25 *Sentinel*, 14 May 1914.

26 *Sentinel*, 19 February 1920.

27 Ibid.

28 McLaughlin, "Orange-Canadian Unionists," 100.

29 A copy of the signatures to the Ulster Covenant may be viewed in the Public Records Office of Northern Ireland, Belfast. For a new perspective

on the Ulster Volunteer Force see Timothy Bowman, *Carson's Army: The Ulster Volunteer Force, 1910–22* (Manchester: Manchester University Press, 2007).

30 Seamus Smyth, "In Defence of Ulster: The Visit of Sir Basil Brooke to North America, Spring 1950," *Canadian Journal of Irish Studies* 33.2 (2007): 10–18.

31 Report of secretary of state for external affairs on the Brooke visit, 6 June 1950, Library and Archives Canada, 9908-T-2-40, RG 25, vol. 3981. I am indebted to Mr Fred McEvoy of Ottawa for drawing my attention to this document.

32 Report on the visit of the lord mayor of Belfast to Toronto, September 1958, Public Records Office of Northern Ireland, Belfast, CAB 9F/198.

2. A Tale of Two Cities: Belfast and Toronto

1 Mark G. McGowan, *The Waning of the Green: Catholics, the Irish, and Identity in Toronto, 1887–1922* (Kingston and Montreal: McGill-Queen's University Press, 1999), 6.

2 Interestingly, the history of Orange celebrations in Toronto is as long as that of St Patrick's Day celebrations in Montreal. St Patrick's Day parades have been held in Montreal since 1824 and were a regular feature of Toronto life until 1879, when, due to recurring public violence, it was agreed to discontinue them. The tradition of St Patrick's Day parades recommenced in Toronto a century later in 1977.

3 McGowan, *The Waning of the Green*, 316. Gregory S. Kealey, "The Orange Order in Toronto: Religious Riot and the Working Class," in Gregory Kealey and Peter Warrian, eds., *Essays in Canadian Working Class History* (Toronto: McClelland and Stewart, 1973), 13.

4 For a discussion of the growing confidence of the Toronto Catholic community see Brian P. Clarke, *Piety and Nationalism: Lay Voluntary Associations and the Creation of an Irish-Catholic Community in Toronto, 1850–1895* (Kingston and Montreal: McGill-Queen's University Press, 1993).

5 Hector Charlesworth, *Candid Chronicles: Leaves from the Notebook of a Canadian Journalist* (Toronto: Macmillan, 1925), 57.

6 McGowan, *The Waning of the Green*, and Clarke, *Piety and Nationalism*.

7 McGowan, *The Waning of The Green*, 7.

8 Ibid., 5. See also John S. Moir, "Toronto's Protestants and Their Perceptions of Their Roman Catholic Neighbours," in Mark G. McGowan and Brian P. Clarke, eds., *Catholics at the Gathering Place* (Toronto: Canadian Catholic Association, 1993), 313–41.

9 Population data for the early period of Belfast's history are derived from Raymond Gillespie and Stephen Royle, eds., *Belfast Part 1, to 1840. Irish Historic Towns Atlas No. 12* (Dublin: Royal Irish Academy, 2003), 10.

10 J.C. Beckett et al., *Belfast, the Making of the City, 1800–1914* (Belfast: Appletree Press, 1983), 17.

11 Jonathan Bardon, *A History of Ulster* (Belfast: Blackstaff Press, 2001), 147.

12 Beckett et al., *Belfast*, 19–21.

13 G.P. deT. Glazebrook, *The Story of Toronto* (Toronto: University of Toronto Press, 1971), 64.

14 John Duncan quoted in ibid., 73

15 Francis Stewart quoted in ibid., 73.

16 Brenda Collins, "Irish Emigration to Dundee and Paisley during the First Half of the Nineteenth Century," in J.M. Goldstrom and L.A. Clarkson, eds., *Irish Population, Economy and Society* (Oxford: Oxford University Press, 1981), 195–212.

17 One of the best interpretations of the industrializing cities is still that crafted by Asa Briggs, *Victorian Cities* (New York: Harper and Row, 1963).

18 The rate of growth of the Catholic population 1861–1901 was less than that warranted by rates of natural increase, notwithstanding the high mortality rates that affected the poorer classes of both religions.

19 C.J. Houston and W.J. Smyth, *Irish Emigration and Canadian Settlement: Patterns, Links and Letters* (Toronto: University of Toronto Press, 1990), 43–78.

20 Boston was, of course, a much larger city. In 1850 it had 136,881 inhabitants as compared with 30,775 in Toronto.

21 The 1871 Census of Canada included for the first time a question on ethnic origins as well as the traditional question on place of birth.

22 Houston and Smyth, *Irish Emigration*, 229.

23 C.J. Houston and W.J. Smyth, "The Irish Abroad: Better Questions through a Better Source, the Canadian Census," *Irish Geography* 13 (1980): 1–19.

24 This calculation is based on a number of assumptions. It is assumed that the ratio of Irish-born : total British born [11,305 : 30,775] is replicated in the proportion of Irish descent : total Canadian-born in 1851 [6,358 : 10,423]. If so, the total number of persons of Irish birth and origin in Toronto in 1851 would have been in the region of 17,663, or 57.4 per cent of the total population of the city. Catholics in the city numbered 7,940, and if French Canadians (467) and 3 per cent of Scots (63) are deducted, a probable population of 7,410 Irish Catholics may be established. This translates as 42 per cent of the total population of the Irish in the city. A version of this methodology was developed in William J. Smyth, "The

Irish in Mid Nineteenth-Century Ontario," *Ulster Folklife* 23 (1977): 97–105. The methodology was later refined by Donald Harman Akenson, *The Irish in Ontario: A Study in Rural History* (Kingston and Montreal: McGill-Queen's University Press, 1985), 28–30.

25 Frank Norman Walker, *Sketches of Old Toronto* (Toronto: Longmans, 1965), 85.

26 Edith Firth, *The Town of York, 1815–1834* (Toronto: University of Toronto Press, 1966), lxxxvii.

27 Charles Dickens as quoted by Peter G. Goheen, *Victorian Toronto, 1850 to 1900* (Chicago: University of Chicago Press, 1970), 55.

28 A discussion of the early history of Orangeism in Toronto is to be found in C.J. Houston and W.J. Smyth, *The Sash Canada Wore: A Historical Geography of the Orange Order in Canada* (Toronto: University of Toronto Press, 1980), 18–20.

29 Hereward Senior, *Orangeism: The Canadian Phase* (Toronto: Ryerson Press, 1966).

30 Hereward Senior, "The Genesis of Canadian Orangeism," *Ontario History* 60 (1968): 13–29.

31 Hereward Senior, "Ogle Gowan, Orangeism, and the Immigrant Question 1830–1833," *Ontario History* 66 (1974): 193–210.

32 Mark G. McGowan, *Death or Canada: Irish Famine Migration to Toronto, 1847* (Toronto: Novalis Publishing, 2009).

33 Ibid., 98.

34 Gregory S. Kealey, *Toronto Workers Respond to Industrial Capitalism, 1862–1892* (Toronto: University of Toronto Press, 1980), 115.

35 Brian Clarke, "Religious Riot as Pastime: Orange Young Britons, Parades and Public Life in Victorian Toronto," 109–128, in David A. Wilson, ed., *The Orange Order in Canada* (Dublin: Four Courts Press, 2007), 114.

36 Congregation for Divine Worship and the Discipline of the Sacraments, *Directory on Popular Piety and the Liturgy: Principles and Guidelines* (Rome: Liberia Editrice Vaticana, 2002), 118. I am indebted to Msgr Dermot Farrell for bringing this to my attention.

37 Clarke, *Piety and Nationalism*, 185–7.

38 Clarke, "Religious Riot."

39 Ian Budge and Cornelius O'Leary, *Belfast: Approach to Crisis: A Study of Belfast Politics, 1613–1970* (London: St Martin's Press, 1973), 25.

40 A particularly good analysis of the 1857 riots and the role of clerical extremists is to be found in Sean Farrell, *Rituals and Riots: Sectarian Violence and Political Culture in Ulster, 1784–1886* (Kentucky: Kentucky University Press, 2000), 147–9.

41 Bardon, *A History of Ulster*, 352.
42 A.C. Hepburn, *A Past Apart: Studies in the History of Catholic Belfast, 1850–1950* (Belfast: Ulster Historical Foundation, 1996), 235.
43 A.C. Hepburn and B. Collins, "Industrial Society: The Structure of Belfast, 1901," in Peter Roebuck, ed., *Plantation to Partition: Essays in Ulster History in Honour of J.L. McCracken* (Belfast: Blackstaff Press, 1981), 210–29.
44 F.W. Boal, R.C. Murray, and M.A. Poole, "Belfast: The Urban Encapsulation of a National Conflict," in S.E. Clarke and J.L. Obler, eds., *Urban Ethnic Conflict: A Comparative Perspective* (Chapel Hill: University of North Carolina Press, 1976), 10.
45 Hepburn, *A Past Apart*, 72.
46 Ibid., 119.
47 Stephan Thernstrom, "Immigrants and Wasps: Ethnic Differences in Occupational Mobility in Boston, 1890–1940," in Stephan Thernstrom and Richard Sennett, eds., *Nineteenth Century Cities: Essays in the New Urban History* (New Haven: Yale University Press, 1971), 125–65.
48 Oscar Handlin, *Boston's Immigrants* (New York: Little, Brown and Co., 1976), 243.
49 Goheen, *Victorian Toronto*, 115–38.
50 Ibid., 153.
51 Ibid., 171.
52 Ibid., 213.
53 Clarke, *Piety and Nationalism*, 23.
54 McGowan, *The Waning of the Green*, 21.
55 Hepburn, *A Past Apart*, 68–87.
56 Ibid., 124.
57 Rev. Jean Jamot, "Census of City Wards, circa Early 1860s," Archives of the Roman Catholic Archdiocese of Toronto.
58 Clarke, *Piety and Nationalism*, 19. The occupational classification is based on that of Goheen, *Victorian Toronto*.
59 Houston and Smyth, "The Irish Abroad." This study is derived from a systematic sample of the ethnic groups in St David's Ward, Toronto, 1860. The occupational classification is based on that of Goheen, *Victorian Toronto*.
60 A. Gordon Darroch and Michael D. Ornstein, "Ethnicity and Occupational Structure in Canada in 1871: The Vertical Mosaic in Historical Perspective," *Canadian Historical Review* 61.3 (1980): 305–33.
61 McGowan, *The Waning of the Green*, 34.
62 Jamie Swift, *An Enduring Flame: The History of the Toronto Gas Workers* (Toronto: n.p., n.d). I am indebted to Professor Gunter Gad for drawing

this source to my attention. Glasgow Rangers was the Protestant soccer team, whose supporters were frequently involved in sectarian fights with Catholic followers of Glasgow Celtic.

63 The four were respectively Ferguson, Henry, Kennedy, and Frost. See Eric Kaufmann, "The Orange Order in Ontario, Newfoundland, Scotland, and Northern Ireland: A Macro-Scale Analysis," in Wilson, ed., *The Orange Order*, 42–69.

64 Letter from Lt Col. Baptist Johnston, OBE, to Sir Robert Gransen, secretary of the Northern Ireland Cabinet, 19 May 1950, Public Records Office of Northern Ireland, Belfast, PM/11/7.

65 Hereward Senior, *Orangeism in Ireland and Britain, 1795–1836* (London: Routledge and Kegan Paul, 1966), 76.

66 Manuscript 1798 Register of Orange Warrants, House of Orange, Belfast. The *Belfast Newsletter*, 18 February 1800, referred to LOL 145 as being located in Belfast.

67 *Belfast Newsletter*, 14 July 1797.

68 *Rebellion Papers*, Dublin, Irish National Archives.

69 Quoted in Senior, *Orangeism in Ireland*, 184.

70 The data for 1833 are taken from the 1835 British parliamentary inquiry into Orangeism. Those for 1858 are derived from the Register of Orange Warrants held by the House of Orange, Belfast.

71 Data for 1900 and 1909 are derived from the Belfast Orange Directories for those years.

72 A useful description of the Toronto response to the Irish Home Rule crisis is to be found in Robert McLaughlin, "Orange-Canadian Unionists and the Irish Home Rule Crisis, 1912–1914," *Ontario History* 98.1 (2006): 68–101.

73 Manuscript letter, Sam McIlroy to Mr Shanks, Minnesota, June 1912, Public Records Office of Northern Ireland, Belfast, D/2709/1/72-80.

74 The resolution of LOL 2159 was published in Dublin by the *Irish Times*, 19 March 1912.

75 The letter from the master of LOL 1319 Co Donegal to the Toronto lodge is to be found in the Toronto Reference Library, Baldwin Room, L35, series xviii.

76 Jim Cusack and Henry McDonald, *UVF* (Dublin: Poolbeg Press, 1997), 210–15.

77 The concept of a double minority was first developed by John S. Moir, "The Problem of a Double Minority: Some Reflections on the Development of the English-Speaking Catholic Church in Canada in the Nineteenth Century," *Histoire Sociale/Social History* 4 (1971): 53–67.

78 Archbishop Lynch, letter to Irish archbishops, 1864, Archives of the Roman Catholic Archdiocese of Toronto, L.AE07.03

79 McGowan, *The Waning of the Green*, 107.

80 Ibid., 107

81 Ibid., 109.

82 Ibid., 108. I am indebted to Professor McGowan for providing me with a copy of this reference.

83 The mass took place on 17 March 2005, and Bishop Lacey, retired auxiliary bishop of the Toronto Archdiocese, was the guest preacher. I am indebted to Ms Rosaleen Daly for facilitating my attendance at the ceremony.

84 Hepburn, *A Past Apart*, 242

85 Donald H. Akenson, *Small Differences: Irish Catholics and Irish Protestants, 1815–1922* (Kingston and Montreal: McGill-Queen's University Press, 1988), 132.

86 R.C. Harris, *The Reluctant Land* (Vancouver: University of British Columbia Press, 2008) contains a reflective summary view of Harris's arguments honed over several decades.

87 Maurice Gerard Craig, *Ballad to a Traditional Refrain* (Dublin: private printer, 1942).

88 *Evening Telegram*, 12 July 1893.

89 As quoted in Christopher Armstrong and H.V. Nelles, *The Revenge of the Methodist Bicycle Company: Sunday Streetcars and Municipal Reform in Toronto, 1888–1897* (Toronto: P. Martin Associates, 1997), 6.

90 Armstrong and Nelles present an excellent and spirited analysis of the municipal debate.

91 C.S. Clarke, *Of Toronto the Good* (Toronto: Toronto Publishing Co., 1898).

92 Jesse Edgar Middleton, *Toronto's 100 Years* (Toronto: Dominion Publishing Co., 1934), 134. The data on churches are derived from the city directories of the time.

93 Ernest Hemingway to Isabel Simmons, 24 June 1923, as reprinted in Carlos Baker, ed., *Ernest Hemingway: Selected Letters 1917–1961* (Princeton: Princeton University Press, 1981), 88.

94 Ernest Hemingway to Ezra Pound, 13 October 1923, reprinted in ibid., 93.

3. Toronto Orangeism: The Nature and Structure of the Orange Order

1 Paul Bew, *Ireland, The Politics of Enmity, 1789–2006* (Oxford: Oxford University Press, 2007), viii.

2 The common appeal of these bodies is illustrated by the fact that both the Orange Order and its sworn enemy, the revolutionary United Irishmen, had both borrowed ritual and symbols from Masonry, and both late eighteenth-century Irish bodies included Masons among their founding members.

3 Manuscript registers for the national jurisdictions are maintained in respective Orange archives in Belfast and Toronto.

4 For a more detailed analysis of the geographical spread of the Order see C.J. Houston and W.J. Smyth, *The Sash Canada Wore: A Historical Geography of the Orange Order in Canada* (Toronto: University of Toronto Press, 1980), 56–83.

5 The *Sentinel* for 27 July 1899 contained a historical summary of the evolution of the Toronto County Lodge on the occasion of its fortieth jubilee.

6 Ibid.

7 Hereward Senior, *Orangeism in Britain and Ireland, 1795–1836* (London: Routledge and Kegan Paul, 1966), 215.

8 In 1850 a long-term opponent of Gowan and an unrepentant Canadian Orangeman, George Nichols, published a pamphlet, *The Position of Ogle R. Gowan Esquire, in Connection with The Orange Institution In Ireland, &c., containing correspondence and other important documents* (Woodstock: n.p., 1850). It contained a number of sworn affidavits from lodge masters in Co Antrim accusing Gowan of embezzlement.

9 George Nichols, deposition before the Legislative Assembly of Upper Canada, 1841.

10 Gerald M. Craig, ed., *Lord Durham Report* (Toronto: McClelland and Stewart, 1963), 98.

11 Louis Hartz, *The Founding of New Societies* (New York: Harcourt, Brace and World, 1964).

12 A history of these developments within the Irish Grand Lodge is to be found in C.S. Kilpatrick, Wm Murdie, and David Cargo, eds., *History of the Royal Arch Purple Order* (Belfast: Orange Order Research Group, 1993).

13 A copy of this letter was reprinted in the *Sentinel* in a special edition commemorating the centenary of the foundation of the Grand Orange Lodge of British America, 26 June 1930.

14 Proceedings of the Imperial Grand Orange Council, New York, 1900, 68. A copy is held in the Orange Archives in Toronto.

15 Senior, *Orangeism in Britain*, 92.

16 *Sentinel*, 16 March 1899.

17 Minute Book, LOL 215, 1838, Orange Archives, Toronto.

18 Houston and Smyth, *The Sash*, 113.

19 Minute Book, LOL 215, 12 July 1854.

20 Minute Book, LOL 215, 2 April 1856.

21 Minute Book, LOL 215, 5 December 1856.

22 Minute Book, LOL 215, 27 August 1858.

23 Minute Book, LOL 215, 16 September 1853.

24 By-laws and Regulations of the Loyal Orange Temperance Lodge No. 301, Toronto, 1848.

25 Ibid.

26 Fragments of the early by-laws of LOL 328 are contained within the Perkins Bull Collection, Provincial Archives of Ontario.

27 By-laws 1872, LOL 328, Perkins Bull Collection, Provincial Archives of Ontario.

28 The Registry of Orange Warrants is held by the Orange Archives in Toronto.

29 A full version of the initiation oath is included in Houston and Smyth, *The Sash*, 120.

30 Minute Book, LOL 154, 10 July and 11 September 1893, Toronto Reference Library, Baldwin Room, L35, series iv.

31 Correspondence received by LOL 342, 1889, Provincial Archives of Ontario, F4409, box 6.

32 Miscellaneous correspondence, Toronto County Orange Lodge, 1918, Toronto Reference Library, Baldwin Room, L35, series i.

33 Correspondence, 21 October 1913 of LOL 857, Toronto Reference Library, Baldwin Room, L35, series xviii.

34 By-laws of LOL 301, Toronto, 1847, Perkins Bull Collection, Provincial Archives of Ontario.

35 By-laws of LOL 342, 1874, Provincial Archives of Ontario, F4409, box 12.

36 For a discussion of the Orange insurance scheme, see Houston and Smyth, *The Sash*, 127–34.

37 Minutes of the Toronto County Orange Lodge executive committee, February 1903, Toronto Reference Library, L35.

38 Correspondence, 24 January 1890, LOL 342, Provincial Archives of Ontario, F4409, box 12.

39 The official name of the paper changed a number of times, but it was generally known as the *Sentinel*. Gordon Keyes and Norman Ritchie, *The Sentinel, 1875–1974* (Toronto: British American Publishing Company, 1975).

40 *Sentinel*, 5 January 1899.

41 Minute Book of the Toronto County Orange Lodge, 1922–43, Toronto Reference Library, Baldwin Room, L35.

42 *Mackenzies British, Irish and Canadian Gazette*, July 1838, as published at www.canadianorangehistoricalsite.com, accessed 31 October 2007.

43 *Copies of Dispatches from Sir George Arthur, relating to Orange Lodges in Canada, since the 17th day of May 1837*. Ordered to be Printed by The House of Commons, 17 August 1839.

44 Senior, *Orangeism*, 48.
45 Leslie Saunders, *The Story of Orangeism* (Toronto: Britannia Printers, 1941), 32.
46 For a good discussion of the early activities of the Orange Young Britons
    see Brian Clarke, "Religious Riot as Pastime: Orange Young Britons,
    Parades and Public Life in Victorian Toronto," 109–128, in David A.
    Wilson, ed., *The Orange Order in Canada* (Dublin: Four Courts Press, 2007).
47 Peter G. Goheen, "The Assertion of Middle-Class Claims to Public Space
    in Late Victorian Toronto," *Journal of Historical Geography* 29.1 (2003): 73–92.
48 Correspondence from Eastern District to LOL 711, May 1935, Toronto
    Reference Library, L35, series xviii, box 4.
49 File pertaining to LOL 551 Toronto, Provincial Archives of Ontario, box 27,
    F4409.
50 *Sentinel*, 17 July 1930.
51 Correspondence to the county secretary, 4 June 1936, Toronto Reference
    Library, Baldwin Room, L35, series xx.
52 Minutes of Council, 25 June 1900, Toronto City Archives.
53 *Sentinel*, 26 April 1921.
54 *Globe*, 13 July 1879.
55 For a discussion of the Orange landscape of Canada see Houston and
    Smyth, *The Sash*, 134–41. Also, C.J. Houston and W.J. Smyth, "Fraternalism
    and the Newfoundland Landscape," *Canadian Geographer* 3 (1981): 23–8.
56 *Sentinel*, 27 July 1899.
57 Financial Records of the County Orange Lodge of Toronto, 1906–17, Toronto
    Reference Library, L35.
58 Minutes of Toronto County Orange Lodge, 7 May 1924, Toronto Reference
    Library, L35.
59 Correspondence of LOL 140 to county secretary, 31 December 1945, Toronto
    Reference Library, L35, series xviii, box 4.
60 Details of the sale of Victoria Hall are contained in the minutes of the
    Toronto County Grand Lodge, September–October 1970. Details on the
    Davisville building were derived from a personal communication with a
    former officer, October 2004.
61 *Sentinel*, 7 November 1912.
62 Alex Rough, at www.canadianorangehistoricalsite.com, accessed 31 October
    2007.
63 Toronto City Directory, 1856, xliv.
64 Toronto City Directory, 1859–60, 280.
65 The development of Queen Street West and the presence of halls were
    explored in an insightful photographic exhibition mounted by Patrick J.
    Commins in St Lawrence Market, February 2007.

66 *Sentinel*, 26 April 1921.

67 Minutes of LOL 551, 1 June 1871, Provincial Archives of Ontario, F4409, box 27.

68 By-laws of Gideon's Chosen Few, Loyal Orange Benevolent Lodge 342, 26 November 1874, Provincial Archives of Ontario, F4409, box 12.

69 *Sentinel*, 29 January 1920.

70 *Sentinel*, 1 July 1920.

71 *Sentinel*, 24 August 1899.

72 A historical sketch of LOL 3115, written by Dominic Di Stasi, was published privately by the Toronto County Orange Lodge, 1980.

73 *Sentinel*, 17 July 1902.

74 By-laws LOL 342, 1874, Provincial Archives of Ontario, F4409, box 12.

75 Records of LOL 375 contained in Toronto County Lodge file 1921–2, Toronto Reference Library, Baldwin Room, L35, series xviii.

76 Christopher Armstrong and H.V. Nelles, *The Revenge of the Methodist Bicycle Company: Sunday Streetcars and Municipal Reform in Toronto, 1888–1897* (Toronto: P. Martin Associates, 1997), 6.

4. Power, Patronage, and Public Employment within the Protestant City

1 J.M.S. Careless, ed., *Colonists and Canadians, 1760–1867* (Toronto: Macmillan, 1971). See especially the chapter by Michael Cross, "The 1820s," 149–73. A useful but partial history of the Family Compact is also to be found in Henry Scadding, *Toronto of Old*, first published in 1873 but reprinted in an edited and abridged format by F.H. Armstrong (Toronto: University of Toronto Press, 1966). Scadding was born in York in 1823 and was the son of Governor Simcoe's estate manager.

2 It was popularly believed that Irish Protestant immigrants, especially those from the vicinity of Ballymena, were favourably received by those in charge of hiring in the Eaton stores in Toronto. Timothy Eaton had come from the same Ulster heartland in the mid-nineteenth century. The specificity of the geographical background has been exaggerated, but there is good anecdotal reason to believe that Eaton's was partial to Irish Protestants seeking employment.

3 Prior to Phillips, the most renowned reform politician in the city was William Holmes Howland, mayor 1886–8. Desmond Morton, *Mayor Howland: The Citizen's Candidate* (Toronto: Hakkert, 1973).

4 Alfred Connable and Edward Silberfarb, *Tigers of Tammany: Nine Men Who Ran New York* (New York: Burrows and Wallace, 1967).

5 A good discussion of the political tactics employed by Gowan is to be found in Hereward Senior, *Orangeism: The Canadian Phase* (Toronto: Ryerson Press, 1966), 13–40.

6 *Globe*, 15 September 1894.

7 *Sentinel*, 1 January 1920.

8 Rev. James George, *The Mission of Great Britain to the World, Or Some of The lessons Which she is Now Teaching* (Toronto, 1867), as quoted in Carl Berger, *The Sense of Power: Studies in the Sense of Canadian Imperialism, 1867–1914* (Toronto: University of Toronto Press, 1970), 103.

9 For a recent interpretation of the 1847 arrivals see Mark G. McGowan, *Death or Canada: Irish Famine Migration to Toronto, 1847* (Toronto: Novalis Publishing, 2009). Also, Brian P. Clarke, *Piety and Nationalism: Lay Voluntary Associations and the Creation of an Irish-Catholic Community in Toronto, 1850–1895* (Kingston and Montreal: McGill-Queen's University Press 1993), 16

10 Michael Cottrell, "Irish Catholic Political Leadership in Toronto, 1855–1882: A Study of Ethnic Politics," PhD thesis, University of Saskatoon, 1988, 135.

11 Dufferin to Argyll, 27 November 1872, Dufferin Papers, Public Records Office of Northern Ireland, Belfast.

12 Cottrell, "Irish Catholic Political Leadership," 321.

13 *Irish Canadian*, 19 April 1876.

14 17 July 1869, Archbishop Lynch Papers, Archives of the Roman Catholic Archdiocese of Toronto, AE02/21. This correspondence is quoted in Cottrell, "Irish Catholic Political Leadership," 275.

15 Gerald Stortz, "John Joseph Lynch, Archbishop of Toronto: A Biographical Study of Religious, Political and Social Commitment," PhD thesis, University of Guelph, 1980, 118.

16 *Telegram*, 8 March 1879.

17 Stortz, "John Joseph Lynch," 25.

18 J.L.P. O'Hanly, *The Political Standing of Irish Catholics in Canada: A Critical Analysis of Its Causes, with Suggestions for Its Amelioration* (Ottawa: n.p., 1872).

19 The 1871 census did in fact record a marginal decrease in the proportion of Catholics in the Ontario population from 18.5 to 16.9 per cent, but the scale of change does not undermine the statistical relativities upon which O'Hanly's argument was constructed.

20 Michael J. Cottrell, "Political Leadership and Party Allegiance among Irish Catholics in Victorian Toronto," in Mark G. McGowan and Brian P. Clarke, eds., *Catholics at the Gathering Place* (Toronto: Canadian Catholic Association, 1993), 62.

21 Mark G. McGowan, *The Waning of the Green: Catholics, the Irish, and Identity in Toronto, 1887–1922* (Kingston and Montreal: McGill-Queen's University Press, 1999).
22 *Irish Canadian*, 11 December 1884.
23 *Irish Canadian*, 4 December 1884.
24 *Irish Canadian*, 4 December 1884
25 *Globe*, 12 November 1894.
26 *Globe*, 14 November 1894.
27 Gordon T. Stewart, "Political Patronage under Macdonald and Laurier, 1878–1911," *American Review of Canadian Studies* 10.1 (1980): 3–26.
28 Ibid., 5.
29 Ibid., 7.
30 Alan Gordon, "Patronage, Etiquette, and the Science of Connection: Edmund Bristol and Political Management, 1911–1921," *Canadian Historical Review* 80.1 (1999): 1–31.
31 Ibid., 8.
32 Edmund Bristol Papers, Provincial Archives of Ontario, F68.
33 Gordon, "Patronage," 10.
34 Stewart, "Political Patronage," 8.
35 Edmund Bristol Papers, Provincial Archives of Ontario, F68.
36 William Mack Papers, Provincial Archives of Ontario, MU3299.
37 *Irish Canadian*, 28 August 1884.
38 *Irish Canadian*, 7 and 12 November 1885.
39 *Irish Canadian*, 8 May 1884.
40 William Jenkins, "Patrolmen and Peelers: Immigration, Urban Culture, and 'the Irish police' in Canada and the United States," *Canadian Journal of Irish Studies* 2.29 (2002): 10–26.
41 Nicholas Rogers, "Serving Toronto the Good," in Victor L. Russell, ed., *Forging a Consensus: Historical Essays on Toronto* (Toronto: University of Toronto Press, 1984), 116–41.
42 Minutes of Toronto City Council, Appendix B, 1908, Toronto City Archives.
43 Toronto City Clerk's Department, Employees' Salaries, 1917–34, Toronto City Archives, 145128–20.
44 Correspondence from LOL 2340 to Mayor Thomas Foster, 8 June 1925. A copy is located in the Archives of the Roman Catholic Archdiocese of Toronto.
45 Ibid.
46 Minutes of Toronto City Council, 10 May 1948, Toronto City Archives.
47 Gordon A. Darroch and Michael D. Ornstein, "Ethnicity and Occupational Structure in Canada in 1871: The Vertical Mosaic in Historical Perspective," *Canadian Historical Review* 61.3 (1980): 305–33.

48 Gordon Darroch, "Half Empty or Half Full? Images and Interpretations in the Historical Analysis of the Catholic Irish in Nineteenth Century Canada," *Canadian Ethnic Studies* 25 (1993): 5.
49 Clarke, *Piety and Nationalism*, 21.
50 Ibid., 23.
51 William M. Baker, *Timothy Warren Anglin, 1822–96: Irish Catholic Canadian* (Toronto: University of Toronto Press, 1977), 243.
52 *Irish Canadian*, 13 November 1884.

5. The Emergence of a New Order

1 This description was applied by J.M.S. Careless, *Toronto to 1918* (Toronto: James Lorimer and Company, 1984), 149.
2 Christopher Armstrong and H.V. Nelles provide a witty and insightful analysis of late Victorian culture in the city in *The Revenge of the Methodist Bicycle Company: Sunday Streetcars and Municipal Reform in Toronto, 1888–1897* (Toronto: P. Martin Associates, 1997).
3 Peter G. Goheen, "The Assertion of Middle-Class Claims to Public Space in Late Victorian Toronto," *Journal of Historical Geography* 29.1 (2003): 73–92. Goheen is incorrect in stating that the Orange Order was excluded from the week's parades.
4 A broadside entitled "Semi-Centennial of Toronto" is retained in the 1884 Broadside collection in the Toronto Reference Library.
5 This practice incurred the condemnation of the *Irish Canadian*, 17 July 1884.
6 This directory was located in 1977 in the archives of the Order in Toronto.
7 This duplication was most prevalent in smaller lodges where a past master might also be returned as a serving treasurer or committee man.
8 *Sentinel*, 20 July 1893.
9 Cecil J. Houston and William J. Smyth, *The Sash Canada Wore: A Historical Geography of the Orange Order in Canada* (Toronto: University of Toronto Press, 1980), 105.
10 Gregory S. Kealey, *Toronto Workers Respond to Industrial Capitalism, 1862–1892* (Toronto: University of Toronto Press, 1980), 108.
11 *Forms to Be Observed in Private Lodges of the Loyal Orange Institution of British America* (Toronto, 1869).
12 The manuscript register is held in the Orange archives in Toronto. It has a continuous listing of all warrants issued since 1830 for all of Canada with the exception of New Brunswick and Newfoundland, which maintained separate registers for much of their history.
13 Careless, *Toronto to 1918*, 124.

14 Houston and Smyth, *The Sash*, 104–11.
15 Gregory S. Kealey, "Orangemen and the Corporation: The Politics of Class during the Union of the Canadas," in Victor L. Russell, ed., *Forging a Consensus: Historical Essays on Toronto* (Toronto: University of Toronto Press, 1984), 41.
16 Peter Goheen, *Victorian Toronto, 1850 to 1900* (Chicago: University of Chicago Press, 1970), 229–30, and Mark G. McGowan, *The Waning of the Green: Catholics, the Irish, and Identity in Toronto, 1887–1922* (Kingston and Montreal: McGill-Queen's University Press, 1999), 295–6.
17 For an analysis of the occupational categories of the Canadian censuses, see Peter Baskerville and Eric Sager, "Finding the Workforce in the 1901 Census of Canada," *Social History/Histoire Sociale* 20 (1987): 521–38.
18 A variant on the classification of Canadian occupations is to be found in Gordon A. Darroch and Michael D. Ornstein, "Ethnicity and Occupational Structure in Canada in 1871: The Vertical Mosaic in Historical Perspective," *Canadian Historical Review* 61.3 (1980): 305–33, but their scheme was devised for the 1871 census. That devised by Goheen takes into consideration the industrial transformation that was underway two decades later.
19 An excellent overview of the industrial identity of Toronto and the scale of its largest employers is to be found in Kealey, *Toronto Workers*, 299–318.
20 Ibid., 98–123.
21 Ibid., 324–5.
22 Houston and Smyth, *The Sash*, 132.
23 There were fifty-six doctors in the Order in 1894. In that same year there were fifty-five lodges in the city.
24 By-laws of LOL 342, Provincial Archives of Ontario, F4409, box 2.
25 Provincial Archives of Ontario, F4409, box 6.
26 Gordon T. Stewart, "Political Patronage under Macdonald and Laurier, 1878–1911," *American Review of Canadian Studies* 10.1 (1980): 3–26, 8.
27 Alexander Muir's "The Maple Leaf Forever" was published in Toronto in 1867.
28 Finance Book of the County Orange Lodge of Toronto, 1888.
29 Toronto County Orange Lodge, minutes, 1934. I am indebted to Ms Fiona Smyth for confirming the relationship with St Albans.
30 Eric P. Kaufman, "From Deference to Defiance: The Transformation of the Orange Order since 1950," paper delivered to the Institute for Social Change, University College Dublin, March 2005. Kaufman established that the background of the Belfast District Officers in 1901 was: professional 8 per cent, petit-bourgeois 46 per cent, skilled 38 per cent, unskilled 8 per

cent. Comparable figures for Toronto in 1894 are: 11 per cent, 51 per cent, 26 per cent, and 12 per cent.

31 Kealey, *Toronto Workers*, 109.
32 Houston and Smyth, *The Sash*, 84–112.
33 Ibid., 103.
34 Ibid., 105–11.
35 Kealey, *Toronto Workers*, 180–5.
36 In an interesting piece of genealogical research, Sheldon and Judith Godfrey, *Burn This Gossip* (Toronto: Duke and George Press, 1991), have argued convincingly that George Benjamin, an early grand master of the Order in Canada, was in fact a Jew.
37 Rare exceptions did sometimes emerge in the census. George Whittaker, LOL 791, was recorded as married to Mary, a Catholic. Michael Basso, a native of Italy and a member of LOL 275, was described as Anglican in the census, but he was sharing lodgings with his brother and nephew, both of whom were returned as Catholics.
38 A good description of the Palatine migrations to Canada is to be found in Patrick J. O'Connor, *People Make Places: The Story of the Irish Palatines* (Limerick: Ireach na Mumhan Books, 1989).
39 Careless, *Toronto to 1918*, 143.
40 Minutes of Toronto City Council, appendix A, 1894 and 1895.
41 *Globe*, 6 January 1895.
42 *Globe*, 13 July 1888.

6. The Climax and Onset of Decline of the Orange Order

1 See letter dated 10 February 1934 from J.L. Hughes to Archbishop McNeil seeking to arrange a meeting between the archbishop and a former Presbyterian minister who wished to "lecture on unity and harmony between all Canadians." The letter was signed "Wishing Your Grace all happiness. I am, yours hopefully, James L. Hughes." McNeil Papers, Archives of the Roman Catholic Archdiocese of Toronto, MN AE21.16.
2 1908, McEvay Papers, Archives of the Roman Catholic Archdiocese of Toronto, ME AA02.26.
3 Kenyon's description of the matter is lodged with the McNeil Papers in the Archives of the Roman Catholic Archdiocese of Toronto, MN A1 21.17. The matter was also the subject of a lengthy article in the *Sentinel*, 3 August 1920.
4 City Clerk's Department, Employees' Salaries 1917–34, Toronto City Archives, 145128-20.

5 *Evening Telegram*, 12 July 1920.
6 Annual Report of the Chief Constable of the City of Toronto, 1907, Toronto City Archives.
7 Stephan Thernstrom as referenced in William Jenkins, "Patrolmen and Peelers: Immigration, and Urban Culture, and 'the Irish Police' in Canada and the United States," *Canadian Journal of Irish Studies* 28.2 (2002): 10–27.
8 Ibid., 20.
9 Jesse Edgar Middleton, ed., *The Municipality of Toronto* (Toronto: Dominion Publishing Co., 1923), 778.
10 *Sentinel*, 8 December 1954.
11 *Evening Telegram*, 12 July 1920.
12 Census of Canada, 1921, vol. 3.
13 *Globe and Mail*, 14 July 1902. A detailed account of the events associated with the funeral is to be found also in the *Sentinel*, 17 July 1902.
14 Jesse Edgar Middleton, ed., *The Municipality of Toronto*, 780–9.
15 Magherafelt Purple Star LOL 864, minutes of meeting on 17 November 1939, Orange Archives, Toronto.
16 Minutes of the Toronto County Lodge, 27 June 1924, Toronto Reference Library, Baldwin Room, L35, series xxi.
17 Report of the County Orange Lodge, 28 July 1938, Toronto Reference Library, Baldwin Room, L35, series xx [series xxi].
18 *Sentinel*, 16 July 1914.
19 Middleton, *The Municipality of Toronto*, 776.
20 Rod McQueen, *The Eatons* (Toronto: Stoddart, 1998), 81.
21 *Evening Telegram*, 12 July 1920.
22 Circular dated 7 November 1914 issued by the Toronto County Lodge, Toronto Reference Library, L35.
23 Minutes of the Toronto County Lodge, 23 July 1936, Toronto Reference Library, L35.
24 A useful summary of the taxation provisions for separate schools in Ontario is to be found in Claire Hoy, *Bill Davis: A Biography* (Toronto: Methuen, 1985), 264–76.
25 An updated list was published regularly by Leslie Saunders's monthly periodical *Protestant Action* throughout 1946 and distributed to the lodges. Copies of the publication are to be found with the Toronto County Lodge Papers in the Toronto Reference Library, L35.
26 *Irish Canadian*, 3 January 1901.
27 *Sentinel*, 6 January 1925.
28 A good overview of the urban politics of the time is to be found in James Lemon, *Toronto since 1918* (Toronto: Lorimer, 1985).

29 Peter Oliver, *G. Howard Ferguson: Ontario Tory* (Toronto: University of Toronto Press, 1977), 51.
30 Correspondence of F. Daul, Imperial Grand Orange Council of the World, to James Craig, 1925, Public Records Office of Northern Ireland, Belfast, PM/6/1.
31 *Evening Telegram*, 12 July 1920.
32 *Sentinel*, 17 July 1930.
33 Proceedings of the Grand Orange Lodge of British America, Orange Archives, Toronto, 1906, 16.
34 This was the technique pioneered in C.J. Houston and W.J. Smyth, *The Sash Canada Wore: A Historical Geography of the Orange Order in Canada* (Toronto: University of Toronto Press, 1980).
35 Cecil J. Houston and William J. Smyth, "The Orange Order and the Expansion of the Frontier in Ontario, 1830–1900," *Journal of Historical Geography* 4.3 (1978): 251–64.
36 The quotation is taken from a letter written by Hocken to a trade unionist and has been published by A. Rough on the Orange web site, www.canadianorangehistoricalsite.com, accessed 31 October 2007.
37 *Sentinel*, 29 January 1920.
38 Annual returns 1917, County Orange Lodge, Toronto Reference Library, Baldwin Room, L35, series xvii.
39 *Sentinel*, 19 July 1921.
40 For a fuller exploration of this membership analysis see Cecil J. Houston and William J. Smyth, "The Faded Sash: The Decline of the Orange Order in Canada, 1920–2005," in David A. Wilson, ed., *The Orange Order in Canada* (Dublin: Four Courts Press, 2007), 170–92.
41 A good discussion of the effect of the Depression on the city is to be found in Lemon, *Toronto since 1918*, 59–79.
42 Toronto County Orange Lodge, minutes, 1932, Toronto Reference Library, Baldwin Room, L35, series xvii.
43 Annual Returns of Eastern District Lodge, 1937, Toronto Reference Library, L35, series xvii.
44 Ibid.
45 These certificates are to be found in the County Orange Lodge material held by the Toronto Reference Library, L35.
46 Twenty-fifth anniversary history of Aughrim Rose of Derry LOL 2159, n.p., Toronto Orange Archives.
47 Annual Proceedings, Grand Orange Lodge of British America, Saint John, 1927, 13.

48 Correspondence of the Grand Orange Lodge of British America, Immigration Department, 22 January 1929.
49 Annual Proceedings, Grand Orange Lodge of Ontario West, 1946, 13.
50 A discussion of this settlement process is to be found in Houston and Smyth, *The Sash Canada Wore*, 44–8.
51 Open letter of H. Birmingham, provincial grand master of Ontario West, 1946, Toronto Reference Library, Baldwin Room, L35, series xviii.
52 In 1901 Catholics in Toronto numbered 23,699 and in the same census 4,069 persons of French and Italian origin were registered. Assuming that almost all of these two latter groups were Catholic, and allowing for a small number of Catholics from among the Scots and Germans, it is probable that the Irish accounted for about 80 per cent of the overall Catholic population of the city.
53 A brief history of the lodge, written in 1980 by Dominic Di Stasi, then grand master of the Canadian Order, is held in the Orange Archives, Toronto, n.p.
54 Letter to all lodge secretaries in Toronto from Garibaldi LOL 3115, Toronto Reference Library, Baldwin Room, L35, series xviii, box 4.
55 *Sentinel*, 20 July 1899.
56 Annual Proceedings, Grand Orange Lodge of British America, 1916, 13, Orange Archives, Toronto.
57 Toronto County Lodge, misc. correspondence, 10 February 1933, Toronto Reference Library, L35.
58 M.J. Quinn, *Debunking the Orange Terror*, pamphlet in the Catholic Archdiocesan Archives, Archives of the Roman Catholic Archdiocese of Toronto, MN AE21.09.

7. The Faded Sash: Toronto and Orangeism

1 Northrop Frye, "Culture and Society in Ontario, 1784–1984," in Jean O'Grady and David Staines, eds., *Northrop Frye on Canada*, vol. 12 of *The Collected Works of Northrop Frye* (Toronto: University of Toronto Press, 2003), 618.
2 Randall White, *Too Good to Be True: Toronto in the 1920s* (Toronto: Dundurn Press, 1993), 25.
3 Mayor H.C. Hocken quoted in G.P. deT. Glazebrook, *The Story of Toronto* (Toronto: University of Toronto Press, 1971), 164.
4 Frye, "Culture and Society in Ontario," 619.
5 Allan Anderson, "Toronto Is Growing Up," *Mayfair* (March 1949): 49–54.

6 The correspondence of Leslie Saunders to the editor (25 April 1949) and the reply (3 May 1949) are to be found in the Toronto Reference Library, Baldwin Room, L35, series xviii.

7 *Mayfair* (July 1949): 40.

8 Saunders letter, 25 April 1949.

9 Legislation Committee Minutes, County Orange Lodge, 30 May 1949, Toronto Reference Library, Baldwin Room, L35, series xx.

10 *Globe and Mail*, 12 July 1949.

11 *Globe and Mail*, 23 March 1949.

12 *Telegram*, 28 March 1946. The term "left-hander" was a colloquial description applied to Catholics.

13 Ibid.

14 *Telegram*, 22 March 1946.

15 The reception was opposed by aldermen W.H. Collings, W.H. Butt, W. Howell, and M. Wilson. Report of Provincial Grand Lodge of Ontario West, 15 May 1946, Orange Archives, Toronto.

16 Minutes of the Toronto County Orange Lodge, 1946.

17 Minutes of Toronto County Orange Lodge, February 1859.

18 Petition of LOL 140 to the County Lodge, 1947, box 13, Loyal Orange Lodge Papers, Toronto Reference Library.

19 Bro Hardy Small to the Legislation Committee, April 1942, Loyal Orange Lodge Papers, Toronto Reference Library.

20 The text of this letter is reprinted in Leslie Howard Saunders, *An Orangeman in Public Life* (Toronto: Britannia Printers, 1980), 117.

21 *Globe and Mail*, 8 December 1954. The paper reflected on the letter as a probable contribution to the rejection of Saunders by the electorate in 1954.

22 *Globe and Mail*, 10 July 1954.

23 *Globe and Mail*, 29 June 1954.

24 *Globe and Mail*, 12 June 1954.

25 *Globe and Mail*, 28 September 1954.

26 *Globe and Mail*, 13 January and 1 February 1955.

27 *Globe and Mail*, 3 December 1954.

28 *Globe and Mail*, 30 November 1954.

29 Ibid.

30 *Globe and Mail*, 4 December 1954.

31 The *Globe and Mail* had used its editorial strength to oppose Saunders and support Arthur Brown, a Liberal, for the position. It dismissed Phillips as "a kindly man who would be Mr Toronto." *Globe and Mail*, 4 December 1954.

32 Personal communication of senior Orange officer with the author, October 2004.
33 *Globe and Mail*, 8 December 1954.
34 Ibid. Phillips was inspired to transform the public architecture of Toronto by a critical review of the city that had been published a short time before by the distinguished architect Frank Lloyd Wright.
35 The survey is contained in a file of correspondence originating in the mayor's office and is held by the Toronto City Archives, file 26, subseries 3, *Council Powers and Procedures*.
36 Legislation Committee Minutes, April 1942, County Orange Lodge Minutes, Toronto Reference Library, Baldwin Room, L35, series xx.
37 Legislation Committee Minutes, 28 October 1943.
38 Legislation Committee Minutes, 30 April 1943.
39 Address of Rev. Dr Campbell to the Legislation Committee, 30 May 1946.
40 Legislation Committee Minutes, 30 September 1946.
41 *Gospel Witness and Protestant Advocate* 24.37 (1946).
42 Legislation Committee Minutes, 20 September 1946.
43 Legislation Committee Minutes, 29 November 1946.
44 Ibid.
45 *Protestant Action*, July 1945.
46 *Maclean's*, February 1981.
47 A fuller analysis of Brooke's visit is to be found in Seamus Smyth, "In Defence of Ulster: The Visit of Sir Basil Brooke to North America, Spring 1950," *Canadian Journal of Irish Studies* 33 (2007): 10–18.
48 *Globe and Mail*, 24 April 1950.
49 *Telegram*, 17 May 1950.
50 Correspondence of Sir Basil Brooke to Loftus Reed, May 1950, CAB Papers, Public Records Office of Northern Ireland, Belfast.
51 Autobiographical sketches of Senator Joseph Cunningham, Public Records Office of Northern Ireland, Belfast, D1288/1A.
52 The manuscript records of LOL 342 are held in the Provincial Archives of Ontario, F4409, box 12.
53 The manuscript records of LOL 711 are held in the Toronto Reference Library, Baldwin Room, L35, series x.
54 The manuscript records of LOL 404 are held in the Provincial Archives of Ontario, F4409, box 19.
55 Hughes uttered these remarks in 1918 and they met with strong criticism from his colleagues in the Orange leadership. The quote is reprinted at www.canadianorangehistoricalsite.com.

Conclusion

1 Personal communication from his son, Professor Tom McIlwraith, Department of Geography, University of Toronto.
2 Donald MacRaild, *Faith, Fraternity and Fighting: The Orange Order and Irish Migrants in Northern England, c. 1850–1920* (Liverpool: Liverpool University Press, 2005).
3 Robert D. Putnam, *Bowling Alone* (New York: Simon and Schuster, 2000).
4 Ibid., 64.
5 Eric P. Kaufmann, *The Orange Order: A Contemporary Northern Irish History* (Oxford: Oxford University Press, 2007).

Index